The Merchants' Capital

As cotton production shifted toward the southwestern states during the first half of the nineteenth century, New Orleans became increasingly important to the South's plantation economy. Handling the city's wide-ranging commerce was a globally oriented business community that represented a qualitatively unique form of wealth accumulation – merchant capital – that was based on the extraction of profit from exchange processes. However, like the slave-based mode of production with which they were allied, New Orleans merchants faced growing pressures during the antebellum era. Their complacent failure to improve the port's infrastructure or invest in manufacturing left them vulnerable to competition from the fast-developing industrial economy of the North, weaknesses that were fatally exposed during the Civil War and Reconstruction. Changes to regional and national economic structures after the Union victory prevented New Orleans from recovering its commercial dominance, and the former first-rank American city quickly devolved into a notorious site of political corruption and endemic poverty.

Scott P. Marler is an associate professor of history at the University of Memphis, where he teaches courses in U.S., southern, and Atlantic world history. A former editor at the *Journal of Southern History*, his work was a finalist for the Allen Nevins Dissertation Prize of the Economic History Association, and he has also won awards from the St. George Tucker Society and the Louisiana Historical Association.

Advance Praise for *Merchants' Capital*

"*The Merchants' Capital* is one of the most impressive contributions to the literature on the political economy of the nineteenth-century South to have appeared in some time. This broadly conceived and well-researched study of the Crescent City's business community is at once rigorously argued and elegantly written. Marler's long-awaited book is a worthy successor to classics such as Harold D. Woodman's King Cotton and his Retainers and Roger L. Ransom and Richard Sutch's One Kind of Freedom."
  — Peter A. Coclanis, Albert R. Newsome Distinguished Professor of History, University of North Carolina, Chapel Hill

"Tracing the history of New Orleans and its merchant class from the days of the slave-based Cotton Kingdom through the Civil War and Reconstruction, Scott Marler offers a new perspective on economic development - and lack thereof - in the Southern economy. He places the city's history firmly in the setting of the international cotton trade, but shows how local factors, including the merchants' own short-sightedness, contributed to the long-term decline of New Orleans as a mercantile center. A valuable contribution to Southern history."
  — Eric Foner, DeWitt Clinton Professor of History, Columbia University

"We've waited a long time for an in-depth history of the antebellum South's most powerful and dynamic business community. There have been dissertations and articles about New Orleans merchants, and more specialized studies of banking in the Crescent City, but not until Scott Marler's prodigiously researched book has there appeared a full-scale treatment of the subject. Well written and shrewdly insightful, *The Merchants' Capital* will become a well-thumbed history of a vital subject."
  — Lawrence N. Powell, Professor Emeritus of History, Tulane University

"Scott Marler combines deep research with conceptual acuity in an impressive analysis of the Deep South's stunted political economy across the nineteenth century. Shining a much-needed searchlight on the businessmen of New Orleans and its hinterland, *The Merchants' Capital* explains why New Orleans did not take off like many other North American cities but rather declined into the 'city that care forgot'."
  — Adam Rothman, Georgetown University

"*The Merchants' Capital* tells the riveting story of New Orleans' precipitous economic and political decline during and after the Civil War, from the nerve center of the Cotton Kingdom to a backwater notorious for corruption and poverty. Scott Marler provocatively sets this narrative in a larger context of global economic change. All students of slavery and the South should read this book."
  — Gavin Wright, William Robertson Coe Professor of American Economic History, Stanford University

"This splendid book offers a meticulous historical study of merchant capitalism in ... New Orleans, a unique port city in the South ... This wonderful study contributes to both southern history and business history and should be required reading in undergraduate and graduate courses."
  — Elena V. Shabliy, Southern Historian

CAMBRIDGE STUDIES ON THE AMERICAN SOUTH

Series Editors:

Mark M. Smith, *University of South Carolina, Columbia*

David Moltke-Hansen, *Center for the Study of the American South, University of North Carolina at Chapel Hill*

Interdisciplinary in its scope and intent, this series builds upon and extends Cambridge University Press's long-standing commitment to studies on the American South. The series not only will offer the best new work on the South's distinctive institutional, social, economic, and cultural history but will also feature works in a national, comparative, and transnational perspective.

Titles in the Series

Robert E. Bonner, *Mastering America: Southern Slaveholders and the Crisis of American Nationhood*

Ras Michael Brown, *African-Atlantic Cultures and the South Carolina Lowcountry*

Christopher Michael Curtis, *Jefferson's Freeholders and the Politics of Ownership in the Old Dominion*

Scott P. Marler, *The Merchants' Capital: New Orleans and the Political Economy of the Nineteenth-Century South*

Peter McCandless, *Slavery, Disease, and Suffering in the Southern Lowcountry*

Johanna Nicol Shields, *Freedom in a Slave Society: Stories from the Antebellum South*

Brian Steele, *Thomas Jefferson and American Nationhood*

Jonathan Daniel Wells, *Women Writers and Journalists in the Nineteenth-Century South*

PLATE 1. Edgar Degas, *A Cotton Office in New Orleans* (1873). Reproduced by permission of the Musée des Beaux-Arts, Pau, France.

PLATE 2. Edgar Degas, *Cotton Merchants in New Orleans* (1873). Reproduced by permission of the Fogg Art Museum, Harvard University, Cambridge, Massachusetts.

The Merchants' Capital

New Orleans and the Political Economy of the Nineteenth-Century South

SCOTT P. MARLER
University of Memphis

CAMBRIDGE
UNIVERSITY PRESS

CAMBRIDGE
UNIVERSITY PRESS

32 Avenue of the Americas, New York NY 10013-2473, USA

Cambridge University Press is part of the University of Cambridge.

It furthers the University's mission by disseminating knowledge in the pursuit of education, learning and research at the highest international levels of excellence.

www.cambridge.org
Information on this title: www.cambridge.org/9781107557543

First published 2013
First paperback edition 2015

A catalogue record for this publication is available from the British Library

Library of Congress Cataloguing in Publication data
Marler, Scott P.
The Merchants' Capital: New Orleans and the Political Economy of the Nineteenth-Century South / by Scott P. Marler.
    pages cm. – (Cambridge studies on the American South)
Includes bibliographical references and index.
ISBN 978-0-521-89764-8 (hardback)
1. New Orleans (La.) – Commerce – History – 19th century.   2. New Orleans
(La.) – Economic conditions – 19th century.   3. Southern States – Commerce –
History – 19th century.   4. Southern States – Economic conditions –
19th century.   5. Southern States – Economic policy.   I. Title.
HF3163.N5M25   2013
330.9763'3505–dc23   2012043468

ISBN 978-0-521-89764-8 Hardback
ISBN 978-1-107-55754-3 Paperback

For Candice,
mia bella Luna

Contents

Illustrations

Plates

Figures

Tables

Acknowledgments

The debts accumulated in the creation of this work extend back many years. During my undergraduate studies, Robert Fisher (now at the University of Connecticut) took me under his wing when I was fresh from military service. Bob soon directed me to his friend Bruce Palmer at the University of Houston–Clear Lake, who helped me to begin understanding the many ironies of southern history. I will always be grateful to Bob and Bruce for the many hours they spent teaching me to read American history with a critical eye. Bruce also introduced me to Joe Austin, who now teaches history at the University of Wisconsin–Milwaukee. Comrade Joe's friendship has now sustained me for much longer than either of us really cares to remember. Thanks, too, to Marjo Avé-Lallemant for her outstanding teaching and support.

During graduate work at Rice University, a succession of department chairs looked out for me, especially Peter C. Caldwell, to whom the analysis of merchant capital herein owes a great deal. Allen J. Matusow took time to direct me through extensive readings in U.S. economic history, and his later criticisms helped keep my arguments honest; thanks also to Martin J. Wiener and Thomas L. Haskell for putting up with "the last Marxist." I will always be very grateful to Michael Maas, Paula Sanders, and Alex Lichtenstein for their constant encouragement and sound advice. Charles A. Israel, Bethany L. Johnson, and Carolyn Earle Billingsley exemplified the high standards expected of us, as did Martin Woessner, Ron Haas, Ann Ziker, Benjamin Wise, Luke Harlow, and Gregory Eow. Finally, I owe a debt of special gratitude to my dear friend Melissa A. Bailar, associate director of Rice's Humanities Research Center, for her assistance with all matters French, her sympathetic ear, and our countless afternoon jogs around the campus perimeter.

Several years of editorial service to the *Journal of Southern History* gave me the privilege of working with Evelyn Thomas Nolen, Patricia Burgess, Patricia Bellis Bixel, Elizabeth Hayes Turner, Bethany L. Johnson, and Randal L. Hall.

It also allowed me to work on a daily basis with the finest boss one could ever hope for: John B. Boles, who also served as my thesis advisor. As his many students would undoubtedly attest, John is truly the proverbial "gentleman and a scholar." I probably owe him most of all, but as with Bob Fisher and Bruce Palmer, I can only promise to keep trying to "pay forward" those debts with my own students during the years ahead.

My service at the *Journal* helped allow me to form relationships with scholars throughout the profession. John C. Rodrigue and Sylvia Frank Rodrigue are, quite simply, the finest academic couple I know, to whom my gratitude is matched only by my respect. Barbara J. Fields, Harold D. Woodman, Gavin Wright, and James Oakes deserve special mention for their generosity – all the more so because I spend so much time debating their brilliant scholarship. Similar thanks are in order to Walter Johnson, Brian Schoen, Jon Wells, and Frank Towers, and also to my fellow Louisiana historians Lawrence Powell, Michael A. Ross, Emily Clark, and Judith Fenner Gentry. Among the many other scholars I wish to thank are Bertram Wyatt-Brown, Douglas Ambrose, Eric Arnesen, Aaron Anderson, Peggy Hargis, Thavolia Glymph, Jennifer Green, Richard Kilbourne, Bo Morgan, Bill Scarborough, Louis Kyriakoudes, Charles Banner-Haley, Jay Mandle, David L. Carlton, and Orville Vernon Burton. And although our personal interactions were rare, this book, along with my broader understandings of southern history, were profoundly influenced by the work of the late Eugene D. Genovese. My deepest gratitude, however, is reserved for three outstanding historians who have also become good friends: Peter A. Coclanis, Louis Ferleger, and Mark M. Smith. All of the aforementioned scholars welcomed me into the "Great Conversation" that constitutes the historical profession, and they frequently challenged me to rethink and sharpen my analyses. However, let me stress that none of them should be held responsible in any way for the arguments herein. Any deficiencies that remain are entirely "my bad."

To acknowledge all of my colleagues at the University of Memphis, I'd have to list practically the entire Department of History. Particular thanks to Walter R. Brown, Beverly Bond, Charles Crawford, Peggy Caffrey, Aram Goudsouzian, Sarah Potter, Susan Eva O'Donovan, and Kent Schull, but especially to our remarkable chair, Janann M. Sherman. Jan has not only made it her mission to provide constant support to her junior faculty, but she has successfully fostered a team-oriented department culture that makes for a fantastic work environment. Jan is now on the cusp of retirement, and she will be greatly missed by us all. I am also grateful for research funding and a sabbatical leave awarded by the University of Memphis's College of Arts & Sciences.

Sarah Bentley, Angela Brown, and Francine Ariz Mendez of Rice's Fondren Library were enormously helpful, as were archivists elsewhere, among them Faye Phillips, Judy Bolton, and Tara Laver (Louisiana State University's Hill Memorial Library); Wayne Everard (New Orleans Public Library); and Leon Miller (Tulane University's Howard-Tilton Memorial Library). I also benefited from the highly professional staffs at the Library of Congress, the Baker Library of Harvard Business School, and the Historic New Orleans Collection. My work also benefited from travel and research grants from Harvard University, the Economic History Association, the Business History Conference, the European Business History Association, the Historical Society, and the Pitman and Nolen Funds at Rice University. Earlier versions of Chapters 3, 4, 7, and 8 appeared in *Louisiana History*, *Civil War History*, the *Journal of Urban History*, and *Agricultural History*, respectively, and are reproduced by permission. All excerpts from the invaluable R. G. Dun & Company Collection archived at the Baker Library of Harvard Business School are reproduced by express permission of Dun & Bradstreet, Inc.

At Cambridge University Press, Mark M. Smith and David Moltke-Hansen recruited my work for their new series in southern studies, and I will always be very grateful to my legendary editor, Lewis Bateman, for his advice, encouragement, and patience during the lengthy process of completing this book. Finally, special thanks to Mrs. Sydney Touchstone, who graciously allowed me to stay at her home adjacent to Audubon Park during research trips to New Orleans; my mother, Kathy Jo Weber; my father, Larry J. Marler; my longtime "surrogate family," Jane Andrews and Dr. Joe Wood; and my close friends outside of academia: Don Parker, David Perwin, Andy Reese, Vicki Fowler, and Diana Villarreal – not to mention, Oswald and Emily. Let me end with two women who have made all the difference to me: my grandmother, Inez Killen Marler (1919–2004), a southern tenant farmer's daughter; and my remarkable spouse, Candice L. Hawkinson. However, this book is rightfully dedicated to Candice, for I simply could not have done any of it without her support and love. As she can surely attest, *via ovicapitum dura est*.

Introduction

Merchants of the Cotton South in the Age of Capital

Cultural depictions of the business elites who were so influential to the mid-nine-teenth-century Atlantic world are fairly rare; most artists who seemed interested in such men tended to portray them as hopeless philistines. (Here one thinks of Dickens's calculating Mr. Gradgrind; or, on the other side of the Atlantic, the repressed Wall Street broker in Melville's "Bartleby the Scrivener.") Even fewer men of commerce appeared in contemporary depictions of the American South, whose slave-produced cotton provided much of the fuel for the industrial revolu-tion then underway. Harriet Beecher Stowe's northern-born slaveholder Simon Legree, a name synonymous with villainy to this day, was more a Louisiana planter than a businessman per se, although some scholars now maintain there was little difference between the two. And while George Washington Cable, a New Orleans native, opened his 1881 novella "Madame Delphine" with a refer-ence to "the activity and clatter of a city of merchants," those merchants played only supporting roles in his scathing narratives about local culture.[1]

There is one striking depiction of nineteenth-century southern business-men notable for its verisimilitude, and it is also set in Cable's New Orleans: French artist Edgar Degas's 1873 portrait of *A Cotton Office in New Orleans* (Plate 1). This famous painting depicts fourteen men during a routine day at a cotton-trading firm in the "Crescent City," a popular nickname for the South's then-largest city derived from its location on a sharp bend near the base of the Mississippi River. Because of its uniquely realistic portrayal of business-men at work (a realism mostly at odds with the impressionist school of art

---

[1] George Washington Cable, "Madame Delphine," in *Old Creole Days* (1885 ed.; repr., New York, 1964), 15. Examples of studies that blur the long-accepted distinction between planters and businessmen in the antebellum South are James Oakes, *The Ruling Race: A History of American Slaveholders* (New York, 1982); and Drew Gilpin Faust, *James Henry Hammond and the Old South: A Design for Mastery* (Baton Rouge, 1982), esp. chap. 6.

that Degas would soon help establish), scholars have frequently reproduced *A Cotton Office in New Orleans* to illustrate studies of new industrial regimes during the nineteenth century. Yet most such uses of Degas's painting have been unintentionally ironic. Rarely discussed are the contexts behind the portrait: the circumstances of its production, the actual firm and men it depicted, and the local and regional economic milieu in which it was set – all of which tend to contradict the themes of triumphant industrial capitalism that these historians imply the painting represents.[2]

For example, Degas's depiction of New Orleans cotton merchants adorns the cover of Eric Hobsbawm's classic study of the mid-nineteenth-century Western world, a period he memorably labeled the "Age of Capital." In this book, Hobsbawm elaborated a classical Marxist perspective on industrial development in the core regions of Europe (England, France, Germany) and the northern United States. Industrialism, in this view, fostered the formation of two new classes largely defined by their relationships to each other in the nascent economic order: the proletariat, who owned only their own commodified labor power; and the bourgeoisie, a class defined by its ownership of the means of production and employment of wage labor. But in the American South, the dominance of plantation slavery had long suppressed the full emergence of these two classes, even in metropolitan settings such as New Orleans. In fact, the sedentary Crescent City gentlemen in Degas's painting, whose use was presumably intended to typify the thrust of Hobsbawm's arguments about mid-nineteenth-century industrial change, represented a far older and less dynamic form of wealth based on the extraction of profit from exchange differentials – that is, "buying cheap and selling dear." Karl Marx referred to this qualitatively distinct form of wealth accumulation as "merchant capitalism," which was a term commonly accepted by other political economists both before and after he wrote. Unlike industrialists, who derived their profits from the organization of production itself, merchant capitalists usually operated at a cautious remove from production processes, instead concerning themselves mainly with their ability to exploit differences in commodity values in geographically separated markets.[3]

---

[2] Art historians have been more attentive to the circumstances behind Degas's painting, but they are clearly on less familiar turf when explicating its socioeconomic context. The best of these studies is Marilyn R. Brown, *Degas and the Business of Art: A Cotton Office in New Orleans* (University Park, PA, 1994). See also Christopher Benfey, *Degas in New Orleans: Encounters in the Creole World of Kate Chopin and George Washington Cable* (Berkeley, CA, and other cities, 1997); and Gail Feigenbaum [ed.], *Degas and New Orleans: A French Impressionist in America* (New Orleans, 1999). Subsequent references to the Musson–Degas family's activities in this introduction will be drawn from these three works. Two other examples of mainstream historians' use of *A Cotton Office in New Orleans* are Thomas L. Haskell and Richard F. Teichgraeber III, eds., *The Culture of the Market: Historical Essays* (New York, 1993); and D. A. Farnie and D. J. Jeremy, eds., *The Fibre that Changed the World: The Cotton Industry in International Perspective, 1600–1990s* (Oxford, and other cities, 2004).

[3] Eric Hobsbawm, *The Age of Capital, 1848–1875* (1975; paperback ed., New York, 1979). This study will rely heavily on the category "merchant capital," but in keeping with the more empirical

Merchant capitalists were, in many ways, a conservative lot. Although often chary of direct involvements with production, once they had established consistently profitable relationships on the production end of the commodity chain, they became dependent on those forms and very reticent to see them change. Such was the case with the mercantile firm in Edgar Degas's 1873 painting. Michel Musson, the seated figure in the front left foreground, was Degas's uncle, and like his father before him, he had been involved with the cotton trade in New Orleans for many years. Musson was a "factor," a commercial intermediary between southern slave-plantation owners and the distant textile manufacturers for whom cotton served as raw material. But even though he was never directly interested in planting himself, Musson, like many other New Orleans cotton factors, had been a slaveholder before the Civil War. Many antebellum merchants had routinely invested in slaves, which gave them a crucial financial stake in the maintenance of the South's "peculiar institution" at a time when it was under increasing siege from the very industrial capitalists who were the main subject of Hobsbawm's book.[4]

The importance of the Crescent City's mercantile community to the U.S. and Atlantic economies during the nineteenth century once led the distinguished historian Clement Eaton to declare that "New Orleans is the ideal city for the study of the business class of the Southern states." Eaton understood that the hundreds of businessmen like Michel Musson who comprised the city's "gentlemen of commerce" represented the largest concentration of merchant capital in the "Old South," with the port of New Orleans handling a disproportionate share of commodity flows to and from the region. Surprisingly, though, subsequent scholars have been slow to fulfill the promise of Eaton's commonsensical insight. Indeed, more studies have been produced about Edgar Degas's experiences in New Orleans than about the Crescent City business community

bent of historical method, its relevance will first be demonstrated throughout the course of the narrative body of the work, with a sustained examination of its more theoretical aspects deferred to the epilogue, where its use by such diverse thinkers as Adam Smith, Karl Marx, and Max Weber are discussed. For now, though, it is worth noting that merchant (or "mercantile") capital was long regarded as a distinct and important category in a great deal of twentieth-century historiography, from "progressive historians" such as Louis M. Hacker to more staid early business historians such as N. S. B. Gras, Henrietta Larson, and George Rogers Taylor. As the practice of economic history became more reliant on quantitative methods, however, the use of such categories fell from fashion – as did studies of political economy more generally. Only recently has the rise of the "new institutional economics" held out the possibility of a much-needed synthesis that takes greater account of these older and still quite valid concerns over the sociopolitical contexts of economic development; see Peter A. Coclanis and Scott Marler, "The Economics of Reconstruction," in *A Companion to the Civil War and Reconstruction*, ed. Lacy K. Ford (Malden, MA, 2005), 342–65.

4 The evolution of cotton factorage in the United States is the subject of Harold D. Woodman's classic study *King Cotton and His Retainers: Financing and Marketing the Cotton Crop of the South, 1800–1925* (Lexington, KY, 1968). On the late medieval and early modern roots of factorage more generally, see N. S. B. Gras, *Business and Capitalism: An Introduction to Business History* (New York, 1939), chap. 3.

itself, and thus Eaton's injunction remains true today. By describing the epochal "Age of Capital" as it was experienced by Louisiana merchants, this study aims to begin filling this surprising historiographical gap on the American South and the Atlantic world.[5]

Part I focuses on what is broadly termed the antebellum era. Like the South more generally, Louisiana was located on the nonindustrial periphery of the Atlantic world, yet the commodities produced on its slave plantations, along with the New Orleans–based commercial agents who shepherded them to national and global markets, played a crucial role in the new forms of capitalist development taking root elsewhere. In the first chapter, the development of New Orleans's merchant community during the first half of the nineteenth century is examined. Close attention is paid to some of the unique aspects of New Orleans, such as its unusual location and demographic composition, particularly the ethnocultural diversity that was a vestige of the city's lengthy Eurocolonial past. Because of its advantageous site near the base of the Mississippi River system, the city grew rapidly as an export point for agricultural products, but tensions between American migrants to the city and Creole residents of Spanish or French heritage diminished the cohesiveness of its merchant community. For example, Michel Musson's father (and Edgar Degas's grandfather) was a slaveholder of French origin who had fled the Haitian revolution in 1809 for New Orleans, where he resumed making his fortune in mercantile activities ranging from Mexican silver and New England ice to southern sugar and cotton. Despite setbacks after the national financial panic of 1837, merchants and bankers thrived on the city's monopolistic position over the fast-growing cotton trade during the 1840s. Yet the wealth they accumulated from southern staple crops caused them to downplay their city's loss of the upriver grain trade to competition from new canal and lake routes that linked midwestern states to urban markets on the northeastern seaboard. Thus, even as the regional economy continued growing during the 1850s, the city's merchants became overly dependent on slave-produced commodities from the southern countryside, and their stake in the perpetuation of the increasingly controversial labor system that underpinned plantation agriculture grew accordingly. But despite

[5] Clement Eaton, *The Mind of the Old South* (1964; rev. ed., Baton Rouge, 1967), 69. Despite its importance, there has been no sustained historical study of Louisiana's nineteenth-century merchant community. This neglect remains apparent in Youssef Cassis' recent study *Capitals of Capital: A History of International Financial Centres, 1780–2005*, trans. Jacqueline Collier (New York, 2007), in which New Orleans goes entirely unmentioned. Robert Earl Roeder's fine unpublished dissertation, "New Orleans Merchants, 1800–1837" (Harvard University, 1959) ended with the Panic of 1837. Significant if narrower contributions to the subject have been made by George D. Green, *Finance and Economic Development in the Old South: Louisiana Banking, 1804–1861* (Stanford, CA, 1972); Elliott Ashkenazi, *The Business of Jews in Louisiana, 1840–1875* (Tuscaloosa and London, 1988); and Richard H. Kilbourne Jr., *Debt, Investment, Slaves: Credit Relations in East Feliciana Parish, Louisiana, 1825–1885* (Tuscaloosa, AL, and London, 1995).

its support for slavery (also reflected in its notorious slave markets), the city's cosmopolitan character caused New Orleans to be widely disparaged as corrupt and dissolute by most southerners. Particular disdain was directed toward the city's commercial elites, whose multinational composition and extensive connections with the North made them more distrusted than those in other regional seaports such as Charleston, South Carolina.[6]

Their reputations were further undermined by the high prices Crescent City factors charged for goods sold to their clients in the countryside. Excessive charges and inefficiencies associated with their handling of outbound commodities also struck many planters as evidence that New Orleans merchants' share of the wealth generated in the countryside had made them not only rich, but also arrogant and lazy. As discussed in Chapter 2, such attitudes were reinforced during the antebellum decades by the failure of city merchants to implement much-needed improvements to their port's infrastructure. In particular, their inept efforts to promote local railroad construction seemed to confirm that the ease of river transportation fostered complacency among mercantile elites. A few prominent members of the New Orleans commercial community, like the northern-born banker James Robb, publicly deplored the city's unique failure to sponsor railroad and industrial development, warning that the lack of such investments bode ill for New Orleans's long-term economic prospects. But although men such as Robb and commercial publisher J. D. B. De Bow sometimes blamed aspects of the fickle, speculative, and migratory nature of merchant capital for these failures, they proved less willing than outsiders to explain the regional dearth of fixed-capital investments, particularly in manufacturing enterprises, as a consequence of the southern system of slave labor.

As Crescent City merchants remained fixated on still-booming Atlantic cotton markets rather than on internal economic development during the 1850s, others began to take advantage of their inattention. The loss of the western grain trade had provided an early signal that New Orleans's river-based "natural advantages" might not be enough to ensure its continued dominance, but now the city's formerly secure hold on its plantation hinterlands also started to come under siege. Competition from other cities played a role, but commercial erosion appeared from within as well. Chapter 3 discusses the growing importance of the hundreds of country stores scattered throughout the Louisiana interior. Although such antebellum stores have been downplayed by historians who emphasize the dominance of the urban-based factorage system, rural and small-town merchants in Louisiana benefited from anti–Crescent City

---

[6] For a suggestive look at eighteenth-century South Carolina merchants see Peter A. Coclanis, "The Hydra Head of Merchant Capital: Markets and Merchants in Early South Carolina," in *The Meaning of South Carolina History: Essays in Honor of George C. Rogers Jr.*, eds. David R. Chesnutt and Clyde N. Wilson (Columbia, SC, 1990), 1–18. See also the valuable essay by French historian Pierre Gervais, "Neither Imperial, Nor Atlantic: A Merchant Perspective on International Trade in the Eighteenth Century," *History of European Ideas* 34 (December 2008), 465–73.

sentiments during the years prior to the Civil War. By increasingly selling goods on credit and marketing the crop production of small farmers, such storekeepers laid strong foundations for their expanded importance to the southern agricultural economy after the Civil War.

As described by Eric Hobsbawm and many others, the development of industrial capitalism played a decisive and often-causative role in many of the political and military events of the mid-nineteenth century, from the European revolutions of 1848 through the Franco-Prussian War of the 1870s. The same holds true for industrial development in the United States, where two divergent regional labor systems fostered conflicts between North and South on multiple fronts. Part II of this study focuses on the Louisiana merchant community's role in the South's withdrawal from the federal Union and the bloody civil war that followed. Chapter 4 discusses commercial attitudes toward the secession movement in Louisiana in late 1860 and how most New Orleans merchants rallied behind the new Confederate nation the following year. However, the city's long-standing and lucrative connections to Atlantic markets complicated the support offered by certain segments of the business community, most notably among its powerful banking sector. Furthermore, the local economy quickly began suffering as a result of the war, particularly after a Federal naval blockade of southern seaports was instituted in May 1861.

The blockade and its effects prompted significant policy divisions between the New Orleans merchant community and the Confederate government. Frustrated by the failure of European governments to intervene in the war on behalf of the South, New Orleans merchants sought to use "King Cotton" as a diplomatic weapon by spearheading a region-wide cotton embargo during the summer of 1861. Although Crescent City businessmen hoped their action would prompt Great Britain and France to break the blockade, the embargo they organized was contrary to the cautious foreign policies then being pursued by the Confederate government, which feared that such economic coercion would prove counterproductive. An earlier proposal for an official embargo had been quashed in the Confederate Congress when advanced by the Louisiana sugar planter Duncan F. Kenner, who had extensive connections to the Musson–Degas family in New Orleans and France. As the Great Powers continued to dither over intervention, regional conditions worsened and hundreds of merchants fled New Orleans, which fell to Union forces in May 1862 and never reverted to Confederate control for the duration of the war.

Their support for southern independence during the Civil War brought the Musson–Degas family even closer together. Michel Musson, who served as a Confederate quartermaster in pre-occupation New Orleans, convinced Edgar Degas's father, a French private banker, to invest heavily in Confederate bonds, and another brother published a passionate public letter in support of slavery to the French emperor Napoleon III. Soon after the city's surrender to troops commanded by the domineering Union general Benjamin F. Butler, Musson sent his daughters (including Estelle, who was widowed when her husband, a nephew of Confederate president Jefferson Davis, was killed in the battle of Corinth in late 1862) to safe refuge in France. During Butler's controversial eight-month rule over New Orleans, which is the subject of Chapter 5, Crescent City merchants found themselves villainized and targeted by the demagogic Massachusetts general. Butler proved especially vindictive toward Crescent City banks, which had shipped most of their ample bullion reserves out of the city before its surrender.

The strict reign of "Beast" Butler over New Orleans represented in many respects the continuation of the war by other means, and his administration exacerbated the anti-Federal attitudes held by most of the city's white residents. The consequences of his draconian regime among the business community were of particular importance, since merchants' pragmatic desire for the resumption of commerce might have been manipulated to enlist their support for the South's postwar "reconstruction," a period discussed in Part III. In New Orleans, the process of federal Reconstruction began in earnest in 1863 under the command of Butler's replacement, General Nathaniel P. Banks, another political general from Massachusetts. However, as described in Chapter 6, most Crescent City merchants continued to be frozen out of federal attempts to reestablish the flows of cotton and other commodities to Atlantic markets. Despite General Banks's less overtly hostile administration over the city, the corruption first apparent under Butler worsened and grew more diffuse in the wake of his departure, especially as interbelligerent trading became more prevalent. Upon the war's conclusion in 1865 and during the years afterward, the former mercantile and financial elites of New Orleans gradually began to realize the severe consequences permanently wrought by the war on their earlier commercial dominance. Drawn by exorbitant wartime prices for cotton, an influx of opportunistic speculators now successfully competed with the remaining resident merchants for the southern trade. Most of these arrivistes were northerners, but also among them was Edgar Degas's brother René, the rather indolent-looking man slouched in a chair reading a newspaper in Degas's 1873 portrait. As Reconstruction-era politics in New Orleans devolved into violent factionalism between racist Confederate veterans and federally backed Republicans, Crescent City merchants' political influence was reduced to ineffective calls for "good government," as well as bitter criticisms of "carpetbaggers" and newly empowered freedpeoples.

Like the portrait of the famous 1864 naval battle between the CSS *Alabama* and USS *Kearsarge* that Edgar Degas included on the back wall of his uncle's cotton office in the upper right corner of his 1873 painting, the Confederacy's defeat in the Civil War continued to hover over New Orleans merchants such as Michel Musson for many years to come. In fact, at the very moment that Degas painted his piece in late January 1873, Musson's firm was on the brink of financial failure, and its dissolution was officially announced within weeks. Chapter 6 examines how the fate of merchants like Musson and many others paralleled the rapid economic decline of New Orleans during and after Reconstruction. The city's banking sector never recovered from the wartime blows it had suffered, which contributed to a severe capital shortage in the wider postbellum South. Furthermore, cross-lines trading during the war had provoked a sharp rise in overland transportation routes, which worked to the long-term advantage of interior cities like Memphis at the Crescent City's expense. Postwar attempts to resecure the upriver grain trade that the city's businessmen had ceded decades before proved an ineffective panacea for New Orleans's many economic woes. As a result of numerous interrelated changes to the structures of regional, national, and global commerce, the fortunes of the quondam "Queen City of the South" plummeted during and after the Civil War. Neither before nor since has a first-rank American city fallen from economic grace so swiftly and decisively.

Even the revival of southern cotton production, which grew well beyond its pre-1860 levels before the end of the century, could not save the former factorage community of New Orleans. Unlike the "gentlemanly capitalists" of nineteenth-century Great Britain, who were able to preserve most of their City–based wealth and influence in the face of ascendant industrialism, the blows suffered by Crescent City merchants such as Michel Musson proved too numerous and powerful to be absorbed. However, the culture and practices of merchant capitalism did persist in postbellum Louisiana and the South, albeit in greatly changed form. Because of the dispersal of postemancipation cotton production from the gang labor of plantation slavery into thousands of individuated small-farming units under sharecropping, the rural and small-town furnishing merchant assumed a pivotal role in the agricultural economy of the "New South" during Reconstruction, a role they continued to play through the Great Depression and the restructuring of southern agriculture during the New Deal. Although other historians have described the importance of rural merchants to the postwar South, Chapter 8 builds on the discussion in Chapter 3, as well as on the foundations laid by historians Roger L. Ransom and Richard Sutch in their influential 1977 study of "the economic consequences of emancipation." Ransom and Sutch used econometric modeling to assert that rural merchants in the Cotton South enjoyed "territorial monopolies" as a result of their dispersal throughout the countryside. Using aggregate data and methods similar to those of Ransom and Sutch, this chapter examines the different ways that "country stores" developed in discrete local environments within Louisiana after the Civil War, with important implications for historians' understandings of the postbellum southern economy.[7]

---

[7] Roger L. Ransom and Richard Sutch, *One Kind of Freedom: The Economic Consequences of Emancipation*, 2nd ed. (New York and other cities, 2001), esp. chaps. 6–8. On the persistence, adaptation, and significance of "gentlemanly capitalism" to industrializing Great Britain, see P. J. Cain and A. G. Hopkins, "Gentlemanly Capitalism and British Expansion Overseas I: The Old Colonial System, 1688–1850," *Economic History Review* 2d ser., 39 (November 1986), 501–25. See also Geoffrey Ingham, *Capitalism Divided? The City and Industry in British Social Development* (New York, 1984); and Martin J. Wiener, *English Culture and the Decline of the Industrial Spirit, 1850–1980* (Cambridge, UK, and other cities, 1981).

Although Edgar Degas never depicted these rural and small-town merchants in his art, they were later memorably portrayed in William Faulkner's epic descriptions of the Snopes and Varner clans in neighboring Mississippi. However, during his 1873 visit to New Orleans, Degas did produce another, far less well known painting that also featured his uncle in his cotton office. In *Cotton Merchants in New Orleans* (Plate 2), a painting that Degas himself thought was "better art," Michel Musson is the top-hatted figure stooped pensively over the table of cotton. The wall portrait of the Confederacy's naval loss hovers over this scene as well, yet the overall style is far less photographic than in the previous painting and clearly presages the French impressionism that Degas would soon help make famous. Although the heaped cotton is greater in quantity, it has now grown less distinct, even less substantial, than before. Indeed, Musson's hands seem to sink into the pile as if he were unable to firmly grasp either the cotton or his own current misfortunes with which it is inextricably bound. In contrast to the crowded office of the earlier portrait, this time there are only two other figures besides Musson. To the right, a derby-hatted man is only partially visible from behind the wall, almost seeming to emerge from the Civil War hanging itself – perhaps one of the many anonymous speculators who had invaded the city along with the northern armies? The other figure is red-bearded and dressed in a light suit in the southern style. Art historians have surmised that this man is probably General Frederick N. Ogden, who was a partner in the cotton business with Musson's son-in-law, both of whom were also prominent in the White League, a well-organized local paramilitary group. The charismatic Ogden, who had been a constant presence in the Musson offices and household during Degas's visit the previous year, led the white resistance that briefly overthrew the carpetbag government of Louisiana in 1874. In fact, Michel Musson addressed the assembled throng on Canal Street that September afternoon before they set off toward the Mississippi River for their showdown with the Republican-backed "Metropolitans." This event (which is discussed in Chapter 6) has been widely viewed by historians as seminal in prompting weakened northern support for federal efforts to maintain Reconstruction governments in the South by military force, a failed process that officially ended just a few years later.

In all of these senses, then, it is difficult not to view Degas's lesser-known painting as representative of the precarious state of his uncle's fortunes, about which the young artist was undoubtedly aware. More broadly, the other two figures in this more liminal work seem to typify the "new men" largely responsible for the changed and decimated condition of the New Orleans–based factorage system. In the epilogue, the significance of the newly dispersed culture of merchant capitalism for economic underdevelopment in the postbellum South is broadly assessed in a transatlantic context. Merchant capital, a qualitatively distinct form of wealth and investment, had made the Crescent City a dominant player in national and global commodity markets for most of the nineteenth century, but during and after the Civil War, it was exiled from its urban stronghold by the literal armies of industrialism and forced to seek refuge among the impoverished hamlets of the southern countryside. Even more so than Degas's similarly themed piece from Reconstruction-era New Orleans, which has been misleadingly appropriated by historians of industrial capitalism, *Cotton Merchants in New Orleans* provides a shrewd figurative expression of the swift decline of this last bastion of the old Atlantic world economy – and the system of southern slavery under which it had thrived – during the "Age of Capital."

There is a great deal that the study of merchant capitalism in Louisiana, both in New Orleans and the interior parishes, can add to our understanding of the nineteenth-century South. Such a study should help to repopulate the historiographical Old South with more than just masters and slaves, thereby better illuminating the often-contentious relationships between city and countryside before and after the Civil War. It should also cast fresh light on debates concerning the socioeconomic ramifications of plantation slavery. Much recent scholarship has relied heavily on the notion of a "market revolution" to portray a convergence of classes and interests in the antebellum United States, but such perspectives are hard-pressed to explain why the nation became so bitterly divided that it ultimately engaged in four years of bloody civil war. This study, by contrast, remains convinced by the testimony of most northern, southern, and foreign contemporaries about the growth of "irreconcilable conflicts" between the North and South during the 1850s, focusing on how southern merchant capital helped buttress the system of plantation slavery and thereby helped inhibit processes of class formation, urbanization, and fixed-capital investments that typified modernization elsewhere. It is also skeptical of a similar historiographical consensus that views elites' attitudes and actions in the postemancipation era through the lens of global capitalist development. Rather than creating a bourgeois "New South," postbellum merchants formed political and economic alliances with planter-landowners that institutionalized racism and fostered new forms of labor exploitation, all of which demonstrably suppressed southern economic development for nearly a century after the Civil War.[8]

This study of southern merchants will not only have implications for comparative regional development in the United States, but by situating their actions in wider international contexts, it should also contribute to our understandings of what is now called "the Atlantic world." Recent scholarship in this vein has done a great deal to revise and advance our knowledge of the connections between transatlantic slavery and early capitalism, but the vast majority

---

[8] A recent collection that promotes a "convergence" view of the antebellum South's business culture is L. Diane Barnes, Brian Schoen, and Frank Towers, eds., *The Old South's Modern Worlds: Slavery, Region, and Nation in the Age of Progress* (New York, 2011). For a discussion and critique of the similar consensus about capitalism's pervasive influence in the "New South," see Scott P. Marler, "Fables of the Reconstruction: Reconstruction of the Fables," *Journal of the Historical Society* 4 (Winter 2004), 113–37.

of these studies have focused on the rise and consolidation of the various exchange processes that constituted the Atlantic world. Although merchants and commodities networks are widely acknowledged to have played key roles in these processes, surprisingly few historians have pushed the Atlantic heuristic framework much past the late eighteenth century. Historians have seemed reluctant to venture beyond the early nineteenth-century anticolonial uprisings in Latin America and the Caribbean, despite the fact that entrenched systems of African slavery in the Americas, which are probably the defining theme of the Atlantic concept, did not meet their revolutionary demise until much later in the century – including, of course, the emancipation that occurred in the Civil War South. In this sense, focusing on merchant capital's role in the slave-based transnational cotton trade initiates a conversation centered not so much on the origins and growth of the Atlantic world than on the conditions that constituted its less understood decline. In so doing, this study should also contribute to business history, a subdiscipline that has long seemed to accept the orientation of modern economics toward production rather than distribution. As two historians of cotton's role in the Industrial Revolution have recently declared, it is astonishing that "the role of merchants has been largely neglected" by scholars, even though their "rehabilitation ... [has] the potential to transform wide swathes of economic history." This study will seek to contribute toward alleviating that long-standing neglect.[9]

---

[9] Douglas A. Farnie and David J. Jeremy, "Cotton as a World Power," in *Fibre that Changed the World*, 8. Though the subject has long been out of fashion, older studies routinely emphasized the importance of merchant capital to American economic development. Three classic examples are Robert G. Albion, *The Rise of New York Port, 1815–1860* (1939; repr., Boston and New York, 1967); Louis M. Hacker, *The Triumph of American Capitalism* (New York, 1940); and George Rogers Taylor, *The Transportation Revolution, 1815–1860* (1951; repr., New York, 1968); but see also Glenn Porter and Harold C. Livesay, *Merchants and Manufacturers: Studies in the Changing Structure of Nineteenth-Century Marketing* (1971; repr., Chicago, 1989). A valuable and important exception to Atlantic scholars' neglect of the late nineteenth century is Rebecca J. Scott, *Degrees of Freedom: Louisiana and Cuba after Slavery* (Cambridge, MA, 2005).

PART I

THE ANTEBELLUM ERA

I

Merchants and Bankers in the "Great Emporium of the South"

In April 1861, the South's leading commercial journal, *De Bow's Review*, which was based in New Orleans, published an unsigned letter titled "We Must Develop Southern Industry." Without alluding to the national political crisis that would erupt into civil war that very month, the author described his "apprehensions" about "the future of the cotton and tobacco growing Southern States." He believed that the region's economy was overdependent on exports of cotton, and he noted that "Great Britain and France are now earnestly engaged" in efforts to develop other sources for the lucrative crop. Although cotton plantations were akin to "a vast gold mine," the writer was skeptical of economies reliant on the production and extraction of natural resources. Those that did, he argued, had demonstrated a historical propensity for "purchasing all the necessaries of life" from external sources at the expense of their own industrial development, which ultimately left them "poor and dependent." The author feared that the South risked the same fate. "The experience of the last forty years has proved that cotton-growing countries do not accumulate permanent wealth," he wrote, because "mercantile capital emigrates to commercial and manufacturing countries to work out its continued accumulation."[1]

Despite the enormous prosperity generated by cotton cultivation in the South during the 1850s, similar economic concerns had provided grist for *De Bow's Review* since the journal's founding in 1846. Native Cassandras often

[1] "We Must Develop Southern Industry," *De Bow's Review* 30 (April 1861), 497–8; see also Stephen Colwell, *The South: A Letter from a Friend in the North, with Special Reference to the Effects of Disunion upon Slavery* (Philadelphia, 1856), 36–7. For a recent account of the nineteenth-century global cotton trade that emphasizes European attempts to develop new sources for the staple, see Sven Beckert, "Emancipation and Empire: Reconstructing the Worldwide Web of Cotton Production in the Age of the American Civil War," *American Historical Review* 109 (December 2004): 1405–38.

warned readers that by failing to reinvest profits from the cotton trade in home industries and infrastructure, instead using them to buy foodstuffs and manufactured goods from outside the region, the South was neglecting to establish a foundation for long-term growth. But this author's particular fears about the fickle, inherent tendency of "mercantile capital" to disregard residentiary investments displayed a keen historical awareness of the problems the region faced. His critique seemed to display familiarity with classical political economy, such as the well-known treatise *The Wealth of Nations* (1776), in which Adam Smith had elaborated the contributions to economic development made by different forms of capital. As opposed to the productive wealth "put into motion" by (nonslave) agriculture and manufacturing, Smith maintained that capital "employed in the trade of exportation has the least effect." Presaging the writer's concerns in *De Bow's Review*, Smith had argued that the wealth created by long-distance commodities exchanges "seems to have no fixed or necessary residence anywhere, but may wander about from place to place, according as it may either buy cheap or sell dear." Smith did admit, however, that urban entrepôts "situated near either the sea coast or the banks of a navigable river," such as London and Amsterdam, could derive enormous profits "from the most remote corners of the world ... by performing the office of carriers between distant countries and exchanging the produce of one for that of another." "A city might in this manner grow up to great wealth and splendour," he wrote, even while merchant capital's transitory character left "the country in its neighborhood" mired in "poverty and wretchedness."[2]

By the mid-nineteenth century, Adam Smith's insights into such geographically favored Atlantic trading enclaves applied with particular force to the port of New Orleans, which was the only true metropolis in the slave South. In an 1852 U.S. Senate report on the nation's commerce, special investigator Israel D. Andrews recognized the city's role as the chief citadel of southern merchant capitalism. New Orleans, Andrews wrote, is "eminently a place of exchange and distribution":

For commercial purposes, New Orleans occupies a very superior and commanding situation. It is the natural entrepôt for supplies destined to all parts of the Mississippi Valley, as well as the depot for those products of that salubrious region which seek a market seaward.

During the antebellum era, because of the city's location at the base of the enormous Mississippi River system, half of all the South's cotton production routinely passed through the hands of New Orleans merchants on its way to textile manufacturers in the North and Europe. Although cotton and sugar

---

[2] Adam Smith, *The Wealth of Nations*, ed. Andrew Skinner (New York and other cities, 1986), 463–5 (first two quotations on p. 465; third quotation on pp. 463–4), 502 (final quotations). For further elaboration about merchant capitalism both as a category of classical political economy and as a later historiographical problematic, see the epilogue herein.

exports were the main source of its commercial dominance, New Orleans was also important for its slave markets, for its retailing of imported goods, and as a bulk-break point for midwestern and regional foodstuffs – all of which were redistributed to the plantations and stores of the southern interior by the city's large, hierarchical community of merchant capitalists: banks, factorage houses, commission agents, wholesalers, and retailers.[3]

The businessmen of New Orleans were not a unified class, however. In fact, they were frequently a quarrelsome lot. After spending several weeks in New Orleans and its environs during the 1850s, Frederick Law Olmsted doubted whether "there is a city in the world where the resident population [is] so divided in its origin, or where there is such variety in the tastes, habits, manners, and moral codes of the citizens." The city's merchants were also often "divided" among themselves by market competition and conflicting institutional demands. Bankers did not always see eye to eye with cotton factors, nor factors with wholesalers, wholesalers with shopkeepers, nor any of them with each other – not to mention disagreements with their rural clientele. But a high degree of class cohesion has never been a hallmark of merchant capitalists. As a group, historically they have been characterized as "parasitic" on classes more directly responsible for the organization and maintenance of production (in the antebellum South, the slaveowning plantation elite), as well as "conservative" in their reluctance to exploit the transformative potential of the wealth they controlled.[4]

This chapter provides an overview of New Orleans and its rapid commercial growth during the first half of the nineteenth century, with an emphasis on its mercantile and financial community. The business practices, ethnocultural backgrounds, and other relevant aspects of this community are discussed, as

---

[3] [Israel D. Andrews], *Report of Israel D. Andrews on the Trade and Commerce of the British North American Colonies, and Upon the Trade of the Great Lakes and Rivers*, Senate Executive Document No. 112 (32 Cong., 1st Sess.) (Washington, DC, 1853), 753 (cited hereinafter as Andrews, *Report on Trade and Commerce*). This study tends to treat New Orleans banks as part of the congeries of institutions representing southern merchant capitalism. However, although the advent of international banking was closely linked historically to the growing need for reliable instruments of long-distance exchange, it should be noted that banking (or "interest-bearing") capital rapidly evolved according to its own imperatives, thereby developing an identity apart from the merchant capitalism that originally fostered it; see, for example, Karl Marx, *Capital*, Vol. III, trans. David Fernbach (1981; repr., London, 1991), 440–79. As will be shown herein, the distinct priorities and interests of New Orleans banks were often at odds with those of southern merchants, planters, and politicians.

[4] Historians Elizabeth Fox-Genovese and Eugene D. Genovese characterized merchant capitalism as "parasitic" and "conservative" throughout their neglected work *Fruits of Merchant Capital: Slavery and Bourgeois Property in the Rise and Expansion of Capitalism* (Oxford and other cities, 1983), esp. chap. 1, "The Janus Face of Merchant Capital"; see also the epilogue herein. Frederick Law Olmsted, *The Cotton Kingdom: A Traveller's Observations on Cotton and Slavery in the American Slave States*, ed. Arthur M. Schlesinger (New York, 1953), 235. On rural Louisiana merchants see Scott P. Marler, "Merchants in the Transition to a New South: Central Louisiana, 1840–1880," *Louisiana History* 42 (Spring 2001), 165–92.

are some of the particular individuals and firms that comprised it. Increasing "apprehensions" about the city's and region's long-term economic prospects, such as those expressed by the anonymous author in *De Bow's Review*, will highlight the differences and similarities among these "gentleman capitalists." This portrait of antebellum Louisiana's economy and merchants' role in it will serve as a foundation for the chapters that follow, in which the fortunes of this community are traced through the prosperous 1850s and their subsequent decline during the Civil War and Reconstruction.

Although New Orleans only had a population of about 10,000 inhabitants at the beginning of the nineteenth century, the city had been linked into the Atlantic world since its founding by the French in 1718. Even as colonies along the eastern seaboard of North America thrived (and eventually chafed) under British mercantilist policies, eighteenth-century New Orleans was more important for its strategic location as the southern anchor of the Mississippi Valley than for the minor economic activities sponsored by its French and Spanish rulers – as well as growing numbers of British and American interlopers. During this period the city first became known for involvements with Latin America and the Caribbean, earning a reputation as a center for international intrigues that it would maintain for years to come. However, staple-crop agriculture was slow to develop in the enormous, sparsely populated Louisiana territory during the eighteenth century (French attempts to grow tobacco were a minor exception); most of its commerce centered on animal hides, naval stores, and other low capital–intensive goods.[5]

The transformation of New Orleans from a small trading outpost on the periphery of the Atlantic world occurred under American auspices in the decades after the fledgling U.S. government purchased the Louisiana territory from France in 1803. During his tenure as George Washington's secretary of state, Thomas Jefferson had been quick to recognize the strategic importance of the Mississippi River and its southern outlet to American interests. Casting a covetous gaze in 1790 toward the interior territory then controlled by Spain, Jefferson insisted that "we have a right to some spot as an entrepôt for our commerce," adding that "a disinterested eye, looking on a map, will remark how conveniently" New Orleans is situated "for the purpose." When he became president a decade later, Jefferson made acquisition of the Louisiana territory, recently retroceded by Spain back to France, a diplomatic priority. Writing to Robert R. Livingston, the U.S. minister to Napoleonic France, in 1802, Jefferson sought to impress the importance of obtaining Louisiana upon his ambassador:

There is on the globe one single spot, the possessor of which is our natural and habitual enemy. It is New Orleans, through which the produce of three-eighths of our territory

---

[5] New Orleans's early commercial development is described in John G. Clark, *New Orleans, 1718–1812: An Economic History* (Baton Rouge, 1970); see also Lawrence N. Powell, *The Accidental City: Improvising New Orleans* (Cambridge, MA, 2012).

must pass to market, and from its fertility it will ere long yield more than half of our whole produce and contain more than half our inhabitants.

Here Jefferson articulated an early version of the soon-to-be popular argument that the natural advantages of New Orleans's location ensured its eventual commercial dominance. But although such geographic determinism had some validity, it also carried the kernel of what would become an ill-advised complacency in the face of technological, commercial, and demographic changes.[6]

The early years of the nineteenth century were difficult for New Orleans. The territory's status as a pawn in Old World warfare led one cotton merchant to complain in April 1803 that it was "high time our Fate should be decided, this long state of suspence Being of the Greatest prejudice to us, without Money, or any Regulation [sic]." But despite Jefferson's peaceful acquisition of Louisiana and its subsequent admission as a state in 1812, the transition to an American-controlled regime proved to be prolonged and painful for the mercantile community at New Orleans. Hostilities between Great Britain and the United States during the Jefferson and Madison administrations demonstrated merchant capital's vulnerability to political disruptions. Beginning in 1807, a series of embargoes and other acts prohibiting commercial intercourse with foreign nations severely affected the export-oriented businesses of New Orleans, especially its nascent cotton trade with England. These acts were highly unpopular with Crescent City merchants and encouraged lawlessness, as many sought to evade restrictions by engaging in blockade-running and other illicit commerce. Vincent Nolte, a German-born merchant, later recalled the difficulties posed to "the enterprising mercantile spirit" by the enforced "absence of business" prevalent upon his arrival to New Orleans in late 1811. The long-simmering conflicts between Great Britain and its former colonies erupted into war the following year, causing many city merchants to overcome their reservations about U.S. foreign policies and fight alongside Colonel Andrew Jackson when the war culminated with the defeat of British forces at New Orleans in January 1815. One of those merchants, Maunsel White, established such a close relationship with Jackson during the siege that he ended up serving as the New Orleans factor of the Tennessee planter-politician well into the 1840s.[7]

---

[6] Thomas Jefferson to Robert R. Livingston, April 18, 1802, in *The Writings of Thomas Jefferson*, comp. and ed. Paul Leicester Ford (New York, 1897), VIII, 144; Secretary of State [Jefferson] to William Short, August 10, 1790, in *The Papers of Thomas Jefferson*, ed. Julian P. Boyd (Princeton, NJ, 1965), XVII, 122. Two recent works by historical geographers that closely examine New Orleans's "site and situation" are Peirce F. Lewis, *New Orleans: The Making of an Urban Landscape*, 2nd ed. (Santa Fe, NM, and Harrisonburg, VA, 2003); and Richard Campanella, *Time and Place in New Orleans: Past Geographies in the Present Day* (Gretna, LA, 2002).

[7] On Maunsel White see Louisiana, Vol. IX, 87, in R. G. Dun & Co. Credit Reports Collection (Baker Library Historical Collections, Harvard Business School; cited hereinafter as Dun & Co., Louisiana, with appropriate volume and page numbers); and Clement Eaton, *The Mind of the Old South* (rev. ed., Baton Rouge, 1967), 71–2. Vincent Nolte, *The Memoirs of Vincent Nolte, or Fifty Years in Both Hemispheres*, trans. Burton Rascoe (1854; repr. New York, 1934),

Although Vincent Nolte fought on the American side at New Orleans, he objected when a few hundred bales of high-quality cotton that he owned were confiscated for use as impromptu parapets against British shells. (The irony of New Orleans merchants literally seeking safe haven behind cotton bales seemed lost on Nolte, but it was an effective tactic that would be repeated in Louisiana during the Civil War a half-century later.) The remarkable Nolte, the scion of a well-established European mercantile family, personally embodied many of the transnational qualities of Atlantic merchant capitalism. He had first visited New Orleans in 1806 as an agent of the allied English and Dutch merchant-banking houses of Baring Brothers and Hope & Company, and he would continue to do business in the city off and on through the 1850s. In his usually candid and detailed memoir published in 1854, Nolte offered little insight into the reasons why he chose to fight with the Americans at New Orleans, but the fact of his service, like that of other merchants, contradicted what Thomas Jefferson, probably echoing Adam Smith, had written about such gentlemen of commerce in 1786. "Merchants are the least virtuous [citizens]," he had quipped, "and possess the least of the *amor patriae*." (It is worth noting that Alexander Hamilton, Jefferson's principal rival, held merchants in much higher esteem.)[8]

Throughout his memoir, Nolte commented on the changing composition and character of the city's mercantile community. He was not enamored with the hundreds of American businessmen, mainly from the upper Atlantic seaboard, who flocked to New Orleans after its acquisition by the United States; upon his return in 1811, Nolte blamed "the spirit of low cunning and adroitness which they [had] introduced" for the city's "moral retrogression" during his absence. Nolte contrasted the boorish opportunism of American merchants with the "openness, good faith, and sincerity in ... mercantile intercourse" of the Creole community of French and Spanish origins. Although Nolte's friend Benjamin Latrobe, one of the most perceptive observers of early national New Orleans, was more attuned to Creole peculiarities, he believed both groups were gradually adopting characteristics of the other and converging to form a single "money-making community" that was "in an eternal bustle."[9]

187 (quotations), 198–9, 206; Clark, *New Orleans, 1718–1812*, pp. 324–8; John F. Merieult (New Orleans) to Bird, Savage & Bird (London), April 25, 1803, document no. 2007.0257.2 in Louisiana Manuscripts Collection, Williams Research Center, Historic New Orleans Collection, New Orleans, LA (hereinafter cited as HNOC).
[8] Thomas Jefferson to Jean Nicolas Démenieur, January 24, 1786, in *Papers of Thomas Jefferson*, X, 16. For Hamilton's more sanguine view of merchants' disinterestedness, see his Federalist No. 35, in *The Federalist Papers*, ed. Clinton Rossiter (New York, 2003), 210–11; see also Stanley Elkins and Eric McKitrick, *The Age of Federalism: The Early American Republic, 1788–1800* (New York and Oxford, 1993), 106–12. Nolte, *Memoirs*, 17–19, 82–6, 216; see also Benjamin Henry Boneval Latrobe, *Impressions Respecting New Orleans: Diary and Sketches, 1818–1820*, ed. Samuel Wilson Jr. (New York, 1951), 42–6, 73–4. On the use of cotton bales as ramparts during the 1863 Federal siege of Port Hudson, Louisiana, see Edward Bacon, *Among the Cotton Thieves* (Detroit, 1867), 136, 211–12, 227–36.
[9] Latrobe, *Impressions Respecting New Orleans*, 32; Nolte, *Memoirs*, 90, 184–5.

Over time, Creole businessmen became more frequent targets of criticism. One visitor remarked in 1851 that "if the commercial prosperity of New Orleans had always depended on Creole enterprise, I fear the purchase of Louisiana would not have been so highly lauded as now." Later in the century, New Orleans native George Washington Cable, himself the son of a wholesale grocer and a mercantile clerk as a young man, repeatedly skewered the city's wealthy Creoles for their indolence in his literary and historical works. In an 1844 letter to his wife back in Georgia, John G. Dunlap, a clerk recently arrived to New Orleans, had expressed such sentiments more obliquely, characterizing one of his employers as a "young Creole … who does not seem to care much about business." "By all accounts," William Kingsford wrote in 1858, "there are two societies" in New Orleans, "which the differences of language and religion tend to perpetuate." While such comments have led some to consider the divisions between Creoles and Americans to be the leitmotif of Louisiana history, an overemphasis on ethnocultural factors threatens to obscure what one scholar called the "peaceful coexistence" of the state's diverse groups of merchants during the nineteenth century. Historian Thomas N. Ingersoll also believes such differences have been exaggerated; for him, slavery and its racial hierarchies were the glue that bound elite New Orleanians together.[10]

Nevertheless, vestiges of the city's Eurocolonial past exerted a profound influence on the development of its business community and would continue to do so over the course of the century. As early as 1806 Thomas Ashe claimed that particular commercial sectors in the city were dominated by groups of differing regional, national, or ethnic origins. By the time of the regional cotton boom that began in the 1820s, New Orleans presented the striking aspect of what one observer called "a world in miniature," and Benjamin Latrobe described how merchants' various national origins created an "incessant … gabble of tongues" around the city's crowded levees and coffeehouse bourses. The global nature of the commerce flowing through New Orleans helped it retain this multicultural character for the duration of the antebellum era. For example, a New York businessman complained in 1851 that the persistence of the Napoleonic Code meant that "the merchant … can never so habituate himself to the legal ways of Louisiana that he can steer his way among the shoals

---

[10] Thomas N. Ingersoll, *Mammon and Manon in Early New Orleans: The First Slave Society in the Deep South, 1718–1819* (Knoxville, TN, 1999), 254–61; John G. Clark, "New Orleans and the River: A Study in Attitudes and Responses," *Louisiana History* 8 (Winter 1967), 121–2 (quotation). The most adamant statement of the importance of Creole/American divisions is Joseph G. Tregle Jr., *Louisiana in the Age of Jackson: A Clash of Cultures and Personalities* (Baton Rouge, 1999), which follows a path blazed by George Washington Cable, especially in *The Creoles of Louisiana* (1884; repr., New York, 1970). William Kingsford, *Impressions of the West and South during a Six Weeks' Holiday* (Toronto, 1858), 55; John G. Dunlap to Beatrice [Dunlap], November 10, 1844, in Dunlap Correspondence, Folder 3 (Howard-Tilton Memorial Library, Tulane University, New Orleans, LA); A. Oakey Hall, *The Manhattaner in New Orleans; or, Phases of Crescent City Life* (New York, 1851), 108.

and breakers of commercial currents without consulting a lawyer's chart and compass." A few years later, British visitor James M. Phillippo insisted that "no other city in the world ... presents greater contrasts of national manners and language." The frequency of such comments reveals that the complex texture of this "world in miniature" and its stratified commercial culture not only made New Orleans unique within the South, but also distinctive even when compared to other port cities of the Atlantic world.[11]

Although the oft-noted "gabble of tongues" was the most conspicuous marker of ethnocultural differences in New Orleans, religious affiliations were also important. Inhabitants of French and Spanish origins ensured a larger institutional presence for the Catholic Church in southeastern Louisiana than anywhere else in the South, although by the 1840s "high-church" Protestant denominations, particularly Presbyterians, as well as the anti-evangelical Congregational Unitarian Church, provided an effective counterweight to Roman influence among newly arrived Anglo-American merchants and professionals. There was also a growing Jewish contingent in the city, many of whom, as elsewhere, were associated with the mercantile trades. Judah Touro, who fought on the American side during the War of 1812 and later made substantial contributions to poor-relief efforts in the city, downplayed his Jewish background during his decades as a resident merchant in the wholesale and commission trades. Judah P. Benjamin, whose Hebraic origins would help make him a controversial figure in the Confederate government, first established himself as a commercial lawyer in New Orleans in the 1830s before branching out to become a prominent (if only erratically successful) sugar planter in cross-river Jefferson Parish.[12]

Adding to the ethnic mix in the sole southern metropolis were thousands of African Americans. The city's slave markets were the main clearinghouse for plantation labor on the southwestern cotton frontier, but many served as domestic servants in merchants' upper-class households, Creole and American alike. New Orleans was also home to the largest concentration of free blacks

[11] James M. Phillippo, *The United States and Cuba* (London, 1857), 306; Hall, *Manhattaner in New Orleans*, 77; Latrobe, *Impressions Respecting New Orleans*, 18; unidentified 1822 city directory quoted in "The Former and Present Times and Trade of New Orleans," *De Bow's Review* 7 (November 1849), 420; Thomas Ashe, *Travels in America Performed in the Year 1806* (London, 1809), 251–62 (quotation on 259–60). Although New Orleans was the South's largest and most ethnically diverse city, it should be noted (*pace* Joseph G. Tregle Jr.) that the rapid pace of nineteenth-century immigration made high percentages of foreign-born residents common in other U.S. urban areas. Foreign-born whites constituted around half of New York City's population in 1850, and in 1860 they accounted for a similar proportion of residents in Chicago, Cincinnati, St. Louis, and Milwaukee; see Allan Pred, *Urban Growth and City-Systems in the United States, 1840–1860* (Cambridge, MA, 1980), 30–1.

[12] Robert D. Meade, *Judah P. Benjamin: Confederate Statesman* (New York, 1943), 38–45, 60–1; Bertram Wallace Korn, *The Early Jews of New Orleans* (Waltham, MA, 1969), 83–8, 217–21; William W. Chenault and Robert C. Reinders, "The Northern-born Community of New Orleans in the 1850s," *Journal of American History* 51 (September 1964), 241–2.

in the antebellum South. Notable among them were Creole men of French-Caribbean descent such as the wealthy merchant-tailor Francois Lacroix: highly cultured, light-complexioned individuals who usually took great pains to distinguish themselves from the darker-skinned blacks who typically made up the ranks of slaves. Indeed, some of these free blacks were slaveholders themselves, as was Lacroix.[13]

Just above blacks on the nineteenth-century ladder of racial caste were the growing numbers of poor European migrants to the city, especially Irish, Italians, and Germans. Most of these penniless arrivals filled out the ranks of day-laborers, particularly on the city's docks. Indeed, Frederick Law Olmsted observed that "free men have very much gained the field of labour in New Orleans to themselves," and they jealously guarded this turf against competition from slaves. Some of these migrants, however, were able to carve out places for themselves as petty shopkeepers or in the artisanal trades. As the immigrant population assumed ever-greater importance to fractious municipal politics, such ambitious and successful *petit bourgeois* capable of appealing to the working class without greatly offending the conservative sensibilities of native business elites – men such as Abdil Crossman, a hatter; Charles M. Waterman, a hardware dealer; Gerard Stith, a typographer; and John T. Monroe, a former stevedore – found themselves elected to terms as mayors of the city during the late antebellum era.[14]

Compounding the city's distinctive cosmopolitan aura were its seasonal residents. Israel Andrews noted in his 1852 report that New Orleans's steady population growth (it had doubled roughly every dozen years over the

---

13 On Francois Lacroix see Loren Schweninger, *Black Property Owners in the South, 1790–1915* (Urbana, II, 1990), 118; and "The World of Francois Lacroix" (2002), an online exhibition with primary documents by the Louisiana Division of the New Orleans Public Library, at http://nutrias.org/exhibits/lacroix/title.htm (accessed November 23, 2011). On free-black refugees from Haiti and Cuba to New Orleans, see Adam Rothman, *Slave Country: American Expansion and the Origins of the Deep South* (Cambridge, MA, 2005), 74–9, 91. On slavery in antebellum New Orleans see Ingersoll, *Mammon and Manon in Early New Orleans*; Walter Johnson, *Soul by Soul: Life Inside the Antebellum Slave Market* (Cambridge, MA, and London, 1999); Roger W. Shugg, *Origins of Class Struggle in Louisiana: A Social History of White Farmers and Laborers during Slavery and After* (1939; rpt., Baton Rouge, 1968), 24–5 and Appendix, Tables 3 and 4 (pp. 318–19); and Richard C. Wade, *Slavery in the Cities: The South, 1820–1860* (New York, 1964), 17–18, 24–5, and passim.

14 "Administrations of the Mayors of New Orleans" (typescript dated 1931; Special Collections, Howard-Tilton Memorial Library, Tulane University, New Orleans, LA; cited hereinafter as HTML-Tulane); Shugg, *Origins of Class Struggle in Louisiana*, 146–8; Olmsted, *Cotton Kingdom*, 233; see also Richard Campanella, *Bienville's Dilemma: A Historical Geography of New Orleans* (Lafayette, LA, 2008), 168–9; and William L. Barney, *The Road to Secession: A New Perspective on the Old South* (New York, 1972), 72, 113. British political economist John E. Cairnes cited another American observer's claim that "nearly all the heavy out-door work in the city of New Orleans is performed by whites"; John E. Cairnes, *The Slave Power: Its Character, Career, and Probable Designs* (1862; repr., Columbia, SC, 2003), 38; see also Samuel Cartwright, "How to Save the Republic and the Position of the South in the Union," *De Bow's Review* 11 (August 1851), 195.

previous half-century) was all the more "extraordinary" because the city's merchants have "always been somewhat migratory." Many businessmen avoided outbreaks of cholera and yellow fever by traveling to New Orleans from Europe and the North only for the fall marketing season. Similarly, every fall and winter, well-to-do plantation owners from around the lower Mississippi Valley relocated their families to the city, where they competed for pride of place with the more sedentary merchant population. Their appearance marked the advent of the busy social season, which culminated with the balls and other festivities associated with Mardi Gras during the weeks before Lent, usually in February. (The creeping Americanization of the traditionally Catholic Mardi Gras festival – a process well under way by the 1850s, when the Mystic Krewe of Comus was formed by the city's Anglo-American business elite – provides a good measure of the ways that cultural differences between merchants were smoothed over in the urban environment.) All told, the city's commercial life was enriched by the constant arrival of steamboats that disgorged itinerant visitors to the "Queen City of the South": drummers (as traveling salesmen were called), country-store owners, upcountry planters, and other transients who made pilgrimages to New Orleans to transact business. This parade of vulnerable visitors also attracted, like bees to honey, a free-floating mercenary army of card sharks, swindlers, and other scoundrels who preyed on these unsuspecting rubes. The international merchant Vincent Nolte noted the presence of such "offscourings of the northern States" in his 1854 memoir. "New Orleans," a Boston business associate told him, "as everybody knows, is a regular rendezvous for all sorts of rogues and rabble."[15]

The stays of rascals and respectable visitors alike were often punctuated by outbursts of debauchery in the Crescent City's numerous dens of gambling, prostitution, and strong liquor. Antebellum accounts frequently mentioned the prevalence of vice in New Orleans – not least of all among its upper-class residents. An anonymous 1849 pamphlet by "a resident" deplored the "immense number of drinking houses in every part of the city" and how the "practice of almost constant drinking through the day pervades all classes of society." Perhaps the most notorious of the city's sensual delights were "quadroon balls," where exotic mixed-race concubines consorted publicly with their white patrons. Alexis de Tocqueville, who attended one of these balls during a brief visit in 1832, was shocked by the "incredible laxity of morals" he felt

[15] Nolte, *Memoirs*, 88; Robert C. Reinders, *End of an Era, New Orleans 1850–1860* (New Orleans, 1964), 155–8; Reid Mitchell, *All on a Mardi Gras Day: Episodes in the History of New Orleans Carnival* (Cambridge, MA, 1995), 23–8. Of nineteen founding members of the Pickwick Club, a private club that grew out of the new Krewe of Comus in 1857, sixteen were merchants; Augusto P. Miceli, *The Pickwick Club of New Orleans* (New Orleans, 1964), 17–19. Andrews, *Report on Trade and Commerce*, 753; for two antebellum visitors' comments on New Orleans's seasonal population, see James Robertson, *A Few Months in America* (London, 1855), 66; and Robert Russell, *North America: Its Agriculture and Climate* (Edinburgh, 1858), 253.

was promoted by such racial intermingling. In 1857 another European visitor, James Phillippo, lamented that the "stigma attached to profligacy [was] so slight" among the "aristocratic portion of the community." The following year, a northern traveler declared "there undoubtedly is a greater love of pleasure [in New Orleans], and a more determined enjoyment of ease, than is met with at the North." Frederick Law Olmsted also attended a quadroon ball during his stay, but his assessment of the city's hedonistic subculture was both less prurient and more insightful. "[A]lthough the facilities for licentiousness are much greater" in New Orleans, he wrote, the resultant "evils" are intensified in northern cities by the "very intrigues, cloaks, hazards, and expenses" that "exasperate [young men], and increase its degrading effect on their character, producing hypocrisy ... and giving them habits which are inimical to future domestic contentment and virtue." Olmsted implied psychological advantages to the ways that wealthy southerners could embrace their sins of the flesh in Crescent City society, whereas their bourgeois Yankee counterparts, to their detriment, had to repress and disavow feelings and actions of which they were deeply ashamed.[16]

Still, some resident businessmen managed to resist the city's panoply of vices. In an 1857 letter, commission merchant James Wyche described his struggles to maintain "moral firmness enough to withstand the temptations with which I am daly [sic] thrown into contact" in a city he called "the most dissipated place in the world." "I don't like New Orleans," Wyche declared, "and only remain here because I think I can in a few years be able to say that I am independent of the world in regard to pecuniary concerns." Such unflattering estimates of the moral character of antebellum New Orleans, whether by residents or outsiders, was long a matter of grave concern to city boosters. But resident publisher J. D. B. De Bow also opposed the type of rootless opportunism represented by merchants such as Wyche, feelings he first made clear in an early number of his southern business journal in 1846. Not only did New Orleans need to overcome its ill-repute as a "great charnel-house" of "disease and death" that resulted from inadequate public health and sanitation, but De Bow also maintained that "we have had a worse reputation still," one that he blamed squarely on short-sighted commercial interests:

Our city has been considered a great depot of merchandise, one vast warehouse in which every inhabitant is a mere transient adventurer, without any kind of local feeling or bond of union, constituting together a heterogeneous mass of material from all the world.... Something higher must be aimed at than mere trade or commerce, high as these may be. *A society must be formed, social institutions promoted,... and a fixed and settled order of things secured.*

[16] Olmsted, *Cotton Kingdom*, 239; Kingsford, *Impressions of the West and South*, 54; Phillippo, *United States and Cuba*, 310; G. W. Pierson, [ed.], "Alexis de Tocqueville in New Orleans," *Franco-American Review* 1 (1936), 36; [Anonymous], *New Orleans as It Is: Its Manners and Morals ...* (Utica, NY, 1849), 53–5.

De Bow, along with a handful of public-spirited city merchants like Maunsel White and Glendy Burke, tilted at this windmill for many years. As Olmsted observed, the long-standing divisions and hierarchies of New Orleans society "injure[d] civic enterprise" and complicated the city's ability to address the many pressing concerns attendant to rapid urban growth.[17]

Other nineteenth-century American cities faced similar problems, to be sure, but in New Orleans, such difficulties seemed worse than elsewhere. While the cultural differences between Creoles and Americans noted by contemporaries and later historians probably contributed to the city's fractious political milieu, there were other important reasons for the lack of a "fixed and settled order of things" in antebellum New Orleans. Shannon Lee Dawdy has recently traced the roots of Crescent City residents' contempt for government authority to its geographic isolation on the periphery of the eighteenth-century Atlantic world, which created and sustained a culture that she terms "rogue colonialism." Even as New Orleans's commercial importance grew during the early nineteenth century, extralegal attitudes and activities persisted. In 1819 Benjamin Latrobe claimed that "there is no country so favorably situated as to the facility of smuggling as Louisiana." He probably had in mind the notorious pirates Jean and Pierre Laffite, who operated throughout the bayous, creeks, and inlets south and west of New Orleans and headed a criminal syndicate widely known to be allied with city merchants, bankers, and other 'legitimate' business interests. The Laffite brothers remain local heroes to this day.[18]

During the antebellum decades, this heritage of nose-thumbing lawlessness combined with the rapid growth of cotton production in the Old Southwest to help lend the city a decidedly frontier character, a persistent "rugged individualism" that gave New Orleans higher rates of violence than comparable American cities. Some antebellum visitors noted the dissonance between intra-gentlemanly violence and the rarified social airs assumed by Crescent City commercial elites. But as Latrobe remarked, "slavery brings with it many things which seem contradictory," and indeed, it was the city's deepening involvements in the regional system of plantation slavery over the first half of the nineteenth century that most strongly reinforced its status as one of the last bastions of exchange-based capitalism in the rapidly industrializing Atlantic

[17] Olmsted, *Cotton Kingdom*, 235; J. D. B. De Bow, "The Moral Advance of New Orleans," *De Bow's Review* 2 (November 1846), 349 (emphasis in original). Many businessmen's initial response to the mid-1853 yellow fever outbreak, which killed thousands in New Orleans, was to downplay the epidemic for fear it would injure the impending crop marketing season; see John Duffy, *Sword of Pestilence: The New Orleans Yellow Fever Epidemic of 1853* (Baton Rouge, 1966); and Ari Kelman, *A River and Its City: The Nature of Landscape in New Orleans* (Berkeley, CA, and other cities, 2003), 94–100. James Wyche to O. A. Otey, January 26, 1857, in Wyche and Otey Family Papers, Folder 9 (Southern Historical Collection, Wilson Library, University of North Carolina–Chapel Hill; cited hereinafter as SHC).

[18] Latrobe, *Impressions Respecting New Orleans*, 137; William C. Davis, *The Pirates Laffite: The Treacherous World of the Corsairs of the Gulf* (Orlando, FL, and other cities, 2005); Shannon Lee Dawdy, *Building the Devil's Empire: French Colonial New Orleans* (Chicago, 2008), chap. 6.

world. Ironically, these processes of industrialization were fueled largely by the millions of bales of slave-produced cotton shepherded through New Orleans. There, however, the relatively effortless profits from this trade lulled businessmen into complacent habits that suppressed the investment patterns and class cohesion that undergirded economic modernization in free-labor urban environments in Europe and the North. Like the migratory tendency of "mercantile capital" noted in the letter he published just before the outbreak of the Civil War, De Bow's complaint against "transient adventurers" in New Orleans reflected his awareness of the peculiar and detrimental market mentalities fostered and buttressed by plantation slavery in the South.[19]

Although the city's economy had long centered on its status as an entrepôt for commodities moved through the Mississippi River system, New Orleans's excessive dependence on the cotton trade evolved gradually over the first half of the nineteenth century. Moreover, the significance of this overreliance was obscured by several factors, not least of which was the prosperity that increased commerce promoted in the city and its hinterlands. Because of the simultaneous shift of the locus of production from the Atlantic seaboard toward the southwestern interior, especially to the young states of Alabama, Mississippi, and Louisiana itself (these three states' share of total U.S. cotton production grew from 22.7 percent in 1821 to 58.6 percent in 1839), the rapid growth of cotton culture beginning in the 1820s proved greatly advantageous to the established commercial channels flowing through New Orleans, where annual receipts of cotton increased from less than 40,000 bales in 1816 to nearly a million by 1840. Fueled by the seemingly insatiable demand of British textile mills, the value of exports from New Orleans during the same period increased nearly sevenfold, and as a result, the city briefly overtook New York during the 1830s as the nation's leading export point. New Orleans merchants used their transatlantic connections to expand the city's banking facilities during this period. In so doing, they played an instrumental, if rarely acknowledged, role in southwestern economic development by making capital and credit available to underwrite regional land and slave purchases. Hundreds of new firms and investors flocked to the city during these initial boom years, which lasted until the national financial panic of 1837.[20]

[19] Edward Sullivan, *Rambles and Scrambles in North and South America* (London, 1852), 224–5; Phillippo, *United States and Cuba*, 309. The comparatively high rates of urban violence in New Orleans are discussed by Dennis Rousey, *Policing the Southern City: New Orleans, 1805–1889* (Baton Rouge, 1996), chap. 3, esp. 81 n. 26; on similar endemic violence in the Louisiana countryside, see Samuel C. Hyde Jr., *Pistols and Politics: The Dilemma of Democracy in Louisiana's Florida Parishes, 1810–1899* (Baton Rouge, 1996). On the frontier character of antebellum New Orleans see Tregle, *Louisiana in the Age of Jackson*, 42–5; cf. Alexis de Tocqueville's famous comments on "Why Americans Are So Restless in the Midst of Their Prosperity," in *Democracy in America*, introduction by Alan Ryan (New York, 1994), Book II, chap. 13.

[20] On the westward shift of U.S. cotton production before the Civil War and its effects on New Orleans receipts, see Stuart Bruchey, comp. and ed., *Cotton and the Growth of the American Economy, 1790–1860: Sources and Readings* (New York and other cities, 1967), 80–1. Data on

The pace of southwestern expansion slowed considerably after the Panic of 1837, with severe effects in New Orleans. One historian has estimated that the panic forced a majority of the city's factorage houses into bankruptcy, with larger firms hit hardest because of the wider extent of their commitments. Some well-known merchants such as Maunsel White and Glendy Burke managed to recover after several years, but during the interim, dozens of smaller firms had stepped into breaches created by the failure of established houses. One such firm solicited business in a circular that declared, "Not having engaged in any speculations, we are certainly entirely free from the embarrassments which unfortunately prevail so generally." Commission merchants Wood & Simmons also claimed to have weathered the "disastrous cotton operations of the past season" when seeking to establish themselves as purchasing agents for a New England textile manufacturer in 1839. Similarly, although the firm of Schmidt & Werner admitted "the prevailing duress in every branch of trade" in an 1838 letter to a London cotton buyer, they nevertheless felt that "prospects ... remain fair" and should "enable us to do an extensive and profitable business for you and your friends."[21]

Cotton production itself, however, was barely damaged by the panic. After a sharp drop during 1838–9, production surpassed two million bales for the first time the following season, and the general trend remained one of growth through the Civil War (Figure 1.1). But the lessons learned during and after the Panic of 1837 inaugurated a period of "retrenchment" among New Orleans merchants during the 1840s. The rush of would-be planters to the Southwest had begun to slow by this time, since much of the best real estate in the region was now settled, cleared, and in use as plantations, especially along the Mississippi and Red Rivers. The rapacious land speculation that had accompanied the 1830s boom became less attractive for many merchants. (The U.S. annexation of Texas would soon ignite another western "land grab," but its effects

states' production shares are derived from ibid., Table 3-D; and total export values from ibid., Table 3-M; see also Taylor, *Transportation Revolution*, 196–8. An excellent recent overview of the expansion of cotton culture in the Old Southwest is Rothman, *Slave Country*. On the pre-1840 expansion of New Orleans banking and commercial institutions see Robert Earl Roeder, "New Orleans Merchants, 1800–1837" (Ph.D. diss., Harvard University, 1959), 118–19, 295; and George D. Green, *Finance and Economic Development in the Old South: Louisiana Banking, 1804–1861* (Stanford, CA, 1972), 20–6.

21 Schmidt & Werner to F. Huth & Co., August 15, 1838, in Cotton Trade Series (Mss 537), No. 12 (HTML-Tulane); Wood & Simmons to Charles H. Dabney, September 23, 1839, in New Orleans Cotton Brokers' Correspondence (Mss 132), Folder 9 (HTML-Tulane); printed circular with letter, S. & W. J. Bryan to John McKowen, October 25, 1837, in John McKowen Papers (Mss 1353), Louisiana and Lower Mississippi Valley Collections, Hill Memorial Library, Louisiana State University, Baton Rouge, LA (hereinafter cited as LLMVC); Roeder, "New Orleans Merchants," 117, 234–6. For the post-1837 travails of Maunsel White see "Pioneers of the Southwest, No. 1: Maunsel White, of Louisiana," *De Bow's Review* 25 (October 1858), 480–1; and Dun & Co., Louisiana, IX, p. 87. On Glendy Burke's failure and recovery after 1837, see ibid., p. 91; and "Gallery of Industry and Enterprise: Glendy Burke, of New-Orleans, Merchant," *De Bow's Review* 11 (August 1851), 219.

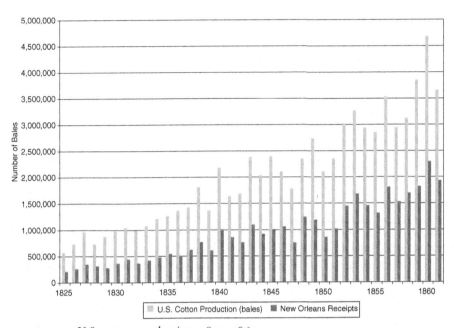

FIGURE I.I. U.S. cotton production, 1825–1861.
Source: Data are derived from E. J. Donnell, *Chronological and Statistical History of Cotton* (1872; repr., Wilmington, DE, 1973).

were dispersed by the near-simultaneous California gold rush.) Other factors obliged merchants to be more careful with their resources. Cotton prices suffered a sharp decline during the 1840s: after averaging 13.57 cents per pound during the 1830s, they dropped nearly 40 percent during the following decade and bottomed out at an antebellum low of 6.22 cents in 1845 (Figure 1.2). Commission merchants, whose income was based on a fixed percentage of sale values (typically, 2.5 percent), saw their profits decline as a result, although some were able to make up the difference because the continued growth of production meant larger sales volume.[22]

[22] Price data are compiled in E. J. Donnell, *Chronological and Statistical History of Cotton* (1872; repr., Wilmington, DE, 1973). Harold D. Woodman, *King Cotton and His Retainers: Financing and Marketing the Cotton Crop of the South, 1800–1925* (Lexington, KY, 1968), 49–51; Gavin Wright, *The Political Economy of the Cotton South: Households, Markets, and Wealth in the Nineteenth Century* (New York, 1978), 15; Merl E. Reed, *New Orleans and the Railroads: The Struggle for Commercial Empire, 1830–1860* (Baton Rouge, 1966), 58 (quotation). Robert W. Fogel and Stanley L. Engerman identified a long-term decline in cotton prices between 1802 and 1861, but they also demonstrated how sharply prices during the 1840s deviated below even these downward trend values; Fogel and Engerman, *Time on the Cross: The Economics of American Negro Slavery* (New York, 1974), 91–3. Without denying the downward spike during the 1840s, Gavin Wright has emphasized the stability of inflation-adjusted prices for cotton during the nineteenth century; Wright, *Political Economy of the Cotton South*, 90–7.

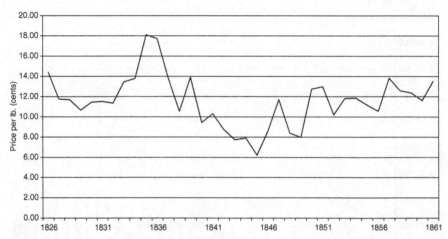

FIGURE I.2. Annual cotton prices in New Orleans, 1826–1861.
Source: Data are derived from E. J. Donnell, *Chronological and Statistical History of Cotton* (1872; repr., Wilmington, DE, 1973).

Probably the major force behind the stabilization of the regional economy centered on New Orleans, however, was the end of the soft money and easy credit that had fueled the speculative frenzy preceding the Panic of 1837. No sector of the New Orleans commercial community had been hit harder by the panic than the city's banks, nor was any sector more compelled to reform its policies in favor of stability afterward. During the 1830s the city's banking institutions had grown even faster than the cotton trade they supported. The number of banks in New Orleans had increased from four to sixteen between 1830 and 1837, which included the chartering of the two largest state banks in the nation, the Union Bank (1832) and the Citizens Bank (1833). Aggregate banking capital in Louisiana rose eightfold during the same interim, from around $5 million to more than $40 million. Competitive pressures had caused these banks to loan out their capital unwisely, much of it on the basis of rising land values in the region. The onset of the national financial panic in the spring of 1837 – and the consequent deflation of the real-estate bubble – thus found New Orleans banks badly overextended. Nearly all of them were forced to suspend operations, some permanently, and their subsequent desperate efforts to collect outstanding notes at a time of sharply declining cotton prices promoted a disastrous ripple effect among city merchants and their rural clientele.[23]

---

[23] "The Louisiana Bank Act of [1842]," *Bankers Magazine*, 3d ser., 12 (November 1877), 346–7; Stephen A. Caldwell, *A Banking History of Louisiana* (Baton Rouge, 1935), 59–61; Green, *Finance and Economic Development*, 25. On the role of banking capital in the "speculative mania

The popular Jacksonian-era animus against banks had its political analogue in Louisiana, where the situation was exacerbated by the growing perception of a division between country and city interests. The seat of state government was then still located in New Orleans, where prominent merchants and their political allies collaborated closely in the establishment and control of new banks during the early 1830s. But many planters resented what they considered to be a mutually reinforcing relationship between city merchants, bankers, and politicians, which was believed to promote corruption and a monopoly of credit in factors' hands. There was some truth to these charges. Louisiana's new "property banks," such as the Union and Citizens Banks, benefited from what one scholar has called the "extraordinarily large" state subsidies of the bond issues that underlay their aggressive capitalization. Furthermore, despite the ostensible purpose of these quasi-public institutions to make credit directly available to agricultural interests, mercantile control of the banks ensured that the bulk of investment capital continued to be parceled out to the countryside by commercial middlemen, which one planter condemned as a "system of robbery [by] our commission houses." Indeed, historian Robert E. Roeder examined the city's largest property banks and concluded that they had provided little direct credit to Louisiana planters during the 1830s; instead, their loans were frequently "used by merchants … to speculate in urban real estate without tying up much of their capital."[24]

Anti-bank sentiment in Jacksonian Louisiana was further complicated by the Creole/American distinction and the xenophobia often closely associated with it. Complaints about the control of one city bank or another by particular ethnic factions had been common since territorial days, but as the institutional matrix of New Orleans merchant capitalism expanded in size, complexity, and global reach during the 1830s, popular prejudices were even more frequently expressed against the powerful banks that seemed to epitomize these trends. One citizen of Donaldsonville, for example, denounced "the influence of foreign capital working through New Orleans banks" in an 1831 letter to the Baton Rouge *Gazette*. Indeed, as of 1837, more than half of the Crescent City's banking capital, over $20 million, was imported from sources overseas, especially from Great Britain and France. The enormous Union and Citizens Banks

of the Thirties" for southwestern land investments, see Lewis C. Gray, *History of Agriculture in the Southern United States to 1860* (2 vols., 1933; repr. Gloucester, MA, 1958), II, 898–900.

[24] Roeder, "New Orleans Merchants," 295–6, 347–9 (quotation on p. 349); Henry W. Huntington to William N. Mercer, April 4, 1837, quoted in Green, *Finance and Economic Development*, 28. On the unusually close relationship between state and private interests in Louisiana banking, see ibid., 109–11 ("extraordinarily large" on p. 109); and Larry Schweikart, *Banking in the American South from the Age of Jackson to Reconstruction* (Baton Rouge, 1987), 57–8, 138–40; on the property banks unique to Louisiana see Irene D. Neu, "J. B. Moussier and the Property Banks of Louisiana," *Business History Review* 35 (Winter 1961), 550–7. For the mercantile orientation of antebellum southern banking more generally, see Eugene D. Genovese, *The Political Economy of Slavery: Studies in the Economy and Society of the Slave South* (New York, 1965), 21–2.

accounted for more than $12 million of this foreign investment, and nearly another fifth of the city's aggregate bank capital came from non-Louisiana U.S. investors, mainly in New York.[25]

The same writer also linked foreign influence in Louisiana banking to "the remnants yet of Spanish feodality" in "our social system." Though he did not single out anyone in particular with this parting shot, many readers probably understood it to be an oblique reference to Edmond Jean Forstall, a well-known Creole commission merchant who was highly influential in New Orleans financial circles. The controversial Forstall was one of the towering figures of merchant-led plantation development in the nineteenth-century Southwest, with a lengthy and exceptional career that spanned from the early national period through Reconstruction. Born in 1794 to a New Orleans mercantile family closely associated with Spanish colonial authorities, by the 1820s Forstall was well established in a British-connected commission firm, one that retained him as a managing partner when it mutated into the New Orleans branch of the Paris-based merchant-banking house of M. Lizardi & Co. in the 1830s. Although he usually represented himself as a commission merchant (he also later tried his hand at sugar planting), Forstall was deservedly best known for his many involvements with Louisiana banking and international finance. First named a bank director at the tender age of twenty-four, Forstall soon became a moving force behind the establishment of Louisiana's major property banks: its first, the Consolidated Association of Planters, in 1829, followed by the Union and Citizens Banks in the early 1830s. However, both his Creole origins and international connections combined to make him a frequent target for anti-foreign sentiments. Forstall was forced out as comptroller of the Consolidated Association Bank in 1830 because of his connections to London's Baring Brothers; similarly, he later fell victim to an American-led purge of Creole directors at the Union Bank; and most famously, he was compelled to resign the presidency of the Citizens Bank in 1838 in the face of accusations that he had improperly steered bank business through the Lizardis, whom he still served as New Orleans agent.[26]

Widespread resentment against Forstall was stoked by his imperious manner, which was typified in a peremptory 1842 circular he wrote on behalf of Citizens Bank. Having been rehired to oversee the bank's liquidation, Forstall

[25] Data on the sources of New Orleans bank capital in 1837 are from Green, *Finance and Economic Development*, 80 (Table 3.2). Baton Rouge *Gazette*, January 29, 1831, quoted in Shugg, *Origins of Class Struggle in Louisiana*, 30. On merchants' close involvement with Louisiana banking during the territorial and early national periods, and the ethnocultural controversies that sometimes resulted, see Clark, *New Orleans, 1718–1812*, pp. 342–9.

[26] Irene D. Neu, "Edmond Jean Forstall and Louisiana Banking," *Explorations in Economic History* 7 (Summer 1970), 384–9; Roeder, "New Orleans Merchants," 288–9, 328–34. Forstall remained the New Orleans agent for the Barings through the late 1860s. By the time of his death in 1873, Forstall's sons had assumed the position, and as late as 1875, they were reportedly still serving as "agents for several capitalists in Europe"; see Dun & Co., Louisiana, X, 530–1.

demanded that the bank's stockholders – "many of our most prominent and wealthy citizens" among them – immediately concede their debts and divulge their annual crop production and all "income ... from the property you have mortgaged to the Bank for your stock." Nevertheless, there were multiple ironies at work in Forstall's poor reputation among his fellow Louisianians, city merchants and country planters alike. For example, critics asserted that Forstall's Creole ties unfairly helped advance his banking schemes, especially with regard to his relationship by marriage to Louisiana governor A. B. Roman. Yet without Governor Roman's support, the state guarantees that backed bond issues by the property banks might never have passed legislative muster; and absent those de facto subsidies, Forstall would not have been able to market the bonds successfully to European investors. By the same token, the esteem with which international firms such as the Barings, the Lizardis, and Hope & Company of Amsterdam regarded Forstall may have been a political liability in New Orleans, but without their confidence in him, it is unlikely they would have seen fit to augment the city's banking capital for the benefit of brash, often-hostile American merchant-bankers such as Connecticut-born Samuel Jarvis Peters of the Commercial Bank of New Orleans (est. 1833), who was a major rival of Forstall's. Here the patrician European cotton merchant Vincent Nolte spoke for his class of Old World "gentlemanly capitalists" when he dismissed Yankee arrivistes to New Orleans such as Peters as crass opportunists insufficiently averse to risk.[27]

The conflicting business cultures in New Orleans emphasized by Nolte also serve to highlight perhaps the foremost irony of Forstall's career. Although he personified for many the anti-bank sentiments legitimated by the events of 1837, in fact, Forstall always sought to govern the banks with which he was associated according to consistently articulated principles that stressed stability and accountability. Only after he was forced out did the merchant-directors of these banks begin to systematically engage in the riskier practices that brought about their downfall during and after the Panic of 1837. Indeed, Samuel J. Peters's public disagreements with Forstall in the 1830s centered on the former's defense of the expansive, "easy-money" system of accommodation credits, which Peters felt was the primary function of banks to provide. Even though his Commercial Bank went into forced liquidation in 1843, Peters and his American allies represented the wave of New Orleans's commercial future. (Peters soon landed on his feet as president of the prestigious Louisiana State Bank, which he served until his death in 1854). Yet it was the Creole

---

[27] Nolte, *Memoirs*, 90. On Samuel J. Peters' rivalry with Forstall, see Roeder, "New Orleans Merchants," 290, 366; Green, *Finance and Economic Development*, 41, 75; and Neu, "Forstall and Louisiana Banking," 389. Printed circular signed by E. J. Forstall, Citizens Bank, to Eliphalet Slack, December 5, 1842, document no. 2007.257.36 in Louisiana Manuscripts Collection (Mss 579), HNOC. A wealthy Iberville Parish sugar planter, Slack had subscribed to the failed bank for more than $18,000 worth of stock.

Forstall's highly conservative approach to "sound banking" that was ultimately enshrined into law in the wake of the Panic of 1837. Passed after several years of partisan wrangling, the Louisiana Bank Act of 1842 allowed New Orleans banks to finally resume business, but only on the basis of regular governmental oversight of their operations, restrictions on the types of investments in which they could engage, and carefully specified reserve ratios of metallic assets to liabilities (such as note issues). These strict reserve requirements in particular made Louisiana's banking system the model for subsequent reforms in several other states. The Boston-based *Bankers Magazine* later called the 1842 law "among the most enlightened pieces of banking legislation to be found on the statute books of any country" and recognized Forstall as "the gentleman most influential in framing this act."[28]

On his home turf, however, Forstall not only had to shoulder an unjust share of public opprobrium for the financial excesses of the previous decade, but then, adding insult to injury, he also found himself roundly condemned during the 1840s by merchants and planters who opposed the contraction of money and credit that accompanied the state banking reforms with which he was associated. Their complaints against the insufficiency of bank-sponsored capital in New Orleans reached a crescendo by the early 1850s, and historian George D. Green has agreed with such critics that Forstall's reforms probably did overcontract the regional money supply during the 1840s. But the Act of 1842 was explicitly designed to allow New Orleans banks to keep providing the short-term accommodation credits on which commercial interests relied, even as it did so at the expense of other long-term investment opportunities, notably in manufacturing. Moreover, other historians have pointed out that Forstall's highly conservative metallic reserve ratios, so admired by later bankers, were then largely possible only because of the atypical situation of New Orleans with regard to specie imports; much of the silver and gold mined in Latin America during this period, which had previously been shunted directly overseas to Spanish coffers, ended up being stored in Crescent City vaults after Mexico threw off its colonial yoke in the 1820s. Regardless, and even though the Act of 1842 later combined with subsequent legislation to provoke

---

[28] "Louisiana Banking Act of [1842]," 347, 352 (quotations). Most historians of American banking, such as Fritz Redlich and Bray Hammond, have also attributed the genesis of the act to Forstall, and even Forstall himself, usually modest, believed that he deserved credit for the principles behind it; see the balanced discussion in Neu, "E. J. Forstall and Louisiana Banking," 391–5. Some scholars have downplayed Forstall's role by emphasizing the political context that shaped the legislation during the five years of controversy prior to its final passage; see Green, *Finance and Economic Development*, 121–7; and John M. Sacher, *A Perfect War of Politics: Parties, Politicians, and Democracy in Louisiana, 1824–1861* (Baton Rouge, 2003), 86–94, 105. For Samuel J. Peters' ill-timed defense of easy money, see his *An Address to the Legislature of Louisiana, Showing the Importance of the Credit System on the Prosperity of the United States, and Particularly Its Influence on the Agricultural, Commercial, and Manufacturing Interests of Louisiana* (New Orleans, 1837); see also Rita Katherine Carey, "Samuel Jarvis Peters," *Louisiana Historical Quarterly* 30 (April 1947), 439–80.

the unintended consequence of creating a banking oligopoly in New Orleans, Forstall's reforms clearly stabilized the antebellum Louisiana economy by making the city's vital financial sector less vulnerable to market fluctuations and periodic panics.[29]

However unpopular they may have been among some New Orleans merchants (and some bankers too), statutory measures to prevent the reoccurrence of speculative abuses by the city's financial institutions were doubtless regarded as a necessary dose of bitter medicine by others. These reforms created a secure, prosperous, and internationally esteemed banking system in Louisiana for the duration of the antebellum era. Combined with a trend toward greater specialization among the city's commodities firms, such institutional changes helped provide a cushion of safety for the increasingly complex framework of global exchange centered on New Orleans. Given the continued health of the cotton economy reflected in sustained production increases, many merchants found that they again had cause for optimism about the Crescent City's future once the dust had settled after the Panic of 1837.[30]

Although there were other reasons that merchants thought the city's economic prospects remained good, gradually unfolding trends would prove these to be less well founded than the improved stability of its markets. Most important was the still-common belief that New Orleans's location at the base of the Mississippi River system ensured the city's commercial destiny. For example, an 1841 article in *Hunt's Merchants' Magazine* on the global importance of the American cotton trade noted the disproportionate benefit redounding to

[29] Bray Hammond, *Banks and Politics in America from the Revolution to the Civil War* (Princeton, NJ, 1957), 680–5, esp. 681; on New Orleans's growing trade with Mexico during and after the 1820s, see James Winston, "Notes on the Economic History of New Orleans," *Mississippi Valley Historical Review* 11 (September 1924), 208–11. Green, *Finance and Economic Development*, chaps. 4 and 5, esp. 159–61; see also Schweikart, *Banking in the American South*, 139–42. Green's study of antebellum Louisiana banking is excellent in most respects, but only slightly less so than Schweikart (whose libertarian ideology is overtly proclaimed), Green prioritizes the ostensibly value-free conclusions of neoclassically derived econometric analysis, pausing frequently to condemn nonquantitative "moralizing" by both contemporaries and later historians. (His favorite target among the latter is Eugene D. Genovese.) But as the rise of the new institutional economics has shown in the decades since Green wrote, mainstream historians' emphases on frequently nonquantifiable variables related to process and context – for example, the distribution and consolidation of political power – can offer much-needed correctives to economists' preference for static (ahistorical) and abstract (nonempirical) models, however internally consistent those may sometimes be. See the discussion in Peter A. Coclanis and Scott Marler, "The Economics of Reconstruction," in *A Companion to the Civil War and Reconstruction*, ed. Lacy K. Ford (Malden, MA, 2005), 342–65.

[30] On the growing differentiation of mercantile functions in New Orleans during the 1830s, see Woodman, *King Cotton*, 25–9; and Roeder, "New Orleans Merchants," 206–19; for similar national trends toward specialization during the period see Glenn Porter and Harold C. Livesay, *Merchants and Manufacturers: Studies in the Changing Structure of Nineteenth-Century Marketing* (Baltimore, 1971). On the resistance of some New Orleans bankers to the 1842 reforms, see Green, *Finance and Economic Development*, 123–8.

the port of New Orleans from the expansion of agriculture in the southwestern states. But at the beginning of the 1840s, faith in the city's natural geographic advantages was reinforced by the seeming diversity of other products and services, besides cotton, that New Orleans merchants provided to the region, the nation, and the world. Like cotton, some of these other commodities were part of the wider antebellum consolidation of a regional plantation economy based on slave labor. Rice and tobacco were two such products, but more prominent than these was sugar. The cultivation of sugar in Louisiana had expanded rapidly beginning in the mid-1820s, and aided by technological improvements in refining, the commodity (along with its ancillary product, molasses) quickly become one of the mainstays of New Orleans commerce. After receiving de facto price support from the federal government in the form of the Tariff of 1842, production more than doubled again during the subsequent decade, and the aggregate value of sugar receipts at New Orleans even approximated that of cotton on a few occasions during these years of slack prices for the latter. More so than cotton, sugar growing was a capital-intensive form of agriculture that benefited from economies of scale. The quintessential Atlantic world staple crop, sugar's importance to New Orleans was magnified by the relative contiguity of its production in the nearby parishes of the deltaic coastal plains, and its planters' enormous wealth thus often translated into prominence in both Louisiana politics and Crescent City high society.[31]

Although increasingly antiquated in a "free-labor" age, the southern system of slavery worked to the advantage of New Orleans–based merchant capitalism in other ways. Among the most important were the city's infamous slave markets, the South's largest, which grew in tandem with the spread of cotton production. After imports of Africans were banned in 1808, hundreds of thousands of slaves from the Upper South, especially Virginia and Maryland, were shipped to the booming plantation belt of the Old Southwest during the first half of the nineteenth century. The consensus among recent historians is that nearly a million forced migrants were involved in this interstate slave trade. However, because there were several ways that slaves could be transported and sold, not to mention other important slave markets (such as Natchez, Mississippi), it is difficult to quantify how much of the domestic slave trade centered on New Orleans. One way to conceptualize the problem is to consider it in light of Steven Deyle's recent estimate that the internal slave trade contributed $12 to $17 million annually to the southern economy during the 1840s and 1850s. These figures, which probably err on the high side, pale before the value of slave-produced

---

[31] J. Carlyle Sitterson, *Sugar Country: The Cane Sugar Industry in the South, 1753–1950* (Louisville, KY, 1953), 24–30; Richard J. Follett, *The Sugar Masters: Planters and Slaves in Louisiana's Cane World, 1820–1860* (Baton Rouge, 2005). See also Follett's perceptive discussion of how the structure of their interactions with merchants and factors inhibited sugar planters' class cohesiveness in "'Give to the Labor of America, the Market of America': Marketing the Old South's Sugar Crop, 1800–1860," *Revista de Indias* 65 No. 233 (2005), 117–46. "The American Cotton Trade," *Hunt's Merchants' Magazine* 4 (March 1841), 218.

crops; receipts of cotton alone at New Orleans in 1845–6, when prices were at their lowest, were valued at $33.7 million. On the other hand, Deyle's estimates do not take full account of the "multiplier effects" that plantation slavery had on Crescent City commerce. The thriving retail sector of New Orleans (whose 1,881 stores in 1840 were the main reason that Louisiana had the highest per capita investment in retailing in the United States) drew most of its strength from the provision of supplies such as dry goods, hardware, and foodstuffs to regional slave plantations, as did the city's large wholesale trade.[32]

Referring to factorage houses' dual intermediary role in the commerce generated by the plantation system – supply provisioning and crop marketing – Gene Dattel has recently claimed that slaves were "largely invisible during these transactions." But the frequent use of slave property as financial collateral casts doubt on this assertion, and slave trading was also "visible" to merchants in other ways. City factors not only routinely brokered slave purchases for their rural clients, but they also often speculated in slaves themselves – sometimes for resale, sometimes for hiring out as rental properties. Michael Tadman has estimated that up to 7,500 slaves were sold annually in New Orleans during the 1850s, most of which occurred from November to April – a daily average of about forty. These transactions were not confined to the roughly two dozen slave-trading depots interspersed throughout the commercial district. Describing the "pyramidal network ... that stretched from the slave pens through the city's hotels and barrooms," historian Walter Johnson has declared that it "must have seemed that slave traders were everywhere in antebellum New Orleans."[33]

[32] Steven Deyle, *Carry Me Back: The Domestic Slave Trade in American Life* (New York, 2005), 139–40; see also Andrews, *Report on Trade and Commerce*, 756–7; James L. Huston, *Calculating the Value of the Union: Slavery, Property Rights, and the Economic Origins of the Civil War* (Chapel Hill, 2003), 32–3; cf. Fogel and Engerman, *Time on the Cross*, 47–53. Figures on the New Orleans retail sector in 1840 are derived from census data compiled in Lewis E. Atherton, *The Southern Country Store, 1800–1860* (Baton Rouge, 1949), Tables I and II (pp. 41–2), which indicate per capita investment in Louisiana retail stores was nearly double that of its nearest competitors, including northern states such as New York and Pennsylvania; see also Harry A. Mitchell, "The Development of New Orleans as a Wholesale Trading Center," *Louisiana Historical Quarterly* 27 (October 1944), 955–6.

[33] Johnson, *Soul by Soul*, 51–2; Tadman's estimates as cited in Deyle, *Carry Me Back*, 150, 325 n. 18; Robert H. Gudmestad, *A Troublesome Commerce: The Transformation of the Interstate Slave Trade* (Baton Rouge, 2003), 25–34; and Judith Kelleher Schafer, "New Orleans Slavery in 1850 as Seen in Advertisements," *Journal of Southern History* 47 (February 1981), 34. For an example of a New Orleans merchant's involvements with slavery, including his ownership of slaves as rental properties, see Joseph Slemmons Copes Papers, esp. Box 6 (HTML-Tulane); and Johnson, *Soul by Soul*, 34–5. See also David Goldfield, "Cities in the Old South," in Goldfield, *Region, Race, and Cities: Interpreting the Urban South* (Baton Rouge, 1997), 210–11. Gene Dattel, *Cotton and Race in the Making of America: The Human Costs of Economic Power* (Chicago, 2009), 61. On the use of slaves as collateral for commercial credit, see Richard H. Kilbourne Jr., *Debt, Investment, Slaves: Credit Relations in East Feliciana Parish, Louisiana, 1825–1885* (Tuscaloosa, AL, and London, 1995), chap. 3.

Although this conclusion seems confirmed by visitors' ubiquitous references to slave trading in the city, New Orleans's total share of the domestic slave trade remains unclear. Another way of approaching this problem is by combining Tadman's estimates of annual slave sales in New Orleans during the 1850s with his more carefully compiled decennial figures for the numbers of forced migrants. Thus considered, a reasonable estimate would be that Crescent City markets accounted for at least 20 percent of the domestic slave trade – not equal to the city's monopolistic hold on cotton exports, but substantial nevertheless. All told, the extensive involvements of New Orleans merchants with plantation slavery buttress Walter Johnson's appeal for greater emphasis on the South's "peculiar institution" as a form of capital accumulation – the neglected flip-side of historians' standard focus on it as a labor system.[34]

By the end of the antebellum era, particularly after the cotton boom of the 1850s, New Orleans's economic dependence on the southern slave system and its products was obvious to most observers, but during the early 1840s, the situation had looked different. Then, the slave-based regional economy still appeared as only one strand of a wider web of commercial relationships that resulted from the city's location at the base of the Mississippi River system. Its advantageous geographic situation made the city not only a vital export point for interior products, but a gateway for imported goods as well. While foreign imports usually averaged less than a quarter of the value of exports from antebellum New Orleans, these figures did not include the city's receipts via coastwise packets, particularly manufactured goods from the Northeast. Firm data on the coastwise trade is unavailable, but most evidence indicates that it was substantial. In his detailed 1852 report on U.S. internal commerce, for example, Israel D. Andrews declared that "a statement fairly exhibiting the movement of merchandise coastwise would show a domestic importation into the southern cities having a much nearer ratio than the foreign importations to their export trade." The dry-goods trade was especially significant: New York City firms established branches in the Crescent City to take advantage of demand for ready-to-wear clothing. During the 1830s, New York's growing involvements in such trades helped prompt a series of southern commercial conventions that invariably condemned the region's mercantile dependence and urged direct imports from overseas. Yet when the largest of these early conventions assembled in Charleston in 1839, the absence of any representatives from Louisiana seemed to reveal the indifference of New Orleans merchants. Many of them were apparently satisfied with the status quo, especially given their

[34] Johnson, *Soul by Soul*, 231 n. 20; Michael Tadman, *Speculators and Slaves: Masters, Traders, and Slaves in the Old South* (Madison, WI, 1989), 12 (Table 2.1); Herman Freudenberger and Jonathan Pritchett, "The Domestic United States Slave Trade: New Evidence," *Journal of Interdisciplinary History* 21 (Winter 1991), 459–63.

city's recent emergence as the southern anchor of a robust triangular commerce between the nation's three great regions.[35]

More than anything else, New Orleans's river-based trade with the states of the upper Mississippi and Ohio Valleys promoted the illusion of a healthy and well-diversified local economy at the beginning of the 1840s. The steady westward movement of frontier settlement away from the Atlantic seaboard that had reshaped the South during the early nineteenth century was even more pronounced in the case of the former territories of the Old Northwest and the upper reaches of the Louisiana Purchase. During the 1830s the rate of population growth in the West had been more than twice that of the southern states; as a result, the region's share of national population in 1840 surpassed the South's for the first time. Fueled by generous federal policies toward the sale of public lands, western population growth was accompanied by an enormous expansion in the region's agricultural production of foodstuffs such as wheat and corn, and prices for these commodities generally either rose or remained fairly stable during the antebellum period because of steadily increasing demand for them in both national and global markets. The outlines of a mutually beneficial economic division of labor between the regions had thus become gradually apparent by the 1840s: the Northeast focused on overseas commerce and, increasingly, manufacturing; the South specialized in raising staple crops like tobacco, sugar, and especially cotton; and the West produced the grain that fed them all.[36]

---

[35] Robert G. Albion, *The Rise of New York Port, 1815–1860* (1939; repr., Boston and New York, 1967), chap. 6, esp. 104–6, 117–21; Herbert Wender, *Southern Commercial Conventions, 1837–1859* (Baltimore, 1930), 30–1. For a condemnation of southern commercial dependence on New York from this period, see "A Scheme for Rebuilding Southern Commerce," *Southern Literary Messenger* 5 (January 1839), 2–12. On the dry-goods trade in New Orleans see Harry A. Corbin, *The Men's Clothing Industry: Colonial through Modern Times* (New York, 1970), 32–7. The city's antebellum export-import position is discussed in Reinders, *End of an Era*, 40–2; and Reed, *New Orleans and the Railroads*, 62–3. Andrews, *Report on Trade and Commerce*, 850. Several years before Andrews' report, William L. Hodge claimed that "if the whole of the foreign and coasting trade of both ports are taken into view, it might be a matter of doubt whether the bulk and possibly the value of merchandise that enters and leaves the mouth of the Mississippi is not fully equal to that" of New York City, and he cited estimates of "coastwise importations at New Orleans" between $30 and $35 million; Hodge, "New Orleans," *De Bow's Review* 2 (July 1846), 54.

[36] The literature on western settlement and the economic expansion it promoted during the first half of the nineteenth century is enormous. Two classic studies that remain useful are Frederick Jackson Turner, *The United States, 1830–1860: The Nation and Its Sections* (1935; repr., New York, 1950); and Douglass C. North, *The Economic Growth of the United States, 1790–1860* (1961; repr., New York, 1966). Population data is derived from North's Appendix II, Table L-IX (p. 257); more generally, see his discussion of western agriculture in chap. 11. More recent scholarship, along with helpful bibliographies, is reflected in Jeremy Atack and Peter Passell, *A New Economic View of American History from Colonial Times to 1940*, 2nd ed. (New York, 1994), chaps. 6–10.

The ability of western farmers to meet the demand for foodstuffs elsewhere, however, was contingent on the facility with which their crops could be transported to consumers in markets hundreds or thousands of miles away. At least through the end of the early national period, the movement of bulk-intensive food crops by overland routes had been prohibitively slow and expensive, causing most markets to remain stubbornly local or regional in character. The growth of cities on the Atlantic coast and elsewhere was limited by their dependence on their immediate hinterlands for foodstuffs. Improvements in distribution networks – the bailiwick of the merchant capitalist, yet so often relegated to a mere "factor of production" by twentieth-century economists – were thus essential to the development of a national economy. In this respect, the assumption of U.S. sovereignty over the sprawling Louisiana territory in the early nineteenth century allowed the Mississippi River and its tributaries to begin serving as a linked series of natural highways for interior and interregional trade. The advent of steamboats made such commercial flows, both downstream and up, even more cost- and time-efficient.[37]

To many observers, not least of all its own merchants, New Orleans seemed uniquely poised to exploit the opportunities thus offered. Entrepreneurs such as John McDonogh moved quickly to seize an intermediary share of the profits from the products that suddenly poured downriver for coastwise transshipment to upper Atlantic ports. Competition forced many city merchants to act aggressively to secure a portion of this burgeoning trade. As late as 1828, a traveler in Illinois reported encountering New Orleans agents buying up produce crops for shipment downriver. But the value of interior receipts at New Orleans doubled roughly every decade after the War of 1812 and reached nearly $50 million by 1840 (Figure 1.3). As a result, a certain complacent belief in the city's "natural advantages" came to the fore. Typical of this attitude was one Louisiana newspaper's reaction to the New York legislature's 1817 passage of the bill authorizing construction of the Erie Canal. It accused the Empire State of "a jealous eagerness to deprive us ... of the advantages arising from our geographical position."[38]

Two decades later, the development of steamboat-based commerce had done little to dispel such beliefs. In 1837, for example, a local paper trumpeted the long-standing refrain that "New Orleans is destined to be the greatest city

---

[37] George Rogers Taylor, *The Transportation Revolution, 1815–1860* (1951; repr., New York, 1968), chap. 7, esp. 135–6. See also Louis B. Schmidt, "Internal Commerce and the Development of [a] National Economy Before 1860," *Journal of Political Economy* 47 (December 1939), 798–822.

[38] *Louisiana Gazette and New Orleans Mercantile Advertiser*, April 29, 1817, quoted in Clark, "New Orleans and the River," 119–20; James Stuart, *Three Years in North America* (2 vols., 1828; rev. ed., Edinburgh, 1833), II, 303–4, 375, 384; Lewis E. Atherton, "John McDonogh and the Mississippi River Trade," *Louisiana Historical Quarterly* 26 (January 1943), 37–43. The value of New Orleans interior receipts cited in the text are from North, *Economic Growth of the U.S.*, Table A-IX (p. 250).

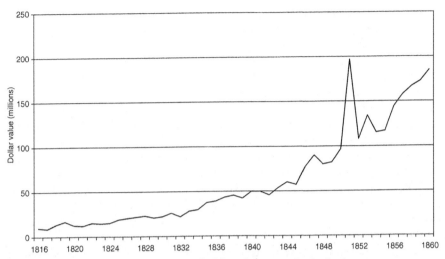

FIGURE I.3. Value of interior receipts in New Orleans, 1816–1846.
Source: Chart based on data compiled in Douglass C. North, *The Economic Growth of the United States, 1790–1860* (1961; repr., New York, 1966), 250 (Table A-IX).

in the Western Hemisphere" because of its site at the base of the Mississippi River. However, with city merchants increasingly focused on their plantation clients in the lucrative southern trade, the traffic in crops from the distant upper Mississippi and Ohio Valleys became an afterthought. Not only was it believed that the natural advantages of river transport still assured New Orleans a large share of this trade, but the built-in demand for foodstuffs that inhered to urban and regional growth meant that such commerce could be safely left to the workings of the free market. Such confidence seemed borne out by continued if unspectacular increases in flour and pork receipts at New Orleans during the 1840s. Corn receipts grew more impressively, quadrupling to 4.9 million bushels, but most had been forwarded to New Orleans from farms in Louisiana and other southern states, not from free-state producers upriver. Unlike wheat, corn was widely grown throughout the South, since it served as the main staple of slaves' and poor whites' diets.[39]

---

[39] Annual produce receipts at New Orleans from 1840 to 1849 are given in John G. Clark, *The Grain Trade of the Old Northwest* (Urbana, IL, 1966), Table 15 (p. 163). Diane Lindstrom has estimated that up to two-thirds of the corn received at New Orleans in the 1840s came from Tennessee and Kentucky; Lindstrom, "Southern Dependence upon Interregional Grain Supplies: A Review of the Trade Flows, 1840–1860," *Agricultural History* 44 (January 1970), 111. It should be noted, however, that Louisiana corn output nearly doubled during the decade to over 10 million bushels, with small farmers in the eastern Florida parishes and the Attakapas region usually marketing their surpluses of corn and other produce crops in New Orleans; Gray, *History of Agriculture in the Southern United States*, II, 1040 (Table 52); Hyde, *Pistols and Politics*, 28–30. On the importance of corn to the antebellum South, see the comments

Statistics showing sustained growth in the bulk and value of western produce received at New Orleans, however, tended to obscure crucial alterations
to the extent and structure of this trade. Most important was the failure of the
city's river-borne grain receipts to keep pace with the massive expansion of
western agricultural production. For example, the 4.9 million bushels of corn
received at New Orleans in 1849 were a miniscule portion of that year's non-
southern production of more than 240 million bushels. The completion of the
Erie Canal in 1825, followed by others in Illinois, Indiana, and Ohio during
the 1830s, allowed western commodities to flow to eastern markets via the
inland seas of the Great Lakes system. Despite the city's earlier scorn toward
such artificial improvements, the success of the burgeoning canal system of
the Old Northwest in diverting western commerce from New Orleans was
extremely rapid. The situation was especially grim in wheat products: twelve
times more wheat was received at Buffalo alone in 1845 than at New Orleans.
By the mid-1840s the combined tonnage of products shipped eastward via the
Great Lakes surpassed that transported down the Mississippi River (whose
totals also included cotton and other southern goods), and by 1853, 62 percent
of western tonnage made its way to market via the lakes, with only 29 percent
still sent downriver.[40]

This proportion shrank further during the 1850s, when even the lake routes
began to face competition from new east–west railroad systems between
Chicago and New York. In the meantime, the merchants of New Orleans proved
unwilling to confront the growing imbalance in favor of the Great Lakes trade.
In large part, complacency about the river's diminishing share of western production reflected their preference for the fast-growing commerce generated by
southern plantations. Although the number of dealers in foodstuffs remained
substantial (an 1854 municipal census revealed 73 wholesale firms devoted
to western produce in the two main districts of the city), these firms began
to assume a subordinate role in the city's mercantile hierarchy. In 1845 one
New Orleans commission merchant declared that he was abandoning western
produce entirely to concentrate on cotton and sugar, because the former trade
"costs more than it brings in." On the other hand, factors' role as purchasing
agents meant that many of them had to continue buying interior produce for
resale to their plantation clients upriver. Some merchants relied on city dealers
for such purchases; others made extra efforts on behalf of their rural customers by seeking lower prices for goods like pork and twine from wholesalers in
other cities. Either way, merchants' cession of the western trade was doubly
disadvantageous to New Orleans: the growth of upriver competitors such as

---

throughout Olmsted, *Cotton Kingdom*; and Sam Bowers Hilliard, *Hog Meat and Hoecake:
Food Supply in the Old South, 1840–1860* (Carbondale, IL, 1972). New Orleans *Picayune*,
February 20, 1838, quoted in Clark, "New Orleans and the River," 120.
[40] Bruchey, *Cotton and the Growth of the American Economy*, 85; "Contests for the Trade of the
Mississippi Valley," *De Bow's Review* 3 (February 1847), 102; Gray, *History of Agriculture in
the Southern United States*, II, 1040 (Table 52).

St. Louis and Louisville was buttressed by the business directed their way; and the already high price of goods at New Orleans, a source of constant grousing by rural consumers, were further inflated as more profit-taking intermediaries insinuated themselves along the lengthened commodity chain.[41]

Higher costs, along with other drawbacks of doing business at New Orleans, became notorious by the end of the decade. For example, as shipments of grain competed with cotton and sugar for space on the city's poorly maintained riverfront docks and levees, *De Bow's Review* noted that excessive spoilage caused prices for flour shipped coastwise from New Orleans to lose an esti-mated twenty-five to fifty cents a barrel in eastern markets, and claimed that "the injury is much greater" in unprocessed commodities. Adding further insult to this literal injury were the frequent delays caused by obstructions on the Mississippi above and below New Orleans, not to mention the "extravagant cost" of river-borne freight, which was said to be five times as high as for the Lake Erie route by 1851. Moreover, as one customer complained that same year, "wharfage fees, port charges, & c. [at New Orleans] are infinitely too high" compared to other ports.[42]

Such complaints were not limited to the diminishing western trade. Of greater concern to merchants by the late 1840s were the consequences of higher costs, rampant corruption, and other abuses in the port's bread-and-butter, the cotton trade. A comparative survey of global trade in 1840 had already dem-onstrated that New Orleans was the most expensive U.S. port for shipping cotton. According to this study, the combined average fees for drayage, storage, commissions, and freight for a hundred bales of cotton forwarded to Liverpool from New Orleans totaled $55.31, with another $65.36 for insurance. The equivalent rates from Mobile were $46.74 and $63.88; from Charleston, $43.81 and $34.40; and from New York City, $39.25 and $48.27. These fig-ures seemed to show that merchants in the nation's leading export point for cotton were managing to defy basic market laws, since the greater volume of business they handled should have resulted in a competitive price advantage

---

[41] The higher prices of goods at New Orleans can be traced in Arthur C. Cole, *Wholesale Commodity Prices in the United States, 1700–1861* (Cambridge, MA, 1938), esp. 65–76, 170–9. For examples of Crescent City factorage firms buying interior products from wholesalers else-where see Bull, Hart & Schultz (St. Louis) to Watt & Desaulles, January 7, 1852; and Todd & Richardson (Louisville) to Watt & Desaulles, July 12, 1851, both in Mrs. Frank M. Besthoff Collection (MSS 388; HTML-Tulane). J. V. Payne to Moses Payne, February 17, 1845, quoted in Clark, "New Orleans and the River," 133. The number of grocers and western produce dealers are from my compilation of data collected in City of New Orleans, Treasurer's Office, Census of Merchants, 1854 (microfilm 89–239, NOPL; hereinafter cited as New Orleans Census of Merchants, 1854). On railroad competition with canal-lake routes during the 1850s, see Taylor, *Transportation Revolution*, 84–103.

[42] "Why New Orleans Does Not Advance," *De Bow's Review* 11 (October–November 1851), 388–9; "Thoughts on a Rail-Road System for New Orleans, No. II," *De Bow's Review* 10 (May 1851), 510; "Contests for the Trade of the Mississippi Valley," 104. See also Robert Royal Russel, *Economic Aspects of Southern Sectionalism, 1840–1861* (Urbana, IL, 1924), 112, 136–7.

over other ports. Instead, the situation only worsened during the years ahead, and objections were directed toward New Orleans intermediaries from both the producing and consuming ends of the commodity chain. Planters grumbled about the high cost of goods advanced on credit by their factors, as well as about grading, weighing, baling, and other city practices that chipped away at their profits. Across the Atlantic in Liverpool, cotton buyers were disgruntled with the grading and baling procedures of New Orleans merchants. Although most were quick to exercise their prerogative to adjust invoices for cotton considered beneath the stated par, the disreputable practice of "plating" – packing a thin outer layer of superior cotton around a lower grade – remained a frequent source of overseas complaints against Crescent City merchants.[43]

Such problems did not go unacknowledged. As late as October 1859, a meeting of the city's leading merchants sought "to redress certain abuses and grievances existing in connection with the cotton trade in New Orleans." But the best they could do was to urge voluntary compliance with solutions they recommended, and key problems were left unresolved: a consensus could not be reached on controversies over weighing, and drayage issues were deferred in favor of extant municipal ordinances. Institutional innovations that had been established in other markets might have helped. In particular, a cotton exchange with the authority to standardize grading and other practices, as was provided to western produce by the Chicago Board of Trade, was badly needed, but none was formed in New Orleans until the 1870s. Given the disproportionate amount of cotton that flowed through the city (receipts averaged over half of total production during the 1850s; see Figure 1.4), it is tempting to blame these persistent problems on the usual complacency of the monopolist. As one historian pointed out, merchants had little incentive to tamper with the status quo, since their fixed commissions meant they "were always assured of a profit barring a complete collapse of the market."[44]

---

[43] For complaints from overseas buyers see the statement by the Liverpool Chamber of Commerce, October 23, 1857, excerpted in Bruchey, *Cotton and the Growth of the American Economy*, 204–5; and Jones, Mann & Fisher to G. Burke & Co., February 23, 1849, in Besthoff Collection (HTML-Tulane). For examples of planters' complaints see Leo Tarleton to Watt & Desaulles, September 28, 1852, in ibid.; and R. Abbey, "Cotton and the Cotton Planters," *De Bow's Review* 3 (January 1847), 8–19. Price data on cotton shipped from New Orleans and other ports are from J. F. Entz, *Exchange and Cotton Trade between England and the United States* (New York, 1840).

[44] Reinders, *End of an Era*, 44 (quotation); "Cotton at New Orleans," *Hunt's Merchants' Magazine* 42 (January 1860), 105–6 (quotation on p. 105). The high transactions costs that resulted from the slow pace of institutional innovation in the American cotton trade are noted in Lance E. Davis and Douglass C. North, *Institutional Change and American Economic Growth* (Cambridge, UK, and New York, 1971), 193–7. Institutional marketing reforms in midwestern and southern commodities are contrasted in Morton J. Rothstein, "The International Market for Agricultural Commodities, 1850–1873," in *Economic Change in the Civil War Era*, eds. David T. Gilchrist and W. David Lewis (Greeneville, DE, 1965), 64–71; on the Chicago Board of Trade see William Cronon, *Nature's Metropolis: Chicago and the Great West* (New York, 1991), 106–19.

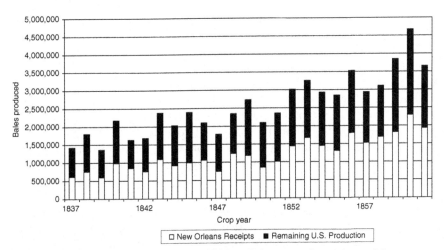

FIGURE 1.4. U.S. cotton production and New Orleans receipts, 1837–1861.
Source: E. J. Donnell, *Chronological and Statistical History of Cotton* (1872; repr., Wilmington, DE, 1973).

Their failure to address endemic problems at the port also reflected the lack of class cohesion among Crescent City merchant capitalists. The highly atomized, speculative, informal, and personalist nature of the antebellum New Orleans commercial community, exacerbated by long-standing ethnocultural divisions, prevented city businessmen from agreeing on and effectively implementing reforms and other improvements that could have alleviated the many obvious shortcomings in the port's handling of the southern commodities trade. Of course, a wide-ranging and well-funded program of reforms might also have given New Orleans merchants a fighting chance at retaining a greater share of the grain trade with upriver western states too. But the state government's support for commercial improvements had been sporadic and weak during the 1840s, mainly because of the unpopular public debts that had resulted from the bank bond issues it had guaranteed prior to the Panic of 1837. By the early 1850s, however, the political tides had shifted again toward business-minded Whigs, and another revised state constitution was in the offing, one that would somewhat loosen earlier banking restrictions and allow more government support of improvement projects. The post-Jacksonian reascendance of "government by gentlemen" prompted one New Orleans commission house to rhapsodize in a fall 1852 circular that "even our own State, after a Rip Vanwinkle slumber, has at length awakened to a proper sense of her own best interests, and commenced in earnest such improvements" that would soon return Louisiana to the "high rank ... which her favored position entitles her to [sic]."[45]

---

[45] Printed circular, G. W. Shaw & Co., September 1, 1852, in Cotton Trade Series, No. 15 (Mss 537; HTML-Tulane). A useful review of improvement controversies through the early 1840s

This faith in the city's geographically "favored position" for the Mississippi Valley's commerce was a hard habit to shake, even for seasoned observers such as Israel D. Andrews, despite the evidence he amassed to the contrary in his 1852 report. Noting the "serious inroads made upon a trade [to] which the merchants of New Orleans formerly supposed they had a prescriptive right," Andrews echoed and even amplified the Crescent City firm's sanguine claims about the future. The recent diversion of commerce "from its *natural* and accustomed channels" by canals and railroads, he wrote, had been "too startling not to arouse the whole community to a sense of taking the proper steps to avert ... the loss of their trade and commercial importance." Andrews also echoed the views of local merchants that government should play a leading role in sponsoring capital-intensive improvement projects.[46]

By the early 1850s, regional differences in the availability and deployment of investment capital had become more obvious, and some commentators brandished these disparities as a means of deflecting responsibility for the rickety southern infrastructure epitomized by the port of New Orleans. In Louisiana, statutory restrictions on capital were made the scapegoat for the declining western trade. In 1852, for example, *Bankers' Magazine* reprinted a critical article from the New Orleans *Commercial Bulletin*, one of the chief organs of the city's mercantile elite. "The banks of New Orleans are the most solvent in the world," it declared, "but what then?" Because the availability of commercial credit is "so cramped by silly, injudicious legislative provisions," the paper argued, "we are daily losing a trade which naturally belongs to us, which is making others rich at our cost, and which is exhausting our resources and cramping our energies." The previous year, an unsigned piece in *De Bow's Review* had been more frank in admitting New Orleans's many competitive disadvantages with respect to Great Lakes routes. But at the same time, its author sought to focus attention on the effects of the conservative Louisiana financial system adopted in 1842 and further tightened in the new state constitution of 1845. The superior ability of "banking facilities at the East" to accommodate western commerce, the author astutely observed, "are doing as much to draw trade from us as [are] the canals and railways which Eastern capital is constructing."[47]

---

is the biographical sketch of a two-term governor from the period in "Gallery of Industry and Enterprise: A. B. Roman, Agriculturalist," *De Bow's Review* 11 (October–November 1851), 436–43. For state political developments in general, see Shugg, *Origins of Class Struggle in Louisiana*, chap. 5 ("Government by Gentlemen").

[46] Andrews, *Report on Trade and Commerce*, 342–3 (quotations). The historically close relationship between merchant capitalists and established state regimes is described in Maurice Dobb, *Studies in the Development of Capitalism* (1947; rev. ed., New York, 1963), 97–109, 161–5; see also the review essay "Merchant Capital and State Power: Jacob Price on the Tobacco Trade and Its Political Consequences," in Fox-Genovese and Genovese, *Fruits of Merchant Capital*, 61–75. On the political division of New Orleans into three competing municipal districts from 1836 to 1852, and the harmful effects it had on the city's credit, see Reinders, *End of an Era*, 51–5; and Reed, *New Orleans and the Railroads*, 31, 81–2.

[47] "The Course of Trade on Rail-Roads," *De Bow's Review* 11 (October–November 1851), 521; "Banking Capital in New Orleans," *Bankers' Magazine* 7 (December 1852), 468–9 (quotations

There was a great deal of truth behind this author's brief and evenhanded assessment. Not only did he avoid apologetics for New Orleans's ill-advised neglect of port-related abuses, but more importantly, neither did he make the routine genuflections toward the city's "natural" advantages for the upper valley's commerce. Instead, he called attention to the role of human-directed institutions and the conscious strategies that were shaping regional and national economic development – and in the process, leaving New Orleans and her complacent merchants well behind. In many ways, a corollary to the conventional wisdom about the "natural" channels of trade was to regard western agricultural growth and the "artificial" transportation improvements nurturing it as a form of benign, gradually evolving coincidence – an economic equivalent of "manifest destiny." Even later generations of historians have not been immune to this way of thinking. Most would reflexively acknowledge the importance of what George Rogers Taylor famously termed the "transportation revolution," yet few have paid sufficient attention to the social contexts underlying nineteenth-century technological changes. But it is important to bear in mind that the history of technology concerns more than just the sudden appearance of useful inventions – the byproducts of "Yankee ingenuity," to use one clichéd but common example. More broadly defined, it concerns the human application of techniques – what environmental historians now call "artifice" – to shape and control the world around them to their perceived advantage. In this sense, people innovate technologies not only by creating new gadgets, but also by willfully rearranging and reorganizing practices that have acquired the false imprimatur of the "natural" through familiarity, prejudice, custom, and habit.[48]

New Orleans's role as gatekeeper to the western interior was one such habit, the product of decades of navel-gazing by armchair geographers and smug Crescent City merchants. Those beliefs had been reinforced by the city's remarkable growth and prosperity during the first half of the nineteenth century. But the author in *De Bow's Review* saw through this tempting mirage, as did De Bow himself, who had written scathingly earlier that year that "the Mississippi River lulls the mind of New Orleans into a sort of stupid fatalism." They both understood that concentrated capital in an industrial age had no need to respect "natural advantages": the aggressive new breed of businessmen

---

on p. 469). A British banking journal concurred in 1861 that "the weak point of the western trade by way of New Orleans is thus the absence of banking facilities" able to accommodate it; quoted in Reinders, *End of an Era*, 43.

[48] It is worth noting that George Rogers Taylor's classic study of the "transportation revolution" concludes with several insightful but neglected chapters in which technological improvements appear less as a *deus ex machina* of American economic history than as tools used in purposeful human struggles over the control of natural resources. A well-contextualized view of U.S. technological development is Ruth Schwartz Cowan, *A Social History of American Technology* (New York, 1997). For a recent example of an environmental history that examines the consequences of human "artifice" in New Orleans, see Kelman, *A River and Its City*; cf. my critique in "Après Le Déluge: New Orleans and the New Environmental History," *Journal of Urban History* 32 (March 2006), 477–90.

who controlled "Eastern capital" were using it to literally reinscribe national maps with the canals and railroads that now patterned the western landscape. But the author also realized that these were just the most obvious manifestations of a revised commercial geography that was redirecting flows of people and commodities – as well as capital. By gradually creating a sophisticated, complex, and flexible national financial system centered on New York – one that furnished interior farmers and merchants with capital and credit that New Orleans and the South could not – these businessmen were fashioning strong institutional bonds among all northerners, eastern and western alike. In this sense, then, eastern capitalists had not just diverted a western trade that the cotton-besotted merchants of New Orleans apparently felt they could afford to lose. More important, the city's declining upriver commerce seemed to be symptomatic of momentous ongoing shifts in the sectional balance of the nation's political economy.[49]

To be sure, fears about the growing reach of "Eastern capital" sometimes had the taste of sour grapes, and indeed, the mid-decade rise of the "King Cotton" perspective can be seen as a stubborn effort to reassert southern commercial supremacy on the playing field of ideas. But for many observers in New Orleans, the problem increasingly centered on the reasons for the apparent failures of resident capitalists to reinvest their profits in local and regional economic development. After all, the city remained one of the nation's wealthiest during the 1850s and was reputedly home to more millionaires than any other. Even though its share of the total upriver trade had declined during the 1840s, the real value of western products received at New Orleans had actually continued to rise, and the recovery of cotton prices after a decade-long slump, along with sustained production growth in southern commodities, augured the beginning of an economic boom that would surpass that of the early 1830s. Rising prices for slaves and land, the twin pillars of southern plantation agriculture, also reflected the South's economic resurgence after the doldrums of the 1840s.[50]

Louisiana probably benefited from the 1850s economic boom more than any other southern state. The 1860 national census revealed that the aggregate value of real and personal property in the state more than doubled during the

[49] "Thoughts on a Rail-Road System for New Orleans, No. II," 505. Some scholars have started to recontextualize the story of "how the West was won" as a key battlefield of the nation's rapidly changing and highly contested political economy. Three good examples are Cronon, *Nature's Metropolis*; Sven Beckert, *The Monied Metropolis: New York City and the Consolidation of the American Bourgeoisie, 1850–1896* (New York, 2001); and William G. Roy, *Socializing Capital: The Rise of the Large Industrial Corporation in America* (Princeton, NJ, 1997).

[50] On national economic expansion during the 1850s see North, *Economic Growth of the U.S.*, chap. 15; on its effects in New Orleans see Reinders, *End of an Era*, 37–49. For the ways that the increasing value of western produce received at New Orleans masked its proportional decline in real terms, see Clark, *Grain Trade of the Old Northwest*, 231–6. On the ideology of "King Cotton" (a term coined by David Christy in 1855) and its pronounced influence in New Orleans, see Chapter 4 herein.

decade, rising from $243 million to $602 million (both regional highs), with $42 million in personal property in Orleans Parish alone. With its intermediary role for southwestern products apparently still secure, the commercial sector of New Orleans thrived during the 1850s. An invaluable but previously neglected census of Crescent City businesses conducted by the municipal government in 1854 provides a detailed snapshot of the prosperous New Orleans business community during the pivotal decade before the Civil War (Table 1.1). Over 4,000 businesses operated in the two main districts of a city that had just over 100,000 free white inhabitants as of 1860. Most of these were small firms in the city's retail sector, which provided a wide range of specialized goods and services, from apothecaries and upholsterers to tailors and rag-pickers. At the pinnacle of New Orleans's commercial economy, however, was its mercantile sector. Previous estimates based on listings in city directories have sometimes underestimated the size of this sector, but the municipal census of 1854 identi-fied nearly 600 commission houses engaged in the commodities trade, with several dozen more specialized firms providing ancillary services such as ship-ping and storage.[51]

Also supporting the mercantile sector in New Orleans were its public and private financial institutions, which were geared mainly to the provision of banking, exchange, and insurance services for the commodities trades. The mercantile and financial sectors were closely intertwined. While the long career of Baring Brothers' agent Edmond Forstall best illustrates this overlap between commodity trading and banking, Maunsel White had served as a director of the Second Bank of the United States branch in New Orleans before its dis-solution, and Glendy Burke was president of the Canal Bank during the late 1840s. However, the 1854 municipal census shows that firms in the financial

---

[51] On the aggregate value of property in Louisiana see *Eighth Census of the United States (1860)*, Vol. I: *Population and Other Statistics* (Washington, DC, 1864), 294–5, 303. For examples of earlier estimates of the number of antebellum New Orleans firms engaged in the southern com-modities trade, see Eaton, *Mind of the Old South*, 72–3; Shugg, *Origins of Class Struggle in Louisiana*, 25, 319–20; and Reed, *New Orleans and the Railroads*, 5. The discrepancy between such estimates and my count based on the 1854 municipal census is probably attributable to the fact that listings in city directories like Mygatt's, Gardner's, and Soard's were solicited advertise-ments, for which a considerable number of merchants apparently declined to pay; cf. Woodman, *King Cotton*, 13 n. 16. Furthermore, even the more complete 1854 municipal census does not reflect all the mercantile firms in the city. For example, Dr. Joseph Slemmons Copes, a resident commission merchant from the Second District, was not listed in the census's block-by-block count, even though other sources confirm his mercantile activities at the time; see Copes Papers (HTML-Tulane); and Dun & Co., Louisiana, XI, 210–11. Although the 1854 census did include service providers such as artisans and innkeepers, interestingly, it did not count professionals – most notably, attorneys and physicians. Copes probably avoided enumeration (and the licensing tax) by declaring doctor as his primary occupation. Also, the outlying Third District of the city has not been included in these figures. A review of the municipal census for this district's busi-nesses revealed that few, if any, commission merchants were located in this essentially suburban area, although its inclusion would admittedly add a few hundred more retailers to the city's totals for that sector.

TABLE 1.1. *Number of Commercial Firms by Sector, 1854, New Orleans, Louisiana, First District (French Quarter) and Second District (American)*

Sector	First District	Second District	Total Number of Firms
1. Trade			
Mercantile	158	425	583
Shipping	6	30	36
Storage/Processing	2	40	42
Total	166	496	662
2. Financial			
Banking/Exchange	2	35	37
Insurance	1	8	9
Real Estate	0	8	8
Total	3	51	54
3. Wholesale			
General	16	68	84
Produce	10	63	73
Dry Goods	0	14	14
Total	26	140	166
4. Retail			
Goods	879	858	1737
Artisanal	199	407	606
Other Services	320	393	1106
Total	1398	1658	3449
5. Manufacturing			
Total	10	31	41
Grand Totals	1603	2376	4372

Source: Compiled by author from City of New Orleans. Treasurer's Office, Census of Merchants. 1854 (microfilm # 89–239, New Orleans Public Library).

sector were few in number. An ironic consequence of the controversial banking reforms of the 1840s had been to encourage oligopolistic growth among the handful of chartered institutions that had managed to regain solvency after the Panic of 1837. In response to this situation, the Whiggish state constitution of 1852, while retaining most of the earlier restrictions specifying reserve ratios and the composition of portfolio assets that had earned New Orleans banks a much-needed reputation for stability, finally allowed charters to again be issued for new state banks. At about the same time, the legislature also authorized the limited establishment of privately held "free" banks in Louisiana. But despite such revisions to state banking policies, by the mid-1850s there were still only a dozen chartered banks in Louisiana, all headquartered in New Orleans, and although free banks helped make more credit available, they probably never represented more than a quarter of the city's banking capital. Rather than relying on banks' highly regimented practices for their needs, many merchants found it more convenient to make recourse to exchange brokers – "shrewd, cunning" men such as Jacob M. Barker, many of whom skirted the boundaries of legality with near-usurious rates.[52]

Furthermore, during a time when northeastern interests were perfecting their ability to augment their investment capital from overseas sources, outside holdings of Louisiana bank securities, whether from U.S. or European sources, were still strongly discouraged: foreign holdings alone of such local stocks declined from nearly $21 million in 1837 to just over $2 million two decades later. Although New Orleans banks' specie holdings in 1860 were second in the nation only to New York's (with many of which they maintained correspondent ties that facilitated the extensive coastwise commodities flows between the two cities), financial capital in the South's premier commercial center nevertheless remained highly concentrated, intensely regional when not merely local in character, and subject to close, often-hostile legislative regulation during the boom years of the 1850s.[53]

In light of the enormous capital resources at their disposal from the cotton trade alone, George D. Green has argued that a less restrictive Louisiana banking system might have helped New Orleans keep a larger share of western agricultural output and thus a more diversified economy. However, Green's contention, based as it is on the abstract models that most economists prefer, ignores the political realities of the day. The city, much like the South as a whole, had squandered much of its credit with foreign investors during and after the Panic of 1837. Although full repudiation of the state's obligations to European bondholders had barely been avoided in Louisiana, the anti-foreign sentiments that undergirded that movement continued to be expressed in state politics throughout the 1840s and 1850s. In the case of New Orleans, the foolish trifurcation of the city into competing municipal districts had nearly caused default on international loans held by the Barings, among others. In short, despite its continuing importance as an entrepôt for the global cotton trade, not only did the state of Louisiana discourage foreign investment, but just as important, the city had cemented an overseas reputation as a risky place

---

[52] On the increasing number of city exchange dealers see Roeder, "New Orleans Merchants," 218–19; for a critical report on exchange broker and private banker Jacob M. Barker, see Louisiana, Vol. 10, p. 373 (quotation), R. G. Dun & Co. Collection. In an otherwise fawning 1877 article on the antebellum Louisiana banking system, *Bankers' Magazine* criticized the lack of functional differentiation among New Orleans banks during the 1850s compared to those in the North; see "The Louisiana Bank Act of [1842]," 349–50. On Glendy Burke's various activities in the financial sector see Dun & Co., Louisiana, IX, 91; for Maunsel White's bank directorship see Green, *Finance and Economic Development*, 92.

[53] Green, *Finance and Economic Development*, 35–36, 80–1 (Tables 3.2 and 3.3). 133–5; Schweikart, *Banking in the American South*, 134–43; cf. Genovese, *Political Economy of Slavery*, 21–2. On northern use of foreign investment capital, particularly in western railroads, see Roy, *Socializing Capital*, 99–100.

to invest capital over the long term. The conservative financial system inaugurated by Forstall was thus probably about the best the city could hope for insofar as it promoted stability in local markets prone to wild price fluctuations and financial panics.[54]

Furthermore, it is not clear that a less restrictive credit system favoring western agriculture would have overcome the other disadvantages under which New Orleans labored: the suicidal port charges, the deteriorating docks and warehouses, the ramshackle levee system, navigational obstructions in the Mississippi River, political stalemates and corruption, poor sanitation and disease, and the lack of railroads. All of these failures were neither coincidental nor the fruits of misgovernment. Instead, they were systemic failures, the consequences of the qualitative type of capitalism represented by New Orleans merchants, whose limited horizons left them unable to muster the political will – much less commit sufficient capital – to mount the multipronged offensive necessary to retain an adequate share of western agricultural output. However, even as the city headed into the most prosperous decade in its history, some observers in New Orleans attributed the local decline of the western trade to the inherent shortcomings of its merchant community. As a result, they believed that municipal and state governments should help promote interregional flows of people and capital such as those that were benefiting the West. An aggressive campaign of railroad construction, they thought, was just the spark needed to ignite industrial development in New Orleans and Louisiana, which would provide the region with a healthier, more diversified economic base. Their efforts to understand and overcome the provincial cast of the Crescent City's lucrative but oddly stagnant exchange-oriented economy are the subject of Chapter 2.

---

[54] Green, *Finance and Economic Development*, 49–65. On the travails of foreign bondholders in the South after the Panic of 1837, see Leland Hamilton Jenks, *The Migration of British Capital to 1875* (New York, 1927), 85–108; and Ralph W. Hidy, *The House of Baring in American Trade and Finance: English Merchant Bankers at Work, 1763–1861* (Cambridge, MA, 1949), 219–26.

2

New Orleans Merchants and the Failure of Economic Development

Debates over banking policy in Louisiana provided a popular platform for addressing broader questions about the inadequacy of home-based economic development in the city, the state, and the South during the antebellum era. While there seemed to be a general consensus about the need for such development, there were many different ways to diagnose the problem and suggest remedies. Some ranged well beyond Louisiana's banking system and criticized the shortcomings of wealthholders, especially tight-fisted New Orleans businessmen. In so doing, they often identified qualitative habits, mentalities, and other characteristics endemic to most merchant capitalists. At the same time, however, because of Crescent City merchants' deep entanglements with plantation slavery – a subject that was mostly off-limits for censure – there was a countervailing tendency not to push one's analyses too far in the direction of a systemic critique of the southern economy.

Probably the most common platform for discussing New Orleans merchants' investment patterns during the 1850s was railroad development. Although the first short-line railroad in the South had been constructed northward from St. Francisville, Louisiana, in 1831, the state had lagged significantly behind the region and nation in its use of the new technology during the years after the Panic of 1837, with less than ten miles of completed track laid in the state during the 1840s. Rail construction in Louisiana was made far more difficult by its swampy, bayou-crossed terrain, especially around the desired terminus of New Orleans. As a result, frequent cost overruns contributed to political conflicts that also hampered railroad development: different projects and routes competed for transitory legislative favor, and the coordination of projects with other state governments, such as Mississippi, also proved cumbersome. But as rail systems expanded across the more favorable terrain of the Old Northwest beginning in the 1840s, criticism of Louisiana's developmental failures mounted, and responsibility for them increasingly focused less on logistical or political bottlenecks than on the paucity of financial support by New Orleans capitalists.[1]

In September 1850, for example, a Crescent City newsweekly worried that "the freights arriving in our port by the river are not commensurate with the rapidly increasing amount of the products of the Western States – a fact which is justly attributable to the superior enterprise of eastern capitalists in the construction of Rail Roads...." Although concerned about the local impact of projected southern railroads intended to connect Tennessee and northern Alabama with competitor ports on the Atlantic coast such as Charleston and Savannah, the paper reserved its greatest fears for the city's declining share of the western trade. "If the products of the Valley of [the] Mississippi are carried to Eastern ports, and, through the same channels, the millions and multiplying millions of that vast region of country receive their foreign supplies for domestic consumption, the fate of New Orleans is sealed." This was a gloomy (if nevertheless prescient) analysis, so the author tried to continue in a more positive vein:

This need not be so. New Orleans may accomplish much to countervail the losses she has sustained, and will sustain.... We want only the enterprise of other cities. How long shall we rest supinely, and see drained from us the very aliment which is necessary for our vigorous existence and growth? ... We hope soon to see the enterprise of our citizens exhibited on a more enlarged scale than heretofore. We do earnestly hope to see our men of capital awakened to the importance of at once pushing forward such enterprises....

Even then, the editor did not consider rail construction in and around New Orleans to be itself a sufficient panacea for the city's economic woes. Instead, he promoted railroads as only one component of a broader program of muchneeded – and doubtlessly, quite expensive – local development.[2]

Sentiments favoring railroads and other improvements would become commonplace in the New Orleans commercial press over the next few years. But complaints about banking restrictions notwithstanding, the problem was not really about a deficit of capital, since the cotton trade continued to generate large fortunes among Louisiana merchants and planters alike. Instead, the crux of the issue became how these men opted to deploy their accumulated wealth. But while it was acceptable to criticize the state for not sponsoring improvement projects, or even to gently prod "men of capital" to be more active in doing so, it took far more chutzpah to condemn wealthy southerners for being socially irresponsible with their property. Only in the privacy of his diary did Crescent City banker Samuel J. Peters, the old rival of Edmond J. Forstall, feel

[1] Merl E. Reed, *New Orleans and the Railroads: The Struggle for Commercial Empire, 1830–1860* (Baton Rouge, 1966), 12–19, 58–61; Lawrence H. Larsen, "New Orleans and the River Trade: Reinterpreting the Role of the Business Community," *Wisconsin Magazine of History* 61 (Winter 1977–8), 121; "West Feliciana [Railroad]: A Century Old," *Illinois Central Magazine* (March/April 1931), 3–5.
[2] New Orleans *News-Letter and General Weekly Review*, September 14, 1850.

free to disparage "men of means" who "are afraid to part with their money for public improvements as long as they can shave notes at the rate of fifteen per centum per annum." "By their short-sightedness," Peters complained, "our city and state are the sufferers, and of course they also."[3]

It took a brave, perhaps even brash, individual to express such thoughts publicly – one like the private banker James Robb. If the Creole merchant-financier Forstall can be regarded as the preeminent figure of New Orleans commerce during the earliest wave of its nineteenth-century expansion, the controversial American Robb similarly personifies its trajectory through the boom years of the 1850s. Yet despite the renown that each man gained, their careers also showed them to be highly exceptional in their local and regional contexts. In Robb's case, his well-publicized efforts to promote railroad development do not exemplify a wider strength of progressive-minded reform among urban businessmen in the antebellum South. Instead, what little he and others were actually able to achieve reflects the limits of southern merchant capitalism and its ingrained resistance to change.[4]

Born in Pennsylvania in 1814, Robb had arrived in New Orleans during the momentous year of 1837. Though he had little money at first, he quickly distinguished himself as a savvy dealer in the city's informal financial underworld of exchange brokers. Taking advantage of the depressed state of currency and other paper obligations in the years following the Panic of 1837, Robb bought up the depreciated securities of the New Orleans Gas Light & Banking Company and had soon accumulated a controlling share of that publicly chartered improvement corporation, which he then served as president until 1856. In the meantime, he continued to establish himself as a private banker and also began to dabble in local politics, serving a term in 1845 as an alderman from the Second Municipality (the "American" district, below Canal Street). It was during this period that accusations of questionably timed dealings first arose, which would dog him throughout his career. His bank had extended a one-year loan of $150,000 at 7 percent interest to the Second Municipality just a month before he was elected alderman, and after quitting office the following year, he then sued his own municipality for nonpayment of the loan. Robb obtained a favorable judgment, and only the last-minute intervention of Samuel J. Peters's state-chartered bank prevented the sale of the municipal corporation's assets at public auction to satisfy his claim. Whether or not he was guilty of any impropriety, the incident provided an early indication of Robb's feelings about two matters at the crux of business/state relations in a democratic republic, each

---

[3] Entry, March 31, 1852, Samuel J. Peters diary, quoted in Reed, *New Orleans and the Railroads*, 85.

[4] For historical portraits of urban businessmen in the Old South that emphasize their "progressive" orientation, see Clement Eaton, *The Mind of the Old South* (rev. ed., Baton Rouge, 1967), chap. 4; Jonathan Daniel Wells, *The Origins of the Southern Middle Class, 1800–1861* (Chapel Hill, 2004); and Frank Towers, *The Urban South and the Coming of the Civil War* (Charlottesville, VA, 2004).

of which would be a hallmark of his career: the rights, privileges, protections, and responsibilities that he felt pertained to private property; and his equally fervent belief in the necessity for unimpeachably sound credit on the part of government. On a more personal level, the incident also served notice that the blunt-spoken Robb could be indifferent, almost ungentlemanly, toward the possibility of offending his fellow urban elites.[5]

Within ten years of his arrival, then, James Robb had become one of the wealthiest men in New Orleans, and beginning in the early 1850s, he used this influence to become the city's most outspoken proponent of railroad development. After a series of embarrassing false starts that earned the city scorn from outsiders for its apparent complacency, the New Orleans railroad movement finally gained serious momentum during the spring of 1851, when Robb was elected president of a group seeking to establish a line running north from New Orleans to Jackson, Mississippi, and from there, eventually also into Tennessee and Kentucky. The members of the group read like a "Who's Who" of New Orleans commerce, particularly its Anglo-American contingent: bankers such as Robb, Samuel J. Peters, Robert M. Davis, and Peter Conrey Jr.; insurance executives such as Joshua Baldwin; planters-cum-businessmen such as Judah P. Benjamin and Maunsel White; and a host of prominent commission merchants including Glendy Burke, H. S. Buckner, R. W. Montgomery, J. P. Harrison, J. C. Cammack, Sheppard Brown, and P. N. Wood, among others. Committees were formed, meetings were held, and by April the group had prepared a detailed proposal for the New Orleans, Jackson, & Northern Railroad, which called for an initial capital stock of $2 million. But according to the Ways and Means Committee chaired by Robb, government support for the project would be crucial. For one thing, the state legislature would have to amend a statute of Jacksonian vintage that limited the capitalization of corporations to $500,000. During the interim, books were opened to accept individual subscriptions for company stock, which were to be payable only after the law's amendment.[6]

However, the committee also warned that relying on voluntary subscriptions to raise the requisite capital had proven insufficient in the past. Despite the groundswell of elite support for this most current effort, not to mention the copious financial dividends it was projected to pay, the organizers still did not

---

[5] The most detailed study of Robb's career is Harry Howard Evans, "James Robb, Banker and Pioneer Railroad Builder of Antebellum Louisiana," *Louisiana Historical Quarterly* 23 (January 1940), 170–258. Originally a 1935 master's thesis at Louisiana State University, Evans collected considerable evidence on his subject, mainly from the contemporary press. Although he relied too heavily on accounts favorable to Robb to support less-than-objective conclusions such as "James Robb was as liberal and generous a man as ever lived" (p. 246), Evans' study remains useful with proper caution. Somewhat less hagiographic views of Robb can be found in Reed, *New Orleans and the Railroads*, chap. 7; and Larsen, "New Orleans and the River Trade," 120–1. Here it is also worth noting the strong resemblance between James Robb and the character Preston Dillard in the classic Bette Davis film *Jezebel* (1938), which was set in early 1850s New Orleans and starred Henry Fonda as Dillard.

[6] Evans, "James Robb," 198–206, 213; Reed, *New Orleans and the Railroads*, 88–91.

believe that this venture's ability to attract investors with deep wallets would be any different. This assessment seemed confirmed when the stock issue was first offered in May 1851. While Robb himself initially signed on for $25,000, others seemed less willing to put their money where their mouths were: such well-known men of means as White, Burke, and Buckner subscribed for just $5,000 each and others for even smaller amounts. As aroused and united in favor of the railroad as New Orleans merchant capitalists now professed to be, this was clearly no way to raise $2 million. Robb's committee thus advanced a fairly radical scheme that relied on state authority essentially to coerce the expected capital shortfall from its landholding citizenry. They proposed that municipal and parish governments oversee the collection of new taxes on real estate, payment of which would entitle citizens to receive shares of stock in the railroad corporation.[7]

Over the next few years, Robb would be the indefatigable point man for the New Orleans, Jackson, & Great Northern Railroad, pledging increasing amounts of his own money to keep the project afloat, and he continued to stump widely on its behalf even after most others had returned their attention to the booming cotton trade. Probably the most important of Robb's speeches, however, was one that he delivered in New Orleans in April 1851, just after the group's plans, including the sure-to-be controversial real estate tax, had been submitted for public consideration. In this lengthy speech, Robb sought to explain and justify these proposals, but as its title implied, "The Condition of Things in New Orleans and the Remedy" was also a wide-ranging excursus that contained a blistering critique of the city's political economy. Robb used his highly publicized speech as a means to discuss the many problems confronting New Orleans during the 1850s, and in the pages that follow, it will serve as a similar point of departure. His speech deserves close attention for its frank condemnation of how wealth was accumulated and deployed in the Crescent City. It provides insights into what "progressive" southern merchant capitalists believed was the necessarily close relationship between business and government, while it also offers apologetics for the glacial pace of capital formation in the city's commercial sector. Especially in this latter regard, however, Robb's speech is sometimes revealing for what he chose *not* to say. Such evasiveness, along with his occasionally strained logic, indicates the limits of systemic self-criticism that southerners could accept as legitimate during a decade of escalating national political tensions. Those limits seem to have been internalized even by the otherwise fearless, northern-born Robb, who was easily the most determined, candid, and visionary champion of southern industrial development to emerge from the mercantile community of antebellum New Orleans.[8]

---

[7] Evans, "James Robb," 205, 211–14, 227; Reed, *New Orleans and the Railroads*, 83–5, 89–90.

[8] Robb's April 18, 1851, speech before the Southwestern Railroad Convention in New Orleans was "of so much interest and value," according to *De Bow's Review*, "as to be incapable of any division," and was thus reprinted there in its entirety as "Speech of James Robb, Esq., on the

In typically frank fashion, Robb began his speech with the proposed real estate tax, which he knew would prove unpopular in many quarters. He admitted that the group had recommended such a tax (at a rate as yet unspecified) partly because previous "appeals to the liberality and sense of duty and of pride of our capitalists had failed" to generate sufficient subscriptions. But rather than dwelling on this failure, Robb tried to shift attention toward other factors that he felt were "insufficiently understood" and more relevant to the need for a real estate tax. The chief reason a tax was now necessary, he believed, was the poor standing of New Orleans's public credit, since "other communities were enabled, through their foreign credit, to raise any sum required for public improvement." But this "was not so in New Orleans," Robb said. He claimed that outstanding city debts from before the Panic of 1837, combined with newer obligations by the still-divided three municipalities, totaled at least $7 million, and furthermore, that the city had been lax about making timely payments on these debts, especially to overseas bondholders.[9]

Of course, this was a subject about which Robb had some first-hand experience. But although he did not mention his 1846 lawsuit against the Second Municipality, Robb repeatedly returned to the city's poor credit in his speech. He described his "shame" when, during a trip to London the previous summer, one of its "greatest bankers" had asked him "why, with her immense commerce, did not New Orleans pay the interest on her public debt?" Robb compared regional underdevelopment with the "extensive system" of public works in New England, the success of which he attributed to the "unlimited extension of her credit" in global bond markets. Finally, he argued that weak public credit adversely affected the city's overall business climate, producing "a general demoralization" that injured commerce and suppressed local investment.[10]

Although it was true that the city suffered from its poor credit rating in national and foreign financial markets, Robb misrepresented the degree to which improvement projects elsewhere, particularly railroads, depended on government support rather than on consortiums of capital assembled and controlled by private interests. In fact, as Israel D. Andrews would note in his report the following year, the need for the state to organize and fund improvement projects was now fairly unique to the South. Andrews argued that the new Louisiana constitution, as well as the long-overdue reunification of New Orleans under a single municipal government, constituted an "extraordinary revolution ... in the political organization of that city and the State" that would

Condition of Things in New Orleans and the Remedy," *De Bow's Review* 11 (July 1851), 77–80. This version of Robb's speech will be used for all quotations herein, though it was also published in other venues, such as the New Orleans *Daily Delta*, April 22, 1851.

[9] Robb, "Condition of Things in New Orleans," 77 (all quotations). On the city's division into three competing municipalities from 1836 to 1852 and its long-term consequences, see Richard Campanella, *Bienville's Dilemma: A Historical Geography of New Orleans* (Lafayette, LA, 2008), 157, 162–3.

[10] Robb, "Condition of Things in New Orleans," 79 (all quotations).

likely result in massive public improvements to help recapture the upper valley trade. It is interesting that he, like southern merchants generally, agreed that government needed to play a leading role in such projects. "In the southern states," Andrews declared without explanation, "works of the magnitude proposed cannot be effected by private enterprise...."[11]

By implicit contrast, though, large projects such as railroad systems were somehow being built with far less government support by the new breed of capitalists in the North and Midwest. (They still welcomed land grants and more indirect subsidies, along with foreign investment, just so long as they did not require ceding control over the broad prerogatives of ownership.) The continued reliance of southern Whigs such as Robb on a government-industry alliance showed them to be out of step with trends elsewhere in the country; indeed, one of the less-examined reasons for the sudden collapse of the national Whig Party during the 1850s was its outmoded support for activist economic policies by the state, which conflicted with the laissez-faire ideologies held increasingly dear by northern businessmen. Furthermore, while Robb was also certainly right about New Orleans's poor business climate, the sorry state of the city's public credit probably reflected this environment more than it had created it. Crescent City business culture was not only divided along ethnic lines, but more importantly, what one visitor termed the "spirit of gambling" that animated local commodities markets tended to pit speculators large and small against one another in what Hobbes would have called "omnum bellum contra omnes": a war of all against all. The ephemeral character of incessant mercantile speculation, in other words, undermined the "team spirit" that was increasingly common among the sober and thrifty nouvelle bourgeoisie of industrializing economies, in which intense interfirm competition guided by the Smithian "invisible hand" actually fostered greater class solidarity and, along with it, a healthier collective willingness to sponsor public improvements that benefited them all.[12]

---

[11] [Israel D. Andrews], *Report of Israel D. Andrews on the Trade and Commerce of the British North American Colonies, and Upon the Trade of the Great Lakes and Rivers,* Senate Executive Document No. 112 (32 Cong., 1st Sess.) (Washington, DC, 1853), 342.

[12] Edward Sullivan, *Rambles and Scrambles in North and South America* (London, 1852), 218 ("spirit of gambling"). On the financing, ownership, and operation of U.S. railroads by private capital beginning in the 1840s, see William G. Roy, *Socializing Capital: The Rise of the Large Industrial Corporation in America* (Princeton, NJ, 1997), 98–102; and Alfred D. Chandler Jr., *The Visible Hand: The Managerial Revolution in American Business* (Cambridge, MA, 1977), 89–94. Historian Louis Hartz described how Philadelphia merchants had solicited state involvement with improvement projects intended to shore up their trade position during the 1820s; by the 1840s, however, with the property form of the mixed corporation under siege, the state was compelled to sell its share in public works to private investors, and conflicts between government and business characterized economic policy during the 1850s, particularly with regard to railroads; Louis Hartz, *Economic Policy and Democratic Thought: Pennsylvania, 1776–1860* (1948; repr., Chicago, 1968), 161–75, 267–85, 290–1; on the rising influence of laissez-faire ideology, chap. 7. Although Michael F. Holt admits the role that its promotion of an activist

To some degree, Robb's emphasis on inadequate public credit reflected his predilections as a banker, but it may have also indicated his strategic reticence to dwell at length on the failures of unpopular New Orleans merchants – who, after all, were the likeliest immediate beneficiaries of railroads that they seemed unwilling to capitalize themselves. This becomes clearer in light of the apologetics he offered for the mercantile community in his speech. Robb "begged to correct an error" made by a previous speaker, one whom had described "the merchants of New Orleans … as too torpid and indifferent" to their city's best interests. Robb demurred from this assessment. "[T]he inert state of New Orleans [is] not due to our merchants," he said. He insisted that the city's "toiling, diligent merchants" have "the will, but not the means, to aid all public works," because "their hard-earned means – their capital – is absorbed in high rents, high interest, and by advances to planters." "There is no more enterprising or public-spirited class of merchants in the world than those of New Orleans," Robb concluded, "but taxed and burdened as they are, it is vain to seek help from them."[13]

Lest his wider audience not find these arguments sufficiently persuasive, however, Robb provided them with a villain to blame for the deficiencies of New Orleans capitalists. There were actually "two classes" among the Crescent City elite, he said. The first were its "toiling, diligent merchants"; the other was "composed of the large property-holders, who live upon the princely revenues of their estates, acquired by inheritance, lucky speculation, or by long and successful business." He then elaborated on this subject:

Within the last year, three individuals died in New Orleans, leaving fortunes which amounted to four millions. These persons belonged to a numerous and influential class, who had always opposed all public improvements and enterprises. They would do nothing to advance the city. They produced nothing; they neither toiled nor spinned; but from the hard labor of others, they drew their large resources.

To fund improvement projects, Robb said, the public should not rely on New Orleans's hard-pressed merchants, but rather on "those who have capital to spare – those who derive princely revenues from the merchants' toils – who, while they produce nothing in reality, hold and enjoy all the wealth in the community." He and his group thus proposed a real estate tax as a means of

---

state had in defining the Whig Party, he skates around the supercession of this view as a reason for the party's rapid collapse in the mid-1850s; Michael F. Holt, *The Rise and Fall of the Whig Party: Jacksonian Politics and the Onset of the Civil War* (New York, 1999), 66–70, 951–61. John Ashworth identifies the Whig Party's "suspicion of *laissez-faire*" as a marker of its "older paternalism associated with the dominance of merchant capital"; John Ashworth, *Slavery, Capitalism, and Politics in the Antebellum Republic*, Volume 1: *Commerce and Compromise, 1820–1850* (New York, 1995), 365; see also Eric Foner, *Free Soil, Free Labor, Free Men: The Ideology of the Republican Party before the Civil War* (New York, 1970), 168–76.

[13] Robb, "Condition of Things in New Orleans," 77. Inconsistencies of punctuation have been silently corrected herein.

"putting the live coal on the backs of the dormant enterprise and liberality of this class of our citizens."[14]

Robb's attempt to deflect responsibility for New Orleans's shortcomings onto a class of urban rentier capitalists was a fairly ingenious strategy. His assault on unproductive wealth resonated with a wider audience accustomed to directing similar opprobrium onto the fortunes acquired by mercantile middlemen in the Crescent City. His reference to recently deceased citizens who personified this class pandered to popular prejudices against long-time city resident John McDonogh, an exceedingly odd millionaire despised for his antisocial miserliness, despite bequeathing his fortune for the establishment of public schools in New Orleans and Baltimore. "How easily even the most ultra Louisianians could put on the imported virtues of the North when they could be brought to bear against the hermit," George Washington Cable later observed of such prejudices. These attitudes were more pronounced in New Orleans because of the exaggerated social context in which the city's antebellum commercial culture was embedded, but Robb's attack centered less on atypical characters such as the land speculator McDonogh than it did on the rentier class as a whole. Real estate in New Orleans was widely believed to be controlled mainly by Creoles and absentee owners overseas, especially in France, and in this sense, Robb was exploiting long-standing ethnocultural divisions in the city on behalf of the Anglo-American community he represented. He was also tapping into the rising tide of xenophobia that would culminate locally and nationally in the nativist political parties of the mid-1850s.[15]

Robb was correct that the real estate sector absorbed a great deal of wealth in antebellum New Orleans. The 1860 census would reveal a staggering $62 million worth of real estate in Orleans Parish – nearly a quarter of the total valuation of land in Louisiana. Just sorting out complicated title claims, which were mostly vestiges of colonial-era land grants of oft-contested legitimacy, had become a thriving cottage industry for local attorneys. Such increased transaction costs contributed to exorbitant real estate prices in an urban market where new development was restricted by the city's awkward, bowl-like topographical situation between river and lake. Nevertheless, Robb again elided facts

---

[14] Ibid., 77–8.
[15] Two nineteenth-century accounts that discuss concentrated real estate holdings among Creoles and foreigners in antebellum New Orleans are *Biographical and Historical Memoirs of Louisiana* (2 vols.; Chicago, 1892), 184, 186; and George Washington Cable, *The Creoles of Louisiana* (1884; repr., New York, 1970), 210–13, 254. Leon C. Soulé, "The Creole-American Struggle in New Orleans Politics, 1850–1862," *Louisiana Historical Quarterly* 40 (January 1957), 54–83. Cable, "Jean-Ah Poquelin," in *Old Creole Days* (1885 ed.; repr., New York, 1964), 142 (quotation). On John McDonogh, who had died in October 1850, see A. Oakey Hall, *The Manhattaner in New Orleans; or, Phases of Crescent City Life* (New York, 1851), 187–90; on his death and the controversial disposition of his estate, see *The Last Will and Testament of John McDonogh* (New Orleans, 1851); and Arthur G. Nuhrah, "John McDonogh: Man of Many Facets," *Louisiana Historical Quarterly* 33 (January 1950), 129–35, 143.

that would not have reflected well on the Crescent City mercantile community that his speech partly sought to absolve. Merchants had long been prime players in the city's real estate markets. During the 1830s they had monopolized property-bank resources intended for rural development to further their own speculations in city properties. To be sure, many Creoles still drew income from properties owned by virtue of their long-time residence in the city, but other foreign nationals, more recently arrived in New Orleans, had built up such holdings using profits originally derived from other commercial activities. For example, after Francois Lacroix, a native of St. Domingue, had securely established himself in the city's clothing trades during the 1830s, he gradually began buying up local property, and by 1860 his holdings were valued at more than $200,000. Like Lacroix, other free blacks in antebellum New Orleans, such as grocer J. Camps and exchange broker Bernard Soulié, accumulated large urban real estate portfolios as a lucrative sideline to other trades. Free people of color probably found such investments appealing not only because of their steadily rising values, but also because they offered opportunities for wealth enhancement that circumvented the racial ceilings inhibiting their ability to operate and advance in the city's exclusivist mercantile social circles. By the same token, though, racism probably caused such Creole entrepreneurs in New Orleans to be resented all the more when they acted as landlords for white businessmen.[16]

However, local real estate investments also attracted many non-Creole residents whose primary pursuits were commercial. John McDonogh had commenced his career in early nineteenth-century New Orleans as a successful all-purpose merchant in the river trade, but his land speculations in and around the city, as well as in the countryside, soon proved a lucrative calling better suited to his increasingly reclusive ways. Ironically, Crescent City slave dealers found themselves nearly as shunned in the upper reaches of "polite" society as were free blacks (and John McDonogh), and perhaps as a result, they also sometimes invested heavily in real estate. Bernard Kendig, for example, was well known as one of the wealthiest slave traders in antebellum New Orleans, yet in the 1860 census, he not only reported ownership of $64,000 in landed property, but he also listed real estate broker as his occupation.[17]

[16] Loren Schweninger, *Black Property Owners in the South, 1790–1915* (Urbana, IL, 1990), 117–18. Free blacks held an estimated $2.5 million in New Orleans real estate in 1850; see Arnold R. Hirsch and Joseph Logsdon, eds., *Creole New Orleans: Race and Americanization* (Baton Rouge, 1992), 100. Roeder, "New Orleans Merchants," 107–11, 349–50; *Eighth Census of the U.S.* (1860), I, 303. Intense legal conflicts between Creoles and Americans over riverfront property rights in New Orleans during the early national period are discussed in Ari Kelman, *A River and Its City: The Nature of Landscape in New Orleans* (Berkeley, CA, and other cities, 2003), 28–49.

[17] Richard Tansey, "Bernard Kendig and the New Orleans Slave Trade," *Louisiana History* 23 (Spring 1982), 159–78, esp. 177. Robert Evans Jr. used quantitative methods to confirm the social ostracism of slave dealers in his article "Some Economic Aspects of the Domestic Slave Trade, 1830–1860," *Southern Economic Journal* 27 (April 1961), 329–37; see also Walter

Contrary to James Robb's portrait of "two classes" of commercial elites in the Crescent City, even respected commission merchants from the American district seemed to regard real estate as the safest and most profitable place to invest their trade-derived incomes. The Jewish businessman Judah P. Touro was another wealthy resident who had been in the city since before the War of 1812, in which he had fought under Colonel Jackson alongside other merchants. Like McDonogh, Touro also had a reputation for miserliness in his personal affairs, but unlike him, he retained many friends and associates in the American mercantile community, owing to both his philanthropic activism and his lifelong involvement in the city's wholesale and consignment trades. Touro did tend to steer clear of speculation in commodities markets, however, and upon his death in 1854 the bulk of his million-dollar estate proved to be composed of various real estate properties in New Orleans.[18]

Most of Robb's allies in the ambitious new railroad venture had similarly large holdings of local real estate. Indeed, this unsurprising fact came to light only a few days after Robb's speech. In an attempt to drum up support for the real estate tax, a local newspaper published figures intended to show how much the chief mercantile backers of the railroad project stood to be assessed if such a levy were adopted. H. S. Buckner and Judah P. Benjamin owned over $200,000 in local property; Glendy Burke and R. S. Montgomery were said to own a hundred dollars in real estate for every dollar of personal property they controlled; and even James Robb himself would face assessment on holdings valued at $100,000. The editorial, friendly to their cause, was meant to demonstrate the sacrifices that wealthy city merchants were willing to make in support of the common good, so it did not mention the contradiction between those merchants' real estate holdings and the drift of Robb's much-praised argument the week before. However, skeptics probably noted that, if taxed at a 3 percent rate (which was the amount eventually agreed upon, with payments to be staggered over six years), the financial contributions to the project being provided by individual Crescent City merchants, whether through mandatory taxes or voluntary subscriptions, were still pitifully low, especially in light of their enormous declared wealth and the disproportionate benefits likely to accrue to them if the venture succeeded.[19]

The distinction that Robb tried to make between merchant and rentier capital in New Orleans thus collapsed upon close examination. Real estate was actually a tempting, logical, and common investment for most successful

---

Johnson, *Soul by Soul: Life Inside the Antebellum Slave Market* (Cambridge, MA, and London, 1999), 24–5. Lewis E. Atherton, "John McDonogh – New Orleans Mercantile Capitalist," *Journal of Southern History* 7 (November 1941), 453–4, 477–80.

[18] Bertram Wallace Korn, *The Early Jews of New Orleans* (Waltham, MA, 1969), 78–90, 217–21; Vincent Nolte, *The Memoirs of Vincent Nolte, or Fifty Years in Both Hemispheres*, trans. Burton Rascoe (1854; repr. New York, 1934), 206.

[19] New Orleans *Daily Delta*, April 30, 1851. For the 3 percent municipal tax passed in June 1852, see Evans, "James Robb," 227.

city merchants. As working capital, real property earned them more than gold drawing interest in a bank, both in terms of the rental income-stream it provided and its steady rise in value over time. In the latter sense, land was an eminently fungible yet stable asset (indeed, it remained the basis of all other wealth, according to some contemporary economic theorists), one that provided merchants' portfolios with an excellent conservative counterweight to their riskier activities in volatile Atlantic commodities markets. Compared to newer forms of capital deployment, especially manufacturing, which required successful owners to pay close attention to the myriad details of production processes, real estate was a more natural fit within the conventional parameters of the sedentary, speculative, exchange-oriented mentality of gentlemanly merchant capitalists. Robb's villainization of Crescent City rentiers to justify a real estate tax was largely a rhetorical strategy, one that also obscured the fact that their proposal was intended for parishes throughout Louisiana, and as such, would likely be stoutly resisted by the plantation owners on whom it would fall most heavily.[20]

Seen in this light, Robb's attempt to distinguish between rentiers and merchants encountered further problems when considered in the context of the antebellum South's agricultural economy, in which capital took two primary forms: land and slaves. New Orleans merchants invested heavily in both, and their investments in the former were not confined only to urban real estate. Merchants' investments in rural properties sometimes took speculative form, as with New Orleans cotton factor Joseph Slemmons Copes, who actively traded land in northwest Louisiana and Texas. But the peculiar nature of southern slave society, with its emphasis on premodern forms of status and hierarchy, often compelled merchants to buy rural properties in an active attempt to "refeudalize" themselves in the manner of the plantation lord, which testified to the continuing truth of Adam Smith's observation that "merchants are commonly ambitious of becoming country gentlemen." For example, from a humble beginning in his family's mercantile business, Isaac Franklin parlayed his success as a New Orleans slave dealer to become one of the largest cotton plantation owners in the state. Even some of the more "progressive" merchants in antebellum Louisiana, both Creole and American, pursued careers as planters after first establishing themselves as urban entrepreneurs. Sugar planting was the most common attraction for New Orleans merchants thus inclined, partly because its production was situated close enough to the city to allow them to keep an eye on their interests there. Edmond J. Forstall, Maunsel White, and

[20] Although the trend in contemporary economic theory, epitomized by Adam Smith and Karl Marx, was toward an emphasis on the costs and benefits of value-added industrial production in urban environments, hindsight should not prevent historians from understanding that such views remained highly contested in the mid-nineteenth century. Thinkers who emphasized the importance of land and/or agriculture, such as the French Physiocrats (Francois Quesnay) or British political economist David Ricardo, were still very influential – and understandably, all the more so in the stubbornly nonindustrial South.

Judah P. Benjamin were all examples of men prominent in the Crescent City commercial milieu who branched out into sugar planting, albeit with mixed degrees of success. The low esteem with which businessmen were regarded helped make such stories common in the antebellum South; yet by the same token, it is revealing that counterexamples of planters abandoning agriculture for trade vocations are exceedingly rare.[21]

Even though Robb evaded the inconvenient fact of New Orleans merchants' extensive real estate holdings in his April 1851 speech, he did acknowledge that such investments showed how wealth generated in local commodities markets was often unproductively employed – that is, when it remained in the city at all. For besides its "toiling, diligent" resident businessmen, Robb noted that the city's "commercial class" was composed of "foreign agents and factors, who came here in the winter, boarded in hotels at $50 a month, ... and, when they had accumulated enough, fly off, or send their money away to be spent in distant countries." Here Robb added his voice to the chorus of complaints about the migratory nature of merchant capital in New Orleans, which drained the pool of funds available for local improvements. The large proportion of northern migrants alone, permanent residents or not, enabled capital extraction and fostered hostility toward the city in the plantation districts. But although historians have also tended to emphasize the number of non-natives, whether foreigners or northerners, in New Orleans's antebellum trade sector, the 1854 municipal census reveals, somewhat surprisingly, that these firms were composed mainly of self-declared residents of the city. In the American district, where the cotton trade was centered, only 27 percent of 355 commission houses reported having nonresidential partners. Robb seemed aware of this, commenting that it was "a great mistake in supposing that the transient population of our city is so large." What he objected to, however, was that so many transients came to New Orleans only to extract capital rather than to spend it.[22]

---

[21] J. D. B. De Bow believed that most southerners regarded "the trading and manufacturing spirit as essentially servile"; De Bow, "Importance of an Industrial Revolution to the South," *De Bow's Review* 12 (May 1852), 556. Robert D. Meade, *Judah P. Benjamin: Confederate Statesman* (New York, 1943), 59–61; Irene D. Neu, "Edmond J. Forstall," in *Banking and Finance to 1913*, ed. Larry D. Schweikart (New York, 1990), 186–201; Eaton, *Mind of the Old South*, 58–62, 75–80 (on Maunsel White); Wendell Holmes Stephenson, *Isaac Franklin: Slave Trader and Planter of the Old South, with Plantation Records* (Baton Rouge, 1938). New Orleans merchant Joseph S. Copes's speculations in Texas land began in the late 1830s and continued until his death in 1885; see the copious correspondence throughout the Joseph Slemmons Copes Papers (HTML-Tulane). Adam Smith, *The Wealth of Nations*, ed. Andrew Skinner (1776; New York and other cities, 1986), 507 (quotation).

[22] Robb, "Condition of Things in New Orleans," 78–9. For an earlier description of transient businessmen in the city, see Benjamin Henry Boneval Latrobe, *Impressions Respecting New Orleans: Diary and Sketches, 1818–1820*, ed. Samuel Wilson Jr. (New York, 1951), 146–7. Residential data on merchants are derived from City of New Orleans, Treasurer's Office, Census of Merchants, 1854, Second District (microfilm no. 89–239, New Orleans Public Library).

Robb compared the situation to that in New York City, where the number of commercial visitors was much higher, yet the money they spent locally helped "support a hundred trades and professions." Although their city also was largely a commercial one, New Yorkers had wisely fostered a more flexible and diversified economy that derived greater benefits from the capital that passed through it. The trains and ships that carried cargo and visitors alike were locally built and owned; its wholesale and retail dealers not only imported more goods directly from overseas, but they also sold far more that were produced nearby; and its bankers and merchants were both favorably inclined to lend financial and marketing support to new industrial enterprises, from small manufactories to enormous projects such as railroads. By contrast, while goods flowed in abundance through New Orleans – by river and sea, inbound and outbound – the city was mostly a waystation for commodities. Practically nothing was added to the value of goods received at New Orleans, unless one counted the near-medieval tariffs exacted by virtue of simply passing through the port. Nevertheless, the sheer volume of trade the city handled left its businessmen satisfied with the fixed charges of the middleman (plus whatever the less principled could finagle on the side), and its practical monopoly on southwestern products, combined with the still-common belief that its geographic position would ensure this dominance indefinitely, promoted arrogant attitudes toward the need for change. Such shortsightedness, Robb claimed, had already "lost to New Orleans nine-tenths of her natural advantages," which he found particularly "alarming" with regard to the declining upriver trade with the West.[23]

Moreover, even the prosperity engendered by the export of southwestern products was dangerously superficial. Here Robb first bemoaned the city's "want of an external commerce," by which he meant that "conducted by ships owned here, and plying between this and foreign ports, and exchanging the produce of our valley for articles of foreign production needed by our people." One might have expected an urban economy based on long-distance exchange to have developed at least a robust transportation sector of its own, from shipbuilding to freight forwarding, but New Orleans had not. There were no home-based shipping lines linking the city directly to European markets, a

Unfortunately, the municipal census-takers failed to solicit the residential status of owners and partners in the First District. The percentage cited is based only on firms designated as commission merchants (which constituted the majority of businesses in this district), not brokers, factors, dealers, or other trade-related descriptions. There does not seem to be any good reason that respondents to the census might have falsified the presence of nonresidential partners, since no apparent benefit or liability attached to their answers. On northern-born residents in New Orleans and southerners' attitudes toward them, see Chapter 4.

[23] Robb, "Condition of Things in New Orleans," 79. On New York–based antebellum economic development see Robert G. Albion, *The Rise of New York Port, 1815–1860* (1939; repr., Boston and New York, 1967); Sven Beckert, *The Monied Metropolis: New York City and the Consolidation of the American Bourgeoisie, 1850–1896* (New York, 2001), 24–9; and Glenn Porter and Harold C. Livesay, *Merchants and Manufacturers: Studies in the Changing Structure of Nineteenth-Century Marketing* (Baltimore, 1971), 62–78.

source of frequent planter complaints against mercantile inaction. The coastwise carrying trade, both on the Gulf and the Atlantic, was monopolized by New England–owned companies. On the nation's rivers, of the 601 steamboats then plying the interior, only 113 were of Crescent City registry, about the same number as from Cincinnati and Pittsburgh. During the 1840s, while Louisville was tripling its steamboat tonnage and St. Louis's more than doubled, the Crescent City added barely a fifth to its own. Finally, the city had no railroads. New Orleans had thus failed to develop either the institutions or the infrastructure needed to ensure a reciprocal commerce with even its plantation hinterlands over the long term. "Save a small trade with both Mexico and Texas," claimed Robb, New Orleans was "entirely destitute of this extensive and enriching branch of commerce."[24]

At the same time, however, Robb again pointed out that "no city ever grew great by commerce alone." Even in "the most favorably located cities in the world," he said, "prosperity was transient, evanescent, compared with that of towns ... where industry and labor were cultivated and flourished – where the mechanical and productive arts were encouraged." "Everything used here [is] manufactured abroad," Robb lamented. His hat, his chair, his bed – all were "the product of the industry of some distant people." Again, New Orleans's economy drew only the limited benefits of the intermediary from the resale of goods produced elsewhere, and the price markups passed along by city retailers and factors were much resented by interior consumers. Frustrated by high prices, increasing numbers of rural storeowners, and even some planters with ready cash, had begun making semi-annual shopping expeditions to eastern markets. Besides earning a reputation for price gouging, Crescent City merchants drained off local capital and helped strengthen competitors' economies when they purchased from New York, or even worse, from wholesalers in Border South cities such as St. Louis and Louisville.[25]

[24] Robb, "Condition of Things in New Orleans," 78; Albion, *Rise of New York Port*, 107–11; James P. Baughman, "The Evolution of Rail-Water Systems of Transportation in the Gulf Southwest, 1836–1890," *Journal of Southern History* 34 (August 1968), 359–63; Robert C. Reinders, *End of an Era: New Orleans 1850–1860* (New Orleans, 1964), 44; Joseph G. Tregle Jr., *Louisiana in the Age of Jackson: A Clash of Cultures and Personalities* (Baton Rouge, 1999), 18. Data on steamboat registry and tonnage by city are from Andrews, *Report on Trade and Commerce*, 733–4, 744. Alexis de Tocqueville attributed the South's inferior merchant marine capabilities to the incompatibility of slave labor with maritime service; Tocqueville, *Democracy in America*, introduction by Alan Ryan (New York, 1994), 399 n.70. With this in mind, it is suggestive to compare the underdeveloped state of locally owned ocean transport in antebellum New Orleans with the role of English merchant capitalists in spearheading the use of free wage labor on their ships during the eighteenth century; see Marcus Rediker, *Between the Devil and the Deep Blue Sea: Merchant Seamen, Pirates, and the Anglo-American Maritime World, 1700–1750* (New York and other cities, 1987), 74–84, 149–51.

[25] Country storekeepers' purchases from northern markets are discussed in Chapter 3 herein; see also Lewis E. Atherton, *The Southern Country Store, 1800–1860* (Baton Rouge, 1949), 113–24. Robb, "Condition of Things in New Orleans," 78–9.

Robb was greatly concerned by the city's lack of a significant manufacturing sector, an absence confirmed by the available data. The 1854 municipal census-takers did not even bother to regard manufacturers as economic enterprises distinct from the mercantile firms they had been statutorily empowered to count, as they had with professional service-providers such as lawyers and physicians. In any case, the results were meager: of more than 4,000 New Orleans businesses in 1854, only forty-one were "manufactories" (Table 1.1). Except for five iron foundries and a few others, most were probably little more than artisanal workshops on a slightly more intensive scale, such as makers of soap, chocolate, perfumes, umbrellas, and baskets. The paucity of factory-style production in antebellum Louisiana was also corroborated by the 1860 national census, when only 16 of more than 100,000 free white male respondents in the state reported "manufacturer" as their occupation. (To be fair, there were several dozen more listed instead as producers of specific items such as pianos, pumps, trunks, and trusses.) A paltry $3 million was invested in manufacturing in Orleans Parish in 1849, and even after a decade of agitation, this figure, adjusted for inflation, had barely budged upward at all ten years later. As urban historian Allan Pred has pointed out, New Orleans's dearth of manufacturing made it unique among major American cities. While the changing composition of urban workforces elsewhere in the United States reflected rapid prewar transitions to industrialization, a mere 3 percent of laborers in New Orleans were employed in manufacturing in 1860.[26]

Despite its great concentrations of agricultural and mercantile wealth, New Orleans and the state in which it was situated managed to compile an even worse record in manufacturing development than the South as a whole – and by most every measure the census provides, the antebellum South was an industrial laggard. The region had less than $100 million of capital invested in manufacturing in 1860, nearly a third of it concentrated in Virginia. This constituted less than a tenth of the nation's industrial capital, and it represented only about 5 percent of the aggregate value of regional farms in 1860 – a proportion that shrinks further if one factors in the roughly $3 billion invested in slaves, the

---

[26] Allan Pred, *Urban Growth and City-Systems in the United States, 1840–1860* (Cambridge, MA, 1980), 8. For a valuable summary of the slave South's pronounced urbanization lag, see David L. Carlton, "Antebellum Southern Urbanization," in Carlton and Peter A. Coclanis, *The South, the Nation, and the World: Perspectives on Southern Economic Development* (Charlottesville, VA, 2003), 35–48. The 1850 U.S. census (conducted in 1849) showed $3.0 million in capital invested in manufacturing in Orleans Parish, which would have been worth $3.26 million in 1859 if adjusted for inflation; the 1860 census listed Orleans Parish manufacturing capital at $3.4 million. This data is derived from the Seventh and Eighth Censuses via the University of Virginia's Historical Census Browser, located at http://mapserver.lib.virginia.edu; the CPI-adjusted figure was calculated using the converter on the website Measuring Worth, located at http://www.measuringworth.com (both accessed November 19, 2011). The number of persons in particular occupations in Louisiana is from the published version of the *Eighth Census* (1860), I, 197. Data on manufacturing establishments in the First and Second Districts was compiled from the New Orleans Census of Merchants, 1854.

overwhelming majority of whom were employed in agriculture. In real terms, the South's proportion of national manufacturing capacity actually fell during the 1850s, whether as capital invested, value produced, or employees engaged. Moreover, these statistics were inflated by the census's inclusion of second-stage agricultural processing as "manufacturing": sugar refining, tobacco curing, lumbering, and most of all, the milling of corn and wheat. Ultimately, one need not take sides in earlier historiographical debates over the reasons for the failure of antebellum southern industrialization to acknowledge at least the fact of that weakness.[27]

James Robb certainly recognized the dearth of industry in New Orleans, and he regarded it as anomalous in light of urban development elsewhere. Referring to "the peculiar character of our population," where, he asked, are those "large industrial classes which have built up other towns"? To explain their absence, Robb fell back on the poor state of public credit, which he said "draws around our city a *cordon sanitaire*, which keeps away industry and capital." But this quintessential bankers' rationale was specious. Although "bad management of our public affairs" contributed to a poor business climate, it is unlikely that private investment was suppressed primarily by municipal debt. Robb's emphasis on public credit also reflected his assumption that such enterprises could not rely on local investors. "To create such [an industrial] class in New Orleans," he said, "to draw them here from other countries, it [is] only necessary to extend and facilitate the connection of this city with the great agricultural states" of the West. Here Robb again seemed to exculpate local merchants for the city's developmental failures. Based on his contention that the "hard-earned means" of Crescent City merchants was "absorbed in high rents, high interest, and by advances to planters," Robb argued that resident businessmen had insufficient resources to sponsor manufacturing enterprises. But again, in light of the real and personal wealth these merchants controlled, his excuse rang hollow.[28]

More interesting was Robb's belief that an industrial class capable of establishing a viable manufacturing sector in New Orleans had to be "created" and "drawn here" from the West, the North, or overseas. Having recognized that

---

[27] All data in this paragraph are derived from the Eighth Census (1860), Manufacturing, Historical Census Browser; and Gary M. Walton and Hugh Rockoff, *History of the American Economy*, 9th ed. (Mason, OH, 2002), 213–15. Fine studies of particular industrial projects in the antebellum South, like those by Charles B. Dew and Tom Downey, have had the unfortunate side effect of masking the exceptional nature of such efforts, helping prepare the ground for one recent scholar to assert that "after the Mexican War ... the [South] industrialized rapidly"; Wells, *Origins of the Southern Middle Class*, 14 (quotation); Dew, *Bond of Iron: Master and Slave at Buffalo Forge* (New York, 1994); Downey, "Riparian Rights and Manufacturing in Antebellum South Carolina: William Gregg and the Origins of the 'Industrial Mind,'" *Journal of Southern History* 65 (February 1999), 77–108. An excellent review of the historiography on the economy of the slave South is Mark M. Smith, *Debating Slavery: Economy and Society in the American Antebellum South* (New York, 1998).

[28] Robb, "Condition of Things in New Orleans," 77–9.

the wealth of southern merchants and planters was overwhelmingly invested in land and slaves, Robb strongly implied that the "peculiar character" of merchant capital in New Orleans, and even in the South more generally, stifled the habits and mentalities associated with industrial growth elsewhere. His conviction that outside capitalists were needed to sponsor regional economic development suggested, albeit subtly and gently, that the southern economy's reliance on slave labor had wide-ranging consequences no less profound for being only vaguely understood or acknowledged. However, Robb's speech avoided overt criticism of the South's "peculiar institution," which highlights a persistent problem faced by industrialization's regional champions. These advocates had to tread softly so as not to appear as if they were endorsing critiques of southern slavery that were becoming more commonplace at the time, from the moral thunder of abolitionists to the national political gridlock over U.S. territorial expansion after the Mexican War.[29]

Businessmen in both sections often relied on platitudes about collective interests when dealing with polarized sentiments over slavery, and Robb was no exception. He argued that railroads would provide "iron bonds of mutual interest ... to soften the asperities and prejudices that too often alienate and divide the citizens of our common country." Yet his speech had cautiously acknowledged economic criticisms of slavery that even pragmatic men of commerce had trouble ignoring. Such critiques frequently centered on the ostensible indolence of poor whites, which they attributed to slavery's degrading effect on ideals of manual labor. But even more relevant to industrial promoters such as Robb were lethargic southern attitudes toward public improvements and economic development more generally. As early as 1841, a lead article in *Hunt's Merchants' Magazine* had discussed the growth of northern textile manufacturing, which the author regarded as curious given the South's monopoly on cotton production. Although he did not blame slavery directly, the author did suggest that the poor condition of southern roads and villages "indicate[s] ... a want of thrifty enterprise on the part of the inhabitants," adding that planters' "liberal and free indulgences" with regard to spending left them in constant debt. In spite of "abundant resources," he concluded, "those means which in the hands of some would be a source of vast profit, become in their hands a cause of mere competence."[30]

---

[29] The best review of growing tensions over slavery during the 1850s, especially as centered on territorial expansion, remains David M. Potter, *The Impending Crisis, 1848–1861*, ed. Don E. Fehrenbacher (New York, 1976).

[30] "The American Cotton Trade," *Hunt's Merchants' Magazine* 4 (March 1841), 201–27 (quotations on 225–6); for a southerner's similar comments see M. Tarver, "Domestic Manufactures in the South and West," *De Bow's Review* 3 (March 1847), 200. Robb, "Condition of Things in New Orleans," 80. For criticisms of poor whites, see Frederick Law Olmsted, *The Cotton Kingdom: A Traveller's Observations on Cotton and Slavery in the American Slave States*, ed. Arthur M. Schlesinger (New York, 1953), 327–8, 522–7; Hinton Rowan Helper, *The Impending Crisis of the South: How to Meet It*, ed. George M. Fredrickson (1857; repr., Cambridge, MA, 1968).

This emphasis on the savings and investment patterns of southern wealth-holders presaged Robb's implicit concerns about the differences between the behavior of capitalists in a slave-based regime and those grounded on free-labor relationships. As the author hinted, nowhere was the absence of southern manufacturing more striking than in the cotton industry. In the same journal several years later, northern textile manufacturer Amos E. Lawrence evinced skepticism toward southern efforts to establish cotton mills, partly because of the scarcity of free-labor operatives willing to work in them. In the southern seaboard states, with their depleted agricultural soils, promoters of cotton manufactures such as William Gregg enjoyed limited success using white laborers in the 1850s, but the growth of mill villages was postponed until later in the century. In the booming cotton culture of the Old Southwest, the neglect of textile manufacturing was more pronounced. In New Orleans, which had the largest pool of free labor in the South, not to mention abundant supplies of cotton, only the passive nature of merchant capital prevented the city from becoming, as one writer put it in an 1850 article in *De Bow's Review*, "another Lowell." Although such men sought to "stimulate the slumbering ideas of mercantile men" as to New Orleans's advantages and the opportunities that awaited, scattered efforts to establish cotton manufactures there during the 1850s remained undercapitalized and unsuccessful.[31]

Outsiders were more willing than southern businessmen such as Robb to attribute such failures to the fickle and conservative character of investment under a slave mode of production. As Amos Lawrence insightfully argued, "Though there are many rich men in the cotton-growing States, the number of moneyed men is very small, and they are not usually the projectors of new enterprises." Lawrence's distinction highlights the comparative dimensions of capitalist development in the United States. It was a hallmark of merchant capitalism to be wary of close involvement with ventures whose profitability depended mostly on inputs, especially labor costs, that were built into the production process and thus required intense supervision. Industrialism in this sense, as sociologist Max Weber later described it, represented a new, all-encompassing form of economic life. But merchants everywhere typically preferred the shallower commitments of short-term gambles based on exchange differentials in markets with which they were familiar or well connected. One such "old-school" Philadelphia cotton merchant of the late antebellum era, for example, included a warning in his will about the fixed expenses and problematic entanglements entailed in manufacturing ventures. But the habits of such men were under siege. To paraphrase another nineteenth-century social theorist, the compression of space and time by capital-intensive transportation and

---

[31] "Establishment of Manufactures at New Orleans," *De Bow's Review* 8 (January 1850), 1–20 (both quotations on p. 1); Reinders, *End of an Era*, 44–5; Downey, "Riparian Rights and Manufacturing," 95, 105–6; [Amos E. Lawrence], "The Condition and Prospects of American Cotton Manufactures in 1849," *Hunt's Merchants' Magazine* 21 (December 1849), 628–33.

communication improvements in the North and West made markets denser and information less exclusive. Consequently, as opportunities to wheedle profits in their customary manner decreased, antebellum northern merchants began cautiously investing in factories. Even though manufacturers soon began to generate investment capital either internally or via the growing northeastern financial sector, historians have recognized merchants' roles as "catalysts" during the early stages of American industrial development.[32]

This was not the case with merchants in the slave South, however, where the absence of the external forces impelling adaptation elsewhere combined with more deeply rooted behaviors to mitigate against industrial development. Both *Hunt's* articles suggested that one of these behaviors was the lack of "thrift" among southern wealthholders. In this popular view, which is confirmed by copious anecdotal evidence, the extravagant personal spending of southern planters and merchants was inimical to the savings habits typical of industrial entrepreneurs. In New Orleans, merchants spent liberally on everything from hand-tailored clothes and fine imported spirits to brougham carriages and the high-bred horses that pulled them, all of which provided outward signifiers of their standing in the city's highly stratified commercial environment. Even the tendency of merchants to invest in slaves and real estate partly served a crucial social function. No well-heeled mercantile family could do without domestic servants, and their homes were the most expensively constructed and furnished in the city. For example, even though James Robb preached the industrial gospel, his spending habits rivaled those of any plantation grandee. He owned a home valued at $100,000, and it was appointed with one of the largest private art collections in the nation.[33]

Historians have debated whether such "conspicuous consumption" proves that wealthy southerners behaved "irrationally" in economic terms, but their profligate spending was by no means irrational given the performative context in which elite New Orleanians defined themselves and one another. Indeed, the normativity of this behavior helps explain the stigma attached to those who refused to participate, such as the miserly millionaire John McDonogh. As historian J. G. A. Pocock has suggested, merchants' displays of wealth reflected their devotion to older, classically derived ideals in which property was the "basis of social personality" and denoted civic virtue and rightful authority. The political nature of elite consumption in the antebellum South is also highlighted by

[32] Porter and Livesay, *Merchants and Manufacturers*, chap. 4; Graeme J. Milne. *Trade and Traders in Mid-Victorian Liverpool: Mercantile Business and the Making of a World Port* (Liverpool, UK, 2000), 100. Karl Marx, *Grundrisse: Foundations of the Critique of Political Economy*, trans. Martin Nicolaus (New York, 1973), 539; Max Weber, *The Protestant Ethic and the Spirit of Capitalism*, trans. Talcott Parsons (1904–5; repr., London and New York, 1992), esp. 169–83. [Lawrence], "Condition and Prospects of American Cotton Manufactures," 628.
[33] Evans, "James Robb," 245–6. On domestic slaves as a form of "conspicuous consumption," see Jane H. Pease, "A Note on Patterns of Conspicuous Consumption among Seaboard Planters, 1820–1860," *Journal of Southern History* 35 (August 1969), 389.

other forms of spending that were less overtly pecuniary. Sociologist Thorstein Veblen argued that forms of "conspicuous leisure" were especially common in slave societies, in which time itself was a commodity to be "spent" by elites relieved of the need to work. Gentlemanly capitalists in New Orleans, including Robb, whiled away the hours in exclusive private associations such as the Boston Club, and their more visible activities, from horse-racing to debutante balls, received a great deal of attention in the local press, which helped to publicly establish and maintain their reputations. Banker Samuel J. Peters, grasping opportunist that he was, devoted "an inordinate amount of time" to organizing his busy social calendar, according to one historian. During the late 1850s Peters and his fellow American merchant-elites poured enormous resources into the newly organized Mystic Krewe of Comus, thereby refashioning the raucous Creole-Catholic festival of Mardi Gras into a theatrical platform for displaying their wealth and prestige.[34]

Some economic critiques of slavery went further, judging slaveholders' reckless spending to be a sign of moral decadence. Perhaps, but these critics were on firmer ground by sticking to the consequences such spending had on the regional capital pool. Yet even in this sense, money or time lavishly spent was actually just another form of conservative investment – in one's personal status – and as such, it could pay handsome dividends in the baroque social framework of antebellum New Orleans's commercial culture. Such investments were not within everyone's means, though. Small businessmen often discovered that they did not have the resources to compete on both the social and commercial planes, however intertwined they were. As one New Orleans merchant, J. M. Ellis, wrote to his sister in 1847, "The fact is, I do not go into society here ... because my business will not allow to the expenses attending it."[35]

---

[34] Reinders, *End of an Era*, 153–61; Clark, "New Orleans and the River," 123 (quotation); Stuart O. Landry, *History of the Boston Club* (New Orleans, 1938). On conspicuous leisure in slave societies see Thorstein Veblen, *The Theory of the Leisure Class: An Economic Study of Institutions* (1899; repr., New York, 1953), 29–30, 74–6; cf. Mark M. Smith, *Mastered by the Clock: Time, Slavery, and Freedom in the American South* (Chapel Hill, 1997). J. G. A. Pocock, "The Mobility of Property and the Rise of Eighteenth-Century Sociology," in Pocock, *Virtue, Commerce, and History* (Cambridge, UK, and other cities, 1985), 103–23 (quotation on p. 119). On the performative nature of elite consumption in the Old South, see Rhys Isaac, "Ethnographic Method in History: An Action Approach," in *Material Life in America, 1600–1860*, ed. Robert Blair St. George (Boston, 1988), 53–4. The question of conspicuous consumption was an important sidebar to older debates over the profitability of slavery; see Eugene D. Genovese, *The Political Economy of Slavery: Studies in the Economy and Society of the Slave South* (New York, 1965), esp. pp. 130, 158, 283; Pease, "Patterns of Conspicuous Consumption"; Gavin Wright, "New and Old Views on the Economics of Slavery," *Journal of Economic History* 33 (June 1973), 452–66, esp. 459; and Fred Bateman and Thomas Weiss, *A Deplorable Scarcity: The Failure of Industrialization in the Slave Economy* (Chapel Hill, 1981), 158–63.

[35] J. M. Ellis to Mrs. Samuel T. Tisdale, February 14, 1847, in Ellis Papers (Mss 1363, LLMVC). An excellent point of comparison is London-based British business culture, as described in P. J. Cain and A. G. Hopkins, "Gentlemanly Capitalism and British Expansion Overseas I: The Old Colonial System, 1688–1850," *Economic History Review* 2d ser., 39 (November 1986),

Still, most merchants devoted careful if costly attention to cultivating social standing, in large part because of the economic benefits that followed. One key advantage of being accepted in Crescent City high society was greater access to "inside" information, the possession of which could often determine success or failure in commodities trading. Well-regarded merchants could rely not only on city contacts but also on planter-clients in the countryside for important insights into the size and condition of pending crops. For those lower on the commercial ladder, such as Ellis, the city's coffeehouses were always rife with rumor, and the 1854 municipal census also indicated that at least a half-dozen "intelligence offices" in New Orleans sold market information to help guide traders' decisions about whether to hold out for better prices or bail out before they declined. In either case, the exchange-oriented nature of merchant capital made their fortunes dependent on reliable market reports, more so than were the profits generated internally in industrial regimes. Of course, such information could be mistaken or subject to shrewd manipulation. In 1852 Edward Sullivan noted how rumors passed along by "touts" in the cotton district "differ considerably," with "each man considering his information better than his neighbour's, and backing it accordingly." That same year, another observer complained that "false reports" caused widespread injuries to profits, arguing that everyone would benefit "if greater steadiness could be given to [cotton] prices" through better information. The advent of telegraphic connections between New Orleans and New York in the early 1850s did little to solve such uncertainties about future crops, although on the demand side, they did help dampen national spot-market price fluctuations considerably. However, information from critical overseas markets, especially Liverpool, was still greatly delayed; regular transatlantic telegraphic service was not established until after the Civil War. Furthermore, merchants were slow to embrace the new communications technology. Among other problems, high costs made most telegraphic correspondence too brief for the detailed reports on market conditions that merchants preferred, and their mediation by poorly paid (that is, eminently corruptible) agents also caused many businessmen to distrust such messages.[36]

Their resistance to communications improvements was another aspect of the seemingly willful isolation of Crescent City merchants from national trends, but in James Robb's view, railroads would break down such barriers inhibiting industrial development in New Orleans by promoting interregional transfers

501–25, esp. 508–9. See also Leonard P. Curry, "Urbanization and Urbanism in the Old South: A Comparative View," *Journal of Southern History* 40 (February 1974), 43–60.

[36] Milne, *Trade and Traders in Mid-Victorian Liverpool*, 129–30; Richard B. DuBoff, "The Telegraph and the Structure of Markets in the United States, 1845–1890," in *Commercial and Financial Services*, ed. R. W. Michie (Oxford, 1994), 254–8; "The Telegraph, Part 2," *De Bow's Review* 16 (February 1854), 168; C. F. McCay, "The Cotton Trade of the South" (1852), repr. in *Cotton and the Growth of the American Economy, 1790–1860: Sources and Readings*, ed. Stuart Bruchey (New York and other cities, 1967), 200 (quotation); Sullivan, *Rambles and Scrambles*, 217–18; New Orleans Census of Merchants, 1854.

of people, ideas, and capital. "When they multiplied railroads," he declared in his 1851 speech, "they multiplied industry." Others agreed, seeing railroads as a necessary catalyst for modernizing New Orleans's stagnant economic structure. If regional railroad projects were "consummated," wrote one local editor, the city would undoubtedly find "manufactories established, and steamship lines multiplied." Robb particularly emphasized the importance of reconnecting the New Orleans with the Midwest. The proposed railroad would help the city "reclaim our fugitive trade" with that region, and he promised wider economic benefits as well, such as facilitating longitudinal population flows from the upper Mississippi and Ohio Valleys. Not only would "the teeming valleys of the West ... seek here the articles of necessity and luxury that they require," but Robb also claimed that the ease of rail travel would create "strong inducements which do not now exist to locate here permanently, and our population will acquire a stable character."[37]

To prove Robb's contentions about the ability of railroads to transform and improve local and regional economies, however, the New Orleans, Jackson, & Great Northern line first had to be successfully constructed, which itself would constitute a decisive test of the willingness of Crescent City and Louisiana wealthholders to make financial sacrifices for the common good. Perhaps unsurprisingly, this was a test they failed. This failure was not the fault of James Robb, who worked tirelessly for the next several years on the project's behalf. He did enjoy some early successes with regard to political reforms crucial to the railroad's completion. After getting himself elected to the state legislature in late 1851, Robb began his term the following January by overseeing the passage of bills amending statutory limits on corporate capitalization and repealing the 1836 division of New Orleans's government into three municipalities. Later that year a new city charter drafted by Robb was approved by voters, as was a municipal real estate tax of 3 percent for the purposes of funding New Orleans's share of the proposed railroad. In the summer of 1852, despite resurgent accusations of self-interestedness, Robb also managed the sale in New York of a $2 million bond issue by the newly consolidated city to refinance old municipal debts. With his political goals thus achieved, Robb resigned his legislative seat well before the completion of his term in order to concentrate on the railroad.[38]

Things did not go smoothly thereafter. For one thing, it proved an uphill battle to secure parish-by-parish approval of real estate taxes to fund the project. As expected, many rural landowners accustomed to using the river were skeptical of expensive "socialistic" legislation that mainly seemed to benefit New Orleans–based interests. Further complicating matters were difficulties in obtaining the funds collected from the municipal real estate tax. Not only had

[37] Robb, "Condition of Things in New Orleans," 79; *New Orleans News-Letter and General Weekly Review*, September 14, 1850.
[38] Evans, "James Robb," 186–9, 194–5, 227.

approval of the tax been secured by staggering its collection incrementally over several years, but the sudden local enthusiasm for railroads had actually diluted the capital pool further by directing that the same tax be used simultaneously to finance a line running westward through the sugar parishes and toward the booming Texas market. Robb diplomatically offered his public support for this project, which was spearheaded by the powerful New Orleans factor and sugar planter Maunsel White, though he probably considered it an unwise dilution of limited resources. In any case, his railroad's problems were just beginning. Logistical problems in laying track over swampy, unforgiving terrain slowed construction and caused frequent cost overruns, which gave ammunition to critics and dampened the enthusiasm of earlier supporters. As a result, political difficulties gradually began to hinder the project's momentum. Legislatures in Mississippi and Tennessee had to be prodded to offer financial support for the line running through their territories. In New Orleans, opponents of the project did not find it either difficult or unpopular to contrive various ways to postpone collection of the municipal real estate tax. Beginning in 1854, Robb also encountered increasing challenges to his authority from hostile shareholder factions. These disputes first led him to resign the presidency of the railroad, then later to withdraw from its board of directors. Robb was persuaded to return in 1856, but by then the project, he admitted, "was in a condition of supineness," its directors having made "many and serious mistakes."[39]

Seven years after the project's inception in 1851, the railroad finally reached its initial terminus at Jackson, only about 150 miles from New Orleans. It did not make it out of Mississippi before the Civil War. Robb, disgusted with the outcome and having lost much of his wealth in the Panic of 1857, decamped for Chicago in 1858. By 1860 the project had consumed more than $6 million, over three times its original estimated capitalization. Less than a fifth of that capital came from private subscriptions; government funds made up nearly all the difference. In the end, Robb's vision of restoring close ties with the West and thereby refashioning the Crescent City's commercial economy came to naught. In retrospect, a minor incident in 1854 seemed to encapsulate the railroad's doomed fortunes. A short excursion organized for a trainload of railroad officials and public dignitaries, including Robb and Louisiana governor Paul O. Hebert, had been stranded in the city's swampy hinterlands when the locomotive jumped off the tracks after hitting a cow. The collision between agriculture and industry in the Deep South had produced a pyrrhic victory for the former. Only if the train had been derailed instead by a cotton bale dropped from a slave-driven wagon could the symbolism have been more apt.[40]

[39] James Robb, "Railroad System of the Southwest," *De Bow's Review* 21 (August 1856), 121–5 (quotations on pp. 121, 124). This article was a reprint of a letter from Robb to Louisiana governor Robert C. Wickliffe. See also Robb, "Condition and Prospects of New Orleans, and What She Must Do for Railroads," *De Bow's Review* 12 (May 1852), 543–51. Reed, *New Orleans and the Railroads*, 95–107; Evans, "James Robb," 227–8, 231–43.
[40] New Orleans *Daily Delta*, December 14, 1854; Evans, "James Robb," 248–50.

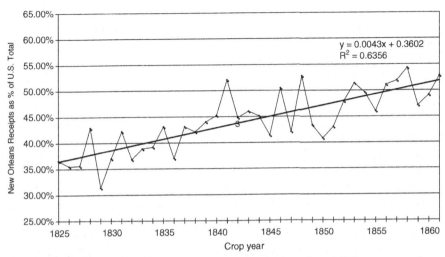

FIGURE 2.1. New Orleans cotton receipts as a proportion of total U.S. cotton production, 1825–1861.

Source: New Orleans cotton receipts derived from data in E. J. Donnell, *Chronological and Statistical History of Cotton* (1872; repr., Wilmington, Del., 1973). The author gratefully acknowledges the help of Donald Parker of Randolph, Mass., with the least-squares correlation on which the trendline in this graph is based.

Hoisted on the petard of their own contradictions with an increasingly isolated slave society that encouraged an odd combination of conservative and opportunistic strategies for capital accumulation and deployment, the hopes of men such as Robb for vigorous industrial development, infrastructural improvements, and institutional reforms had faded well before the advent of the Civil War. In New Orleans such will-o'-the wisps were dispersed within the self-congratulatory atmosphere of prosperity during the 1850s, when the Crescent City enjoyed its own "Great Barbecue," to borrow Vernon Louis Parrington's description of the nation's later Gilded Age. Cotton prices stabilized at more than ten cents per pound, and these relatively high prices proved remarkably inelastic in light of the continued growth of southern cotton production. Total annual output never fell below 2 million bales during the 1850s, and usually hovered near 3 million. And despite many well-publicized complaints, New Orleans remained the chief market and export point for cotton. Indeed, the city's annual cotton receipts averaged more than half of all southern production throughout the decade, and furthermore, these receipts represented a proportion of total output that had grown steadily since the 1820s (Figure 2.1).[41]

---

[41] Cotton price and production data are from E. J. Donnell, *Chronological and Statistical History of Cotton* (1872; repr., Wilmington, DE, 1973). For a contemporary acknowledgement that New Orleans handled "about half" the South's cotton production, see Stephen Colwell, *The Five Cotton States and New York* (Philadelphia, 1861), 9.

Given the cotton-fueled prosperity in New Orleans during the 1850s, the reluctance of its merchants to tamper with what did not seem broken is more understandable. However, it has proven too easy for historians to confuse the armchair exhortations of editors such as J. D. B. De Bow, or the efforts of visionary businessmen such as James Robb, with the meager results that they were able to obtain. Jonathan D. Wells, for example, has recently relied on Whiggish public rhetoric to argue that a commercial and professional "middle class" in New Orleans and other cities was on the brink of achieving a thoroughgoing reform of southern society that aped the manners, morals, and capitalist strategies of free-labor society in the North. Most contemporaries would have been skeptical of such claims, however. "Cities do not thrive well upon Southern soil," argued Stephen Colwell in 1861, because "[t]here is no middle class to build and inhabit them." In fact, as historian Larry Schweikart has recognized, "spokesmen for industrialism ... such as James Robb, were peculiar to the overall intellectual climate" of the antebellum South. Though it is true that propaganda favoring railroads and other improvements was common in the South during the 1850s, even if such verbiage had been worth its weight in gold, it is doubtful whether merchants (or planters) would have rushed to invest their surplus bounty in the preferred manner. The data on southern industrial development during the period certainly do not reflect any such predilection. Moreover, it would have been uncharacteristic of the historical investment patterns of merchant capital had they done so. Instead, merchants recycled profits into further commodity speculations, or into conspicuous consumption, slaves, and real estate – but not into factories, nor into railroads.[42]

Mercantile satisfaction with the status quo was also reflected in their lackluster participation in antebellum politics. In his classic study of nineteenth-century Louisiana, Roger W. Shugg contended that Crescent City gentleman-merchants, allied with large planters, dominated state and local governments before the Civil War. But as historian John M. Sacher has recently shown, merchants never constituted more than 5 percent of state legislators during the antebellum era. Even the most reform-minded shied away from sustained political commitments, preferring to assume the kingmaker role from the comfort of their social clubs. James Robb himself attained public office several times, typically keeping them just long enough to achieve his policy goals before resigning. After the passage of the pro-business state constitution of 1852, Robb was one of several Whig businessmen who declined to stand for office, leading

---

[42] Larry Schweikart, *Banking in the American South from the Age of Jackson to Reconstruction* (Baton Rouge, 1987), 251 (quotation); Colwell, *Five Cotton States and New York*, 29; Wells, *Origins of the Southern Middle Class*, 14–15 and passim. To support his contention that industrialization and urbanization were transforming the South, Wells employs economists' old sleight-of-hand of claiming high growth rates based on expansion from very low base figures; Ibid., 164–70. For criticism of this approach see Peter A. Coclanis and Scott Marler, "The Economics of Reconstruction," in *A Companion to the Civil War and Reconstruction*, ed. Lacy K. Ford (Malden, MA, 2005), 346; see also Scott P. Marler, "Stuck in the Middle (Class) with You," *Historical Methods* 39 (Fall 2006), 154–8.

a New Orleans newspaper to complain that it was difficult to find "capable gentlemen willing ... to surrender their business avocations in the behests of party." Their withdrawal left the field open for the consolidation of political power in New Orleans and Louisiana in the hands of "machine" bosses such as Democratic Party kingpin John Slidell (with whom Robb had a cozy relationship). Although city merchants carped incessantly about the factionalism, corruption, and "mob rule" that characterized tumultuous New Orleans politics during the 1850s, they had helped create the conditions that made it possible. Moreover, despite their anachronistic attachment to activist state commercial policies as typified by the fast-collapsing Whig Party, New Orleans merchants provided lukewarm support at best toward the sorts of taxes, particularly on property, that were needed for capital-intensive improvement projects.[43]

One arena in which New Orleans merchants were quite politically active during the late antebellum era was their entanglement with a variety of overseas adventures, especially in Latin America and the Caribbean. Although partisan divisions sometimes affected their support for particular projects, prominent Whigs and Democrats alike ramped up New Orleans's long-standing predilection toward meddling in Latin American politics. In the wake of the recent war with Mexico, New Orleans Whigs remained out of step with their party's ongoing objections to U.S. militarism, which were often made on racist or anti-Catholic grounds. On the national level, rival Louisiana politicians such as John Slidell and Pierre Soulé both pressured cautious presidential administrations to back expansionist projects during the 1850s, even as local elites made little effort to conceal the financial and logistical support they organized for various filibusters to Cuba and Nicaragua. Although their support for a proposed U.S. annexation of Cuba made little sense to outsiders, Louisiana sugar planters and the Creole merchants allied with them heavily favored it – but so did many Americans, such as the Whig banker Samuel J. Peters. The Boston Club, home of the city's Anglo-American commercial elite (including James Robb, who had banking interests in Havana), also proudly trumpeted its members' efforts on behalf of William Walker's doomed filibuster to Nicaragua in 1857.[44]

---

[43] Reinders, *End of an Era*, 58–59; Leon Cyprian Soulé, *The Know Nothing Party in New Orleans: A Reappraisal* (Baton Rouge, 1961), 40–8, 94–102. New Orleans *Bee*, November 26, 1852, quoted in John M. Sacher, *A Perfect War of Politics: Parties, Politicians, and Democracy in Louisiana, 1824–1861* (Baton Rouge, 2003), 226; Ibid., 211–12, 225, 230. Roger W. Shugg, *Origins of Class Struggle in Louisiana: A Social History of White Farmers and Laborers during Slavery and After* (1939; rpt., Baton Rouge, 1968), chap. 5, esp. 138–41.

[44] Landry, *History of the Boston Club*, 47–8, 55–6; Robert E. May, *Manifest Destiny's Underworld: Filibustering in Antebellum America* (Chapel Hill, 2002). A few years later, Karl Marx recounted John Slidell's career, calling him "the soul of the southern conspiratorial enclave" and "the evil genius of Buchanan's administration"; Marx, "The Trent Affair" (December 1861), rpt. in *On America and the Civil War*, ed. and trans. Saul K. Padover (New York, 1972), 120. Two examples of contemporary bemusement at Louisiana's support for Cuban annexation are Olmsted, *Cotton Kingdom*, 331–2; and John E. Cairnes, *The Slave Power: Its Character, Career, and Probable Designs* (1862; rpt., Columbia, SC, 2003), 294–5.

Foreshadowing the jingoism of American progressives later in the century, even men such as J. D. B. De Bow jumped on the imperialist bandwagon. After the U.S. seizure of Texas and California from Mexico in the late 1840s, scarcely an issue of his New Orleans commercial journal went by without features on the benefits of "manifest destiny" to the South. De Bow wrote in 1852 that the Gulf of Mexico and the adjacent Caribbean should be regarded as a "great Southern sea" centered on New Orleans. Later, De Bow and others backed yet another ill-fated railroad to be controlled by New Orleans interests, this one across the isthmus of Tehuantepec in Mexico. This project, however, put them at loggerheads with powerful New York transportation moguls and their Louisiana allies (namely, John Slidell), who preferred an alternate route. Both sides, however, were lured by the riches to be gained by linking the South with California and the Pacific Rim.[45]

Historian Robert E. May rightly highlighted the "entrepreneurial" dimensions of such extranational proposals, which call to mind similar linkages between merchant capitalism and colonial expansion during the First British Empire. More recently, Matthew Guterl has analyzed the relationships between proslavery racial ideologies and southerners' desires to convert the Gulf into an "American Mediterranean." But New Orleans merchants' intrigues on behalf of southern expansionism were also consonant with the furtiveness of local commercial culture, as well as the city's legacy of privateering and cynicism toward the law. As Guterl writes, "filibustering was high politics conducted through private, unofficial means." Moreover, merchants' support for filibustering may have reflected their ambiguous standing in the southern political economy. Like the similarly belligerent and delusional "King Cotton" perspective that arose in the mid-1850s, Crescent City elites' strident pro-imperialist cheerleading seems at least partly an ideological means of compensating for their unpopularity in the countryside and alleviating the suspicion with which their northern ties were regarded by other southerners.[46]

Most of all, such self-indulgent fantasies showed that the city's merchants had yet to relinquish their geopolitical ambitions for New Orleans to play a leading role on the transatlantic stage. However, their actions prompted conflicts not only with powerful eastern capitalists, but also with their fellow southerners, the U.S. government, and European powers. Historian William W. Freehling has described the tensions that Crescent City overseas adventurism provoked

---

[45] De Bow, "Importance of an Industrial Revolution to the South," 558; see also A. V. Hofer, "The Central American Question," *De Bow's Review* 21 (August 1856), 125–31; May, *Manifest Destiny's Underworld*, 174.

[46] Matthew Pratt Guterl, *American Mediterranean: Southern Slaveholders in the Age of Emancipation* (Cambridge, MA, 2008), 18–35 (quotation on p. 25); Robert F. May, *The Southern Dream of a Caribbean Empire, 1854–1861* (Baton Rouge, 1973), 138–9, 195–9 (quotation on p. 195). England's Lord Palmerston famously declared that "it is the business of government to open and secure roads for the merchant"; as quoted and discussed in Cain and Hopkins, "Gentlemanly Capitalism and British Expansion Overseas, [Part] I," 523.

among South Carolina's "fire-eaters," who felt such sideshows detracted from more important battles over slavery being fought on American soil – a conclusion that De Bow himself seemed to reach just as the Civil War broke out. Like the later Confederate government, the successive administrations of Presidents Franklin Pierce and James Buchanan, otherwise sympathetic to southern goals, repeatedly had to curb excessive foreign-policy meddling by New Orleanians. Pierce dismissed Pierre Soulé as minister to Spain over Cuban affairs, and federal courts initiated anti-neutrality prosecutions in New Orleans against local backers of Walker's Nicaraguan expedition. Finally, New Orleans's aggressive Caribbean designs provoked diplomatic anxieties in Great Britain. In 1858, a British visitor, William Kingsford, described the city's advocacy for Cuban annexation as an outward extension of its elites' long-standing belief in their gatekeeper role at the base of the Mississippi River system, and he worried that Caribbean "commerce could be entirely controlled by New Orleans" if the policy became reality. The previous year, another English traveler had warned that a U.S. annexation of Cuba would create "mischiefs" for Britain "that can scarcely be conceived."[47]

Being at odds with both their own government and their chief overseas trading partner indicates how New Orleans's merchants clung to outmoded conceptions of 'iron-fist' Atlantic colonial relationships that were already being superseded by domestically driven economies with export policies governed by the "velvet-glove" imperialism of free trade. Yet there was also a desperate aura to merchants' support of overseas adventurism that probably reflected the fast-shrinking horizons of the city's economic influence. Here it helps to reemphasize the importance of New Orleans's failure to retain an adequate proportion of the western grain trade for its long-term role in the U.S. urban system. One rationale offered for a U.S. takeover of Cuba was that it would redirect the midwestern trade to New Orleans, from which foodstuffs would be exported to a captive island market. By the 1850s, very little of the midwestern products received at New Orleans were still being forwarded to the Atlantic seaboard via coastal packets; most were retained for local and regional consumption, often simply turned around and shipped back upriver to customers in the plantation districts. But even in terms of those southern markets, New Orleans merchants had begun facing intense competition from other cities

[47] James M. Phillippo, *The United States and Cuba* (London, 1857), 402–3; William Kingsford, *Impressions of the West and South during a Six Weeks' Holiday* (Toronto, 1858), 60–1. May, *Manifest Destiny's Underworld*, 138–43; J. Preston Moore, "Pierre Soulé: Southern Expansionist and Promoter," *Journal of Southern History* 21 (May 1955), 203–23. William W. Freehling, *The Road to Disunion, Volume II: Secessionists at Bay* (New York, 2007), chap. 11, esp. 152–9. For De Bow's sudden lack of enthusiasm for southern expansionism at the outset of the Civil War, see his "The Disruption of the Federal Union," *De Bow's Review* 30 (April 1861), 436. This essay is a revised version of a speech he had made four years before as president of the Southern Commercial Convention held at Knoxville, TN; the original speech's more pro-imperialist stance is evident in the version reprinted by the New Orleans *Daily Delta*, August 20, 1857.

trying to secure larger shares of interior commerce for themselves. This was true not only of midwestern cities such as Chicago and Milwaukee; it also applied to cities on the border between North and South, such as Louisville, Cincinnati, and especially St. Louis. Even southern cities such as Memphis, Mobile, Galveston, and Charleston were seeking to tap into New Orleans's plantation markets. Especially for a city that still harbored pretensions of its predestined importance to the Atlantic economy, the gradual shrinking of New Orleans's hinterlands showed the dangers of relying so heavily on cotton to define its commercial territory.[48]

Lest too much blame be attributed to merchants for New Orleans's problems, it should be pointed out that external seizures of the city's competitive advantages often resulted from developments beyond their control. Moreover, the foundation of southern wealth on staple-crop agriculture – and by extension, on land and slaves – was not so much a situation they created as one they inherited and exploited. As James Robb apparently recognized, the failure of New Orleans merchants to diversify their local economy, particularly through industrialization, reflected a wider socioeconomic context that devalued and discouraged such efforts. Again, older historiography that has fallen somewhat out of fashion would have endorsed Robb's view. Eugene D. Genovese, for example, argued convincingly that there were a variety of deeply rooted, interwoven reasons for the scarcity of industry in the antebellum South, such as elite whites' fears of urban slave rebellions, their racist beliefs in blacks' incompetence, and their distrust of immigrant free labor and its social consequences.[49]

Lately, however, historians have seemed more inclined to find an amorphous national "market revolution" lurking behind every instance of careful bookkeeping and profit-making by planters; as one recent study of elite slaveholders exclaimed, they were "Capitalists All!" But this perspective cannot explain either the nagging fact of southern industrial underdevelopment, or the associated reluctance of regional businessmen to invest in manufacturing, despite public exhortations by well-respected contemporaries like James Robb that

[48] On the nineteenth-century U.S. urban system see Pred, *Urban Growth and City-Systems in the United States*; and William Cronon, *Nature's Metropolis: Chicago and the Great West* (New York, 1991), esp. chap. 6. Albert Fishlow analyzed the changing composition of New Orleans's antebellum grain trade and its consequences in *American Railroads and the Transformation of the Ante-Bellum Economy* (Cambridge, MA, 1965), 269–97; see also John G. Clark, *The Grain Trade of the Old Northwest* (Urbana, Il, 1965), 163–71, 231–6. For an example of the grain-trade rationale for Cuban annexation, see the public letter by John S. Thrasher to Samuel J. Peters in the New York *Times*, May 23, 1854, which was also published in *De Bow's Review* XVII (July 1854), 43–9; see also Richard Tansey, "Southern Expansionism: Urban Interests in the Cuban Filibusters," *Plantation Society in the Americas* I (June 1979), 227–51.

[49] Genovese, *Political Economy of Slavery*, esp. chaps. 7–9; see also William L. Barney, *The Road to Secession: A New Perspective on the Old South* (New York, 1972), 33–7. For an economic historian's acknowledgment that the institution of slavery suppressed southern industrial development, see Gavin Wright, *The Political Economy of the Cotton South: Households, Markets, and Wealth in the Nineteenth Century* (New York, 1978), 107–20.

such enterprises were both desirable and the vanguard of economic growth. The market revolution thesis and its offshoots also tend to gloss over the profound qualitative differences in the composition of northern and southern capital that Robb pointed out in his 1851 speech. It is unusual that scholars who readily acknowledge the obvious distinctions between types of labor – not only between free and slave labor, but *among* those laborers as well – seem inclined to lump "capitalists" into a homogeneous mass. Political economists from Adam Smith to Karl Marx certainly recognized the crucial distinctions attendant to what the latter described as "the division of labor between capitals." By obscuring such differences, the market revolution thesis too often allows a convenient label to replace careful analysis, and thereby undermines even the most tenuous understandings of the contribution of economic factors to the onset of the Civil War.[50]

Merchants in antebellum New Orleans operated in a shared but isolated business culture that generated enormous wealth despite its manifest shortcomings. Their monopolistic position in the cotton trade masked the many ongoing changes that threatened their long-term prosperity. In the context of the slave society in which they were deeply implicated, their peculiar market culture discouraged the investments necessary for the city to modernize its economic base, whether through diversifying into industrial enterprises or buttressing and expanding their trade territory by means of transportation improvements such as railroads. The atomized nature of the marketplace over which they presided also mitigated against class cohesion, which prevented merchants from collectively sponsoring other institutional innovations, such as a cotton exchange, that would have improved the city's future prospects. Instead, New Orleans merchants continued to rely on their abilities to profit from short-term market gains within a closed social milieu organized in many ways more by caste than by class.

The persistence of this personalist commercial culture and the inefficient markets that resulted from it confirms the depth of New Orleans merchants' conservatism and their commitment to increasingly outmoded forms of business practice. In a market in which price swings of a penny per pound could

[50] Karl Marx, *Capital*, Vol. III, trans. David Fernbach (New York, 1981), 392–3; Smith, *Wealth of Nations*, Book III, chap. 5 ("On the Different Employment of Capitals"). In *Masters of the Big House: Elite Slaveholders of the Mid-Nineteenth Century South* (Baton Rouge, 2003), William Kauffman Scarborough titles his chapter on the non-plantation interests of the 300-plus largest southern slaveholders "Capitalists All!" He might have more accurately called it "Capitalists Few," since by his own admission, he could identify non-agricultural interests among only one-fifth of the slaveholders in his highly intensive study, and most of these were conservative forms of investment like banking and real estate; see pp. 218–19. Charles Sellers, *The Market Revolution: Jacksonian America, 1815–1846* (New York, 1991). Two influential studies that anticipated Sellers' thesis with regard to the Old South are James Oakes, *Slavery and Freedom: An Interpretation of the Old South* (New York, 1990); and Harry L. Watson, *Liberty and Power: The Politics of Jacksonian America* (New York, 1990).

bring fortune or ruin, it is not hard to see how cotton speculation in New Orleans, with its secrecy and dependence on keen but largely instinctual judgments, resembled the city's notoriously popular culture of gambling writ large. As one visitor noted in 1852, "People [in New Orleans] make bets about the probable rise and fall in the price of cotton, and book them in the same way as a man does his bets on the 'Derby.'" But the Crescent City's merchant community headed into the Civil War with the economic deck increasingly stacked against them. The predication of regional wealth on land and slaves, which would soon prove disastrous for New Orleans and the South, also required city merchants to play this game with an avid audience hovering over their shoulders. This audience not only consisted of the plantation clients on whose agricultural wealth their profits depended, but it also included a growing number of merchants scattered throughout the countryside. Since these rural and small-town storeowners were to assume great importance in the agricultural and commercial economy of the post–Civil War South, a closer examination of their development in antebellum Louisiana, as well as their relationships with urban factors and rural planters, is now in order.[51]

---

[51] Sullivan, *Rambles and Scrambles*, 217. On the widespread popularity of gambling in antebellum New Orleans, see Tregle, *Louisiana in the Age of Jackson*, 21–2.

3

Rural Merchants on the Cotton Frontier of Antebellum Louisiana

In the summer of 1860 Dr. Joseph Slemmons Copes, a New Orleans commission merchant, took a hiatus from the city's notorious fever season and attended to his firm's interests throughout the thriving cotton regions of the Red River Valley. Harlow J. Phelps, Copes's business partner and son-in-law, had a brother who managed a large store and cotton-forwarding business in Shreveport, Louisiana, that was closely allied with their firm. Shreveport, located on the Red River near the Arkansas and Texas borders, had a growing reputation as a boomtown for the plantation-supply trade; J. W. Dorr, a roving correspondent for the New Orleans *Crescent*, reported from Shreveport that same year that "the place has gone business mad.... There seem to be more stores than residences." The conditions that Copes found among the hundreds of merchants in the valley's interior were only slightly less competitive than in Shreveport. With scarcely concealed satisfaction, Copes, who was also an agent for a northern insurance company, informed his partner that he had convinced one rural storekeeper in central Louisiana to abandon a rival firm and represent his policies instead. The merchant, Copes noted, was also the area postmaster, a position that put him in regular contact with many potential customers. The marketplace tended to reward businessmen like Copes who paid such close attention to detail. Earlier in the year, for example, another newly established customer of Copes & Phelps, an enterprising village store owner in Mississippi, had written them to order a few barrels of apples from the produce markets of New Orleans. The young shopkeeper admitted that "there is little or nothing to be made" from selling fruit, but he explained that a strategically placed barrel "draws customers," and thus "one is enabled sometimes to sell some other articles." The self-described "novice to the business" had shrewdly intuited the concept of what modern retail management theory would call a "loss leader."[1]

[1] N. B. Kelsey (Brookhaven, Mississippi), to Copes & Phelps, January, 11, 18, 1860, and Copes to Harlow J. Phelps, June 28, 1860, in Joseph Slemmons Copes Papers, Box 6 (Mss 733;

Copes & Phelps had interests elsewhere besides the burgeoning Red River Valley. Earlier that year, Copes had traveled to Natchez, Mississippi, to find a new agent for the firm in that area's long-settled plantation district. In a letter carried back to New Orleans by his friend, the Presbyterian minister Benjamin M. Palmer, Copes reported that "as I expected, I have to allow a larger commission for receiving and selling stock" in the crowded Natchez market. Still, he wrote, E. B. Baker "does a leading business with planters and is just the man we want." Of special importance was Baker's willingness to serve as a conduit for sales of "Speer's Iron Hoops" for baling cotton. Copes & Phelps were the exclusive southern agents for this particular brand of clasp, despite their involvement in ongoing patent litigation faced by its Pennsylvania inventor. Since sales to planters through their allied Shreveport house had been brisk, Copes now hoped to tap the potential of the even-wealthier Natchez market.[2]

Joseph Slemmons Copes's 1860 travels exemplified an older type of American businessman: the "all-purpose" merchant who dealt in a wide variety of goods, from local truck-farm crops to manufactured products from distant markets. In the antebellum North, where industrial growth was prompting commercial specialization, such merchants were fast becoming obsolete, but different conditions still obtained in the agricultural South. Besides selling goods to his plantation clients in the land-locked interior, Copes marketed their staple crops and furnished them with seasonal credit. The services that Copes provided to his rural clientele as their "factor" (a term that originated in the late Middle Ages) – along with his agency for a New York–based insurance company and Speer's northern-made iron hoops, as well as his own network of formal and informal agents – all embodied the range of entrepreneurial practices that business historian N. S. B. Gras once called "the most distinctive feature of mercantile capitalism."[3]

Since such businessmen usually operated out of coastal entrepôts such as New Orleans, they have also been called "sedentary" merchants, but Joseph Copes's 1860 travels seem to belie that adjective. Copes was a middling but ambitious commission merchant (a term largely interchangeable with *factor*),

Howard-Tilton Memorial Library, Tulane University, New Orleans, LA; hereinafter cited as Copes Papers, HTML-Tulane); J. W. Dorr, "A Tourist's Description of Louisiana in 1860," ed. Walter Prichard, *Louisiana Historical Quarterly* 21 (October 1938), 1176.

[2] Harlow J. Phelps to Copes, April 28, 30, 1860; Copes to Harlow J. Phelps, May 5, 1860 (quotations), Box 6, Copes Papers. On small-town merchants in antebellum Mississippi, see John Hebron Moore, *The Emergence of the Cotton Kingdom in the Old Southwest: Mississippi, 1770–1860* (Baton Rouge, 1988), 238–42.

[3] N. S. B. Gras, *Business and Capitalism: An Introduction to Business History* (New York, 1939), 117 (quotation); see also Harold D. Woodman, *King Cotton and His Retainers: Financing and Marketing the Cotton Crop of the South, 1800–1925* (Lexington, KY, 1968), 6–14. On the "all-purpose" merchants of the northeastern seaboard see Bernard Bailyn, *The New England Merchants in the Seventeenth Century* (1955; repr., New York, 1964); and on their declining importance see Glenn Porter and Harold C. Livesay, *Merchants and Manufacturers: Studies in the Changing Structure of Nineteenth-Century Marketing* (1971; repr., Chicago, 1989), 15–22.

and increasingly crowded conditions in Crescent City commodities markets caused him to seek out new customers in the southern countryside. (Copes also speculated heavily in real estate, especially in eastern Texas.) Furthermore, businessmen in cities such as Memphis, Mobile, and Galveston were busily establishing relationships with planters in the fast-growing cotton regions of the Southwest, which the convenience of Mississippi River transport had long made tributary to New Orleans. Copes's aggressive efforts to cultivate new commercial relationships in the Red River Valley and the Natchez district partly reflected the encroachment of other mercantile communities on a southern trade to which, as one observer put it in 1852, "the merchants of New Orleans formerly supposed they had a prescriptive right."[4]

Nevertheless, some aspects of New Orleans's long-time dominance of regional commerce appeared secure. It is important to keep in mind the dual role that most Crescent City factors played for their clients: they not only marketed incoming staple crops from rural districts, but they also directed an outward flow of commodities back to those same districts by supplying goods to planters on credit. During the boom years of the 1850s, most large plantation owners in the lower South had begun devoting nearly all their land and slave labor to the maximization of cotton production – an apparently rational investment decision, given bullish market conditions. Yet in so doing, planters forswore self-sufficiency in goods that could have been produced locally, instead choosing to rely on their city factors to furnish them. While factors had long sold luxury goods to status-hungry planters, now they also sold them low-value bulk products such as soap, candles, and most notably, foodstuffs. In an article for *De Bow's Review*, New Orleans merchant J. B. Gribble noted the consequences. "The great crop of 1859–60 was made too much at the expense of corn, etc.," he wrote, "the scarcity of which has had so important a share in bringing about the large indebtedness of our planting community" to city merchants. Tensions often accompanied such indebtedness, especially when factors sought legal protections against crop failures and other misfortunes that might befall their customers. In 1848, H. C. Simrall, a planter in Woodville, Mississippi, "considered [it] altogether unusual" that his Crescent City factor, Joseph Lallande, had recently "declined from making the necessary supplies without a mortgage." However, Simrall's experience was not as "unusual" as he believed. Historian Richard H. Kilbourne has convincingly detailed how the expanding web of encumbrances that Louisiana merchants placed on planters' properties, especially slaves, were crucial to the smooth functioning of the southern financial system during the decades after the Panic of 1837.[5]

---

4 [Israel D. Andrews], *Report of Israel D. Andrews on the Trade and Commerce of the British North American Colonies, and Upon the Trade of the Great Lakes and Rivers,* Senate Executive Document No. 112 (32 Cong., 1st Sess.) (Washington, DC, 1853), 343 (quotation).

5 Richard H. Kilbourne Jr., *Debt, Investment, Slaves: Credit Relations in East Feliciana Parish, Louisiana, 1825–1885* (Tuscaloosa and London, 1995); H. C. Simrall to Joseph Lallande [n.d.

Some planters sought to reduce their supply costs by making semi-annual shopping expeditions to New Orleans, but since such journeys were arduous and time consuming, most large interior planters continued to rely mainly on the credit and provisions available through the city factors who also oversaw the marketing of their crops. Crescent City factors did their best to maintain these semi-reciprocal economic relationships by attending carefully to the needs of their established plantation clients, many of whom could be demanding and difficult. The prominent city merchant Glendy Burke, although reputedly a millionaire, personally reviewed even the most minor inquiries from his firm's customers in the interior. In 1857, one wrote politely asking Burke to provide his son with $120 "to enable him to enter the Law School in your city"; other requests were more peremptory in tone if no less trifling. Burke also heard from rural clients who made no attempt to conceal their ongoing purchases from other merchants. Writing from northern Louisiana in 1851, planter Abraham Kelly uneasily informed Burke that one of his local creditors was "very anxious" to be repaid, so he asked that the proceeds from the recent sale of his cotton crop be sent to him "as soon as possible."[6]

1848], Document No. 2007.257.42 in Louisiana Manuscripts Collection (Mss 579), Williams Research Center, Historic New Orleans Collection, New Orleans, LA (hereinafter cited as HNOC); J. B. Gribble, "The Cotton Interest, and Its Relation to the Present Crisis," *De Bow's Review* 32 (March/April 1862), 282 (quotation). Some economic historians, such as Robert E. Gallman and Gavin Wright, have questioned the conventional wisdom that large southern plantations became steadily less self-sufficient during the late antebellum era. Besides the overwhelming weight of anecdotal and other evidence that runs contrary to their econometric views, however, several objections suggest themselves. For one thing, their studies focus entirely on self-sufficiency in foodstuffs, which leaves open the wide range of other necessities that could have been artisanally produced on plantations, such as soap, but increasingly were not, since such items had become readily available at low cost through factors and local merchants, thus making it more feasible to devote slave-labor resources to cash-crop production. But even with regard to foodstuffs, their arguments are subject to dispute. Dependence on outside sources for food varied widely within the South, but generally speaking, southwestern plantations with ready access to Mississippi River–supplied markets – most notably, in New Orleans – frequently found it more cost-efficient to rely on purchased supplies than to shift labor into food production. Gallman's own evidence seems to bear out these significant intraregional differences, as he found that "unsuccessful" corn-producing plantations in Louisiana outnumbered self-sufficient ones by a 2:1 ratio in 1860. Robert E. Gallman, "Self-Sufficiency in the Cotton Economy of the Antebellum South," *Agricultural History* 44 (January 1970), 5–23, esp. Table 7; Gavin Wright, *The Political Economy of the Cotton South: Households, Markets, and Wealth in the Nineteenth Century* (New York, 1978), 57–74.
[6] Abraham Kelly to G. Burke & Co., February 16, 1851, in Cotton Trade Series, No. 1 (G. Burke & Co.), (Special Collections, Howard-Tilton Memorial Library, Tulane University, New Orleans, LA; hereinafter cited as HTML-Tulane). That same month John Burrus, a planter near Shreveport, asked Burke to promptly forward the funds from his cotton sales because "I am in much need of the proceeds to settle up my little accounts...." Burrus to G. Burke & Co., February 11, 1851, in ibid. See also E. Archinand to G. Burke & Co., October 20, 1857; and C. G. Dahlgren to G. Burke & Co., November 3, 1851, both in ibid. On Glendy Burke see "Gallery of Industry and Enterprise: Glendy Burke, of New-Orleans, Merchant," *De Bow's Review* 11 (August 1851), 218–20. For an example of an interior planter who made an annual shopping pilgrimage to New

Like the 1860 reports by Joseph Copes and J. W. Dorr, Abraham Kelly's letter highlighted another source of competition for the interior trade long dominated by New Orleans firms: the hundreds of small-town and rural stores that dotted the countryside. As early as 1840 there were nearly 600 stores in Louisiana outside of New Orleans, numbers that continued to grow during the decades before the Civil War. These "country stores" competed with urban factorage houses by offering merchandise for local inspection and sale. However, some store owners were not satisfied to serve merely as retail outlets; instead, they sought to make inroads on the other long-standing prerogatives of Crescent City firms: credit provisioning and crop marketing. One such store in the far north-central portion of the state, Bond & Rogers, sent an unsolicited letter to Glendy Burke in 1857 that frankly expressed these intentions. "We wish you to lend us fifteen hundred dollars for the purpose of advancing on cotton," wrote W. H. Rogers. Warning Burke that "strong efforts are being made to control cotton at this point – now, by merchants of your city," Rogers described his store's "prospects [as] bright, if we can get and keep means." Despite his application for some of the near-legendary gentleman-merchant's abundant capital, the storekeeper's attitude toward him was hardly deferential. "We do not think you should charge us the [2.5] per cent for advancing the money," Rogers declared bluntly, "but of course we are willing to pay the usual interest.... Please attend to us immediately." Burke's scrawled notation for the benefit of his clerks to Rogers' somewhat haughty request was terse but compliant: "Accepted."[7]

Although the importance of rural furnishing merchants to the post–Civil War South has long been appreciated by historians, the tendency has been to downplay antebellum stores as either primitive trading posts or mere "appendages" of the city-based factorage system. It is true that such stores increased in numbers and socioeconomic significance after the war; it is also the case that some served as agents for particular New Orleans firms, such as Copes & Phelps's allied store in Shreveport. But as Bond & Rogers' letter to Glendy Burke indicates, even when rural store owners solicited financial support from New Orleans houses, they entered into such agreements with a keen eye on their own bottom lines. Most stores in the countryside were independent ventures, however, so even when their owners made marketing arrangements with New Orleans firms (say, forwarding all the cotton they accumulated to a particular house), they usually did so without ceding control over managerial prerogatives such as inventory maintenance – much less agreeing to any formal division of profits. In other words, the relationships of most rural entrepreneurs

Orleans, see Horace Adams, ed., "Arkansas Traveler, 1852–1853: The Diary of John W. Brown," *Journal of Southern History* 4 (August 1938), 381–3.

[7] Bond & Rogers (Trenton, LA) to G. Burke & Co., October 27, 1857, in Cotton Trade Series, No. 1 (HTML-Tulane). The 1840 national census enumerated the number of stores in the United States, but unfortunately, this effort was not repeated in subsequent censuses; *Sixth Census of the United States*, Vol. 3 (Washington, DC, 1841), 241 (Louisiana data). See also the discussion in Lewis E. Atherton, *The Southern Country Store, 1800–1860* (Baton Rouge, 1949), 41–2.

with city merchants were freely contracted and nonsubordinate, and thus more similar to those between planters and factors than those between employee and employer.[8]

This chapter examines how merchants in rural and small-town Louisiana paved a path for their stores' increased importance after emancipation. These stores were more common in the antebellum countryside than previous historiography would lead one to expect. Like stores after the war, they were second only to churches as gathering places for the dispersed rural population. Their operation as kin- and ethnoculturally based ventures presaged postbellum trends as well. Country merchants also experienced a fairly high degree of social mobility. Although they were often distrusted for their "sharp" business practices, store owners' high community profiles helped them become prominent figures in local society and politics. Many were able to accumulate impressive wealth, which they tended to deploy in ways similar to the conservative investment patterns of their larger mercantile brethren in the city, placing the bulk of their capital in land and slaves. However, social mobility was a two-way street: as with most family-based small businesses, failures were common and sometimes sudden.[9]

Nevertheless, hundreds of rural storekeepers succeeded, thereby establishing a foundation for their enhanced role in the transformed plantation system after the Civil War. (Indeed, as discussed in Chapter 8, numerous stores survived the war intact.) Many flourished by providing goods, credit, and marketing services to yeomen households that were too small to merit attention from New Orleans factors, but whose collective output represented a significant share of regional crop production. Some city merchants may have been aware of the threat that such interior stores presented to their own interests and stability. As early as the Panic of 1819, "heavy failures" had been reported among New Orleans firms because of "country merchants [who] did not meet their payments," and similar debt-collection problems had reoccurred in 1837. Yet whether they succeeded or failed, the relative independence of rural stores from the urban-based factorage system served to highlight crucial weaknesses of the Crescent City's long-standing dominance over commerce in the lower Mississippi Valley.[10]

---

[8] The classic monograph on rural merchants in the antebellum South remains, in Atherton, *Southern Country Store*, a fine study published in 1949. Harold D. Woodman paid little attention to prewar stores in *King Cotton and His Retainers* (see esp. chap. 13 and pp. 190–2), which led Ronald L. F. Davis to comment that "Woodman and Atherton seem to disagree on the extent to which the [antebellum] store served as an appendage of the factorage system"; Ronald L. F. Davis, "The Southern Merchant: A Perennial Source of Discontent," in *The Southern Enigma: Essays on Race, Class, and Folk Culture*, eds. Walter J. Fraser Jr. and Winfred B. Moore Jr. (Westport, CT, 1983), 140 n.15. Woodman admits, however, that the postbellum "furnishing merchant system was heavily freighted with remnants of the antebellum South…."; Woodman, *King Cotton*, 296.

[9] On social mobility among rural and small-town merchants in the antebellum South, see Frank J. Byrne, *Becoming Bourgeois: Merchant Culture in the South, 1820–1865* (Lexington, KY, 2006).

[10] Daniel K. Noyes (New Orleans) to Thomas Noyes, March 19, 1819, Document 2007.0257.16 in Louisiana Manuscripts Collection, HNOC; John McKowen to Seth Beers, July 28, 1837, in

On the eve of the Civil War, Samuel Henarie owned one of the most successful stores in Alexandria, Louisiana, a bustling frontier town of about 1,300
people on the Red River. The traveling reporter J. W. Dorr identified him as one
of Alexandria's "principal dealers," a judgment confirmed by Henarie's frequent
advertisements in the local press, which show that he stocked everything from
carpeting and cradles to saddles and scythes. Henarie catered mainly to the
needs of nearby farmers and planters, with an inventory of "Plantation Goods"
that included "bagging, rope, and twine" for baling cotton and "Linseys and
Kerseys," low-grade fabrics used for slave clothing.[11]

Besides his retail operations, Henarie sought to make himself a player in the
regional cotton trade in other ways. He advertised his willingness to buy cotton from local producers "at the New Orleans quotations, one cent per pound
off," a flat rate that earned him at least 8 to 15 percent upon resale, and he also
offered to make "Cash advance[s] for Cotton." Although his ads were silent
as to the interest rates he charged, Henarie clearly would have expected some
return, especially given the risks entailed in making loans in a precarious agricultural economy. At the time, Crescent City factors charged their plantation
clients interest in the range of 8 to 10 percent, sometimes higher. However, those
who borrowed from Henarie against future crops were mostly yeoman farmers
whose operations did not earn much attention from New Orleans–based commission houses. By serving as the "small farmer's factor," Henarie was able to
consolidate enough cotton under his proxy to deal with New Orleans firms, but
in so doing, the crops he consigned to them became subject to their commission
and shipping charges. The sensible practice would then be for Henarie to pass
these charges along to his customers. Given his penny-per-pound charge on
cash purchases of cotton as a benchmark of what he considered a reasonable
rate of return (one that represented about three to four times the standard 2.5
percent commission charged by factors), a conservative estimate would be that
Henarie profited from his cash advances to small farmers by deducting 10 to
25 percent from their eventual crop sales as a form of interest.[12]

John McKowen Papers (Mss 1353), Louisiana and Lower Mississippi Valley Collection, Hill
Memorial Library, Louisiana State University, (hereinafter cited as LLMVC).

[11] Dorr, "Tourist's Description of Louisiana in 1860," 1156; [Alexandria] *Louisiana Democrat*,
July 13, 1859. On antebellum Rapides Parish see Sue Eakin, *Rapides Parish: An Illustrated
History* (Northridge, CA, 1987).

[12] Woodman, *King Cotton and His Retainers*, 52, 76–83; see also Kilbourne Jr., *Debt, Investment,
Slaves*, 107–9. Woodman notes that the web of usury laws in antebellum Louisiana limited the
maximum allowable interest rate to 10 percent. But these laws seem to have been applied mostly
to banks and the larger commission merchants in New Orleans. Small storekeepers such as
Henarie probably slipped under the net of these laws with little attention or minor adjustments.
In part, this may have been due to the fact that most of these loans to small farmers were probably informally collateralized. The lack of formal security, especially in the case of nonslaveholders, certainly increased Henarie's exposure to the risk of default, but it also allowed him the
leeway to boost his interest rates well past the legally allowable maximum; see Woodman, *King
Cotton*, 52–4; and Kilbourne, *Debt, Investment, Slaves*, 19–21.

In addition to marketing the output of small farms, Samuel Henarie also sold goods on account to "punctual customers," although his ads again failed to mention what he charged his customers for credit. Historian Lewis Atherton maintained that "farmers were not compelled to pay interest on accounts ... settled within the year" at antebellum country stores, but he also acknowledged that these accounts "reflected whatever interest charges storekeepers had to meet in wholesale centers," which were typically 6 to 8 percent on invoices over six months. Moreover, these charges would have been tacked onto the "extremely high" markups built into retail prices, which were often 100 percent or more.[13]

While selling on credit was obviously riskier than relying on cash sales, several decades of confidential field reports from local agents of the Mercantile Agency, a New York–based credit reporting firm known after 1859 as R. G. Dun & Co., reveal the ubiquity of the practice among rural and small-town merchants before the Civil War. However, these reports also show that the difficulties of debt collection in a fickle agricultural economy proved to be the financial undoing of many a rural merchant in Louisiana. For example, Hugh Keenan of Catahoula Parish co-owned a successful country store twenty miles from the parish seat of Harrisonburg. In 1846, the local Dun agent noted that Keenan and his partner "have a large amount due them, but from the partial failure of the cotton crop they can't collect sufficient to meet their engagements." Although Keenan continued to struggle with collections, he managed to stay in business through the mid-1850s. Isaac Fleishman was a Jewish merchant of the same parish who, after "peddling for several years," finally accumulated enough money to open a store in Harrisonburg. The agent was initially impressed with Fleishman's small, safe trade, reporting in 1853 that he "sells principally for cash & [I] believe him to be honest as the rest of the tribe." The agent changed his mind about Fleishman, however, after he took on a partner the following year. "They are too anxious to sell," the reporter wrote, and in June 1855 he advised the agency that "both Jews do a good business, but it is too much on a credit [basis]...." Yet Fleishman & Conn continued selling goods on "accommodating terms," as they advertised in 1857, and their store stayed afloat through the outbreak of the war. Just as Louisiana was seceding from the Union in January 1861, an agent reported that the partners were "solvent but hard-pressed & will be so, as they will not be able to collect their debts." Three months later the local newspaper noted an impending sheriff's sale of land and slaves to satisfy debts held by the firm.[14]

---

[13] Atherton, *Southern Country Store*, 120, 170–1, esp. n. 56; [Alexandria] *Louisiana Democrat*, July 13, 1859. On retail price markups during the antebellum period see Theodore F. Marburg, "Income Originating in Trade, 1799–1869," in National Bureau of Economic Research, *Trends in the American Economy in the Nineteenth Century* (Princeton, NJ, 1960), 320–1, esp. n.16.

[14] Harrisonburg *Independent*, April 3, 1861, and September 23, 1857; Louisiana, Vol. IV, 1–2, R. G. Dun & Co. Credit Reports Collection, Baker Library Historical Collections, Harvard Business School; cited hereinafter as Dun & Co., Louisiana, with appropriate volume and page

Catahoula Parish was part of the fast-expanding cotton frontier in north-ern and central Louisiana during the antebellum era. Bisected on a northwest/southeast axis by the Red River, the rich alluvial lands of the area were relative latecomers to plantation development. The "Great Raft," a mass of floating debris some seventy miles in length, blocked river traffic and slowed agricul-tural development until its removal by engineers under Captain Henry M. Shreve during the Jackson and Van Buren administrations. Although the rivers, bayous, and lakes that punctuated the state's landscape ("an American kind of Netherlands," historian Roger Shugg called it) aided commercial intercourse in the interior, these same natural transportation routes tended to impede railroad development. Louisiana ranked last in the South in track mileage in 1860, and the central portion of the state was especially backward in this regard, despite sitting squarely on the great "migration highway" that brought a steady flow of Texas-bound settlers westward.[15]

Antebellum Louisiana's social structure reflected great disparities of wealth, which was most apparent in the slave-plantation districts of the eastern par-ishes along the Mississippi River, as well as in the sugar parishes in the south-ern part of the state. In 1860, median slaveholding in the state was more than double the regionwide figure, yet more than two-thirds of the state's free whites were nonslaveholders. These patterns of concentrated wealth were duplicated in the interior parishes. In enormous Rapides Parish, the 1860 census reported more than 15,000 slaves to about 10,000 free whites, but less than a third of the nearly 1,800 free households owned slaves, and of these, just over a hundred held fifty or more slaves. As J. W. Dorr noted in his 1860 journey, "wealthy planters" in Rapides Parish clustered along the Red River and its larger tributaries, but as one moved away from the river, the land became hilly, covered by pine woods and low-quality soils. These pine uplands were occupied mostly by yeomen farmers, some of whom were small slavehold-ers. In other central Louisiana parishes, plantation agriculture was even less developed. In Catahoula Parish, less than a third of the land was improved by 1860, and small farms of 100 acres or less outnumbered plantations by a 4:1

---

numbers. It is clear from local newspapers that Dun & Co. misspelled Fleishman's name as "Flashman." The handwritten transcriptions of field reports in the Dun ledgers rely heavily on standardized abbreviations, which are spelled out without brackets when quoted herein. The invaluable Dun & Co. reports are described in James H. Madison, "The Credit Reports of R. G. Dun & Co. as Historical Sources," *Historical Methods Newsletter* (September 1975), 128–31. On the history of the Mercantile Agency see Ray A. Foulke, *The Sinews of American Commerce* (New York, 1941); and James D. Norris, *R. G. Dun & Co. 1841–1900: The Development of Credit-Reporting in the Nineteenth Century* (Westport, CT, and London, 1978).

[15] Roger W. Shugg, *Origins of Class Struggle in Louisiana* (1939; repr., Baton Rouge, 1968), 3, 43–4, 107–9; John F. Stover, *The Railroads of the South: A Study in Finance and Control* (Chapel Hill, 1955), 25; Joel M. Sipress, "The Triumph of Reaction: Political Change in a New South Community [Grant Parish, LA], 1865–1898" (Ph.D. diss., University of North Carolina at Chapel Hill, 1993), 123; J. Fair Hardin, *Northwestern Louisiana: A History* (3 vols.; Louisville, KY and Shreveport, LA, 1937), I, 251–82.

ratio. There were only 327 slaveholders among the parish's 5,538 whites, 188 of whom owned fewer than ten slaves. Nevertheless, cotton production had increased dramatically during the 1850s even in such mixed-farming parishes, and storekeepers such as Henarie and Fleishman predicated their extension of credit to yeoman households mainly on their output of staple crops.[16]

Even in plantation-dominated parishes, rural and small-town stores commonly sold goods on credit during the antebellum era. In the well-developed "sugar bowl" of southern Louisiana, for example, Ascension Parish was home to several dozen stores by 1840, most of them located in and around the parish seat of Donaldsonville. Although the parish was situated less than a hundred miles upriver from New Orleans, many of its stores thrived by catering to large planters, as well as to the surprising number of small farms still intermingled among the plantations that abutted the river. According to the local Dun reporter, Jemplet & Richard, whose store had been in business since the early 1840s, were reportedly "very good collectors" who sometimes profited further from credit extension by allowing debts to "lie in the hands of their customers and charging them 15 percent for it." By contrast, Victor Pugos's even-older "planters' store" in the same parish ran into trouble with collections during the mid-1850s and became "considerably embarrassed" as a result. In Iberia Parish, a more isolated sugar-producing parish located to the southwest, a Jeanerette store's account ledgers showed more than four times more credit than cash sales in 1852–53.[17]

In the cotton parishes farther upriver, the situation was much the same. Peter Lebret was a French immigrant who had established his store in Bayou Sara during the late 1830s. Located on the river about thirty-five miles north of Baton Rouge, Lebret's store initially did a "large business, chiefly [in] cash" by selling goods to the well-established planters of West Feliciana Parish, where landholdings were larger and concentrated among fewer families. By the 1850s, however, Lebret (who took on a partner, William Hearsey, in 1851) was making the majority of his sales on credit. The store's carefully maintained account books indicate that credit purchases accounted for nearly three-fourths of Lebret & Hearsey's sales in 1853 and 1854 (Table 3.1).

At first Lebret & Hearsey enjoyed considerable success with this strategy. In 1853 the local Dun agent reported that they are "the best firm here, no doubt about it." But relying so heavily on credit sales left the firm vulnerable to

---

[16] *Eighth Census of the United States (1860)*, Vol. I: *Population and Other Statistics* (Washington, DC, 1864), 194; Vol. II, 230, 344; Dorr, "A Tourist's Description of Louisiana in 1860," 1160; Lewis C. Gray, *History of Agriculture in the Southern United States to 1860* (2 vols., Washington, DC, 1933), I, 530; Shugg, *Origins of Class Struggle*, 16–33, 329.

[17] Jeanerette, LA, store accounts as tabulated in Atherton, *Southern Country Store*, 53 (Table III); Dun & Co., Louisiana, I, 1 (Victor Pugos and Jemplet & Richard); Sidney A. Marchand, ed., *The Flight of a Century (1800–1900) in Ascension Parish, Louisiana* (Donaldsonville, LA, 1936), 111. This book consists of excerpts compiled from various nineteenth-century newspapers and almanacs.

TABLE 3.1. *Cash and Credit Sales, 1853–1854, Lebret & Hearsey's Store, Bayou Sara, West Feliciana Parish, Louisiana*

	1853			1854	
Month	Cash Sales	Credit Sales	Month	Cash Sales	Credit Sales
Jan	1,172.85	2,588.99	Jan	905.48	2,078.96
Feb	630.15	1,848.16	Feb	625.82	1,666.39
Mar	1,009.40	2,858.49	Mar	732.64	2,711.22
Apr	913.40	2,623.70	Apr	774.87	5,105.24
May	698.75	2,549.49	May	512.13	1,244.05
June	1,061.35	2,460.83	June	540.72	1,274.77
July	737.90	1,729.70	July	454.45	1,062.39
Aug	606.35	1,747.87	Aug	393.40	1,004.24
Sept	140.45	358.47	Sept	363.84	1,186.75
Oct	68.20	336.50	Oct	296.85	1,666.12
Nov	755.94	3,418.71	Nov	608.14	1,858.56
Dec	1,006.05	3,094.72	Dec	179.36	1,305.20
TOTALS			TOTALS		
1853	$8,800.79	$25,615.63	1854	$6,387.70	$22,163.89

Source: Journal, 1853–1854, Volume 9, *Lebret & Hearsey Record Books*, 1838–1875 (Mss 216, Louisiana and Lower Mississippi Valley Collection, Hill Memorial Library, Louisiana State University, Baton Rouge, Louisiana).

disruptions, and in 1855 the Dun reporter noted "there is a large amount due them, and their embarrassments [have] been caused by the difficulty of making collections."[18]

Despite such problems, Lebret's store remained a fixture in the parish through Reconstruction. But even though stores such as Lebret's could boost their sales by offering merchandise on credit, other rural merchants adhered to a "cash-only" policy, especially when first establishing themselves. When Julius Freyhan opened his Bayou Sara store in the late 1850s, he ran his "small business [using] the cash system," causing a Dun reporter to warn in January 1860 that he "will not do much." Freyhan would defy those expectations, however, becoming the largest merchant in West Feliciana Parish by the late nineteenth century. In Catahoula Parish, Schlenker & Dosher's "Cash Store," which had "just opened" in the summer of 1856, advertised that they offered "the lowest

[18] Dun & Co., Louisiana, XXII, 240. On his 1857 trip through Bayou Sara and its twin town just uphill from the river, St. Francisville, Frederick Law Olmsted noted that West Feliciana residences gave evidence of "rapidly accumulating wealth" and "luxury," and that "fewer than fifty negroes are seldom found on a plantation"; Olmsted, *The Cotton Kingdom: A Traveller's Observations on Cotton and Slavery in the American Slave States*, ed. Arthur M. Schlesinger (New York, 1953), 406–9 (quotations on pp. 406 and 408).

cash prices" in Harrisonburg, "which will enable them to sell as low as ... can possibly be afforded."[19]

In Alexandria, Samuel Henarie's riverfront store flourished during the 1850s, but his devotion to credit extension often seemed to threaten its stability. In June 1849 the Mercantile Agency reporter noted the paradox: "Sales larger and collections smaller this season than usual.... All traders here complain of small collections owing to [the] small price of cotton." Still, Henarie's business increased significantly during the boom years of the 1850s, and by 1854 the agent estimated that he "sells about $50m [thousand] yearly," an impressive figure for a small-town store. But by this time, the Dun ledgers also reflect what is apparent in the pages of the *Louisiana Democrat*: Henarie had begun to face considerable competition from new retailers in the area. The stores of Winehill & Brother, R. C. Hetherwick, Jacob Walker, and others now vied for advertising space with Henarie, and each trumpeted their superiority based on lower and fairer prices. In 1860 Winehill's store announced that "we have adopted the One Price System.... You will save 50 per cent by purchasing of us." The previous year, Jacob Walker had made a lengthier and seemingly pointed declaration along the same lines in his weekly advertisement:

"Prompt customers & low percentage" is the motto. Goods might be sold much lower in Alexandria, if merchants were not compelled to tack on extra percentage to cover the losses from bad sales; I have determined to abandon that system, and hereafter sell only for CASH or SHORT GOOD PAPER, by which plan I shall be able to sell LOWER and make more money than those who follow a different practice.

Walker clearly considered his form of business practice not only safer and more profitable, but he also implied that it was somehow more honest as well. According to an 1859 estimate by the local Dun correspondent, Walker was "an upright man" as creditworthy as Samuel Henarie, even though his store's sales were less than half those of Henarie's.[20]

Regardless of whether they sold on cash or credit, antebellum merchants and their stores usually played a prominent role in their rural and small-town Louisiana communities. Country stores served as gathering places for a population widely dispersed throughout the countryside, a place where news, gossip, and opinions about local affairs could be exchanged on their front porches in the summer or around their hot stoves inside during the winter. Some stores sold liquor, which doubtlessly helped facilitate tongue-wagging and encouraged loafing; such stores were more likely to become gendered spaces considered unfit for women. Because of their stores' centrality to community life, rural merchants also frequently served as local postmasters. This position was much sought after, since it ensured a steady flow of potential customers (rural

[19] Harrisonburg *Independent*, June 25, 1856; Dun & Co., Louisiana, XXII, 258.

[20] [Alexandria] *Louisiana Democrat*, March 27, 1860, and July 13, 1859; Dun & Co., Louisiana, XIX, 10 (Walker), 7 (Henarie).

free delivery still being some decades away). The New Orleans factor Joseph Copes acknowledged the advantages of this exposure in 1860 when he persuaded a Rapides Parish merchant and local postmaster to promote the policies of an insurance company that Copes represented. In small villages with several merchants, the competition to serve as postmaster could be intense, and the position was often a political sinecure dependent on party affiliations.[21]

Postal appointments did not always translate into personal esteem, however. Emile Collin, an Ascension Parish storekeeper since 1853, "is unpopular on account of his disagreeable manner," advised the Dun correspondent, who later added that the cantankerous old Frenchman "makes many enemies and gains few customers," in spite of his postal appointment. Collin's example shows how rural merchants' high profiles often caused their characters to be called into question. This was especially true among the clannish and fiercely independent Creole residents of southern Louisiana, who were castigated by Frederick Law Olmsted as "apathetic, sleepy, and stupid," yet also "habitually gay and careless, as well as kind-hearted." In mixed-farming Avoyelles Parish, many poor but self-sufficient Creoles of French descent existed uncomfortably amid the growing number of slave plantations abutting the lower Red River. Olmsted also claimed that many Creole men were "inveterate gamblers," and the prim Yankee's generalization seemed borne out by a local Dun reporter's description of one such merchant, F. Villamarette. Villamarette took advantage of the hunting and trapping culture popular among his Creole brethren by operating a tannery along with his small country store. The Dun agent wrote in 1856 that Villamarette was "honest but addicted to cards," and a series of later reports advised that the merchant's gambling habits were causing his business interests to suffer. His credit rating declined steadily along with them.[22]

Another Avoyelles Parish merchant of questionable character was Auguste Voinchi, a general storekeeper of Marksville who merited one of the lengthiest and most detailed entries in the Dun ledgers from central Louisiana. In 1848, the first entry on Voinchi described him as a thirty-five-year-old married Frenchman who had been in business about a decade. Voinchi's sales were then estimated at $20,000 to $25,000 annually – a considerable figure even

[21] J. S. Copes to Harlow J. Phelps, June 28, 1860, in Box 6, Copes Papers; Atherton, *Southern Country Store*, 192. Historian Thomas D. Clark's descriptions of the social importance of post-bellum southern country stores are in many ways just as apt for the prewar decades; see Clark, *Pills, Petticoats, and Plows: The Southern Country Store* (1944; repr., Norman, OK, 1989), esp. x–xi, 15. On nineteenth-century southern stores as "gendered spaces," see Ted Ownby, *American Dreams in Mississippi: Consumers, Poverty, and Culture, 1830–1998* (Chapel Hill, 1999), 11–13; and Lu Ann Jones, "Gender, Race, and Itinerant Commerce in the Rural New South," *Journal of Southern History* 66 (May 2000), 297–320.

[22] Dun & Co., Louisiana, II, 146 (Villamarette); Ibid., I, 15, 30, 34 (Collin); Olmsted, *Cotton Kingdom*, 327–8 (quotations); see also ibid., 316–17. Interestingly, Olmsted's descriptions of Louisiana Creoles show him to be fairly well disposed toward them, and they do not come across as the "degraded" poor whites he notoriously described elsewhere throughout his southern travel narratives.

for what J. W. Dorr later called a "thriving and busy" village of well under a thousand inhabitants, especially considering that Voinchi's store was one of four "principal mercantile business[es]" there. (The others were also owned by men with French surnames.) But according to the local Dun agent, Voinchi did "the largest business in the place," and his estimated worth more than doubled during the 1850s. As an 1850 report grudgingly acknowledged, there was little reason to deny credit to such a "substantial merchant": "In prosperous circumstances, and so far as resources are concerned [he] is entitled to credit."[23]

Still, the local agent was wary of Voinchi despite his growing wealth, and this distrust was constantly reflected in his reports. In the 1848 dispatch, for example, Voinchi was damned with this faint praise: "Habits good," the agent began hopefully, "save for his propensity to cheat." Although he "pays promptly and is in good credit," Voinchi "overreaches and tricks" and is "not honest." Six months later the same reporter repeated gossip about Voinchi's past in an attempt to justify his judgment of the Frenchman's character. "[Voinchi] is said to have commenced as a pedlar in Bordeaux, France, changed his name from 'Duke' to that which he now [has] and fled to this country with his goods," and thus "no confidence is had in his integrity." By the mid-1850s a different agent, also aware of Voinchi's "smart and cunning" practices, reported that the storekeeper had begun to diversify into real estate, slaves, and less well-regarded forms of profiteering, and by 1860 the reporter estimated that "the old man is … worth fully $50m [thousand] clear and perhaps a good deal more." The last prewar report on Voinchi was in April 1861, and the agent was blunt. "Cannot be trusted – he will take all the advantages that the law will permit and more if possible – a Damn rascal."[24]

The small-town storekeeper Auguste Voinchi is just one colorful example among dozens of similar reports in the Dun ledgers about devious, debt-avoiding, hard-drinking Louisiana merchants. Historian Lewis Atherton, who spent much of his career attempting to rehabilitate the shabby reputations of pioneer store owners in the South and West, concluded that "the overwhelming bulk of contemporary evidence indicates that the [Old] South … respected the occupation." Atherton also claimed there was a "complete absence in … business records of any testimony" showing that storekeepers were poorly regarded by their fellow southerners. But the Dun ledgers, which were unavailable to Atherton (despite his familiarity with the Mercantile Agency), provide copious evidence against his sanguine estimate of public opinion about merchants in the antebellum South. Here one should bear in mind that Dun reports were not furnished by traveling agents from outside the region, but were instead solicited from local correspondents, most often from attorneys keenly attuned to their communities' subjective opinions and objective conditions.[25]

[23] Dun & Co., Louisiana, II, 142; Dorr, "A Tourist's Description of Louisiana," 1147–8.
[24] Dun & Co., Louisiana, II, 142, 156.
[25] James H. Madison, "The Evolution of Commercial Credit Reporting Agencies in Nineteenth-Century America," *Business History Review* 48 (Summer 1974), 167–76; Atherton,

Other contemporary accounts reflect the shaky esteem with which rural merchants were regarded by southerners, even if sometimes unfairly. During his 1857 trip through Louisiana, Olmsted noted that credit-providing store-keepers were frequent targets of local opprobrium. When crop markets were stagnant, farmers "would whine and complain, as if the merchants were to blame for it, and would insist that no one could be expected to pay his debts when prices were so low, and that it would be dangerous to press such an unjust claim." Two other famous antebellum accounts show popular attitudes toward country merchants to have been ambivalent at best. Hinton Rowan Helper's native antislavery polemic, *The Impending Crisis of the South* (1857), directed numerous attacks toward southern store owners, especially those who owned slaves, for undermining regional development by buying their inventories from northern suppliers. "Merchants of the South, slaveholders!" he cried. "You are the avaricious assassinators of your country! ... You are constantly enfeebling our resources and rendering us more and more tributary to distant parts of the nation." Daniel R. Hundley, an Alabama native who would fight for the Confederacy, offered a more balanced if still controversial account of *Social Relations in Our Southern States* in 1860. Even though Hundley admitted that some were hard-working and industrious members of their communities, he was skeptical about the ethics of most southern storekeepers. Presaging postwar complaints against "carpetbagging" merchants, Hundley condemned "the larger and less honest class of storekeepers" whom he called "Southern Yankees." Such merchants, he wrote:

appear to find it almost impossible to acquire that easy, unaffected simplicity of manners, which is the charming characteristic of all classes in the South, the slaves not excepted. Without intending it, they yet appear either too pert and consequential, or else too fawning and sycophantic. They are too frequently patronizingly good-fellowish with the bluff yeomanry, and at the same time most torturingly polite to the wealthy planter. They manage, however, to fleece most of those who deal with them; or else become bankrupt and run away from their creditors....

Apart from the question of their particular nativities, Hundley here characterized most southern merchants – and the market culture their country stores represented – as foreign to the texture of everyday life in the agricultural and preindustrial slave South.[26]

Southern Country Store, 204–5 (quotations). The Dun & Co. ledgers were not donated to Harvard Business School until 1962, over a decade after Atherton published his 1949 study; see Julie Flaherty, "A Good Credit History, Indeed: Opening the Books on American Business, 1841–1891," New York *Times*, August 21, 1999, p. B1. On his familiarity with the Mercantile Agency, however, see Lewis E. Atherton, "The Problem of Credit-Rating in the Antebellum South," *Journal of Southern History* 12 (November 1946), 534–56.

26 Daniel R. Hundley, *Social Relations in Our Southern States* (New York, 1860), 100–17 (quotations on p. 105); Hinton Rowan Helper, *The Impending Crisis of the South: How to Meet It*, ed. George M. Fredrickson (1857; repr., Cambridge, MA, 1968), 21–2, 334–5, 356–9 (quotation on p. 334); Olmsted, *Cotton Kingdom*, 330–1 (quotation on p. 331).

Popular prejudices against rural merchants as outsiders to their communities (and to southern society more generally) were reinforced in other ways. As was also true of prewar New Orleans mercantile firms, many rural stores were operated by owners of shared ethnic origins. But more so than in the multicultural Crescent City, differences of ethnic and national background often appeared stark in the more homogeneous Louisiana countryside, where there was already a widely acknowledged demographic division between the Creole-Catholics clustered in the southern portions of the state and the Anglo-Protestants of the northern and western parishes. In both sections, Jewish merchants in particular tended to stand out among the dominant regional "white" cultures, and all the more so because Jewish farmers were fairly rare. The role of Jewish storekeepers in the South has been often discussed by historians, but again, their attentions have usually focused on the postbellum era. Thomas D. Clark, for example, admired the Jewish merchant as an unsung hero of the postwar southern economy, from the itinerant peddler ("circuit riders for market culture," he called them) to the well-established small-town retailer. Similarly, even though economic historians Roger L. Ransom and Richard Sutch argued that "Jews apparently constituted only a small minority of the merchants" in the Reconstruction-era South that they studied, they admitted that an exceptional number seem to have been concentrated in the lower Mississippi Valley, which confirms the observations of postwar travelers such as Robert Somers and Edward King.[27]

The large number of Jewish merchants in Louisiana, however, had its origins in the antebellum period, when hundreds of surnames of apparent Hebraic origin were listed among the state's rural store owners. Correspondents for the Mercantile Agency rarely failed to mention the ethnicity of their Jewish subjects, and their reports reflected the ambivalence of public opinion about them. While it is too much to say these reporters were entirely "free of feelings of anti-Semitism," as one historian would have it, they did often seem to display grudging respect for Jewish storekeepers' business acumen. For example, referring to one of the Bernstein brothers, who owned stores in Winn and Natchitoches Parishes during the mid-1850s, the reporter called him "as reliable as any Jew ... clever and popular." An 1850 report on recently established store owner David Marks of Harrisonburg claimed that the "Dutch Jew ... will undoubtedly do a safe business," which was obviously an endearing trait from the standpoint of creditors. Isaac Levy and his brother Jacob, who bought an Alexandria store from Samuel Henarie's former partner in 1856, were German Jews who owned "several small stores" throughout Rapides Parish. "The

[27] Robert Somers, *The Southern States Since the War, 1870–1* (New York, 1871), 151; Edward King, *The Great South*, eds. W. Magruder Drake and Robert R. Jones (1875; repr. Baton Rouge, 1972), 274; Roger L. Ransom and Richard Sutch, *One Kind of Freedom: The Economic Consequences of Emancipation* (2nd ed.; New York, 2001), 342–3 n. 34; Thomas D. Clark, "The Post–Civil War Economy in the South," in *Jews in the South*, eds. Leonard Dinnerstein and Mary Dale Passon (Baton Rouge, 1973), 159–69 (quotation on p. 163).

children of Israel worth altogether 30m," deadpanned the agent about them in an 1857 report.[28]

In 1860 the Levy brothers sold their Alexandria store and instituted successful legal proceedings against farmers who still owed debts to it. Such property seizures by merchants provoked hostility among local freeholders, which was exacerbated by anti-foreign sentiments in the case of Jewish store owners. Nevertheless, Jewish merchants seemed to encounter few problems attaining elite status in their communities. Isaac Levy would be appointed to a term on the Alexandria city council soon after the war by the conservative governor James Madison Wells, a former slaveholding planter of Rapides Parish. The Bernsteins of Winn Parish were also respected members of their community. Morris Bernstein was prominent in the parish Democratic Party before the war, and he later served in the Confederate Army. Interestingly, Bernstein, like other Jewish merchants, was also a member of his local Masonic lodge. Although Freemasonry is sometimes mistakenly associated only with Protestantism (largely as a result of its anti-Catholic stances), the presence of prominent Jews such as Bernstein serves to demonstrate that such fraternal societies often served less as arbiters of spiritual doctrine than as exclusionary institutional spaces that sought to include men of commerce among their ranks.[29]

Indeed, whether Jewish or not, store owners in the antebellum Louisiana interior were often leading members of their communities, despite popular anti-mercantile sentiments. Although he had a temperament that a contemporary described as "tolerably explosive," Samuel Henarie was able to parlay his position as one of Alexandria's largest merchants into membership in the Rapides Parish elite. In 1859 he served alongside future southern scourge William Tecumseh Sherman on the founding board of supervisors of the seminary that would later become Louisiana State University. That same year, Henarie's competitor Jacob Walker was appointed as a parish delegate to the state Democratic convention, as was Walker's partner, Henry Klotz. Antebellum merchants were sometimes successful local political office-seekers as well. P. Arthur Hatkinson, a town merchant, was elected mayor of Donaldsonville in 1849, and Bayou Sara storekeeper Felix V. Leake became sheriff of West Feliciana Parish in 1857. Deeper in the countryside, stores typically served as precinct polling stations, which gave their owners a prominent role in the often-heated elections conducted under their isolated auspices. Such political entanglements could sometimes take more sinister form. During the mid-1850s, for example, Ezra Bennett's country store in southern Rapides Parish

---

[28] Dun & Co., Louisiana, XIX, 11 (Levys); Ibid., IV, 3 (Marks); Ibid., XXII, 287 (Bernstein); Clark, "Post–Civil War Economy in the South," 166 (quotation).

[29] *Biographical and Historical Memoirs of Northwestern Louisiana* (Nashville and Chicago, 1890), 495 (Bernstein), 539 (Levy); [Alexandria] *Louisiana Democrat*, February 1 and 8, 1860. On Freemasonry and antebellum political culture see Steven C. Bullock, *Revolutionary Brotherhood: Freemasonry and the Transformation of the American Social Order, 1730–1840* (Chapel Hill and London, 1996).

apparently served as a supply depot and staging ground for paramilitary units training for a Latin American filibuster expedition financed by the Mississippi planter and ex-governor John A. Quitman.[30]

Country merchants' admission to elite status among their communities was in part a byproduct of the considerable wealth that many managed to accumulate. Again, historians' attention has usually focused on the postbellum period, but rural and small-town stores in Louisiana frequently tallied impressive sales totals before the Civil War as well. One study of the Bennett store ledgers claimed to find more than $600,000 in sales receipts during the 1854–55 harvest season. That was an exceptionally high figure, if correct, but sources show that many stores had annual sales in the range of $20,000–$50,000. Samuel Henarie, who had opened his Alexandria store around 1841 in partnership with Duncan C. Goodwin, was estimated to be selling about $30,000 annually by 1845, a figure that had nearly doubled a decade later. Victor Pugos's planters' store in sugar-producing Ascension Parish reportedly did over $50,000 in sales in 1848. That same year, the local Dun correspondent claimed that Peter Lebret's store in West Feliciana Parish enjoyed annual sales in the range of $30,000–$40,000. Lebret's account ledgers for 1853 and 1854, when the store sold over $34,000 and $28,000, respectively, confirm the relative accuracy and stability of his estimate.[31]

By gleaning information from parish tax rolls, Dun reporters were often able to ascertain merchants' wealthholdings more accurately than they could estimate stores' annual sales. Their examinations indicated that, like their larger mercantile brethren in New Orleans, rural store owners tended to invest their wealth in the twin pillars of the antebellum southern economy: land and slaves. Sometimes these investments were limited to town properties and a few slaves used for domestic or commercial purposes, as were those of Jewish merchants Isaac Fleishman of Catahoula Parish and Solomon Weinschenck of Ascension Parish. Although John Whiteman of West Feliciana Parish had only $5,000 in stock in his Bayou Sara store in 1859, he owned $2,600 in real estate and slaves valued at $5,600. His fellow parish store owner and sheriff Felix V. Leake had declared only $1,200 worth of stock-in-trade in 1857, but he also owned $3,000 in real estate and $1,700 in slaves. However, such relatively low levels of capital invested in stores should not be mistaken for poor management. To the contrary, retailing was an attractive form of business to many partly because of the small amount of capital that it typically required. Furthermore, then as now, successful store owners sought to keep their ratio

[30] D. Clayton James, "The Tribulations of a Bayou Boeuf Store Owner, 1836–1857," *Louisiana History* 4 (Summer 1963), 255; Dun & Co., Louisiana, XXII, 245 (Leake); Marchand, ed., *Flight of a Century*, 127, 136–7; [Alexandria] *Louisiana Democrat*, March 27, 1860 (quotation), August 3, 10, and 24, 1859; see also Hardin, *Northwestern Louisiana*, I, 452.

[31] Journal, 1853–54, Vol. 9, Lebret & Hearsey Record Books, 1838–1875 (Mss 216), LLMVC; Dun & Co., Louisiana, XXII, 240 (Lebret); Ibid., II, 1 (Pugos); Ibid., XIX, 7 (Henarie); James, "Tribulations of a Bayou Boeuf Store Owner," 254–5.

of sales as close as possible to their stock-in-trade by emphasizing the rapid turnover of their inventories, although those who bought and sold on credit usually found this goal more difficult to achieve.[32]

Some rural merchants took their investments in real estate and slaves a step further by diversifying into planting. Historian Lewis Atherton argued that "more storekeepers shifted to planting than to any other occupation," finding such interests among 30 percent of the antebellum merchants that he sampled. Daniel Hundley believed that such storekeepers were motivated by a desire to capture some of the high status attendant to planting that eluded them as mere merchants. Perhaps, but it is also likely that many saw an opportunity for greater profits in planting and invested accordingly. Ezra Bennett combined his mercantile interests with cotton and sugar cultivation beginning in the 1840s and eventually became one of Rapides Parish's leading planters. In so doing, he laid the basis for his integrated operations to enjoy even greater success under his son's management after the Civil War. Other merchants also established themselves as slaveowning planters while retaining their retail furnishing trade, thus prefiguring the "plantation stores" that would become common in the postbellum period. Like Bennett, Jacob Lemann of Ascension Parish began integrating his sugar-plantation and store interests in the 1840s, and both would thrive upon his return to the region from New York after the Civil War. In the same parish, John Dominque was "considered the greatest monied man in the Parish" in 1851. His total worth was estimated at $300,000, and although he still maintained "a large country store" that had been in business for many years, the "old Italian" was said to make most of his money "by loaning and sugar planting."[33]

Some rural merchants were less successful at juggling their commercial and agricultural enterprises. After more than a decade of profitable storekeeping, for example, Peter Lebret began buying up land and slaves in West Feliciana Parish during the mid-1840s. In the 1850 census Lebret listed his occupation

---

[32] Dun & Co., Louisiana, XXII, 243 (Whiteman), 245 (Leake); Ibid., I, 2 (Weinschenck); Ibid., I, IV, 4 (Fleishman). It is sometimes maintained that Jewish merchants shied away from slaveholding, but the Dun ledgers indicate that they were just as likely to own slaves as other storekeepers. Contemporary double-entry bookkeeping manuals often emphasized the importance of inventory management to mercantile profits; see, for example, James Bennet, *The American System of Practical Book-Keeping....* (21st ed., 1842; repr., New York, 1976), 15–18, 36. For a condemnation of the effects of credit merchandising on stock turnover, see J. A. Dacus, *A Guide to Success, with Forms for Business and Society* (St. Louis, 1880), 32–3. Stores could still be successful with low amounts of capital in trade; indeed, the national average of capital invested per retail store in 1840 was only $4,300; see Marburg, "Income Originating in Trade, 1799–1869," 318; and Atherton, *Southern Country Store*, 71–4.

[33] Dun & Co., Louisiana, II, 4 (Dominque); Ibid., 1, 21, 35, 58 (Lemann); see also Leslie A. Lovett, "From Merchant to Sugar Planter: The Rise and Success of Jacob Lemann and Son" (unpub. honors thesis, Tulane University, 1990), 14–18; and Elliott Ashkenazi, *The Business of Jews in Louisiana, 1840–1875* (Tuscaloosa and London, 1988), chap. 2. James, "Tribulations of a Bayou Boeuf Store Owner," 243–51; Eakin, *Rapides Parish*, 24–5; Hundley, *Social Relations in Our Southern States*, 115; Atherton, *Southern Country Store*, 203.

as merchant, but in 1851 the Dun agent reported that he owned twenty-nine slaves and was "mak[ing] 75 to 100 bales of cotton every year." At first his store operations continued to do well; in June 1853 Lebret & Hearsey's store was still considered "the best firm here, no doubt about it." Over the next few years, however, Lebret's attention increasingly focused on his plantation to the detriment of his commercial interests, and after an 1855 fire destroyed many of Bayou Sara's tightly clustered riverfront stores, including his own, Lebret spent the next few years engaged exclusively in planting. Although he reopened a small store and woodyard before the war, Lebret listed his occupation as planter in the 1860 census, in which he reported owning fifty-six slaves and a plantation of 1,000 improved acres valued at $20,000. Another West Feliciana Parish merchant, Felix W. Haile, found his planting operations sufficiently profitable that he decided to sell his well-established Bayou Sara drugstore in 1859.[34]

Providing primitive banking services was even more common than planting as a non-retail interest among antebellum storekeepers. There were no state-chartered banks in the Louisiana countryside; all of them were clustered in New Orleans. But the interior economy was unable to run solely on barter, and rural merchants were better placed than anyone else to offer financial services to small farmers and even the occasional large planter. Most important was their willingness to accept and disburse banknotes and other privately issued forms of money that originated from non-local sources, usually at discounts or premiums from their stated face values – a disreputable practice known as "shaving paper." During the period of tight money that accompanied the financial panic of 1837, Mississippi merchant John McKowen journeyed to Bayou Sara, where he did business with newly established storekeeper Peter Lebret. "I took some specie with me," he wrote, "and shaved Mississippi paper with it at a discount of 40 percent." Like the "shrewd and calculating" Auguste Voinchi of Avoyelles Parish, Jacob Lemann of Ascension Parish reportedly "makes a good deal by shaving notes," the Dun correspondent reported in 1851. As did John Dominque of the same parish, Lemann also loaned out his capital at interest to local planters, and their defaults helped him begin accumulating mortgaged plantation properties in the region. Similarly, store owner William H. Dawson of West Feliciana Parish was reported in 1854 to have "money loaned at interest," and he also profited "by dealing in paper."[35]

[34] Dun & Co., Louisiana, XXII, 254 (Haile), 240 (Lebret). 1860 manuscript census data on Lebret as compiled in Joseph Karl Menn, *The Large Slaveholders of Louisiana, 1860* (New Orleans, 1964), 228–9; for his listing in 1850 see U.S. Manuscript Census, 1850, Schedule I, Free Inhabitants, Town of Bayou Sara, West Feliciana Parish, Louisiana.
[35] Dun & Co., Louisiana, XXII, 252 (Dawson); Ibid., II, 146 (Voinchi); Ibid., II, 4 (Dominique), 1 (Lemann); Lovett, "From Merchant to Sugar Planter," 34–7; John McKowen to Seth Beers, July 28, 1837, in John McKowen Papers, LLMVC. On the lack of banking facilities in the antebellum Louisiana interior, see George D. Green, *Finance and Economic Development in the Old South: Louisiana Banking, 1804–1861* (Stanford, CA, 1972), 28–32.

Such financial operations were more closely related to merchants' traditional functions than was an occupational shift into planting. Interestingly, though, few storekeepers seemed interested in deploying their wealth in fixed capital investments such as manufacturing. The Dun ledgers indicate that merchants such as F. Ricord of Avoyelles Parish, who operated a sawmill and leather tannery in combination with his store, were exceptional before the Civil War. In part, the near-absence of rural manufacturing reflected the higher expenses involved in the complex forms of industrial power generation necessary in Louisiana. As one observer later explained, unlike in the northeastern states or even on the lower Atlantic seaboard, "the low topography [of Louisiana] furnishes no water power for the wheels of manufactories." It was also difficult to find skilled mechanics capable of maintaining and repairing steam-powered engines like that at Ricord's sawmill. But the dearth of industrial enterprise among storekeepers held true even for basic farm-processing facilities such as cotton pressing and baling, most of which continued to be handled in major market centers such as New Orleans. The ingrained aversion to manufacturing investments that characterized the wealthy merchant capitalists of the Crescent City was thus duplicated on a smaller scale among antebellum store owners in the state's interior regions. Not until after the war, when rural merchants played an even more prominent role in crop marketing under the decentralized sharecropping regime, did such processing facilities become typical adjuncts to the operations of larger stores in the Louisiana countryside.[36]

When successful rural and small-town merchants expanded their operations before the Civil War, they usually opted to stay with the game they knew best. Some would invest their capital in improvements to their existing stores. (The construction of a brick building often signaled a successful storekeeper's intention to stay put in the area.) Many others, however, sought to increase the geographic scope of their operations by buying out nearby stores or establishing new ones. The ownership of multiple stores was fairly common among rural Louisiana merchants before the Civil War and could be found in all regions of the state – cotton, sugar, and mixed-farming parishes alike. Lewis Mayer, a slave-owning Jewish merchant of Catahoula Parish whose credit-providing store had sales estimated at $30,000 in 1851, also co-owned a firm in Livingston, a distant town in the Florida parishes north of New Orleans, which specialized in marketing tobacco produced by the area's small farmers. Usually, though, multiple stores held under single or pooled ownership were more regionally clustered. Brothers Isaac and Jacob Levy owned "several small stores" throughout Rapides Parish during the 1850s. In Winn Parish, the three Bernstein brothers were not only reportedly "connected with a house in Alexandria" to the south, but they also operated a branch store in the nearby town of Montgomery. In the cotton parishes of the Felicianas, the Levy family

---

[36] Dun & Co., Louisiana, II, 146 (Ricord); William Carter Stubbs, *Handbook of Louisiana, Giving Geographical and Agricultural Features....* (New Orleans, 1895), 5.

had interlocking interests among several stores located in Bayou Sara, Jackson, and Clinton, as well as in neighboring Pointe Coupee Parish.[37]

The dispersal of their capital among multiple locations provides further evidence of the wealth that many storekeepers had at their disposal, but it also reflected the independence that such wealth secured among rural merchants in antebellum Louisiana. Like other occupational classes in nineteenth-century America, most southern merchants practiced their vocations in order to achieve a measure of independence for themselves and their families. Yet although the ideal of self-reliance was deeply ingrained in republican ideology, the particular forms by which independence was pursued and maintained often occurred in a decidedly associational context, as was especially obvious in the informal networks of mutual aid common among immigrant communities. In the case of the antebellum Louisiana interior, such forms of mutuality also found expression in the widespread reliance on kin and ethnocultural solidarity to help merchants successfully establish their stores. Writing about Jewish merchants such as the Levys in mid-nineteenth-century Louisiana, historian Elliott Ashkenazi found that "business connections among family members and in-laws were frequent.... [O]wners looked to familial and ethnic contacts in commercial transactions to protect themselves" from an often-hostile and fickle marketplace.[38]

Stories are legion of newly arrived immigrants to the state starting out with help provided by established kinfolk and then becoming esteemed storekeepers in their communities. Isaac Fleishman and Herman Black, for instance, both began as itinerant peddlers in the 1840s before accumulating sufficient capital to settle down and open their own stores in Catahoula Parish. Two of the most exceptionally successful examples of this career trajectory, however, were Leon Godchaux and Jacob Lemann, both of whom first arrived in New Orleans in the late 1830s with little more than the shirts on their backs. Soon their backs were also encumbered with packs full of goods staked by city merchants that they peddled around the Louisiana countryside, and within a few years, both men were able to establish themselves as prominent storekeepers in the sugar parishes. By the 1850s Lemann was summering in New York and Newport, Rhode Island, and after leaving the region for several years just before and during the Civil War, he and his family would return during Reconstruction to resume their interlocked mercantile and planting interests. Leon Godchaux enjoyed even greater fortune, both as a wholesale and retail dry-goods merchant in antebellum New Orleans and later as a sugar planter. From his humble beginnings as a peddler, Godchaux would die a millionaire in 1899, and the

---

[37] On the Feliciana Levys see Ashkenazi, *Business of Jews in Louisiana*, chap. 3; Kilbourne, *Debt, Investment, Slaves*, 27; and Dun & Co., Louisiana, XXII, 240–1, 260; Ibid., XXII, 287 (Bernsteins); Ibid., XIX, 11 (Isaac and Jacob Levy); Ibid., IV, 1 (Mayer).

[38] Ashkenazi, *Business of Jews in Louisiana*, 105. See also Rowena Olegario, "'That Mysterious People': Jewish Merchants, Transparency, and Community in Mid-Nineteenth-Century America," *Business History Review* 73 (Summer 1999), 161–89.

department-store chain that bore his family's name was still spread throughout Louisiana until the late twentieth century.[39]

The peddler-to-store owner occupational path exemplified the social mobility that often eventuated in financial success for rural storekeepers in Louisiana before the Civil War. Ethnocultural solidarity was not limited to Jewish merchants, though: the Bordelons, a prolific French Creole family of Avoyelles Parish, displayed a similar mutualist mercantile bent that began in the mid-nineteenth century and continued after the war. But shared commercial interests among groups of relatives such as the Bernsteins, Levys, and Bordelons also highlight another common feature of antebellum merchants' pursuit of independence: the degree to which country stores were typically run as "family affairs," often including wives, children, and extended networks of blood relations. Historians have been slow to acknowledge kinship as a category for understanding how social structures were created and maintained among the widely dispersed population of the nineteenth-century South, but the popular animus against merchants was probably diluted in part by their families' inter-relationships with others throughout their rural communities.[40]

Merchants' households were frequently involved in the operation of stores, many of which were attached to the family residence. Furthermore, although business decisions and capital maximization strategies are often assumed to be the exclusive province of men in the public sphere, the Dun records indicate that wives in particular were integral to the operation of many rural Louisiana stores. In Ascension Parish, for example, Solomon Weinschenck's wife "helps him along wonderfully in the business," reported the agency's correspondent in 1851, and John Dominque's wife, "a close, industrious woman," continued to run their store after her husband's death in 1854. In West Feliciana Parish, as Peter Lebret's attention increasingly focused on his burgeoning plantation interests, the Dun agent reported that "his 'wife is the businessman' and attends the store." The Lebrets' unfolding story during the 1850s, however, shows how property disputes involving mercantile families could be especially bitter. Lebret's partner, William Hearsey, had married one of Lebret's daughters in the mid-1850s, and after the family's various business interests took a turn for the worse later in the decade, Lebret and his wife Elise were forced to take out mortgages on some of their slave- and landholdings to satisfy debts to their creditors, including $35,000 owed to the New Orleans commission firm of Bellocq, Noblom & Co. Entries in an 1858–61 Lebret family diary indicate

---

[39] Bennett H. Wall, "Leon Godchaux and the Godchaux Business Enterprises," *American Jewish Historical Quarterly* 66 (September 1976), 50–66; Lovett, "From Merchant to Sugar Planter"; Dun & Co., Louisiana, II, 1, 21 (Lemann); Ibid., IV, 1 (Black), 2 (Fleishman).

[40] On the Bordelon family of Avoyelles Parish, see the references scattered throughout Dun & Co., Louisiana, II, 147–96. An important attempt to assert the importance of kinship to southern social structure before the Civil War is Carolyn Earle Billingsley, *Communities of Kinship: Antebellum Families and the Settlement of the Cotton Frontier* (Athens, GA, 2004); see also Byrne, *Becoming Bourgeois*.

how closely Elise Lebret was involved in "putting the thousands of bills, letters, [and] accounts in order" for these settlements. The diary also reflects the deep "emotional upset" that Elise felt when her daughter, Hearsey's wife, sued the family to recover $20,000 worth of debts for which she and her husband had been held partially responsible.[41]

Under the terms of the state's unique French-derived civil code, wives frequently became parties to property litigation involving stores in nineteenth-century Louisiana. Indeed, one common strategy among storekeepers for protecting their property from seizure by creditors was to assign it to their wives. *Hunt's Merchant's Magazine* had warned its readers of this practice, apparently just barely legal under the Louisiana civil code, as early as 1847. Frustrated correspondents for the Dun agency, who were often attorneys, filed many irate reports about a legal device that they considered a "swindle." For example, Jacob Ringold, a storekeeper of modest means in Alexandria, tried to "cover up his property" from New York–based creditors "by his wife getting judgment for her portion" in 1852. As this report indicates, these strategies often took the unusual form of having the wife sue her husband for her rightful portion of their property. Such circumstances probably lay behind an 1859 sheriff's sale at the Rapides Parish courthouse of a "lot of Dry Goods, 300 yards of various Calico Domestic, and a lot of Groceries," which was intended to satisfy the terms of a recent court decision in favor of one Hester Nathan against her husband Norris.[42]

Cases like these demonstrate that the well-worn path of social mobility traveled by rural and small-town storekeepers in antebellum Louisiana ran two ways, downhill as well as up. Still, either direction on this path seemed to be paved with credit, an issue that had a lengthy and contentious pedigree in American political economy. Credit-providing merchants were frequent targets of criticism because of the dependence that debt fostered among their customers, but less acknowledged were the problems that the culture of credit occasioned among merchants themselves. The Dun ledgers are filled with examples of storekeepers whose credit purchases left them "embarrassed" when unable to meet their obligations. Antebellum commercial journals issued regular warnings about mercantile insolvencies and how to avoid them, and their advice usually centered on some variant of the Shakespearean injunction "Neither a borrower nor a lender be." Despite his criticisms of southern merchants, Daniel Hundley nevertheless sympathized with the "unutterable grief that lies behind

[41] 1858 diary entries, in Lebret Diary, 1858–61 (Mss 3504, LLMVC). The author is grateful to Dr. Melissa A. Bailar of Rice University for translating portions of this diary, which was maintained in French. Mortgage of Peter and Elise Lebret, February 16, 1859, in Mortgage Records, Vol. 9 (1855–1860), 378–81, West Feliciana Parish Courthouse, St. Francisville, LA; Dun & Co., Louisiana, XXII, 240, 254 (Lebret); Ibid., II, 4 (Dominque), 2 (Weinschenck).

[42] [Alexandria] *Louisiana Democrat*, July 13, 1859; Dun & Co., Louisiana, XIX, 10 (Ringold); Francis H. Upton, "Law of Debtor and Creditor in Louisiana, Part IV," *Hunt's Merchants' Magazine*, XVI (February 1847), 165–71.

that smiling mask" of the "Honest Storekeeper" who struggled to make collections and pay off his creditors. "No wonder his head is prematurely gray," he declared. "Wait until we have been similarly tried!"[43]

Antebellum merchants' widespread reliance on credit – whether for purchases, sales, or both – thus often threatened to undermine the independence that most of them sought to achieve. One alternative that rural storekeepers in Louisiana had to dangerous commitments to credit was to substitute another form of dependence instead: serving as agents for better financed outside backers from cities such as New Orleans or New York. Such alliances could take several forms, which were characterized by varying degrees of external control over their stores' operations. At one end of the spectrum, a store could essentially be owned by one or more partners in a mercantile firm located elsewhere, which left the on-site storekeeper as either a profit-sharing partner at best or little more than a clerk for distant owner/managers otherwise. Phelps & Rogers, a planters' store in the "business mad" town of Shreveport, was closely allied in this manner with the New Orleans commission house of Copes & Phelps. James E. Phelps, who managed the Shreveport store, was the brother of Harlow J. Phelps, son-in-law of Joseph Slemmons Copes and the junior partner in his Crescent City firm. Both New Orleans partners made frequent trips to the northwestern corner of the state to meet with planter-clients in that burgeoning tri-state cotton region and coordinate the store's affairs, from inventory maintenance to the locally produced cotton that the store received and forwarded to Copes & Phelps in New Orleans. It is not clear how James Phelps and his partner were compensated for their efforts, but correspondence between the two firms clearly indicates the rural store's subordination to its Crescent City patrons.[44]

Other Louisiana storekeepers, however, managed to limit or equalize their dependence on relationships with New Orleans houses. Solomon Weinschenck's store in Ascension Parish was sustained in part by his simultaneous partnership in a Crescent City commission firm controlled by his father-in-law. Some store owners managed their sales and inventories "on their own hooks," but they also advertised their standing as agents for particular New Orleans firms in the buying and marketing of local crops, as did A. C. Phillips of Rapides Parish. Still other Louisiana stores were connected to more distant firms, especially

---

[43] Hundley, *Social Relations in Our Southern States*, 115–16. For discussions of mercantile insolvency see "Relation of Debtor in Louisiana toward His Creditors," *De Bow's Review* 4 (September 1847), 106–8; "Insolvency among Merchants," *De Bow's Review* 16 (March 1854), 311–19; and "Mercantile Character and Successes," *De Bow's Review* 25 (September 1858), 356–8. See also Edward J. Balleisen, *Navigating Failure: Bankruptcy and Commercial Society in Antebellum America* (Chapel Hill, NC, 2001). For a fine discussion of credit and dependence among eighteenth-century southern slaveholders, see T. H. Breen, *Tobacco Culture: The Mentality of the Great Tidewater Planters on the Eve of Revolution* (Princeton, NJ, 1985), 133–41.

[44] Copes Papers (HTML-Tulane), esp. Boxes 5 and 6 and Correspondence, Vols. 3–6; Dorr, "Tourist's Description of Louisiana in 1860," 1176 ("business mad").

ones based in New York City. The interlocking interests of the Levy and Meyer stores in the Feliciana parishes were linked to New Orleans commercial houses that were themselves closely allied with L. Bach & Co. of New York. Another large general store in Bayou Sara, Myer, Hoffman & Co., reportedly had a "senior partner [who] resides in New York worth $150,000" in 1860. Among the many northern-based houses that had relationships with both urban and rural merchants in the antebellum South, two of the most aggressive were Charles P. Leverich & Co. and Jackson & Co. Leverich's branch office in New Orleans was run by two of his relatives and enjoyed many contacts with store owners and planters throughout the lower Mississippi Valley interior. Jackson & Co. also had branches (sometimes with slightly different named partners) in New Orleans, Charleston, and other southern cities, as well as in Liverpool, England. In 1851 a Dun reporter thus advised that the hardware sold by Victor Pugos's planters' store in Donaldsonville "comes from an English house in New York (Jackson & Co., I think)." Such reports indicate how the tentacles of the Atlantic economy extended deep into the nineteenth-century southern countryside.[45]

Historian Harold D. Woodman has left the impression that such external connections made antebellum store owners little more than appendages to the urban-based factorage system. But although rural merchants necessarily relied on outside sources for their inventories, as well as marketing support (for those who bought and sold crops), antebellum stores that were owned by or served as official agents for city interests seem to have been relatively few in number. The majority of stores in the Louisiana interior before the Civil War were small firms, locally owned and managed, and as such, their proprietors were busily laying the groundwork for the enormous expansion of their influence during and after Reconstruction. Even apart from their business acumen, it would be a mistake to dismiss these rural and small-town merchants as hapless provincials; despite their isolation on the frontier, some were remarkably sensitive to the effects of global events such as the Crimean War on market prices for cotton. Moreover, as is apparent from Bond & Rogers's 1857 letter to the powerful factor Glendy Burke, store owners often displayed a decidedly independent attitude toward their city brethren when they had to deal with New Orleans mercantile houses. Store owner Ezra Bennett of Rapides Parish distributed his business among multiple firms in New Orleans and often sought to play them off against each other to his advantage. In 1843 Bennett grumbled that the insurance rates he had been charged by commission merchant C. Toledano for

[45] Dun & Co., Louisiana, II, 1 (Pugos); 2 (Weinschenck); Ibid., XXII, 254 (Myer, Hoffman & Co.), 240-1 (Levys/Bach). Advertisement for A. C. Phillips in [Alexandria, LA] *Red River Whig*, April 25, 1840. On Jackson & Co. see Woodman, *King Cotton and His Retainers*, 17–18; and Jackson, Riddle & Company Papers (Mss 368, Southern Historical Collection, Wilson Library, University of North Carolina at Chapel Hill). On Leverich & Co. see Charles P. Leverich Papers, 1833–1851 (Mss 222, Woodson Research Center, Rice University, Houston, TX); and Jonathan Daniel Wells, *The Origins of the Southern Middle Class, 1800–1861* (Chapel Hill, 2004), 64.

recent crop shipments to the Crescent City were twice those of another city
house for cotton forwarded "from the Same Place." The previous year he had
pestered another New Orleans firm to buy flour for him. "I know it is out of
your line of business," he admitted, "but you can accommodate a customer."
Bennett also did not hesitate to complain loudly about bookkeeping errors or
the high prices of goods.[46]

The widely noted tendency of country merchants to purchase their inventories from northern and other markets was another means by which storekeepers in antebellum Louisiana asserted their independence from the New
Orleans–based factorage system. Indeed, partly because of the widespread animus in the countryside against the high prices, poor service, and general arro-
gance of Crescent City merchants, store owners often bragged about making
their purchases elsewhere. In 1836, for example, one Catahoula Parish store
advertised that it was "constantly receiving [dry goods] from New York." In
the same parish, the Dun agent noted in 1849 that store owner Lewis Mayer's
"principal debts are in New York," and a decade later, Harrisonburg merchant
David Marks was reported to have "gone to New York to buy winter stock."
Many country merchants like Marks made semi-annual buying expeditions to
wholesalers and auction houses located on the upper Atlantic seaboard, which
led a New Orleans newspaper to complain in 1852 that "our country friends
send their produce to us, but they do not buy of us." In neighboring Rapides
Parish, Jacob Ringold faced "problems with Ross & Leitch [of] New York" in
1853. Perhaps he had been enticed into buying goods on "long credit" by one
of the "drummers" (traveling salesmen) for northern houses who increasingly
blanketed the area, according to one local newspaper. In West Feliciana Parish,
located less than two hundred miles upriver from New Orleans, storekeepers
such as George W. Leet and John Whiteman nevertheless found it advantageous to "purchase principally" from dealers in St. Louis and Cincinnati, which
Peter Lebret often did as well.[47]

<hr />

[46] Bennett to C. Toledano, March 1, 1843; and Bennett to Hall & Blake, January 28, 1842, both
quoted in James, "Tribulations of a Bayou Boeuf Store Owner," 251, 253; Bond & Rogers to G.
Burke & Co., October 27, 1857 (HTML-Tulane); Woodman, *King Cotton and His Retainers*,
chap. 13; cf. Davis, "Southern Merchant," 140 n.15. For a fine example of a small-town merchant's consciousness of global conditions and their impact on his profits, see the 1852–53
letters from P. H. Goodwyn & Son of Memphis, Tennessee (which still had fewer than 10,000
inhabitants) to the New Orleans commission firm Watt & DeSaulles, in Mrs. Frank J. Besthoff
Collection (Mss 388), HTML-Tulane. Such correspondence supports historian Thomas L.
Haskell's contention that merchants' activities in far-flung markets disposed them toward wider
"causal horizons" than others with more traditional, locally oriented mindsets; Thomas L.
Haskell, "Capitalism and the Origins of the Humanitarian Sensibility, Part 2," in *The Antislavery
Debate: Capitalism and Abolitionism as a Problem in Historical Interpretation*, ed. Thomas
Bender (Berkeley and Los Angeles, 1992), 136–60 (quotation on p. 155).

[47] Dun & Co., Louisiana, XXII, 240 (Lebret), 243 (Whiteman), 244 (Leet); Ibid., XIX, 10
(Ringold); Ibid., IV, 1 (Mayer), 3 (Marks); see also Atherton, *Southern Country Store*, 32, 58,
114–15, 124. "Northern Agents," Alexandria *Louisiana Democrat*, January 25, 1860; see also

As tensions between the sections mounted during the antebellum decades, southerners' resentment toward northern dominance of the trade in plantation goods grew as well, and it became touchier for interior storekeepers such as Lott & Ives to trumpet their purchases from New York. Hinton Rowan Helper articulated a version of this hostility when he wrote, "The North is the Mecca of our merchants, and to it they must and do make two pilgrimages per annum.... Instead of keeping our money in circulation at home, ... we send it all away to the North, and there it remains; it never falls into our hands again." Country merchants thus found themselves pinned on the horns of a dilemma, since bypassing the expensive middlemen of New Orleans clearly resulted in lower prices for their customers and more business for their stores. To the chagrin of critics such as Helper, most of them opted to attend to their own bottom lines. In this respect, the comments of General William T. Sherman in 1859 probably echoed the sentiments of many country merchants. Condemning the "double profits and commission[s]" of New Orleans merchants he encountered while furnishing the new Louisiana State Seminary, Sherman insisted that "New York is the great commercial center of America, and it would be in my judgment extreme squeamishness to pay more for a worse article elsewhere."[48]

When an 1855 southern commercial convention held at New Orleans passed a resolution exhorting regional planters to "patronize exclusively our home merchants," the assembled delegates, who mainly represented urban-based mercantile interests, probably had themselves in mind as the beneficiaries of this appeal. However, many planters apparently took such advice to buy "at home" more literally. Rural storekeepers were not alone in their disdain for Crescent City merchants. In 1851, for example, one planter of southern Louisiana publicly censured New Orleans businessmen for the greed and "overweening confidence" that caused them to "drive commerce from [their] doors." But although most of them remained wedded to the convenient seasonal credit extended by their city factors on the strength of coming crops, many planters and their families helped store owners maintain their independence by spending some of their considerable wealth in their own communities. Isaac Franklin's plantation records reflect his estate's reliance on dozens of firms in New Orleans, Louisville, and Cincinnati, but they also show numerous purchases from small businessmen in West Feliciana Parish, including Peter Lebret. Rapides Parish planter and future Louisiana governor Thomas Overton Moore was well-served by his New Orleans factor Aristide Miltenberger, but Moore bought

"The Long Credit of Northern Cities," *Hunt's Merchants' Magazine* 33 (August 1855), 263-4. "Banking Capital in New Orleans," New Orleans *Commercial Bulletin*, undated 1852 article, repr. in *Bankers' Magazine* 7 (December 1852), 469 (quotation); [Alexandria, LA] *Planters' Intelligencer*, May 25, 1836 (Lott & Ives).

[48] W. T. Sherman to G. Mason Graham, December 25, 1859, in *General W. T. Sherman as College President ... 1859-1861*, ed. Walter L. Fleming (Cleveland, OH, 1912), 92-3; Helper, *Impending Crisis of the South*, 22.

liberally from area merchants as well; in 1856, for example, he spent more than a thousand dollars at a store owned by James McCloskey.[49]

Country newspapers earned a steady and much-needed revenue stream from storekeepers' advertisements, and they compensated in part by regularly publishing editorials and other "news" that encouraged readers to patronize local businesses. Tidbits that centered on the arrival of the latest fashions at a given store were clearly aimed at luring female shoppers, and during an era when travel to distant urban markets remained exceedingly difficult, women often responded accordingly. One antebellum account described how women from nearby sugar plantations were carried by boat to the small village of Thibodeaux on designated days to socialize and shop among its several stores. In Bayou Sara, purchases by women who belonged to wealthy plantation families such as the Barrows and Richardsons seem to have comprised the majority of sales in one account ledger of Peter Lebret's store between 1857 and 1862. Wartime deprivations may have prompted some to spend more heavily than usual, as when Mrs. Jared Richardson charged nearly $400 worth of goods on account during one period in 1861. Her bill went unsettled until 1864, by which point Lebret had added eighty-one dollars of interest to the total. Such spending seems to indicate that at least some small-town merchants in antebellum Louisiana carefully attended to a female-centered trade that could be quite lucrative, thereby also calling into question the claim of one recent historian that nineteenth-century southern country stores were always highly gendered environments hostile to women shoppers.[50]

Overall, then, stores in the Louisiana interior displayed considerable strength and independence during the antebellum period. They were also surprisingly

---

[49] Moore's purchases are discussed in Atherton, *Southern Country Store*, 76. Wendell H. Stephenson, *Isaac Franklin: Slave Trader and Planter of the Old South, with Plantation Records* (Baton Rouge, 1938), Part III; for an 1847 payment to "P. Letret" of Bayou Sara, see p. 301. "Why New Orleans Does Not Advance," *De Bow's Review* 11 (October–November 1851), 387–8 (quotations); 1855 resolution as quoted in Olmsted, *Cotton Kingdom*, 331 n. 6. Irritation with the high cost of doing business at New Orleans led even some sugar planters to deal instead with factorage firms in eastern seaports such as Charleston and Baltimore; see Merl E. Reed, "Footnote to the Coastwise Trade: Some Teche Planters and Their Atlantic Factors," *Louisiana History* 8 (Spring 1967), 191–7.

[50] Ledger, 1857–62, Vol. 17, Lebret & Hearsey Record Books (LLMVC); for Mrs. Richardson's 1861 account, see p. 290. My estimate that purchases by women constitute the majority of recorded sales in this ledger is informally derived; but nevertheless, Lebret's records provide a marked contrast to historian Ted Ownby's assertion that "throughout the nineteenth century, the tremendous majority of visitors and customers [to southern general stores] were men," and that the "few ledgers that recorded precisely who visited the stores make clear that the stores were male institutions"; Ownby, *American Dreams in Mississippi*, 11. There are also descriptions of wealthy female customers in Hundley, *Social Relations in Our Southern States*, 108–9; and J. H. Ingraham, *The Sunny South; or, The Southerner at Home....* (Philadelphia, 1860), 425–6; see also Raleigh A. Suarez, "Bargains, Bills, and Bankruptcies: Business Activity in Rural Antebellum Louisiana," *Louisiana History* 7 (Summer 1966), 191. On newspaper editors' alliances with local storekeepers see Atherton, *Southern Country Store*, 199–201.

numerous, especially in light of the rural population's typically wide dispersal, as well as the pull exerted by the nearby presence of the South's only metropolis. Several provisional explanations for this seeming anomaly can be suggested. Historian Roger W. Shugg called attention to Louisiana's "unusual number of small villages for a planting state" before the Civil War. It is difficult to prove this contention using the national census, which counted places as towns only if they held more than a thousand inhabitants, but if Shugg was correct, then perhaps this nascent urban subsystem served as a more conducive environment for small-business growth and stability. Alternatively, successful stores could themselves have fostered town growth around them. Although studies of the economic geography of retailing tend to favor this latter explanation, they also usually rely on the central-place theory of markets, which maintains that a large metropolis typically spurs the growth of medium-to-small distribution nodes on its periphery. However, the economic influence of New Orleans was widely and actively resisted in Louisiana's interior, even in riverside towns such as Donaldsonville and Bayou Sara, whose merchants often purchased their inventories from suppliers in more distant cities such as Louisville, Cincinnati, and St. Louis. Compared to the mutually reinforcing cycles of urban–rural economic development underway in the Midwest, the relationship of New Orleans to its agricultural hinterlands seems to have been peculiarly weak.[51]

Regardless of the explanation, there were undoubtedly a large number of stores in rural Louisiana during the antebellum period. In 1840, when the national census sought to enumerate stores for the only time that century, Louisiana's number of stores per thousand population (7.0) ranked second in the country. This total is boosted, of course, by the inclusion of Orleans Parish, but even when it is subtracted, the resulting average of 2.3 stores per thousand population (which also includes slaves) placed the state second only to Georgia (2.5) in the Deep South, without even adjusting the latter state's figure to account for urban enclaves such as Augusta and Savannah. Although census data are unavailable for the two decades before the Civil War, the Dun records indicate that the number of stores in Louisiana's interior was similarly impressive in 1860, not only in plantation districts but in mixed-farming communities such as Avoyelles Parish, where most free households remained on the margins of the cash-crop economy (Table 3.2).[52]

[51] Shugg, *Origins of Class Struggle in Louisiana*, 43–4 (quotation). On the central-place theory of markets see Brian J. L. Berry, *Geography of Market Centers and Retail Distribution* (Englewood Cliffs, NJ, 1967); and James E. Vance Jr., *The Merchants' World: The Geography of Wholesaling* (Englewood Cliffs, NJ, 1970). On midwestern economic development centered on nineteenth-century Chicago, see William Cronon, *Nature's Metropolis: Chicago and the Great West* (New York, 1991); for his discussion of central-place theory, see pp. 46–54.
[52] The 1840 census data on stores is analyzed in Fred Mitchell Jones, *Middlemen in the Domestic Trade of the United States, 1800–1860* (Urbana, IL, 1937), 56–7; see also Atherton, *Southern Country Store*, 40–2. Both historians derive their figures showing the South well below the national average of 3.4 stores per thousand population in 1840 by including slaves. In Louisiana,

TABLE 3.2. *Stores per Thousand Inhabitants (Free Population) in Selected Louisiana Parishes, 1860*

Parish	Free Population	Number of Stores	Stores per Thousand Free Inhabitants
Ascension	4,108	34	12.0
Avoyelles	5,982	31	5.3
West Feliciana	2,100	23	9.1

Sources: Eighth Census of the United States (1860), Vol. I: *Population and Other Statistics* (Washington, DC, 1864), 194; R. G. Dun & Co. Credit Reports Collection, Louisiana, Vols. II and XXII (Baker Library Historical Collections, Harvard Business School).

The surprising strength of stores in antebellum Louisiana's interior parishes was reflected not only in their numbers, but also in the significant roles their owners played in their rural communities, as well as the independence from the still-dominant New Orleans–based factorage system that many were able to achieve. Particularly important were the successful efforts of storekeepers such as Peter Lebret and Samuel Henarie to insinuate themselves into the burgeoning agricultural economy by providing their customers with credit and crop-marketing services, which established an important foundation for the expansion of their socioeconomic influence in the tumultuous years that followed the Civil War. This foundation has been insufficiently acknowledged by historians of the nineteenth-century South, who have grown increasingly accustomed to emphasizing the radical break (or, to use older terminology, "discontinuity") with the past represented by slave emancipation after the North's victory in the war. Obviously, emancipation transformed the southern economy; few would deny the epochal significance of the sudden destruction of a mode of production that had been entrenched for nearly two centuries. Yet largely because of lessons they learned before the war, rural merchants suddenly found themselves well situated to reap the benefits of those changes. Under the postbellum sharecropping system, staple crops previously raised by slaves on large and mid-sized plantations were produced on smaller, family-based farms, and even as forms of tenancy became the norm among freedpeople, increasing numbers of white yeoman households were also being drawn into what Steven Hahn has called "the vortex of the cotton economy." The gentleman-merchants of New Orleans, who had provided goods, credit, and marketing services to slave plantations, found themselves poorly equipped to lend similar support to thousands of decentralized small-farming units. Rural merchants, however, had cut their credit-provisioning teeth by dealing with the white yeomanry before the war,

if only the free population is counted and Orleans Parish is excluded, there were 5.9 stores per thousand inhabitants in 1840 – well above the national average.

and they were thus better positioned to furnish the needs of small farms afterward.[53]

One should take care not to overstate the broader significance of rural store owners to the antebellum southern economy. Planters were clearly the dominant class in the Old South, and many of them had long undermined ambitious country store owners by "bundling" the crops of their yeoman neighbors with their own consignments to city factors. Moreover, the relatively small size of most stores and their geographic dispersal tended to suppress any incipient class consciousness among rural merchants. Still, even before the war, critics deplored the growing importance of credit-furnishing merchants in the southern countryside. An 1855 commercial convention at New Orleans condemned crop advances as a "dangerous practice" that tended to "establish the relations of master and slave between the merchant and planter"; a few years later, *Hunt's Merchants' Magazine* denounced the same aspects of southern crop marketing as having "no parallel except in a pawn-broker's shop." Although both disparaging metaphors would later be commonly directed against furnishing merchants in the postbellum South, their use in the 1850s highlights the groundwork already laid by rural store owners in states such as Louisiana before the Civil War.[54]

[53] Steven Hahn, *The Roots of Southern Populism: Yeoman Farmers and the Transformation of the Georgia Upcountry, 1850–1890* (New York and Oxford, 1983), 133. Recent historiographical (mis)understandings of the nineteenth-century southern economy are discussed in my article "Fables of the Reconstruction: Reconstruction of the Fables," *Journal of the Historical Society* 4 (Winter 2004), 113–37.

[54] "Banking at the South, with Reference to New York City," *Hunt's Merchants' Magazine* 42 (March 1860), 321; New Orleans commercial convention resolution as quoted in Olmsted, *Cotton Kingdom*, 331 n. 6. For examples of Louisiana planters' long-standing practice of "bundling" small-farm output with their own crop shipments, see ibid., 323–5; J. F. Merieult (New Orleans) to Bird, Savage & Bird (London), April 25, 1803, Document 2007.0257.2 in Louisiana Manuscripts Collection, HNOC; and Samuel C. Hyde Jr., *Pistols and Politics: The Dilemma of Democracy in Louisiana's Florida Parishes, 1810–1899* (Baton Rouge, 1996), 36. Susan Feiner overestimates the independence of the urban factorage system in the Old South's class structure in "Factors, Bankers, and Masters: Class Relations in the Antebellum South," *Journal of Economic History* 42 (March 1982), 61–7.

PART II

SECESSION AND WAR

4

From Secession to the Fall of New Orleans, 1860–1862

Louisiana was one of the antebellum South's chief producers of agricultural products, but its most crucial economic contribution to the region was the enormous commercial traffic steered through the port of New Orleans, a city whose business and financial district constituted one of the most intensely concentrated sites of capital in the mid-nineteenth-century Atlantic world. As plantation development had shifted steadily westward over the antebellum decades, the South's only true metropolis had become its premier banking and mercantile center. At the onset of secession winter in 1860, New Orleans's privileged position at the nexus of slave-based plantation agriculture and transatlantic trade networks thus seemed to herald a leadership role for Louisiana in any new southern government. But even though it would eventually provide the Confederacy with several important statesmen, Louisiana generally suffered from the deep suspicion with which Crescent City mercantile and banking elites were regarded throughout the South. Largely because of its merchants' connections to northern and foreign capital, both contemporaries and historians alike would tend to underestimate the depth of their support for slavery, secession, and the Confederacy. Their commitment to southern goals, born of their long-standing relationships to plantation slavery, has been partly obscured by the independent streak they sometimes displayed toward the Confederate government during the period before the Union occupation of New Orleans in May 1862. Most notably, the New Orleans banks initially resisted aligning their currency policies with those of the Confederate Treasury, and its merchants organized a cotton embargo against the Davis administration's wishes during the summer of 1861.

This chapter examines these and other reactions to government policies by the state's commercial and financial community, situating them within the context of the rapid and largely unique economic deterioration that Louisiana experienced as a result of the unprecedented pressures of secession and war. Understanding their reactions should help illuminate the global ramifications of the American Civil War during what historian Eric Hobsbawm called the "Age of Capital." The Crescent City business community's failed efforts to assert the primacy of "King Cotton" forced them to begin confronting the dependent nature of southern merchant capitalism in an era of ascendant industrialization elsewhere. Ultimately, the South's defeat would confirm New Orleans's standing as one of the last major urban outposts of an increasingly anachronistic, trade-based Atlantic world economy.[1]

Like many other New Orleans merchants in 1860, Dr. Joseph Slemmons Copes believed that intersectional commercial ties would provide a restraining influence on growing tensions. When Copes traveled to the Old Northwest early that year, he reported that there were "scarcely any persons who are not sympathizers with the South" in Ohio business circles. Similarly, a few months before, in an article titled "Commerce as a Peace-Maker," the New Orleans *Delta* had asserted that the powerful New York City business community was "becoming, through the influence of commercial relations ... essentially Southern in sympathies." As the crucial elections of 1860 approached, such beliefs caused Crescent City merchants to appeal to their northern brethren for help in averting a constitutional crisis. At the same time, many Louisiana businessmen also hoped that interregional ties based on the Mississippi River might promote political cooperation between southern and western states.[2]

Events had acquired a terrible momentum of their own, however, and uncertainty over the future began to be adversely reflected in the marketplace. In October, Walter Cox, another Crescent City factor, advised an Arkansas planter-client about the "growing distrust in the commercial mind at the unsettled condition of domestic politics":

In the event of Mr. Lincoln's election, trouble may ensue. Large depreciation in the value of Southern property would not be unlikely. These considerations are ... lending weight to our moneyed transactions and rates are well up. We think that Southern planters and merchants cannot exercise too great a caution until after the deciding election of November.

Already, he concluded, the New Orleans cotton market "has suffered largely on the mere strength of such apprehensions."[3]

[1] Eric Hobsbawm, *The Age of Capital, 1848–1875* (New York, 1974). On the westward shift of southern plantation agriculture during the antebellum decades, see Adam Rothman, *Slave Country: American Expansion and the Origins of the Deep South* (Cambridge, MA, 2005).

[2] E. Merton Coulter, "The Effects of Secession Upon the Commerce of the Mississippi Valley," *Mississippi Valley Historical Review* 3 (December 1916), 280–1; New Orleans *Delta*, September 9, 1859, quoted in Philip S. Foner, *Business and Slavery: The New York Merchants and the Irrepressible Conflict* (Chapel Hill, NC, 1941), 168 (quotation), 171–2; see also Michael Zakim, "The Dialectics of Merchant Capital: New York City Businessmen and the Secession Crisis of 1860–61," *New York History* 87 (Winter 2006), 67–87. Joseph S. Copes to Harlow J. Phelps, January 24, 1860, in Joseph Slemmons Copes Papers, Box 6 (Mss 733; Howard-Tilton Memorial Library, Tulane University, New Orleans, LA; hereinafter cited as Copes Papers).

[3] W[alter] Cox to W. E. Ashley, October 5, 1860, in W. Cox & Co. Letters, 1860–61 (MS-49; Manuscripts Division, New Orleans Public Library, New Orleans, Louisiana; hereinafter cited as Cox Papers, NOPL).

Walter Cox's letter highlights how commercial and financial markets weakened in 1860 as endemic "apprehensions" undermined the wider web of exchange relations. Even more than production-oriented industrialists, commodities merchants such as Cox relied on a stable business climate for the wheels of commerce to run smoothly – that is, for profits to be routinely extracted by common consent at various geographic waystations. Political instability threatened the interlocked structure of contingent promises inherent to long-distance exchange contracts, with uncertainty most immediately reflected in the higher cost of money, and any increases in discrete transaction costs had a ripple effect that affected profit margins all along the extended commodity chain. In contrast to the quixotic hopes of intersectional business cooperation held by Copes and others, one New Orleans newspaper feared that a national political crisis would cause "conflicts of material interests" between the regions to be "almost, if not absolutely, insurmountable."[4]

Abraham Lincoln's victory in the presidential election of November 1860 immediately heightened tensions over the nation's future among New Orleans merchants. By late November, local reporters for the R. G. Dun Mercantile Agency sought to assure their New York patrons that large firms such as John Watt & Co., which enjoyed long-standing ties to millionaire factor Glendy Burke, were "unmoved before the storm that is sweeping so many before it." No New Orleans house "stands firmer" than that of Watt and his Creole partner, Marcel Musson, the correspondent insisted. By early December, however, the city's tri-weekly commercial organ, the *Price-Current*, reported that conditions in the city's money markets were "grow[ing] more and more severe from day to day" because of political concerns. The British consul at New Orleans, William Mure, who also did business as a cotton broker, described the city's "Commercial panic" in a mid-December letter to London. "[O]ver 30 Factorage houses have suspended within the last fortnight," he reported. Although some firms tried to reassure their customers (as well as northern creditors) that these suspensions were only temporary, one merchant admitted that "the panic is infinately [*sic*] worse than that of 1857 on account of the uncertainty over political matters." Anxieties over the probable effects of secession on trade were also reflected in the quickened pace of exports from New Orleans that winter. In spite of the suspensions, Walter Cox observed in January 1861 that the cotton market was "active and buoyant," which he

---

[4] New Orleans *Daily Picayune*, December 12, 1860; Lance E. Davis and Douglass C. North, *Institutional Change and American Economic Growth* (Cambridge, UK, 1971), 20–5. For the notion of "commodity chains" in international commerce see Gary Gereffi and Miguel Korzeniewicz, eds., *Commodity Chains and Global Capitalism* (Westport, CT, and London, 1993). Thomas L. Haskell stressed the importance of "promise-keeping" to the stabilization of commercial contracts beginning in the eighteenth century; Haskell, "Capitalism and the Origins of the Humanitarian Sensibility, Part 2," in *The Antislavery Debate*, ed. Thomas Bender (Berkeley and Los Angeles, 1992), 143–6; see also Nuala Zahedieh, *The Capital and the Colonies: London and the Atlantic Economy, 1660–1700* (Cambridge, UK, and other cities, 2010), chap. 5, esp. 90–113.

attributed to concerns among New York houses about "future supplies" of the staple, and later that month, local newspapers noted the unusually rapid pace of ships leaving the port.[5]

Mercantile uneasiness over the implications of secession has been used to support characterizations of New Orleans business opinion as firmly pro-Union during the crisis of 1860–61. But even though nearly 80 percent of the vote in Orleans Parish went to the two moderate presidential candidates, John Bell and Stephen A. Douglas, such conservatism in favor of a stable status quo was to be expected from southern merchant capitalists, for whom the threat of disruptions to routine trade patterns were anathema. Moreover, it is important to distinguish the real intention behind the support of New Orleans businessmen for Bell's Constitutional Union Party. For most merchants, a vote for Bell did not express unconditional Unionism against southern extremism; instead, they hoped that a Bell administration might be able to negotiate a settlement to the political crisis, as had occurred in the famous Compromises of 1820 and 1850. However, their stance proved wholly contingent on a favorable outcome to the election. After the Republican Party's victory, observers noted an immediate hardening of political attitudes among New Orleans elites. With few exceptions, the local press rapidly closed ranks in favor of withdrawal from the Union, and *De Bow's Review*, the New Orleans–based southern commercial journal, was also strongly pro-secession. A widely discussed Thanksgiving Day sermon in support of secession by the city's Presbyterian Reverend Benjamin M. Palmer (who was friend and pastor to the merchant Joseph Slemmons Copes) lent moral authority to the emergent southern cause. By December, British consul William Mure admitted that he had not expected "to find the feeling in favour of Secession so strong or general as it is in this City and State." Alluding to the business community, Mure reported that "even the motives of interest have [now] given place to antipathy and hostility to the Northern and Western States." The President-elect's pledge to prevent any further extension of slavery in the territories, as well as more radical antislavery intentions that he and his allies were believed to harbor, made him unacceptable to Louisiana's gentleman-merchants. Their support for the "peculiar institution," born of their long-standing ties to the

[5] New Orleans *Daily True Delta*, January 22, 1861; Cox to W. E. Ashley, January 4, 1861, Cox Papers, NOPL; David G. Surdam, *Northern Naval Superiority and the Economics of the Civil War* (Columbia, SC, 2001), 112; Rhorer & Zunts to P. T. Hickman, December 5, 1860, quoted in Woodman, *King Cotton*, 201 (quotation), 205–6. William Mure to Lord John Russell [British Foreign Secretary], December 13, 1860, reprinted as "Financial and Economic Disturbance in New Orleans on the Eve of Secession," ed. Milledge L. Bonham, *Louisiana Historical Quarterly* 13 (January 1930), 32–3; see also Mure's listing under "Commission Merchants and Cotton Factors" in *Gardner's New Orleans, Louisiana, City and Business Directory for 1861* (New Orleans, 1861), 474. New Orleans *Price-Current*, December 1, 1860; entry on John Watt & Co. dated November 8, 1860, in Louisiana, Vol. 9, pp. 91, 100 (quotations on p. 100), R. G. Dun & Co. Credit Reports Collection (Baker Library Historical Collections, Harvard Business School).

planter class, quickly assumed priority over their Whiggish preference for stable government and business-as-usual.[6]

As with misunderstandings of the city's presidential vote, the strong showing of the "Cooperationist" faction in the state's January election for delegates to a secession convention led many contemporaries to overstate Unionist sentiment in Louisiana. Some New York newspapers harped on alleged voting irregularities to assert the existence of a conspiracy that had managed to drag an ostensible Unionist majority into secession. However, the crux of the Cooperationist position on secession was procedural, not oppositionist: its supporters maintained that the South should withdraw from the Union in concert rather than as individual states. In fact, the Cooperationist movement in Louisiana was less an expression of Unionist loyalties or doubts about the South's political course as much as it was an extension of long-standing factionalism centered on the bitter political rivalry between the Slidell and Soulé wings of the Louisiana Democratic Party. "I find that the secessionist movement is if anything stronger here [in New Orleans] than in Mississippi," insisted one Breckinridge supporter in December.[7]

The mistaken conflation of the short-lived Cooperationist movement with unconditional Unionism would have policy consequences during early Reconstruction, when the Lincoln administration severely underestimated pro-Confederate feeling in the state. But even their fellow southrons were not immune to skepticism about Crescent City loyalties. After the January 7 election the New Orleans *Daily Crescent* expressed regret that "the Cooperation party here has caused the South to look upon New Orleans with doubt," while still admitting that "this doubt [is] very reasonable, considering the cosmopolitan character of the city." Hostility toward the wealthy urban businessmen

[6] Mure to Lord Russell, December 13, 1860, in Bonham, ed., op. cit., 32. Palmer's sermon is reprinted in Jon L. Wakelyn, ed., *Southern Pamphlets on Secession, November 1860–April 1861* (Chapel Hill, 1996), 63–77; on Joseph S. Copes and Palmer, see Rev. J. H. McIlvain to J. S. Copes, December 20, 1860, Box 6, Copes Papers. See also Gerald M. Capers, *Occupied City: New Orleans under the Federals, 1861–1865* (Lexington, KY, 1965), 20–2; Willie Malvin Caskey, *Secession and Restoration of Louisiana* (Baton Rouge, 1938), 12–15; and Clement Eaton, *The Mind of the Old South* (rev. ed., Baton Rouge, 1967), 87–8. In a post-election letter to President Buchanan, the powerful Louisiana senator John Slidell grumbled that "seven-eighths" of the Democratic votes for Douglas in New Orleans had been cast by working-class immigrants who were "at heart, abolitionists"; many were also aligned with Slidell's rival, former U.S. senator Pierre Soulé; Louis Martin Sears, *John Slidell* (Durham, NC, 1925), 174. British journalist William Howard Russell later called Slidell "one of the most determined disunionists in the Confederacy," and said of his influence that he "is to the South something greater than Mr. Thurlow Weed has been to the North"; Russell, *My Diary North and South* (Boston, 1863), 237.

[7] Frank Valliant to Marian Rucks, December 14, 1860, quoted in William L. Barney, *The Secessionist Impulse: Alabama and Mississippi in 1860* (Princeton, NJ 1974), 220. John M. Sacher, *A Perfect War of Politics: Parties, Politicians, and Democracy in Louisiana, 1824–1861* (Baton Rouge, 2003), 290–7; Roger W. Shugg, *Origins of Class Struggle in Louisiana: A Social History of White Farmers and Laborers during Slavery and After* (1939; repr., Baton Rouge, 1968), 168–9; Caskey, *Secession and Restoration*, 14–15, 38–41.

who controlled so much of the cotton trade had often appeared throughout the plantation South, and even in Louisiana, many rural citizens had long been frustrated by the perceived domination of state politics by Crescent City commercial interests. As the region withdrew further into a defensive posture over the winter, such attitudes helped undermine any claims that New Orleans might have to serve as the capital of a new southern nation.[8]

Most worrisome to many southerners were the extraregional connections maintained by Crescent City merchants. Some firms were considered little more than appendages of New York–based interests, not only among commodities exporters but also among wholesalers and retailers, especially in the lucrative dry-goods trade. Powerful old houses of European origin, such as the Barings and the Browns, had played a prominent role in New Orleans since its colonial days, and the city's banking community was widely distrusted for its links to northern and foreign capital. Perhaps most troubling to many was the large number of New Orleans businessmen who had been born in the North. Typical of these concerns was a correspondent of John C. Calhoun, who warned him in 1849 about the influence of "Northern agents" (as well as "Foreigners" and "Creoles") on the city's political loyalties. Years before the term *carpetbagger* became a common southern epithet, New Orleans was derided for its community of opportunistic northern-born migrants who had established a foothold for Yankee business culture in the heart of the deep South. Among such migrants were powerful lawyer-politicians such as John Slidell, a native New Yorker who had made his fortune in Louisiana land speculation and whose niece was married to the New York banker August Belmont, himself an agent of the European house of Rothschild. But there was also a plethora of more anonymous middling merchants in the city – men such as Joseph Slemmons Copes, a Delaware native who had moved to New Orleans in 1849. Like others, Copes continued to visit and correspond frequently with his northern friends and relatives. Whether the loyalties of such transplanted businessmen could withstand the pressures of secession and possible war was a question pondered by many southerners during the crisis of 1860–1.[9]

[8] Shugg, *Origins of Class Struggle in Louisiana*, 138–41; New Orleans *Daily Crescent*, January 8, 1861; John G. Clark, "New Orleans and the River: A Study in Attitudes and Responses," *Louisiana History* 8 (Winter 1967), 129–33.

[9] J. D. B. De Bow, "Nativities and Inhabitants of the Leading Cities," *De Bow's Review* 19 (September 1855), 262; William W. Chenault and Robert C. Reinders, "The Northern-born Community of New Orleans in the 1850s," *Journal of American History* 51 (September 1964), 232–47; Sears, *John Slidell*, 5–11, 111–12. See also John Ashworth, *Slavery, Capitalism, and Politics in the Antebellum Republic*, Volume 2: *The Coming of the Civil War, 1850–1861* (New York, 2007), 87–8. On Joseph S. Copes's northern ties see Copes Papers, *passim*. H[enry] W. Conner to John C. Calhoun, January 12, 1849, in *The Papers of John C. Calhoun*, Vol. 26, eds. Clyde N. Wilson and Shirley Bright Cook (Columbia, SC, 2001), 211; Stephen A. Caldwell, *A Banking History of Louisiana* (Baton Rouge, 1935), 89; George D. Green, *Finance and Economic Development in the Old South: Louisiana Banking, 1804–1861* (Stanford, CA, 1972), chap. 3; Ralph W. Hidy, *The House of Baring in American Trade and Finance: English Merchant Bankers*

Businessmen also endured more suspicion than other migrants because the lure of mammon was widely presumed to make them agnostic at best with regard to political affairs. However, such fears were largely misplaced. In fact, the overwhelming majority of Louisiana's merchants, northern-born or not, actively and publicly supported the Confederacy, often at great cost to themselves. Vigilance committees and other warnings to northern business-men attested to the strength of anti-Unionist sentiment in New Orleans dur-ing secession winter. Competition for plantation clients may have undermined New Orleans merchants' cohesiveness as a class, but their alliances with slave-holding planters tended to be more organic and fairly stable. In contrast to the increasingly impersonal ties of northern finance, credit relationships between city factors and rural planters were tightly woven into the southern social fab-ric. When formalized at all, the rolling annual loans extended by New Orleans factors to their planter-clients were routinely collateralized by mortgages on slave property, which gave merchants a vital pecuniary stake in the contin-ued legitimacy of the peculiar institution. Status as well as financial consider-ations also compelled many city merchants to establish themselves as planters when diversifying their investment portfolios. Even "sedentary" merchants such as Copes traveled frequently to maintain face-to-face contact with their rural patrons, and a great deal of intermarriage resulted from such visits, with bonds of kinship further solidifying ties between planters and their city factors. For such reasons, historian Clement Eaton concluded that southern business-men were actually more aligned with "agrarian ideals" than was popularly believed by contemporaries, and it becomes less surprising that only 16 of the 172 most prominent Louisiana Unionists identified by another historian were merchants.[10]

In economic terms, as much as some New Orleans merchants valued the midwestern grain trade, when push came to shove, slave-produced commodi-ties were the city's lifeblood: in 1860, cotton and sugar comprised nearly three-fourths of the value of all receipts at New Orleans. Furthermore, it was not unreasonable for Crescent City businessmen to assume that an independent southern nation might actually improve their long-term fortunes. Independence, they believed, would necessarily foster more direct trade with Europe, thereby

at Work, 1763–1861 (Cambridge, MA, 1949); Edwin J. Perkins, *Financing Anglo-American Trade: The House of Brown, 1800–1880* (Cambridge, MA, and London, 1975), 156–67, 185–8; Harry A. Corbin, *The Men's Clothing Industry: Colonial through Modern Times* (New York, 1970), 32–7; Albion, *Rise of New York Port*, 95–7.

[10] Ted Tunnell, *Crucible of Reconstruction: War, Radicalism, and Race in Louisiana, 1862–1877* (Baton Rouge and London, 1984), Appendix 1; Eaton, *Mind of the Old South*, 58–62; Richard H. Kilbourne Jr., *Debt, Investment, Slaves: Credit Relations in East Feliciana Parish, Louisiana, 1825–1885* (Tuscaloosa, AL, and London, 1995), 73–4; Woodman, *King Cotton*, 34–42; William L. Barney, *The Road to Secession: A New Perspective on the Old South* (New York, 1972), 186–7. For a passionate antebellum defense of southern businessmen's patriotism see "The Merchant – His Character, Position, Duties," *De Bow's Review* 3 (February 1847), 93–7.

allowing profits long siphoned off by northeastern ports to accrue instead to New Orleans merchants and their plantation patrons. This line of thinking prompted some observers outside the region to worry that their debts to northern firms were an incentive for southern merchants to support the Confederacy. But even though the combined debt of Crescent City firms to the North was estimated at $30 million in early 1861, visitors reported that "the great commercial community of New Orleans.... den[ies] that they intend to repudiate" those obligations, despite secession. These attitudes persisted after the city's occupation: a British businessman visiting in October 1862 declared that he failed to encounter "a solitary instance where the slightest disposition was manifested to repudiate, or even compromise[,] either a Northern or a foreign debt."[11]

For most Louisiana merchants, the ingrained habits of intra-mercantile honor died hard. A businessman's reputation for integrity demanded that obligations contracted in good faith be respected. After the war, middling merchant Joseph Copes jumped through hoops, so to speak, to reach a fair settlement of old debts demanded by the unforgiving Ohio manufacturer who had supplied his former profitable trade in iron cotton-bale clasps. Higher up the merchant-capitalist ladder, conservative New Orleans bankers would successfully deploy their political influence during Reconstruction and afterward to prevent the official cancellation of debts contracted before, during, and after the conflict, thereby shoring up tenuous state and municipal-bond ratings in national and foreign markets – at taxpayer expense, controversially, and during a time when southern states such as Virginia and Mississippi were indulging their own popular movements for repudiation. Due to their long-standing position at the southwestern nexus of the Atlantic trading network, New Orleans merchants were more inclined to consider the claims of outside creditors as still legitimate, despite the interruptions of secession and war, than most other southerners. However, although there is no evidence for insinuations that merchants backed secession to gain windfall profits from cancelling their outstanding debts, perceptions are often as important as reality. Many outside observers in early 1861 probably would have agreed with Union general Benjamin F. Butler's later insistence that "the certain confiscation of many millions of debts which the South owed to the North was a great inducement to the commercial classes of the South to go into the Rebellion."[12]

[11] W. C. Corsan, *Two Months in the Confederate States: An Englishman's Travels Through the South*, ed. Benjamin H. Trask (1863; repr., Baton Rouge, 1996), 15; Russell, *My Diary North and South*, 250; John Christopher Schwab, *The Confederate States of America, 1861–1865: A Financial and Industrial History of the South during the Civil War* (New York and London, 1901), 110–13. See also "The Commercial Revulsion," New York *Economist*, repr. in *De Bow's Review* 31 (July 1861), 93–4. For 1860 crop receipts at New Orleans see [Appleton's] *American Annual Cyclopedia and Register of Important Events of the Year 1862* (New York, 1865), 113–14.

[12] Benjamin F. Butler, *Butler's Book: Autobiography and Personal Reminiscences of Major-General Benjamin F. Butler* (Boston, 1892), 321. In a letter to his colleague Karl Marx in May 1862,

Louisiana's withdrawal from the Union in late January 1861 was thus applauded by most local businessmen, as was the seizure of the federal Customhouse at New Orleans, in which more than a half-million dollars in federal bullion was confiscated – by far the single largest appropriation of federal property to result from secession. (Similar seizures by all the other Confederate states combined netted less than $75,000 in specie.) However, merchants were already disturbed by signs that secession was having an adverse effect on commerce. With the books nearly closed on the 1860 harvest, one New Orleans newspaper published a gloomy report on business conditions:

Trade is at a standstill; the importation of merchandise has almost entirely ceased; ... the banks are remorselessly curtailing their discounts; ordinary creditors are endeavoring by all means short of legal pressure to lessen the liabilities of their debtors; stores and manufactories, traders and mechanics are diminishing their expenses by the discharge of hands; ... [E]verybody looks dubious and bewildered, not knowing what to expect or what may happen.

The rapid advent of economic hard times in New Orleans and its interior hinterlands in early 1861 partly reflected the fact that the secession movement coincided with the usual post-harvest slowdown of commerce. But the most serious cause of economic difficulties in Louisiana as the year progressed was the lack of an adequate circulating medium of currency, or "tight money." Commission merchant Joseph S. Copes received several complaints that spring from plantation clients about the sudden scarcity of money; one planter wrote him that "nearly every farmer wishes to buy, but there is [no] money in the country to buy with – at least what there is, is in the hands of a few." Money was also in short supply in New Orleans. Factor Walter Cox was forced to trim a client's order in May because "money is so scarce." "It is extremely disagreeable to be forever prating of the stringency of financial affairs," Cox continued, but "we must bear it with a stiff upper lip until the crop comes in" later in the year.[13]

Frederick Engels offered a conjecture similar in spirit to Butler's. "The fanaticism of the New Orleans merchants for the Confederacy," he wrote, "is simply explained by the fact that the fellows have had to take a quantity of Confederate scrip for hard cash"; Engels to Marx, May 23, 1862, in Marx and Engels, *The Civil War in the United States*, ed. Richard Enmale (2nd ed.; New York, 1940), 245. It is worth noting, however, that both Engels and Butler took the fact of southern businessmen's support for the Confederacy for granted. Caldwell, *Banking History of Louisiana*, chap. 8; Joe Gray Taylor, *Louisiana Reconstructed, 1863–1877* (Baton Rouge, 1974), 260–4; Joy J. Jackson, *New Orleans in the Gilded Age: Politics and Urban Progress, 1880–1896* (2nd ed.; Lafayette, LA, 1997), 34; William Colcord to J. S. Copes, August 14, 1865, and James R. Speer to Copes, September 7, 1865, both in Box 7, Copes Papers; Schwab, *Confederate States of America*, 113.

[13] W[alter] Cox to W. E. Ashley, May 8, 1861, in Cox Papers, NOPL; W. S. Finch to Copes & Phelps, March 18, 1861, in Box 6, Copes Papers; New Orleans *Daily True Delta*, January 28, 1861, as quoted in [Appleton's] *American Annual Cyclopedia and Register of Important Events of the Year 1861* (New York, 1870), p. 429; Richard Cecil Todd, *Confederate Finance* (Athens,

The inadequacies of the U.S. monetary system had been burdensome for inter-regional commerce before the Civil War, but new developments lay behind the severe tightening of Louisiana money markets in 1861. For one thing, fewer com-modities in circulation meant less money in circulation, a problem that would grow steadily worse under Union military pressure both from upriver and in the Gulf. Also, there was a great deal of uncertainty surrounding the value of previ-ous currencies, especially those that had originated outside the South, and the new Confederate Treasury Secretary, Christopher G. Memminger, was slow to address monetary problems. Another factor was the sudden, poorly coordinated shift of the economy onto a war footing, since the massive diversion of funds to military purposes depleted scarce regional monetary resources. In Louisiana, where the government had never enjoyed a reputation for thrift, Governor Moore wasted no time appropriating funds to strengthen the state's prepared-ness for war, causing one newspaper to warn its readers about the "erection of a monstrous superstructure of debt." Yet many parish governments followed the governor's lead by levying new taxes and issuing bonds to support local military mobilization, as did the oft-maligned municipal government of New Orleans.[14]

Probably most of all, however, monetary stringency in Louisiana in 1861 was a result of contractionist policies pursued by the powerful New Orleans banks during secession winter. In 1861 there were a dozen state-chartered banking institutions in Louisiana, all headquartered in New Orleans. By every relevant measure, these dozen institutions easily controlled a larger share of the South's financial resources among themselves than those of any other state. Most notably, the $13.6 million in specie reserves held in New Orleans vaults was greater than that in the rest of the eventual Confederate states combined. These enormous bullion reserves (second nationally only to the $26.4 million distributed among New York's 306 banks) epitomized the impeccably conser-vative practices of New Orleans bankers.[15]

Most of the wide-ranging commerce on which New Orleans and its hin-terlands thrived depended on the city's banks for the notes, bills of exchange,

GA, 1954), 158–9; Schwab, *Confederate States of America*, 143–4. On New Orleans mercan-tile support for secession in early 1861, see Russell, *My Diary North and South*, 237–8; Stuart H. Landry, *History of the Boston Club* (New Orleans, 1938), 61–70; and New Orleans *Daily Crescent*, January 28 and February 7, 1861.

[14] New Orleans *Daily True Delta*, January 28, 1861, quoted in *Appleton's Cyclopedia for 1861*, p. 429; Jefferson Davis Bragg, *Louisiana in the Confederacy* (1941; repr. Baton Rouge, 1997), 48–61; Todd, *Confederate Finance*, 85–6; Douglas B. Ball, *Financial Failure and Confederate Defeat* (Urbana and Chicago, 1991), 28–31, 161–2.

[15] The net capitalization of Louisiana's twelve banks stood at $24.6 million in 1861, a total that was half again greater than that of Virginia ($16.5 million) and South Carolina ($14.9 million), both of which spread their resources more thinly among a greater number of banks (twenty-five and eighteen, respectively). The $17 million worth of deposits in Louisiana banks repre-sented nearly half of the region's total $38.1 million in deposits. Banking statistics are derived from the "General Statement of the Condition of the Banks of the United States" in *Appleton's Cyclopedia for 1861*, p. 462.

and other promissory instruments they issued, all of which served as the closest thing that the region had besides scarce metallic coinage to a universally accepted, relatively non-depreciating currency (or, "good paper"). This broad reliance on New Orleans bank paper, however, left the regional economy vulnerable if the flow of that paper were constricted, which is precisely what happened beginning in the fall of 1860. Even before the November election, New Orleans banks had begun shoring up their financial position in the face of future uncertainty. They decreased their liabilities by steadily retiring their various notes in circulation and sharply limiting the issuance of any new ones. By December the city's banks had stopped issuing new loans entirely, and many firms suddenly could not even obtain the short-term bills of exchange that they used to move the fall cotton harvest, which led some to suspend operations. The situation did not improve in the new year, as the city's banks hewed steadfastly to the policy of reducing their financial exposure. After the banks had sharply cut their notes in circulation by a third between September 1860 and the end of the year, New Orleans money markets enjoyed some minor improvement, only to tighten again in April after the fall of Fort Sumter. The banks' outstanding short-term paper, most of which consisted of the 90-day loans on which the export trade relied, fell more relentlessly between November and April, from $24.4 million to $14.1 million.[16]

Faced with such stringency, it was no wonder that the beleaguered city merchant Walter Cox concluded in May that "what the South chiefly needs [now] is money." "If we can only keep supplied with that 'sinew'," he averred, "we shall thrash the North easily enough." Cox's comment implied that New Orleans banks might better serve the public by maintaining the flow of currency they issued, which would help to smooth the economic dislocations that attended secession and war. These banks were, after all, institutions whose very existence was predicated on the public forbearance implied in their state-issued charters, which also allowed for governmental oversight of their operations. However, the banks were ultimately only quasi-public institutions, and very politically influential ones at that. Regardless of the party in power, Louisiana's government had been dominated since the early 1850s by politicians whose decidedly Whiggish commercial outlook disinclined them to challenge the New Orleans banks.[17]

---

[16] Financial data on New Orleans banks were published regularly in national commercial journals such as *Hunt's Merchants' Magazine*, as well as in the New Orleans *Price-Current*; the 1860–1 figures cited here are collated in Schwab, *Confederate States of America*, 124–5. Russell, *My Diary North and South*, 250; Bragg, *Louisiana in the Confederacy*, 69. William Mure to Lord Russell, December 13, 1860, in Bonham, ed., op. cit., 32–3; Larry Schweikart, "Secession and Southern Banks," *Civil War History* 31 (June 1985), 118–19; New Orleans *Price-Current*, December 1, 1860.

[17] Shugg, *Origins of Class Struggle in Louisiana*, chap. 5, esp. 124–35; Caldwell, *Banking History of Louisiana*, 71–80; Green, *Finance and Economic Development in the Old South*, 118–35; W[alter] Cox to W. E. Ashley, May 8, 1861, Cox Papers, NOPL.

Furthermore, the logic behind the banks' contractionist policies was based on impeccable precedent, since their surfeit of specie had helped the city to withstand the Panic of 1857. It was hard to argue against hard money in the vaults, and in fact, the New Orleans banks' efforts to increase their already ample specie reserves was a crucial component of their contractionist policies. Anticipating the secession crisis, the banks of New Orleans had begun augmenting their specie holdings in September 1860, which were increased by nearly 50 percent before the end of the year. By April 1861 the banks had amassed more than $17 million in bullion reserves. These burgeoning stockpiles of hard money were all the more remarkable for having been accumulated without ever suspending specie payments – a step that many other banks, from South Carolina to New York, had already taken by early 1861 to protect themselves against panic-driven "runs" on their metallic reserves. Thus, when the state board charged with bank oversight reported in January 1861, it did not criticize the banks' contractionist policies; instead, the board praised their maintenance of specie payments as evidence of "the wisdom of our banking system." Brushing aside concerns over the shortage of money being expressed by merchants like Walter Cox, the board insisted that "our commercial community ... [is] ready to submit to severe privations for the sake of preserving the integrity of our currency."[18]

By the late spring of 1861 the New Orleans banks were nearly unique in their maintenance of specie payments, but this now began to strike many observers less as admirable proof of their financial integrity than as a self-serving policy that privileged narrow institutional concerns over those of the new Confederate nation. Although the Louisiana State Bank had contacted Governor Moore in January 1861 to offer an unsolicited $100,000 loan to aid the state in its military preparations, similar evidence of the banks' loyalty to the southern cause had been notably lacking during the first half of 1861. So long as the financial epicenter of the South continued to maintain its reserves exclusively in the form of bullion, the widespread acceptance of newly issued Confederate Treasury notes was significantly hampered. At a southern banking convention held in Richmond in July, the delegates endorsed Secretary Memminger's request to receive and pay out Confederate notes, which, given the suspension of specie payments most had already implemented, would make the government's currency their monetary standard. But representatives of the New Orleans banks were conspicuously absent from this convention, and without their cooperation, Memminger was warned that his notes would continue to circulate well below par value.[19]

[18] *Report of the Louisiana Board of Currency*, January 1861, quoted in Bragg, *Louisiana in the Confederacy*, 68; Schweikart, "Secession and Southern Banks," 118–21; Schwab, *Confederate States of America*, 125; Thomas Prentice Kettell, *Southern Wealth and Northern Profits* (New York, 1860), 94–7.

[19] Gazaway B. Lamar [ed.], *Proceedings of the Bank Convention of the Confederate States Held at Richmond, Va., July 24th, 25th, and 26th, 1861* (Charleston, SC, 1861); Schwab, *Confederate*

Despite these warnings, as well as his ongoing correspondence that year with James D. Denegre, the president of Citizens Bank in New Orleans, Memminger delayed making any effort to enlist the New Orleans banks' voluntary support for his interlinked fiscal and monetary goals. On September 11, Memminger finally addressed a terse letter to Governor Moore and the officers of the New Orleans banks:

The banks throughout the Confederate States, with the single exception of your city, have come forward and with one voice have determined that they will receive and pay [Confederate Treasury notes] out as currency, even to the injury and exclusion of their own circulation.... At New Orleans (the largest and most important city in the Confederacy) the necessity is most urgent that our Treasury notes should be made available.

Moore, who was then desperately seeking increased Confederate military support for the defense of New Orleans, complied immediately with Memminger's request by authorizing the state-chartered banks to suspend specie payments, which they did.[20]

Since records of their internal deliberations are lacking, the reasoning behind the policies of the New Orleans banks during 1861 remains a matter of informed deduction. In light of their political influence, as well as the widespread public backing for Confederate policies reflected in Governor Moore's speedy response to Memminger's request, the banks' official stance that their state-issued charters prohibited them from suspending specie payments seems little more than a convenient excuse. Their absence from the southern banking convention in July was probably an accurate barometer of their determination to keep their operations independent from outside pressures. Though the banks were a vital part of the city's exchange-oriented economy, their cloistered practices and global ties promoted institutional priorities that set them apart from run-of-the-mill merchant capitalists such as wholesalers, commission merchants, and factorage houses. Yet even before Memminger's belated request was received, at least some city bankers had grown wary of the perception that their policies might be obstructing the Confederate war effort. Alluding to the alarming shrinkage of specie reserves in the city since the onset of war in April, an official of the Southern Bank, Thomas Layton, argued in the New Orleans *Daily Crescent* on September 13 that "our leading banks may as well take the bull by the horns first as last, and not wait," urging them to "take steps for

States of America, 127–40; William S. Pike to Governor Thomas O. Moore, January 11, 1861, as reprinted in Lane C. Kendall, "The Interregnum in Louisiana in 1861, Part II," *Louisiana Historical Quarterly* 16 (July 1933), 381.

20 Christopher G. Memminger to Governor Thomas O. Moore, September 11, 1861, in Raphael P. Thian, comp., *Reports of the Secretary of the Treasury of the Confederate States of America, 1861–65* (Washington, DC, 1878), 45–6a. For Memminger's 1861 correspondence with the New Orleans banker Denegre, see Ball, *Financial Failure and Confederate Defeat*, 148 n. 6 and 149 n.11.

making the Government issue currency of the country." Ultimately, the banks' stubbornly independent course of action during much of 1861 helped perpetuate the costly impression that the Crescent City commercial community was less than united behind the new southern nation. And regardless of whether blame for the lack of a coordinated regional monetary policy during the crucial first year after Lincoln's election should reside with the New Orleans banks or with Memminger's procrastination in confronting them, it would not be the last time that southerners' ideological preference for laissez-faire economic policies would undermine Confederate goals.[21]

Although news from the war front was fairly heartening for southerners during much of 1861, the Union strategy of splitting the Confederacy into western and eastern halves at the Mississippi River caused Louisiana to begin suffering the war's effects more swiftly than most other states. The U.S. naval blockade that began in late May reduced seaborne arrivals at New Orleans to a small fraction of their usual number, yet just as worrisome was the steep decline in river-borne steamboat traffic, since the steady shift of antebellum resources into cotton production had left much of the state dependent on the downriver flow of foodstuffs from the Midwest. Even as supplies from both midwestern and ocean-borne sources dwindled, ordinary citizens in New Orleans began to clamor about the effects of "tight money." Beginning in the summer of 1861, the shortage of reliable money for day-to-day transactions caused city streetcar tickets to be widely exchanged as fractional currency, and other small change circulated in the form of minor notes, known as "shinplasters," that were informally issued by private individuals, most notably grocers and tavernkeepers. The novelist George Washington Cable, then a young grocery clerk in New Orleans, later recalled the paradoxical situation that arose that fall: "not merely was the price of food and raiment rising, but the value of the money was going down" as a result of the makeshift currencies in circulation. The grim logic of Gresham's Law ("bad money drives out good") was only exacerbated after the New Orleans banks agreed to suspend specie payments and adopt Confederate currencies in September; despite the banks' public assurances that their financial condition was still sound, many citizens panicked and began hoarding what metallic coinage remained. Just a few days after the specie suspensions were

---

[21] Stanley Lebergott, "Why the South Lost: Commercial Purpose in the Confederacy, 1861–1865," *Journal of American History* 70 (June 1983), 58–74; see also Lawrence N. Powell and Michael S. Wayne, "Self-Interest and the Decline of Confederate Nationalism," in *The Old South in the Crucible of War*, eds. Harry P. Owens and James J. Cooke (Jackson, MS, 1983), 29–45. New Orleans *Daily Crescent*, September 13, 1861. Historian Douglas B. Ball has argued that the failure to compel the New Orleans banks' acceptance of government notes sooner may have contributed to the city's inability to defend itself against Federal naval forces in the spring of 1862. A project to construct several ironclad ships for the city's defense had gotten underway in early 1861, only to grind to a halt in the summer due to a lack of funds to pay workers, who went on strike rather than accept wages in still-tenuous Confederate currency. Ball, *Financial Failure and Confederate Defeat*, 165–6; see also James M. Merrill, "Confederate Shipbuilding in New Orleans," *Journal of Southern History* 28 (February 1962), 87–93.

announced, the *Picayune* published a letter to Governor Moore from "one of our prominent business men" that expressed his concerns about growing discontent among the city's "poor and laboring classes." *De Bow's Review* would soon ascribe the midsummer establishment of a "free market" for poor relief to the New Orleans business community's "usual far-reaching and unstinted benevolence," but well-placed fears of bread riots probably also helped convince them to spearhead its organization. Although the author found it "amusing to see ... many of our rich merchants, with their white aprons on.., working as hard as if their own bread depended on their exertions," his subjects found little humor in the situation, especially since many of the newly indigent masses, according to one diarist, "curse[d] their benefactors heartily."[22]

With the Confederate government preoccupied with problems elsewhere, the Crescent City's best chance of obtaining supplies now rested with its merchants. Procuring goods from the interior, however, required them to face new difficulties, such as mail disruptions, transportation delays, higher insurance rates, and currency shortages. Some New Orleans merchants sought to overcome these obstacles by taking off for the hinterlands in search of goods, yet their efforts prompted a resurgence of old animosities between the countryside and the Crescent City. In October a newspaper in upstate Alexandria noted the appearance of roving "sharpers and Shylocks" from New Orleans in local stores and suggested that any more "trading travelers" on purchasing raids be tarred and feathered. Copes & Phelps received similar reports that fall from their large allied store in Shreveport, where James Phelps claimed that shortfalls prevented him from filling his New Orleans partners' orders. But Phelps also admitted that he was under pressure from his own customers, nervously informing Copes & Phelps that "the countrymen generally are venting their wrath on the merchants," particularly due to shortages of salt. With longstanding resentments now also fueled by scarcity and rising prices – as well as by the disproportionate number of merchants who avoided conscription by paying substitutes to fight in their stead – the escalating anger of the rural majority probably made interior storekeepers such as James Phelps feel isolated and vulnerable indeed.[23]

[22] Kate Mason Rowland and Mrs. Morris L. Croxall, eds., *The Journal of Julia LeGrand: New Orleans, 1862–1863* (Richmond, VA, 1911), 37–8; *De Bow's Review* 31 (December 1861), 559; "A Suggestion as to Small Change," New Orleans *Daily Picayune*, September 18, 1861; George W. Cable, "New Orleans Before the Capture," in *Battles and Leaders of the Civil War*, eds. Robert U. Johnson and Clarence C. Buel (4 vols., 1887; repr., New York, 1956), II, 17; see also Clara Solomon, *The Civil War Diary of Clara Solomon: Growing Up in New Orleans, 1861–1862*, ed. Elliott Ashkenazi (Baton Rouge, 1995), 131; and Elisabeth Joan Doyle, "Greenbacks, Car Tickets, and the Pot of Gold: The Effects of Wartime Occupation on the Business Life of New Orleans, 1861–1865," *Civil War History* 5 (December 1959), 347–62. Bragg, *Louisiana in the Confederacy*, 89–91; *Appleton's Cyclopedia for 1861*, p. 432; Coulter, "Effects of Secession," 289–90; Surdam, *Northern Naval Superiority*, 170.

[23] Phelps & Rogers to Copes & Phelps, December 2, 1861, in Box 6, Copes Papers. Salt provides a fine example of the ways that merchant capitalism had helped suppress the development of

Even as the sectional conflict forced New Orleans merchants to consider how their commercial activities might contribute to the wider regional goal of winning the war, the invisible hand of self-interest led many to resist some Confederate policies. For example, despite his defensive insistence that city merchants were "as anxious as any in the South to assist the Government," New Orleans factor Walter Cox opposed various programs of so-called produce loans, since such a state-controlled marketing system would bypass the entire established machinery of merchant capitalism. Mercantile opposition helped fuel resistance to the program in Louisiana, where a mere 28,000 bales of cotton were pledged toward the August 1861 produce loan by year's end (out of a southern total of 417,000 bales).[24]

The most significant instance of Louisiana merchants' resistance to official Confederate policies, however, was their successful promotion of a voluntary cotton embargo beginning in the summer of 1861. Much ink has been spilled over the South's devotion to "King Cotton diplomacy," a sort of faith-based foreign policy whose guiding tenet was that European economic dependence on southern cotton would eventually compel intervention on behalf of the Confederacy. Yet historians have been slower to acknowledge the disproportionate contributions to this diplomatic strategy made by Louisiana elites like Judah P. Benjamin, John Slidell, and Duncan F. Kenner, among others. Moreover, the New Orleans merchant community took it upon themselves to assume a vanguard role in cotton diplomacy that was not sanctioned by – and was even at odds with – official Confederate foreign policies. Given the global connections that Crescent City bankers and merchants had cultivated for several decades by mediating the flow of regional commodities to transatlantic markets, it is unsurprising that these businessmen would consider themselves the most appropriate stewards of the South's international interests. Yet the eventual failure of the embargo to achieve its progenitors' goals also provides a good measure of the ill-advised hubris of Louisiana's merchants. Their miscalculation was no small matter, since if their strategy had managed to provoke a pro-southern intervention by Europe's "Great Powers," particularly during

---

southern manufacturing before the war. Despite adequate domestic sources in Louisiana and elsewhere in the South, salt had been routinely imported by sea to New Orleans and sold to the interior. The region's antebellum reliance on salt imports was largely an unintended consequence of using the bulk mineral as much-needed ballast for incoming ships; see Ella Lonn, *Salt as a Factor in the Confederacy* (New York, 1933), 22–5; and Surdam, *Northern Naval Superiority*, 13. Alexandria *Louisiana Democrat*, October 30, 1861, repr. in New Orleans *Daily Crescent*, November 4, 1861; Corsan, *Two Months in the Confederate States*, 14. On mail disruptions see L. E. Griffith to Copes & Phelps, July 9, 1861, Box 6, Copes Papers; on transportation delays, Phelps & Rogers to Copes & Phelps, September 14, November 3, 1861, in ibid.; on rising insurance rates, W. Cox & Co. to W. E. Ashley, July 8, 1861, Cox Papers, NOPL; and on interior currency shortages, John T. Ball to Copes & Phelps, November 18, 1861, Box 6, Copes Papers.

24 Walter Cox to W. E. Ashley, July 8, 1861, Cox Papers, NOPL; Todd, *Confederate Finance*, 33–5; Judith F. Gentry, "White Gold: The Confederate Government and Cotton in Louisiana," *Louisiana History* 33 (Summer 1992), 230.

From Secession to the Fall of New Orleans

1861–2, the course of the American Civil War – perhaps even its outcome – might have been substantially altered.[25]

During the 1850s the reliance of European industry, especially in England, on southern cotton had been widely touted as the region's trump card under a scenario of secession or civil conflict. With more than four-fifths of the cotton that fueled British and French textile mills imported from southern slave plantations, the region's planters, politicians, and newspapers frequently expounded the popular sentiment that "Cotton Is King," as one famous book's title put it in 1855. The stake that European powers had in the uninterrupted flow of southern commodities was a constant refrain among New Orleans merchants, especially in *De Bow's Review*, the premier journal of the region's commercial classes. Indeed, just as the secession crisis was erupting, the January 1861 issue featured an article typifying this belief, one whose opening sentence summed up the conviction that would undergird cotton diplomacy over the years ahead. "The secession of these States must necessarily be a peaceful one," author W. D. Chase asserted, "because England, France, [and] the rest of commercial Europe … require that it should be." Even before secession was fait accompli, the commercial and political elites of Louisiana had taken the diplomatic lead based on this belief. In mid-December 1860 the British consul at New Orleans, William Mure, reported that he had been visited by a delegation of "influential gentlemen connected with the State, who assured me that a Southern Confederacy was certain." The men outlined a mutually profitable quid pro quo to Mure: a "most liberal Commercial Treaty" in exchange for British support for a new southern confederacy. The self-appointed delegation was wisely circumspect about brandishing cotton as an economic weapon, but the consul seemed to get the point anyway, privately advising the Foreign Office of his fears that any interruption of trade on "the manufacturing interests of Great Britain will be severely felt."[26]

During the spring of 1861 many southerners were disappointed that recognition of the Confederacy was not immediately extended by European

[25] On Confederate foreign relations the classic work remains Frank L. Owsley, *King Cotton Diplomacy: Foreign Relations of the Confederate States of America* (Chicago, 1931); see also Charles M. Hubbard, *The Burden of Confederate Diplomacy* (Knoxville, TN, 1998); and Howard Jones, *Union in Peril: The Crisis over British Intervention in the Civil War* (Chapel Hill, 1992).

[26] Mure to Lord Russell, December 13, 1860, in Bonham, ed., op. cit., 35–6; W. D. Chase, "The Secession of the Cotton States: Its Status, Its Advantages, and Its Power," *De Bow's Review* 30 (January 1861), 93; David Christy, *Cotton Is King: or, The Culture of Cotton …* (1855; 2nd ed., New York, 1856). In 1858 a widely circulated U.S. Interior Department report written by New Orleans resident John Claiborne had emphasized Europe's dependence on southern cotton; see the discussion in Brian Schoen, *The Fragile Fabric of Union: Cotton, Federal Politics, and the Global Origins of the Civil War* (Baltimore, 2009), 224–5. See also Sven Beckert, "Emancipation and Empire: Reconstructing the Worldwide Web of Cotton Production in the Age of the American Civil War," *American Historical Review* 109 (December 2004), 1405–38, esp. 1408–9; and D. A. Farnie, *The English Cotton Industry and the World Market, 1815–1896* (Oxford, Eng., 1979), 136–8.

governments, but they tended to dismiss such hesitation as a matter of poor timing, since the secession crisis had occurred at the end of the 1860 harvest season. The seasoned British journalist William Howard Russell, who toured the South that spring, met with New Orleans commercial lawyer and sugar planter Judah P. Benjamin, then serving as the Confederate attorney-general, who assured the veteran British journalist that "all this coyness about acknowledging a slave power will come right at last." Indeed, Russell heard so many self-assured prognostications of King Cotton's power to compel his nation's cooperation that he finally became annoyed and offended. "It was scarcely very agreeable," he wrote during his visit to South Carolina, "to find that no considerations were believed to be of consequence in reference to England except her material interests, and that these worthy gentlemen regarded her as a sort of appendage to their cotton kingdom." "Slavery perhaps has aggravated the tendency to look at all the world through parapets of cotton bales," sniffed the proud London *Times* correspondent. After he visited New Orleans at the end of May, Russell reported that "the mercantile community hope the contest will be ended before the next season by the recognition of Southern Independence," but he also described growing concerns over the Federal naval blockade, whose ships first arrived off the Gulf coast during his stay. "The great commercial community of New Orleans ... now feels the pressure of the blockade," he concluded, and thus "depends on the interference of the European Powers next October."[27]

As the summer wore on, hopes born of merchants' faith in King Cotton were increasingly expressed in the form of anxieties, a shift revealed in the correspondence of New Orleans factor Walter Cox. In January, Cox had boasted that "we have an abiding faith in cotton" and opined that the outcome of the political crisis "will make the King more secure even on his throne." Six months later, though, his confidence was beginning to waver. "If England and France do not run Mr. Lincoln's blockade," Cox now worried, "we see no means of cotton paying its debts." With their deep-seated belief in King Cotton shaken but not yet abandoned, the merchants of New Orleans responded as do many religious groups when their devotion is challenged: they adopted a more aggressive approach toward propagating the faith. By midsummer 1861, rather than worrying about the Union blockade's effects on the impending crop-marketing season, merchants proposed to finesse the issue by declaring a cotton embargo instead. (In some ways, the logic seems redolent of the famous retort, "You can't fire me – I quit!")[28]

In July 1861, representatives from the Southwest advanced the first cotton embargo proposals in the Confederate Congress. Rightly fearing that an official

[27] Russell, *My Diary North and South*, 118, 176, 231, 250. On the significance of secession's timing, see Henry Blumenthal, "Confederate Diplomacy: Popular Notions and International Realities," *Journal of Southern History* 32 (May 1966), 170.
[28] W[alter] Cox to W. E. Ashley, January 4 and July 8, 1861, Cox Papers, NOPL.

embargo policy would strike foreign governments as diplomatically coercive, however, the Davis administration managed to quash their plans. Taking these concerns into account, Louisiana's influential representative Duncan F. Kenner then offered a shrewd substitute proposal that would prohibit the shipment of cotton from the rural interior to southern port cities such as New Orleans affected by the blockade. The advantage of such a proposal was that it could be officially justified on grounds of military necessity: by keeping valuable crops scattered on the plantations, they would not be exposed to seizure en masse by Union attacks on southern ports. But Kenner intended for his proposal to have the same effect as an embargo, since crops obviously could not be shipped overseas unless they were first consolidated in coastal entrepôts. Kenner's clever plan would have permitted the Confederacy to gain the advantages of a more assertive approach to King Cotton diplomacy, even while its military rationale would allow the fledgling government to maintain a measure of plausible deniability with foreign powers as to their intentions. But even this roundabout means of declaring an embargo struck the cautious Davis administration as too confrontational, so Kenner's proposal was packed off to die in committee.[29]

Undeterred by the government's cool reception of their representative's scheme, the merchants of New Orleans were now inspired to take matters into their own hands. In late July, 130 of the city's most prominent cotton merchants – among them, the firms of Walter Cox and Copes & Phelps – issued a brief, remarkable circular published in the New Orleans commercial press. In it, the city's merchants collectively urged interior planters "not to ship any portion of their crops of Cotton" to New Orleans, and furthermore, they declared their intention to enforce their proclamation by refusing to receive any crops forwarded to the Crescent City. Less heedful of the diplomatic subtleties entailed in Kenner's proposal, the merchants' manifesto explicitly linked their demands to the Union naval cordon, insisting that the prohibition would not be lifted "until the blockade is fully and entirely abandoned." Although they stopped short of saying that their proclamation was designed to provide an incentive for England and France to come to the Confederacy's aid, the manner by which they invoked the blockade nevertheless made their goals quite clear. Since there was no reason that prohibiting cotton shipments to the city would cause the Union to forego its naval strategy, the merchants' action was evidently intended to compel European intervention.[30]

In New Orleans the diplomatic rationale behind the merchants' ban on cotton shipments to the city was clearly understood, even as references to it

[29] Raphael P. Thian, comp., *Extracts from the Journals of the Provisional Congress and of the First and Second Congresses of the Confederate States of America on Legislation Affecting Finance, Revenue, and Commerce, 1861–65* (Washington, DC, 1880), 46–7.

[30] New Orleans *Price-Current*, July 27, 1861; see also the notice in the New Orleans *Daily Picayune*, July 27, 1861. Interestingly, the signed circular was dated July 17; the ten-day delay probably indicates that the merchants refrained from publishing their statement pending the outcome of Kenner's similar proposal to the Confederate Congress.

remained oblique. In the same issue in which the factors' circular was first published, the local tri-weekly *Price-Current* coyly editorialized that "the objects
to be obtained by these apparently stringent regulations are so obvious that we
shall not refer to them." A few days later, at a large assembly of the city's business and political leaders to organize aid for the Confederate wounded, which
was held at the Merchants' Exchange on July 29, the ubiquitous Reverend
Benjamin M. Palmer offered his blessings to the factors' efforts. "Cotton gives
us immense power," Palmer declared to the gathered merchants, since "the
millions of Europe depend on it for their bread." Referring to the blockade,
Palmer concluded that "this war must soon terminate, or the civilized nations
of Europe must become engaged" on the South's behalf.[31]

Over the next few weeks, what one historian called the "decisive" leadership
role played in the South by the New Orleans merchant community became
apparent, as the cotton factors and associated companies of other southern
ports, such as Mobile, Savannah, and Charleston, quickly followed the Crescent
City's example. The de facto cotton embargo prompted by the merchants' circular was also greeted approvingly by planters. On August 7 the *Picayune*
reprinted a letter from a Louisiana planter to the factorage firm of Wright &
Allen. "Not a bale of cotton will be shipped until the blockade is raised," he
insisted. Claiming to speak for his neighbors, the planter emphasized their confidence in the advice of the city's merchants, "as we know they are as deeply
interested in the welfare of our country as we are."[32]

Yet a report in the same day's paper indicated that such confidence might
not be fully reciprocated. When they had gathered to approve the cotton circular, the city's merchants had also agreed to establish a "black book" in which
they would record all supply and cash advances made to interior planters. No
such public register of debts had previously been deemed necessary for the
largely informal antebellum system of seasonal credit, and adopting one now
offered another sign that the war might be undermining the trust on which
the long-standing planter–merchant alliance was based. Moreover, when the
harvest season began in late August, New Orleans merchants discovered that
they were also having trouble trusting each other. Aided by desperate plantation clients, some were conspiring to evade the prohibition by receiving cotton shipments anyway. Eager to nip this trade in the bud, in September some
ninety-odd factorage firms convinced the governor to criminalize the importation of cotton into the city. In contrast to their July circular, the merchants'
public letter to Moore did not mince words as to the reasons behind their
prohibition of cotton shipments from the interior. If not halted, the "injudicious conduct of the factors and planters" would only "contribute to the

---

[31] New Orleans *Price-Current*, July 27, 1861; New Orleans *Daily Picayune*, July 28 and 30, 1861
(Palmer quotations).
[32] "A Cotton Planter to His Factors," New Orleans *Daily Picayune*, August 7, 1861; Owsley, *King
Cotton Diplomacy*, 28–9 (quotation on p. 28).

maintenance of that quasi-neutrality which European nations have thought it proper to avow...."[33]

Despite scattered blockade-running, the efforts spearheaded by Crescent City merchants to withhold southern cotton from transatlantic markets were remarkably successful. One measure of their effectiveness was the striking decline in official receipts of cotton at the South's most important port during the fall of 1861. Over 1.8 million bales of cotton had been received at New Orleans during the 1860–1 crop season; the following year, the ban on cotton shipments from the interior reduced receipts to a mere 38,880 bales. After other southern ports followed New Orleans's lead, the prohibition had a similarly dramatic effect in reducing the amount of the South's total cotton crop able to reach overseas buyers: during the 1861–2 season, regional cotton exports to Europe dropped to around 1 percent of their normal level, according to one historian's recent estimate. Such figures reveal that New Orleans merchants had indeed managed to inspire a South-wide cotton embargo, even though it remained an officially unwelcome one.[34]

The question now became how the Great Powers, particularly England, would react to the unofficial embargo. Insights into the pressures shaping British diplomacy in 1861 can be gleaned from the columns of an unlikely special London correspondent for Horace Greeley's New York *Daily Tribune* that fall. In an October column for the *Tribune*, Karl Marx noted that "English merchants and manufacturers [had been] extremely slow and reluctant in acknowledging the awkward position of their cotton supplies" during the first half of 1861. "In the innermost recesses of the mercantile mind, the notion was cherished that the whole American crisis, and consequently the blockade, would have ceased before the end of the year," Marx reported. This belief, of course, was similarly dear to the "mercantile mind" in New Orleans, and its power on

[33] "Cotton Factors of New Orleans" to Governor T. O. Moore and Major General D. E. Twiggs, September 23, 1861; and undated proclamation [ca. late September 1861] of Governor Thomas O. Moore, both in *The War of the Rebellion: A Compilation of the Official Records of the Union and Confederate Armies* (Washington, DC, 1900–), Ser. III, Vol. 2, pp. 725–8 (hereinafter cited as *Official Records*); "The Cotton Factors' Movement," New Orleans *Daily Picayune*, August 7, 1861.

[34] Jeffrey Rogers Hummel, "Confederate Finance," in *Banking and Finance to 1913*, ed. Larry D. Schweikart (New York, 1990), 133. Figures on New Orleans cotton receipts are from *De Bow's Review*, 2nd ser., I (January 1866), 49, which is usually among the most reliable sources for such data. Other sources, however, estimated the city's 1861–2 cotton receipts as even lower; see, for example, the figures cited in Owsley, *King Cotton Diplomacy*, 42. Stephen R. Wise, *Lifeline of the Confederacy: Blockade Running during the Civil War* (Columbia, SC, 1988), 74–80. Some New Orleans merchants relocated to Matamoros, Mexico, during the war, where they profited handsomely exporting cotton to Great Britain at highly inflated prices. However, the extent of this trade was fairly minor; a liberal estimate places the total exports from Mexico between 1862 and 1865 at only 320,000 bales, which is less than a fifth of the cotton received annually at New Orleans during the 1850s; see James W. Daddysman, *The Matamoros Trade: Confederate Commerce, Diplomacy, and Intrigue* (Newark, DE, 1984), 61–3, 159–61.

both sides of the Atlantic had been reflected in the relative stability of market prices for cotton during the first several months of 1861. Late that summer, however, agents of New England textile mills appeared in Liverpool and began aggressively purchasing cotton for export back to the United States. British commercial reaction to this unprecedented reversal of transatlantic trade patterns (which was also noted with satisfaction by the New Orleans press) was swift. Marx reported in November that "the Liverpool cotton market has since been in a state of feverish excitement" since the Yankee buyers' arrival, which caused spot prices for cotton to increase nearly 50 percent over their midsummer levels; they would continue to rise through the war's end nearly four years later. But as the comforting notion of a rapid end to the war began falling by the wayside during the fall of 1861, it gradually became clearer that British intervention on behalf of the Confederacy was unlikely, due to considerations of diplomatic civility (the insulting appearance of coercion that inhered to the embargo), domestic political pressures (several generations of public antipathy toward chattel slavery), and even military worst-case scenarios (a possible retaliatory U.S. invasion of Canada).[35]

In light of the claims predicated on King Cotton's ostensible authority over transatlantic commerce, it is also worth stressing the economic reasons that the 1861–62 informal embargo failed to secure British intervention. First, and perhaps most importantly, the much anticipated "cotton famine" never really came to pass with anywhere near the expected force, since British mill-owners had managed to accumulate ample reserve stocks of cotton from the bumper crop of 1860. Furthermore, by the late 1850s many textile manufacturers were convinced that the industry was beginning to suffer a "crisis of overproduction," wherein their ability to churn out finished goods had outpaced demand for these products, especially in glutted overseas markets such as India. In that sense – as was unhelpfully pointed out in public by manufacturers' intellectual allies from the Manchester School of political economy – the southern cotton embargo should be endured, even welcomed, for effectively helping to winnow out weaker firms and reduce excess production capacity. Also contributing to British reluctance to intervene on the South's behalf was the country's growing dependence on King Cotton's northern cousins: wheat, corn, and other grains imported from the United States. Although there were other foreign sources of

---

[35] Karl Marx, "The British Cotton Trade" (September 21, 1861), repr. in Marx, *On America and the Civil War*, ed. and trans. Saul K. Padover (New York, 1972), 62–5 (quotations on pp. 62–3); Marx, "The Crisis in England" (November 1, 1861), in ibid., 81; New Orleans *Daily Picayune*, October 23, 1861. As early as 1856, northerner Stephen Colwell had argued that the South would be foolish to expect British military intervention because of cotton supplies; Colwell, *The South: A Letter from a Friend in the North, with Special Reference to the Effects of Disunion upon Slavery* (Philadelphia, 1856), 31–7. On cotton prices during 1861 see Surdam, *Northern Naval Superiority*, 124, 128–9 (Table 10.2). R. J. M. Blackett, *Divided Hearts: Britain and the American Civil War* (Baton Rouge, 2001); D. P. Crook, *The North, the South, and the Powers, 1861–1865* (New York and other cities, 1974).

grain supplies, any shortfalls provoked by a sudden withdrawal of the American portion would have imperiled the stability of prices at the least, and European governments had learned from experience that tampering with food supplies was one of the surest recipes for political disaster. Another important consideration was the enormous amount of British capital invested in the United States. Most of these investments were concentrated in the Northeast and Midwest, particularly in public debt instruments and capital-intensive enterprises such as the burgeoning railroad system. In a related vein, it is worth mentioning that the powerful British banking community clustered in London had suffered some notable financial reverses in the antebellum South. The city of New Orleans itself had nearly defaulted on its municipal-bond obligations a decade before, only to be bailed out by the House of Baring. But the memory that probably most rankled London bankers was the state of Mississippi's arrogant public repudiation of its mostly foreign-held bonded debt in the 1850s – an action that had been staunchly backed at the time by none other than its then-Senator Jefferson Davis.[36]

Undoubtedly, the highwater mark of possible British intervention was the *Trent* affair during the final two months of 1861. For several weeks beginning in late November, the U.S. Navy's provocative seizure of two Confederate commissioners (one of whom was Louisiana's John Slidell) from a British vessel, the *Trent*, provided grist for the pro-southern propaganda mill in England. Unsurprisingly, this agitation was most intense in Liverpool, a port city whose venerable community of merchant capitalists were not only concerned to resume the flow of southern cotton supplies, but whose former leading role in the international slave trade had left many businessmen reconciled to the South's peculiar institution. With patriotic fervor inflamed by the Americans' violation of British maritime sovereignty, on November 27 the Liverpool cotton exchange was the site of a raucous "indignation meeting" presided over by

---

[36] On most of these points there exists considerable historical literature. On the cotton famine see Eugene A. Brady. "A Reconsideration of the Lancashire 'Cotton Famine,'" *Agricultural History* 37 (October 1963), 156–62; and Van Mitchel Smith, "British Business Relations with the Confederacy, 1861–1865" (Ph.D. diss., University of Texas, 1949), 91–3. On the "crisis of overproduction" in British textiles see Gavin Wright, *The Political Economy of the Cotton South: Households, Markets, and Wealth in the Nineteenth Century* (New York, 1978), 96; and Farnie, *English Cotton Industry and the World Market*, 141–70. On the importance of U.S. grain exports to England see Louis B. Schmidt, "The Influence of Wheat and Cotton on Anglo-American Relations during the Civil War," *Iowa Journal of History and Politics* 16 (July 1918), 400–39; and Crook, *North, South, and the Great Powers*, 268–72. On British investments in the U.S. see Leland H. Jenks, *The Migration of British Capital to 1875* (New York and London, 1927); and William G. Roy, *Socializing Capital: The Rise of the Large Industrial Corporation in America* (Princeton, NJ, 1997), 110, 126–7, 135–40. On the difficulties of London-based banks in the antebellum South, see Hidy, *House of Baring in American Trade*, esp. Part III; on Louisiana and Mississippi see ibid., 330–37, 429–30; and Lebergott, "Why the South Lost," 68. With the exception of this last point, each of these factors also found contemporary expression in Karl Marx's published reports on English attitudes toward the American Civil War.

James Spence, a young merchant who had just published a tract arguing for a pro-southern tilt to British foreign policy, pointing to the recently enacted Morrill Tariff to prove that it was now U.S. policy to "exclude our manufactures ... and monopolize the Southern trade." At the meeting, Spence easily secured the support of Liverpool's cotton merchants for an angry resolution calling on Her Majesty's government to retaliate against the United States for the *Trent* seizures – and in the course of such a reprisal, the merchants also clearly wanted the Royal Navy to breach the Union blockade of New Orleans and other southern ports. Instead, after several weeks of tension, the British government allowed the Lincoln administration to extricate itself from the diplomatic crisis without serious consequences.[37]

Even as its hopes for an end to British neutrality were being raised by the *Trent* affair, however, the Confederate government's cautious stance toward brandishing cotton as a diplomatic weapon remained official policy. In December, Judah P. Benjamin, then serving as Secretary of War, contacted Governor Moore about his support of the New Orleans factors' ban on cotton shipments to the city. Following a lead set by President Davis in his November address to the Confederate Congress, Benjamin adopted a stance of willful ignorance toward the de facto embargo, simply refusing to acknowledge its clear intention to provoke European intervention against the blockade, even though this rationale had been explicitly stated in the factors' public letter endorsed by Governor Moore in September. However, the secretary had apparently gotten wind of Moore's new "pass system," which the governor had proclaimed in conjunction with his agreement to criminalize cotton shipments to the city. This system restricted vessels from leaving the port and running the blockade without official authorization. This smacked too much of a state-sanctioned embargo, so Benjamin reminded Moore that the Confederate government had "hitherto refused to interfere with shipments of produce of all kinds from our ports." In replying his compliance in January, Moore also avoided any reference to the de facto embargo or the reasons behind it.[38]

[37] Marx's account of the Liverpool merchants' meeting on November 27 relied on descriptions from the mainstream English press; see his columns reprinted as "The *Trent* Affair" in Padover, ed., 112–32, esp. 117–18. James Spence, *The American Union* (London, 1861), 30 (quotation), 305–15. Spence would later serve briefly as a commercial agent for the Confederacy, but ironically, he ran afoul of John Slidell; see Todd, *Confederate Finance*, 177–83. For Liverpool's continuing support for overseas slavery during the nineteenth century, see Eric Williams, *Capitalism and Slavery* (1944; repr., Chapel Hill and London, 1994), 161–3.

[38] J. P. Benjamin to Thomas O. Moore, December 24, 1861, in *Official Records*, Ser. IV, Vol. 1, p. 814; Thomas O. Moore to Hon. J. P. Benjamin, January 9, 1862, in ibid., pp. 836–7. Although Benjamin's letters clearly demonstrate that the cotton embargo was never officially sanctioned by the Confederate government, there was confusion on the issue among contemporaries and historians alike. In a November 1861 article published in *Die Presse*, for example, Karl Marx reported that "the Confederacy lends compelling force to [the] blockade with its decision not to export a bale of cotton of its own accord...."; Marx, "Crisis in England," in Padover, ed., *On America and the Civil War*, 80; see also Phillip E. Myers, *Caution and Cooperation: The American Civil War in British-American Relations* (Kent, OH, 2008), 53. Details about

At the same time, the planter-governor took a pointed swipe at the mercantile community of New Orleans, where Benjamin himself had established his fortunes. "[T]his is a city of cotton speculators of all nationalities," he explained, "who care but little for any consideration not immediately affecting results in profits." Moore's cutting remark exemplified the growing stress between New Orleans merchants and their plantation clientele as the new year began. Fierce battles over a "Cotton Planters' Relief Bill" in the legislature dominated Louisiana politics in January 1862. Although in some ways similar to the Confederate produce-loan program, the proposed legislation went considerably further, providing for an issue of $7 million in state treasury notes to serve as an immediately useable currency in exchange for planters' pledged crops. The initial vote in favor of the proposal revealed a stark division between city and countryside, with the sizeable Orleans Parish delegation unanimously opposed. The mercantile community now vigorously urged Governor Moore to veto the bill. The governor was himself a plantation owner, however, and the previous November, he had proposed "stay laws" intended to prevent debt foreclosures, another unpopular measure with merchants. Still, Moore usually seemed well disposed toward city interests and was known to keep close company with several influential New Orleans merchants. The British journalist William Howard Russell had repeated rumors that Moore was "somewhat under the influence of the Hebrews," men such as Aristide Miltenberger, a prominent city merchant and bank director. Miltenberger, who was the planter-governor's factor, personally lobbied Moore to veto "the stay law and Planters' relief bills," claiming that "every man I have spoken to is heart and soul opposed" to the proposals. For a few tense weeks, New Orleans merchants kept up a steady drumbeat of opposition to the bills in the press, until Governor Moore finally vetoed the planters' relief measure on January 21. However, he did approve the new stay laws, despite opposition to these debt-relief measures among both city and interior merchants.[39]

These legislative controversies between planters and merchants contributed to an inauspicious opening of the war's second year in Louisiana. Doubts about the likelihood of foreign intervention became endemic after the disappointing resolution of the *Trent* affair, and having sacrificed an entire marketing season upon the diplomatic altar of King Cotton, some of these doubts

Governor Moore's pass system in the fall of 1861 are sketchy and drawn mainly from the hostile and perhaps inaccurate account provided by Union general Benjamin F. Butler during his tenure in New Orleans the following year; see Butler to Edwin M. Stanton, October [n.d.], 1862, in *Official Records*, Ser. III, Vol. 2, pp. 721–2.

39 New Orleans *Daily Picayune*, January 5, 22, and 24, 1862; Aristide Miltenberger to Governor T. O. Moore, January 14, 1862, in Box 1, Folder 39, Kuntz Civil War Collection, Woodson Research Center, Rice University, Houston, TX; Russell, *My Diary North and South*, 242; message from Governor Thomas O. Moore, November 26, 1861, in *Official Journal of the House of Representatives of the State of Louisiana, Session of November 1861* (Baton Rouge, 1861), 5–6.

now extended to the continued wisdom of the self-imposed cotton embargo. The New Orleans *Picayune* published a long, torturous rationale for abandoning the embargo in February 1862, and comparable intellectual gymnastics were evident in that long-time bully pulpit for King Cotton, *De Bow's Review*. Using the same striking turn of phrase that Walter Cox had employed privately the year before, New Orleans commission merchant J. B. Gribble began an article that spring by professing his "abiding faith in the potent influence of 'King Cotton,'" even while also admitting that he "had anticipated an earlier movement" against the blockade by European powers. Skirting around the de facto embargo endorsed by his own firm the previous summer, Gribble now declared his opposition to "any legislative or conventional action" designed to "[make] other nations feel the want" of southern cotton. "Nothing could be more impolitic," the merchant insisted. "It is clearly in our interest to supply the general demand [for cotton], at a fair and remunerative price."[40]

Pessimistic conclusions about the embargo also gained currency among the most elite members of Louisiana's commercial community: the bankers of New Orleans. Edmond J. Forstall, whose global connections had made him the most prominent representative of the city's powerful banks ever since the 1830s, had first evinced skepticism toward the Great Powers' ability to break the Union blockade during his June 1861 visit with the British journalist William Howard Russell. In January 1862 a gloomy report from Robert M. Davis, the president of the Bank of Louisiana, was forwarded to the government at Richmond. Having spent the previous summer and fall touring Europe, Davis maintained that "our people should not look to any foreign power for relief from the evils of the blockade." Davis argued that the South had "ample means" to reopen its seaports, and he urged the Confederate government to quickly direct resources toward this end. Like Gribble, he now believed all attempts at relieving the worsening economic crisis "must prove futile without opening a market for the sale of our products." The influential banker's discouraging estimate of the unlikelihood of European intervention on the South's behalf indicated that the Crescent City's assertive promotion of King Cotton diplomacy should probably be abandoned.[41]

The embargo also prompted increasing divisiveness among New Orleans merchants during the spring of 1862. A surge of violations of the state-sanctioned ban on cotton shipments compelled Governor Moore to stiffen the criminal penalties for receiving such shipments. These violations also helped prompt New Orleans municipal authorities to form a "Committee on Public

---

[40] J. B. Gribble, "The Cotton Interest, and Its Relation to the Present Crisis," *De Bow's Review* 32 (March/April 1862), 279–86 (quotations on pp. 279, 280–1, 284); "Cotton Exports and Permits," New Orleans *Daily Picayune*, February 7, 1862; see also the similar stance adopted by the New Orleans *Daily Crescent* as discussed in Surdam, *Northern Naval Superiority*, 59–60 and 239 n. 7.

[41] R. M. Davis to J. M. Gladney, January 14, 1862, in *Official Records*, Ser. IV, Vol. 1, pp. 892–3; Russell, *My Diary North and South*, 254, 259–60.

Safety" in late February. This committee of sixty-three citizens, many of whom were prominent bankers (such as R. M. Davis) or merchants (such as Walter Cox), was granted extraordinary powers to assist in the city's defense, a broadly defined goal that included securing outside provisions as well as enforcing the ban on cotton shipments to New Orleans. Aware that such a powerful unelected body smacked of vigilantism, Governor Moore defended them to President Davis as "not a secret organization, but a well-known public association of patriotic and influential citizens." Moore's unsolicited defense implicitly acknowledged the emergence of often-violent conspiratorial enclaves in the months before the city's surrender. New Orleans politics had already earned a reputation for the incidence of "mob rule" manipulated from above during the 1850s, and the war only exacerbated this tendency for extralegal intrigues. In mid-March the Confederate general Mansfield Lovell justified his declaration of martial law in the city by alluding to threats posed by elite-directed factions. Others would later claim that these "secret, diligent, and fierce" elements continued to wield a "rod of terror" even after Lovell's declaration.[42]

As the Union fleet drew closer in April, many businessmen closed up their offices and deserted the city. Those who remained faced a desperate situation, sometimes with near-comic determination. George Washington Cable later drily described the "array of old men" who had marched down the "neutral ground" of Canal Street in a semblance of military drills. "The merchants, bankers, underwriters, judges, real-estate owners, and capitalists of the Anglo-American part of the city," he remembered. "This was the flower of the home guard." Others, however, did not comport themselves with such grim dignity and instead took to quarrelling among themselves. Many retailers stopped accepting Confederate notes, thereby incurring the wrath of the Committee on Public Safety, and threats of mob violence were directed toward city exchange brokers. But the city's plight with regard to foodstuffs prompted the most concern during the weeks prior to the fall. The few commodities that remained by April were the subject of rampant speculation and price-gouging, and Cable later recalled how merchants "turned upon each other" in ugly battles over dwindling stocks of food. President Davis was warned on April 17 that the city was on "the verge of a bread famine," and Governor Moore urged him to support relief plans organized by the merchant-led Committee on Public Safety, though he also felt it necessary to assure the president that "there are no speculators among them."[43]

[42] Cable, "New Orleans before the Capture," 18; General Mansfield Lovell to Judah P. Benjamin, March 22, 1862, in *Official Records*, Ser. I, Vol. 6, pp. 864–6; Thomas O. Moore to President Davis, April 17, 1862, in *Official Records*, Ser. I, Vol. 53, p. 801; Resolution of the New Orleans Common Council, February 20, 1862, in *Official Records*, Ser. III, Vol. 2, pp. 728–9; Bragg, *Louisiana in the Confederacy*, 82. The domination of municipal politics by competing bands of "Thugs" had been described to the British journalist William Howard Russell during his May 1861 visit to New Orleans; see Russell, *My Diary North and South*, 252.

[43] Thomas O. Moore to President [Jefferson] Davis, April 17, 1862, in *Official Records*, Ser. 1, Vol. 53, pp. 801–2; H. M. Spofford to Jefferson Davis, April 17, 1862, in ibid., p. 802; Resolutions

A week later, on April 24, Union ships passed the fortifications below New Orleans. That night, some 15,000 bales of cotton on the levees were set afire, and much of the business district was looted as well. Although the city's banks managed to ship out several million dollars' worth of specie before the occupation, skirmishes were reported between mobs and the Foreign Brigade, which was composed largely of European merchants trying to protect their property. Later reports claimed that a number of "frenzied women and spoliating rowdies" had been prepared to torch the whole city rather than concede it to the Federals, although there were probably not many gentleman-merchants among those two groups. A week later, after protracted negotiations, New Orleans was surrendered to Union forces.[44]

Considering the fall of New Orleans from exile in London, Karl Marx echoed the judgment of his colleague Friedrich Engels that "the moral effect [of the fall of New Orleans] on the Confederates was evidently enormous, and the material effect will have already made itself felt." But both men were mostly mistaken, and on both counts. In terms of its "material effects," the gradual pincer movement of Union forces from above and below had already prevented the city from making any further contribution to the war effort. Even more important, as historian David Surdam has pointed out, the fall of New Orleans relieved the overburdened Confederate government at Richmond of an enormous logistical "headache." Indeed, for several months the Davis administration had acted as if a choice had been made to devote scarce resources to the Confederacy's scattered, overextended armies rather than trying to feed thousands of sedentary residents in the Crescent City. Why not let the hated Federals provision them instead?

Engels was closer to the mark about the depressing "moral effect" that New Orleans' surrender had on the Confederacy, and Marx cited several gloomy accounts in that vein from the southern press. But again, both men missed the main point. The fall of New Orleans actually constituted more of a boost to northern morale than it represented a blow to the South's, and furthermore, its effects in European diplomatic circles on perceptions of the Confederacy's diminishing prospects were of even greater importance. Still, it is true that most Confederate supporters were not pleased about the turn of events in New Orleans. In France, John Slidell was quite distraught, calling the city's

---

of the Common Council of New Orleans, March 22, 1862, in *Official Records*, Ser. 4, Vol. 1, pp. 1013–14; "The Brokers," New Orleans *Daily Picayune*, March 9, 1862; Bragg, *Louisiana in the Confederacy*, 72; Cable, "New Orleans Before the Capture," 15–17 (quotations on p. 15).

[44] James Parton, *General Butler in New Orleans; Being a History of the Administration of the Department of the Gulf in the Year 1862* (New York, 1864), 63 (quotation); Capers, *Occupied City*, 44–5; Todd, *Confederate Finance*, 174; Schwab, *Confederate States of America*, 142–4. Some accounts imply that General Lovell gave an order to set fire to the cotton on April 24–5, which would have been within his discretionary authority, yet this seems to be contradicted by the timing of his dispatches with Richmond; see the various letters between April 25 and May 4 in *Official Records*, Ser. I, Vol. 6, pp. 883–5.

fall "disastrous" in a mid-May letter to Judah Benjamin. Although there is no record of his reaction, Benjamin was probably just as dismayed as Slidell. Even though he had presided over the policy of benign neglect that contributed to the city's fatal isolation during his ill-fated tenure as Secretary of War, Benjamin had first established his reputation in New Orleans's commercial community, and his mansion there, in which his sisters resided, was seized during the Federal occupation.[45]

The "moral effects" of the city's surrender were obviously "enormous" in New Orleans itself; indeed, the city would display the collective psychic scars of the Federal occupation a bit too prominently on its sleeve for decades to come. But attitudes in the city toward the Confederate government were affected as well. General Lovell had sent his 3,000-odd troops packing during the night as the Union fleet approached, which infuriated the citizens thus abandoned. The diary of Julia LeGrand, the daughter of a successful Louisiana planter and a New Orleans resident, offers insights into the reactions prompted by the city's surrender:

We Confederates of New Orleans consider that Louisiana has been neglected by our Government; ... [C]oward 'New Orleans' is the cry. There were no troops left to defend New Orleans, though such an important point. We had no soldiers except the "Confederate Guard," a sort of holiday regiment composed of all the well-to-do gentlemen of the city, who were anxious to show their patriotism on the parade ground, but who never expected to fight. The pomp and circumstance they kept up finely.... [T]hese were our defenders, and General Lovell was given to feasting with them. They were called his pets. When the forts fell ... [they] made haste to pack away their epaulettes and become the most unassuming of citizens on a moment's notice.... Congress was appealed to again and again, but the President and House seemed to keep up a hardened blindness as to its condition.

One should not underestimate the intelligence, political awareness, and fighting spirit of pro-Confederate women such as Julia LeGrand during the Civil War. In occupied New Orleans, such women would soon become notorious for their provocations of Federal troops and officers.[46]

LeGrand's diary entry exemplifies the anger felt by many residents toward the Davis administration, but it is just as interesting for the hostility displayed by this daughter of the southern plantation elite toward the gentleman capitalists of the Crescent City. It is worth keeping this hostility in mind when evaluating the justice of her feelings toward the Confederate government. Could the Davis administration's "hardened blindness" toward New Orleans' plight been in

---

[45] Meade, *Judah P. Benjamin*, 273–5; Slidell to Benjamin, May 14, 1862, quoted in Sears, *John Slidell*, 192; Capers, *Occupied City*, 52; Surdam, *Northern Naval Superiority*, 60; Marx, "The English Press and the Fall of New Orleans," in Marx and Engels, *Civil War in the United States*, 180–83; Engels to Marx, May 23, 1862, in ibid., 243.

[46] Kate Mason Rowland and Mrs. Morris L. Croxall, eds., *The Journal of Julia LeGrand: New Orleans, 1862–1863* (Richmond, VA, 1911), 80–2.

part a reflection of similar sentiments at the upper reaches of the Confederacy? Again, the tone and substance of reactions from Richmond during the months preceding the city's fall seem to indicate that a decision had been made at some point to allow the Federals to take New Orleans. But even if this was strategically sound and necessary, it still seems to have been a curiously easy choice for officials to make. It was more than the logistical problems that the city presented. There was also the barely articulated sense that New Orleans was somehow a little bit disloyal, and much too enamored of the Yankee values of mammon. (The harsh treatment meted out to the Confederate government's most prominent New Orleans representative, Judah P. Benjamin, was typical of these sentiments – just substitute anti-Semitic prejudices for anti-northern ones.) The city had been a step too slow to embrace secession, its banks too arrogant in their disdain for the national interest, and its merchants too quick to meddle in foreign policy. Especially in terms of the latter, one could see how some might have regarded the city's occupation to be just deserts for its overly aggressive promotion of King Cotton diplomacy. Less than a year after the war began, then, the agricultural region's only true metropolis had precious few champions left in the Confederate government – the only authority that really counted – or for that matter, even around the South more generally.

And what "moral effects" did New Orleans' fall have among the city's merchant capitalists – men such as Joseph Slemmons Copes, Walter Cox, Aristide Miltenberger, and Edmond Forstall? The psychological toll on such men of commerce must have been profound. It was not so much the actual property being destroyed – after all, 15,000 bales of cotton was nothing compared with the millions of bales they had shepherded through the port during the decades of New Orleans' dominant role in the Atlantic cotton trade. In the end, the epic scene was probably more devastating to merchants for what it symbolized: the immolation of "King Cotton" upon his riverfront throne in the heart of his sturdiest urban redoubt. Yet some of these same merchants might also have paused to consider that, in fact, all might not be lost. Europe would still need to buy cotton, regardless of the government that ruled over New Orleans. The coming Federal occupation, however distasteful, might at least serve to reestablish some of their former connections with commercial networks in the Northeast. Turning away from the depressing scene on the levee, some might have returned to their shuttered offices to calculate the possibilities – already thinking to themselves, as Julia LeGrand would write in her diary several months later, that "King Cotton dethroned must mount again."[47]

---

[47] Rowland and Croxall, eds. *Journal of Julia LeGrand*, 82.

5

Bankers and Merchants in Occupied New Orleans

The Butler Regime

Among the witnesses to the cotton-torching on the New Orleans levee in late April 1862 was a Cuban-born émigré named Loretta Janeta Velazquez. In an 1876 memoir she recalled the "terribly magnificent spectacle," writing that "it fairly made me shudder to see millions of dollars worth of property being utterly destroyed in this reckless manner." Velazquez showed similar sensitivity to the economic dimensions of the war throughout her memoir. In a chapter about the lucrative wartime contraband trade, for example, she discussed the collusion of Confederate agents with northern mercantile firms, which she insisted was only the tip of an iceberg. "In fact," Velazquez declared, "there is a secret history of the war, records of which have never been committed to paper, and which exists only in the memories of a limited number of people." However, because many war profiteers remained prominent in the business circles of both sections when she composed her memoir, Velazquez believed it unlikely that "this secret history will ever be written out with any degree of fullness...."[1]

Shorn of its conspiratorial overtones, the pro-Confederate Velazquez's comment finds considerable expression in the history of New Orleans during the Civil War and Reconstruction, beginning during the city's eight-month occupation under Union general Benjamin F. Butler. After New Orleans was surrendered to Union forces in late April 1862, some hoped its long-standing role as a commercial fulcrum from which thousands of northern-born residents helped

---

[1] Loretta Janeta Velazquez, *The Woman in Battle: A Narrative of the Exploits, Adventures, and Travels of Madame Loretta Janeta Velazquez....* (Hartford, CT, 1876), 236 (first quotation), and chap. 39 (quotations on p. 459). Some historians have questioned the veracity of Velazquez's account, but see the recent scholarly defense by DeAnne Blanton and Lauren M. Cook, *They Fought Like Demons: Women Soldiers in the American Civil War* (Baton Rouge, 2002), 179–83.

facilitate massive intersectional flows of capital, commodities, and credit would help ease the city's transition back to a federal regime. However, that did not prove to be the case. Butler, the Massachusetts commander appointed to administer the occupied city, was one of Lincoln's "political generals." An opportunistic Democrat known for his recent conversion to the antislavery cause, the demagogic Butler lacked subtlety and tact, to put it mildly. During his eight-month tenure over New Orleans, he refused to extend an olive branch to the city's "old gentlemen of commerce"; instead, he targeted them as implacable foes, disregarding any influence they might have contributed to federal efforts to promote Unionism and restore commerce. In addition, Loretta Velazquez was only one among many contemporaries, southern and northern alike, who condemned the interbelligerent trade that General Butler fostered in conjunction with his brother Andrew, who accompanied him to New Orleans. Probably to avoid appearing to endorse the pro-Confederate sentiments long intertwined with the furious character of local accounts of the Crescent City's early occupation, historians have seemed loath to acknowledge the character or effects of Butler's corrupt regime. But despite its relative brevity, "Beast" (or "Spoons") Butler's tenure over the city ultimately had important local, regional, national, and transatlantic consequences for the cotton trade.[2]

When General Butler assumed command over New Orleans in early May 1862, commercial matters stood high among his priorities. Although the arrival of U.S. forces helped alleviate food shortages that had plagued the city for months, Butler and his troops were mostly greeted with hostility rather than gratitude. During the early weeks of the occupation, Butler responded forcefully to expressions of resistance to federal authority, most notoriously with his "woman order" on May 15. However, he also sought to curb forms of resistance that interfered with his commercial goals. For example, many Crescent City shopkeepers refused to open their shops, so one of Butler's first acts was to order them to resume business or face a hundred-dollar fine. But merchants were slow to obey. In June businessmen were reportedly still "lolling listlessly about," and that fall an English visitor described merchants who "lounged about their empty stores ... until about 2 PM ... and then went home to curse the common foe in peace."[3]

---

[2] Despite his long, fascinating career, Butler's unpleasant character has presented a challenge for biographers, which helps explain why no major study of him has appeared for nearly forty years. The best remains Hans L. Trefousse, *Ben Butler: The South Called Him Beast!* (New York, 1957). On Butler's late but typically attention-grabbing conversion to the cause of slave emancipation, see ibid., 79–84. By 1860 northern consumption of cotton represented nearly a quarter of the southern crop; see *De Bow's Review* 32 (January/February 1862), 122. The rate of domestic growth in cotton consumption had outpaced that of England and France during the 1850s, helping to maintain the upward pressure on market prices during that decade; see David G. Surdam, *Northern Naval Superiority and the Economics of the Civil War* (Columbia, SC, 2001), 142–3.

[3] W. C. Corsan, *Two Months in the Confederate States: An Englishman's Travels Through the South*, ed. Benjamin H. Trask (1863; repr., Baton Rouge and London, 1996), 18; New Orleans *True Delta*, June 21, 1862, quoted in Elisabeth Joan Doyle, "Greenbacks, Car Tickets, and the

Petty shopkeepers, however, were a minor consideration. What Butler had in mind was a resumption of agricultural commerce, especially cotton. He was well aware that more than 2 million bales had passed through the city in 1860 – roughly half the South's entire crop. Butler's desire to restore the cotton trade was not an objective shared by the War Department to which he answered (nor would it ever be, since there was little to recommend it on military grounds), but it was a goal he shared with Secretary of State William Seward, who, despite his distaste for the demagogic Butler, had been ballyhooing the capture of New Orleans as a means of liberating cotton to U.S. diplomatic advantage for several months. But regardless of the appearances thereby engendered, it would be misleading to characterize Union actions as a "cotton grab." Plans to seize New Orleans had been underway since the fall of 1861 and were consistent with its strategy of controlling the Mississippi River. Moreover, Union officials must have known that there was simply not much cotton to be had in New Orleans proper. Apart from the bales burned on the levee prior to the arrival of Federal forces, the embargo on cotton shipments to the city spearheaded by merchants the previous summer had been effective, so the vast majority of the 1861 crop was still being held on interior plantations. If Butler were to restore the cotton trade, he thus had two choices. He could muster his troops and venture into the hostile Louisiana countryside where most cotton was being held. But Butler was not yet authorized to conduct extensive military operations, so the other option was to make the cotton come to him in New Orleans.[4]

Thus commenced the slippery slope of interbelligerent commerce in the Department of the Gulf. Having barely unpacked his bags, Butler tried to

Pot of Gold: The Effects of Wartime Occupation on the Business Life of New Orleans, 1861–1865," *Civil War History* 5 (December 1959), 349; Marion Southwood, *Beauty and Booty: The Watchword of New Orleans* (New York, 1867), 61; Clara Solomon, *The Civil War Diary of Clara Solomon: Growing Up in New Orleans, 1861–1862*, ed. Elliott Ashkenazi (Baton Rouge, 1995), 362; New Orleans *Delta*, May 1, 1862, quoted in [Appleton's] *American Annual Cyclopedia and Register of Important Events of the Year 1862* (New York, 1865), 646 (cited hereinafter as *Appleton's Cyclopedia for 1862*). The *Delta* and the *True Delta* were separate New Orleans newspapers; the former would serve as the semi-official press organ of Union authorities during the occupation years. James Parton, *General Butler in New Orleans; Being a History of the Administration of the Department of the Gulf in the Year 1862* (New York, 1864), 107. This book, written in close cooperation with Butler, was largely intended to defend the general against various charges that had arisen from his eight-month rule over New Orleans.
4 On the genesis of Union naval plans to attack New Orleans and their approval by the Lincoln administration during the fall of 1861, see the detailed account, "The Opening of the Lower Mississippi," by U.S. naval commander David D. Porter, in *Battles and Leaders of the Civil War*, eds. Robert U. Johnson and Clarence C. Buel (4 vols., 1887; repr., New York, 1956), II, chap. 3. In the years after the occupation of New Orleans, Porter became one of the most outspoken critics of interbelligerent commerce in the lower Mississippi Valley, especially the effects of the illicit cotton trade on military discipline. For Seward's expectations with regard to the fall of New Orleans, see *Appleton's Cyclopedia for 1862*, pp. 227–8, 382–3; and D. P. Crook, *The North, the South, and the Powers, 1861–1865* (New York and other cities, 1974), 197–8; on the tepid official British response see Howard Jones, *Union in Peril: The Crisis over British Intervention in the Civil War* (Chapel Hill, 1992), 119–21, 146.

convince planters of his good intentions to buy their cotton, declaring that "all cargoes of cotton and sugar shall receive safe conduct" and their owners "allowed to return" from the occupied city. Although Butler's assurances of safe conduct had little immediate effect among Louisiana planters, Governor Thomas O. Moore realized the temptation might overwhelm considerations of regional loyalty, so from his refuge in Opelousas, he officially forbade such relations. "Trading with the enemy is prohibited under all circumstances," the governor declared. "We cannot exchange our corn, cattle, sugar, or cotton for their gold." These strictures prompted the *Picayune* to complain that the city was being "subjected to a sort of double siege."[5]

Despite its "natural" advantages, New Orleans represented more than just a convenient locale; much of the city's disproportionate influence over agriculture in the Mississippi Valley was based on its interlocked financial and marketing institutions. To make commerce "flow again in its ordinary channels," a more prudent commander would have sought allies among this residual institutional framework. But instead, Butler assumed a hostile posture toward the Crescent City business community – a stance first evident in his dealings with city banks. Antebellum New Orleans had been home to the best-capitalized cluster of banks in the South, ranked nationally behind only New York's. These banks had a reputation as the most conservatively managed in the country, and their overarching concern for stability had been reflected in their cool reception of the secession movement in 1860–1. Most suspicions about the loyalty of the city's business community could be attributed to the aloof attitudes of its bankers, and indeed, if any group in the mercantile structure might have been disposed toward cooperation with Union authorities, New Orleans bankers would have topped the list. Only eight months before had they grudgingly revised their financial policies to offer support for the Confederacy, and then only after being publicly upbraided by Treasury Secretary Memminger. But despite their lukewarm support for secession, Butler did not approach the city's bankers as potential allies. Because he considered New Orleans to be "the banking-house of the rebellion," he tailored his policies accordingly.[6]

5 New Orleans *Daily Picayune*, July 2, 1862; address of Governor Thomas O. Moore to the People of Louisiana, June 18, 1862, in *Official Records*, Ser. I, Vol. 15, pp. 504–10 (quotations on pp. 504–5, 509); *Appleton's Cyclopedia for 1862*, pp. 228, 648; General Orders No. 20 (May 3, 1862) and General Order No. 22 (May 4, 1862), repr. in *Private and Official Correspondence of Gen. Benjamin F. Butler During the Period of the Civil War*, comp. Jessie Ames Marshall (5 vols.; Norwood, MA, 1917), I, 442–3 (cited hereinafter as *Butler Correspondence*).

6 Benjamin F. Butler to Colonel Halbert E. Paine, August 19, 1862, in *Official Records*, Ser. I, Vol. 15, p. 553 (quotation); Douglas B. Ball, *Financial Failure and Confederate Defeat* (Urbana and Chicago, 1991), 164–6. For comparative data on Louisiana's dozen state-chartered banks, all headquartered in New Orleans, see the "General Statement of the Condition of the Banks of the United States" in *Appleton's Cyclopedia for 1861*, p. 462. On New Orleans' dominant position relative to other antebellum southern urban markets see Harold D. Woodman, *King Cotton and His Retainers: Financing and Marketing the Cotton Crop of the South, 1800–1925* (Lexington, KY, 1968), esp. chap. 2; David Goldfield, "Cities in the Old South," in Goldfield, *Region, Race,*

Heartened by Butler's early promises as to the sanctity of property, New Orleans bankers designated a committee to establish his willingness to work with them. Despite his seizures of gold from local banks a few days before, this committee met with the general on May 12. Their discussion that day centered on the status of several million dollars' worth of bullion reserves that the banks had shipped out before the city's occupation. It is worth digressing a moment to discuss these missing specie reserves, aspects of which have remained mysterious. The most intriguing discrepancy concerns their value. Most historians' estimates of the specie removed have ranged between $4 and $6 million. These estimates are usually derived from Confederate records of the monies from New Orleans banks that were secured (and eventually confiscated) by the southern government, which totaled about $5 million – a figure independently confirmed in a June 1862 letter from F. H. Hatch, the exiled Confederate customs collector at New Orleans. Since his figures were based on three shipments then in Confederate possession, his combined total of $4.7 million should represent a minimum baseline for the amount of specie removed from New Orleans. However, when the city's banks had suspended specie payments the previous fall, their collective reserves stood at $14.1 million – so if only $5 million was shipped to the Confederacy, where was the other $9 million? Alluding to this discrepancy, historian Douglas Ball claims the Confederacy "lost" not only its largest city in May 1862, but also "$8 million of gold and silver coin still in the banks' vaults." But there is no indication the banks still had this much bullion on hand after the occupation. In fact, it is likely that several banks had surreptitiously removed their specie reserves for private safekeeping earlier in the spring, when the city's fall was clearly imminent. This seems to be confirmed by an 1877 article in *Banker's Magazine*, which claimed that, besides the specie sent to the Confederacy, two other Crescent City banks had buried $4.5 million underground, and another had sent nearly a million to an unspecified site up the Red River. Estimates of the money shipped out before the surrender of New Orleans – an example of Loretta Velazquez's "secret history of the war" – should therefore be revised well upward, probably by a factor of two or more.[7]

***

and Cities: Interpreting the Urban South (Baton Rouge, 1997), 196–7; and Allan Pred, *Urban Growth and City-Systems in the United States, 1840–1860* (Cambridge, MA, 1980).

[7] "The Louisiana Bank Act of 1844," *Banker's Magazine*, 3d ser., 12 (November 1877), 353; Ball, *Financial Failure and Confederate Defeat*, 127–8 (quotation on p. 127) and Richard Cecil Todd, *Confederate Finance* (Athens, GA, 1954), 165, provide detailed estimates based on Confederate Treasury reports. Less documented but similar estimates can be found in John Christopher Schwab, *The Confederate States of America, 1861–1865: A Financial and Industrial History of the South during the Civil War* (New York, 1901), 142–3; Stephen A. Caldwell, *A Banking History of Louisiana* (Baton Rouge, 1935), 91; and Capers, *Occupied City*, 45. F. H. Hatch to General [P. G. T.] Beauregard, June 13, 1862, in *Official Records*, Ser. IV, Vol. 1, p. 1153; see also the independent confirmation for the Bank of Louisiana in R. M. Davis to W. H. Young, June 9, 1862, in ibid., p. 1148; and Table 9, "Confederate Specie Revenues," in Ball, op. cit., 124. New Orleans *Daily Delta*, May 1, 1862. On the gold seizures of May 10 see ibid., May 11 and 14, 1862.

In their May 12 meeting with Butler, the presidents of two of the city's oldest and largest banks claimed they had removed their specie not because of concerns over a restored federal regime, but rather to secure the funds from looting during a prolonged siege. Now that order had been restored, they said they were willing to retrieve the specie from behind Confederate lines, but emphasized that since it was now in areas "beyond [our] control," they could "only promise to use our best exertions for its return." Their promise to ensure the specie's return was an empty one, since they undoubtedly realized that the Confederate government would never ship it back to an area under Union control. However, they did make persistent pleas for the specie's return over the coming months, and Confederate officials were appalled by their "good faith" efforts, which Hatch considered "to the lasting shame of those gentlemen."[8]

In any case, General Butler was not mollified by these mild collaborationist gestures. He promised "safe conduct" if the banks could "bring back their specie, which they have so unadvisedly carried away," but with two crucial caveats. First, the general expected any specie returned to be "used ... to make good the obligations of the banks to their creditors"; and second, he emphasized that no funds were exempt from his mission to "retake, repossess, and occupy all ... property of the United States." These provisos hinted at the direction that Butler's policies toward the banks were about to take. As he wrote years later, Butler was convinced that "the certain confiscation of many millions of debts which the South owed to the North was a great inducement to the commercial classes of the South to go into the Rebellion," and his vow to reclaim all U.S. property "of whatever name and nature" reflected this view. The outstanding prewar debts of Crescent City firms to northern creditors were estimated to be around $30 million, and Butler considered it his duty to uphold these private claims aggressively against what he believed to be a widespread intention to repudiate their obligations. Butler also sought to "repossess" U.S. government property, including several hundred thousand dollars that had been seized from the New Orleans Custom-house, which he wrongly believed had been deposited in the city's banks.[9]

[8] F. W. Hatch to Gen. Beauregard, June 13, 1862, in *Official Records*, Ser. IV, Vol. 1, p. 1153. W. Newton Mercer and J. M. Lapeyre to Major-General [Benjamin F.] Butler, May 13, 1862, in *Official Records*, Ser. III, Vol. 2, pp. 129–30 (quotations on p. 129); New Orleans *Daily Delta*, May 13, 1862. Mercer was serving as acting president of the Bank of Louisiana, since its president, R. M. Davis, had decamped the city for Richmond. On pre-occupation removal efforts, see Governor Moore to President Davis, April 23, 1862, in *Official Records*, Ser. I, Vol. 53, p. 803. Though no specific instructions from General Lovell with regard to the banks' specie have survived, a subsequent letter, sent with Memminger's approval, indicates official involvement in at least some of its removal; see R. M. Davis to W. H. Young, June 9, 1862, in *Official Records*, Ser. IV, Vol. 1, p. 1148; see also the discussion in Ball, *Financial Failure and Confederate Defeat*, 127–8. Later that fall, the New Orleans banks proposed that England or France be allowed to hold their specie, but this idea was rejected by both Washington and Richmond; see *Butler Correspondence*, II, 517–18.

[9] For Butler's mistaken belief that U.S. government monies seized at New Orleans in early 1861 had been "paid into the Banks by the Secession authorities," see his letter to Secretary of War

The following week Butler dashed any residual optimism the bankers may have felt. Reneging on his earlier pledge to allow Confederate currencies to continue in circulation to prevent a severe monetary shortage, Butler reversed course and proclaimed "all circulation of ... Confederate notes and bills will cease within this department" on May 27. Bankers and citizens alike were greatly agitated by this order – the latter all the more so after banks took out advertisements advising customers to withdraw all funds deposited in Confederate notes or assume the risk of forfeiture under Butler's edict. An infuriated Butler considered this a ploy to shift the burden of his directive onto the backs of the public. On May 19 his wrath took the form of General Orders No. 30, a document as much an ideological salvo as it was a clarification of his preceding order. Butler accused the banks of causing "great distress, privation, suffering, hunger, and even starvation" in New Orleans by "causelessly suspend[ing] specie payments in September last" and "introduc[ing] Confederate Notes as currency." Having managed to legitimize these notes among "the poor and unwary," the banks were trying to "[Foist] the loss from this worthless stuff" onto the public. "They have invested the savings of labor and the pittance of the widow in this paper. They sent away or hid their specie, so that the people could have nothing but these notes with which to buy bread." To "equalize this general loss," he ordered the banks to pay all depositors and creditors in "bills of the bank, U.S. Treasury notes, gold, or silver."[10]

The effect of this order on the banks was devastating, since it made it impossible for them to balance their books. W. N. Mercer invited the general to examine his bank's ledgers, but he refused. Then, on June 6, Butler ordered any bank-held assets of the "so-called Confederate States" turned over to him in specie or banknotes – not as Confederate bills. James Denegre, president of the Citizens Bank, protested, arguing that the banks had been legally compelled to accept Confederate notes. The general was unmoved, however, replying that "this order [had been] submitted to if not with joy, [then] at least not under protest." Butler maintained his stern posture toward chartered banks over the

Edwin M. Stanton, May 16, 1862, in *Butler Correspondence*, I, 491–2; cf. the convincing and detailed description of how those confiscated funds actually made their way to the Confederate Treasury in Todd, *Confederate Finance*, 158–9. On southern prewar debts and repudiation see Schwab, *Confederate States of America*, 110–11; and Todd, *Confederate Finance*, 159–60. Benjamin F. Butler, *Butler's Book: Autobiography and Personal Reminiscences of Major-General Benjamin F. Butler* (Boston, 1892), 321 (quotation); Butler to William N. Mercer and J. M. Lapeyre, Committee, May 14, 1862, in *Official Records*, Ser. III, Vol. 2, p. 130.

[10] General Orders No. 30, May 19, 1862, in *Official Records*, Ser. I, Vol. 15, pp. 437–8. This document is also reprinted in *Butler Correspondence*, I, 504–5. Minor stylistic variations between the two versions have been silently corrected here, with the exception of the bracketed word "foist," which appears nonsensically as "fostering" in the *Official Records* and ungrammatically as "foisting" in the compiled Butler correspondence. General Orders No. 29, May 16, 1862, in *Official Records*, Ser. I, Vol. 15, p. 426; Parton, *General Butler in New Orleans*, 110; several bank notices about withdrawals are also reproduced there.

next several months – and his relationships with private bankers were not much better. He seized $70,000 in gold from the British-connected firm of Samuel Smith & Co. in early May, ostensibly to pay his troops, which resulted in a civil suit that dragged on for years. (Butler eventually lost.) The general also employed spies to study transactions by "Jew brokers" in the city, believing their speculations to be based on "intelligence from Richmond" supplied by Judah P. Benjamin, the Confederate secretary of state from New Orleans.[11]

The general had a better relationship with Jacob Barker, a venerable Crescent City private banker. A cousin of Benjamin Franklin born in Maine in 1779, the elderly Barker had a long, notorious career as an American merchant-financier. After moving from New York to New Orleans in 1834, he had founded his own private bank, and although his Quaker faith disposed him to oppose slavery, the opportunistic Barker was financially implicated in the plantation system. Among his many contacts in the Northeast during the 1850s was a young attorney-politician named Benjamin Butler – a relationship that helps explain why Barker extended several unsecured personal loans to Butler within a few weeks of his arrival, including one of $100,000 in gold. According to Barker's later testimony before a commission investigating corruption in the Gulf Department, Butler borrowed these funds to finance commodity speculations by his brother, "Colonel" Andrew Butler, who had accompanied the general to New Orleans. Barker's recollection was largely corroborated in Butler's 1864 campaign biography, which maintained that Andrew was merely "one of the lucky men who chanced to be in business at New Orleans at the critical moment." By Butler's own estimate, his brother profited around $200,000 from his 1862 speculations; other observers put the figure at more than half a million dollars. Although Butler later claimed he had personally never gained from these transactions, most southerners (and many Federals, too) doubted his claims of pecuniary innocence. Even his own correspondence reveals the general's close, inappropriate involvement with the Barker loans.[12]

[11] Butler, *Butler's Book*, 510; Butler to Salmon P. Chase, July 2, 1862; Butler to Asa S. Blake, July 2, 1862; and Butler to W. B. Dinsmore, July 3, 1862, all in *Official Records*, Ser. I, Vol. 15, pp. 513–14; Dan T. Carter, *When the War Was Over: The Failure of Self-Reconstruction in the South, 1865–1867* (Baton Rouge, 1985), 99; Trefousse, *Ben Butler*, 117; Edwards Pierrepont, *A Review by Judge Pierrepont of Gen. Butler's Defense Before the House of Representatives in Relation to the New Orleans Gold* (New York, 1865); *Official Records*, Ser. I, Vol. 15, p. 503; New Orleans *Daily Delta*, May 14, 1862; Special Order No. 294, August 23, 1862, in *Butler Correspondence*, II, 213. James D. Denegre to Butler, June 11, 1862, and Butler to the Secretary of the Treasury, June 19, 1862, in *Official Records*, Ser. III, Vol. 2, pp. 165–8; General Orders No. 40, June 6, 1862, in *Butler Correspondence*, I, 563; Butler to Mercer, May 22, 1862, in *Butler Correspondence*, I, 481.

[12] Parton, *General Butler in New Orleans*, 108–9; Jacob Barker testimony, in "Report of the Special Commission," September 23, 1865, Old Army Records (RG-94), Vol. 737, pp. 145–6 (microfilm, National Archives; hereinafter cited as Smith-Brady Report); Capers, *Occupied City*, 82–4; Trefousse, *Ben Butler*, 122–4. George S. Denison, a U.S. Treasury Department agent in New Orleans sympathetic to General Butler, wrote that "it is stated by secessionists – and by

Jacob Barker was a rarity in occupation-era New Orleans: a bona fide Union collaborationist. In addition to making large, unsecured loans to the general, Barker also agreed to guard the bullion that Butler had seized from private bankers Samuel Smith & Co., a task that apparently made Barker nervous. "I am particularly anxious to close my agency in that case," he wrote Butler in September. Barker had good reason to be concerned, since his speculations in Confederate currency had earned him threats of violence from a secret local organization called the "Southern Independence Association" in the months before the occupation. However, the octogenarian banker had refused to be intimidated then, and no less determined now, Barker purchased the New Orleans *Daily Crescent*, a newspaper closed down for its pro-Confederate stances. Although Barker used the paper as a platform for his pro-Union positions, even he ran afoul of the general's censorship policies later that fall.[13]

Indeed, the rigidity with which Butler controlled the press forces historians to decipher conspicuous "silences" for clues as to mercantile opinion during this period. The perspective of this influential community had long provided the editorial backbone for conservative papers such as the *Picayune*, the *Crescent*, and the *Price-Current*. One can reasonably speculate that if commercially rationalized collaborationist tendencies or moderate Unionism like

some Union men – that [Andrew Butler] has made a half a million dollars or more." Denison to Salmon P. Chase, August 26, 1862, in "Diary and Correspondence of Salmon P. Chase," *Annual Report of the American Historical Association for the Year 1902* (2 vols., Washington, DC, 1903), II, 312 (hereinafter cited as *Chase Correspondence*). Though he could not prove that the general had "done ... anything for his pecuniary advantage," Denison admitted that Butler "is such a smart man, that it would ... be difficult to discern what he wished to conceal"; Denison to Chase, September 9, 1862, in ibid., 313. For two firsthand southern accounts of Butler & Bro. in New Orleans see Southwood, *Beauty and Booty*; and Velazquez, *Woman in Battle*, 242. For General Butler's close attention to the details of the Barker loans and the transactions they supported, see his exchanges with Richard Fay and J. G. Carney, both of Boston, in *Butler Correspondence*, I, 529–30, 533–5, 585, 593–4, 620–2, 634–5. Jacob Barker has yet to receive the full biographical treatment he merits, but aspects of his Zelig-like career can be traced in [Jacob Barker], *Incidents in the Life of Jacob Barker, of New Orleans ... from 1800 to 1855* (Washington, DC, 1855); R. D. Turner, *The Conspiracy Trials of 1826 and 1827: A Chapter in the Life of Jacob Barker* (Philadelphia, 1864); and "Jacob Barker's Career Recalled," New Orleans *Daily Picayune*, November 18, 1894, p. 25. Barker mentions his correspondence with one "Benjamin F. Butler, Esq." in a letter to Dunlap & Campbell, March 4, 1852, in Jacob Barker Letters (M-183, Special Collections, Howard-Tilton Memorial Library, Tulane University, New Orleans, LA).

13 New Orleans *Daily Delta*, June 5, 1862; Elizabeth Joan Doyle, "Civilian Life in Occupied New Orleans, 1862–65" (Ph.D. diss., Louisiana State University, 1955), 248. On Barker and the Southern Independence Association see "The Brokers," New Orleans *Daily Picayune*, March 9, 1862; and *Butler Correspondence*, I, 513–14; on his safekeeping of the Smith & Co. funds see Barker to Butler, September 29 and 30, 1862, in ibid., II, 337–8. For Butler's suppression of Barker's *National Advocate*, see Special Orders No. 513, November 14, 1862, in *Official Records*, Ser. I, Vol. 15, pp. 595–6; and *Butler Correspondence*, II, 480. On the New Orleans *Daily Delta*, which was seized in May and edited thereafter by two Union officers appointed by Butler, see Parton, *General Butler in New Orleans*, 114–15.

Barker's had been widespread among merchants during Butler's occupation, these opinions would have found expression in the press, since the general would have welcomed rather than censored such views. But in fact, such sentiments were almost never expressed in the press – an absence that suggests New Orleans merchants more or less opposed Butler's regime.[14]

Admittedly, it remains difficult to gauge the depth of mercantile opposition to Federal authority, in part because some of those inclined to collaborate may have been intimidated by Confederate loyalists. Treasury agent George S. Denison, for example, blamed "fear of retribution from the secessionists" for the paucity of pro-Union public sentiment in New Orleans. On the other hand, Butler's strict surveillance policies, which played on white southerners' deepest fears by encouraging slaves to become informers, helped foster covert pro-southern cliques, and these groups were heavily dependent on merchants for support. The influential merchant-banker Edmond Forstall was reputedly "a leading member" of the Southern Independence Association, the group that had threatened Barker. Rumors about merchants' support for such "secret societies" continued to circulate throughout the occupation period.[15]

Nevertheless, the Federals' monopoly on force gave them the upper hand over such revanchist groups in New Orleans, where incidents of organized resistance were practically nonexistent. "Fear of retribution," it seems, was a two-way street with precious little "neutral ground." One British businessman who visited in October 1862 described how "the middle and upper classes of New Orleans" were "amazed at the cool manner in which ... General Butler had disarmed them, and placed them at his mercy." But although these citizens appeared "helpless and cowed," he reported that "they were worse 'rebels' than ever" in private. One "old and wealthy merchant" admitted to him that he and

[14] A similar example that supports this conclusion also involves Jacob Barker, who ran for a U.S. congressional seat from New Orleans in the fall of 1862. In a tightly controlled election in which only about 5,000 votes were cast, Barker's Whiggish but independent Unionism (during the campaign, he once referred to Butler and his troops as "adventurers") managed to garner a mere 453 votes, even among the small group of New Orleans citizens then considered sufficiently loyal to exercise the franchise. George Denison to Salmon P. Chase, December 4, 1862, in *Chase Correspondence*, 337; Willie Malvin Caskey, *Secession and Restoration of Louisiana* (Baton Rouge, 1938), 64. For an example of Butler's suppression of the New Orleans commercial press see ibid., 53; see also Capers, *Occupied City*, 176–8; and the useful description of the political proclivities of New Orleans newspapers in Roger W. Shugg, *Origins of Class Struggle in Louisiana: A Social History of White Farmers and Laborers during Slavery and After* (1939; repr., Baton Rouge, 1968), 340–2.

[15] John Richard Dennett, *The South As It Is, 1865–1866*, ed. Henry M. Christman (Athens, GA, and London, 1986), 308; Butler to William H. Seward, September 19, 1862, in *Butler Correspondence*, II, 308; George S. Denison to "Mother," June 10, 1862, repr. in "Some Letters of George Stanton Denison, 1854–1866: Observations of a Yankee on Conditions in Louisiana and Texas," ed. James A. Padgett, *Louisiana Historical Quarterly* 23 (October 1940), 1183; Parton, *General Butler in New Orleans*, 64. On Butler's use of informers in New Orleans, including slaves, see [Reverend] B. M. Palmer, *The Oath of Allegiance to the United States, Discussed in Its Moral and Political Bearings* (Richmond, VA, 1863), 9.

his compatriots greatly feared confiscation, imprisonment, and exile. Because Federal rule was so harsh, the merchant said, "we *must* grin and abide our time. But the day of reckoning *will* come, and then – look out!"[16]

That "day of reckoning" would be nearly four years in the future – on July 30, 1866, to be precise – but in the meantime, the city's merchant community faced U.S. military authorities not only in a state of mutual hostility but also in greatly diminished numbers. Several contemporary accounts describe the exodus of businessmen from New Orleans during 1861–2, led by those who were young and able-bodied enough to serve in the Confederate military. Others had left as the economic situation worsened, and even more evacuated the city just prior to its occupation. As with the extent of commercial opposition to the Federal regime, it is hard to know how many resident merchants had left by mid-1862, but their overall numbers may have been reduced by more than half of what they had been in late 1860. A rough estimate can be obtained by comparing firms that appeared in the 1861 Gardner's city directory with those listed in two subsequent sources during the early years of the war: the signatories to the July 1861 cotton embargo circular, and those included on General Butler's August 1862 "Schedule B" of firms to be assessed a special cotton-brokers' tax (discussed later). Of 467 "commission firms and cotton factors" in the 1861 city directory, 111 subsequently signed the July 1861 circular, as did another 19 firms that did not appear in the directory. These figures show that at least a quarter – and probably closer to half – of New Orleans mercantile firms had not closed their doors upon secession. (It is worth noting that those who signed the embargo circulars were not Unionists or fence-sitters but had instead publicly cast their lot with the Confederacy.) More than a year later, General Butler was still able to locate and tax seventy-four firms that had appeared in the 1861 directory, plus another twenty not listed but whose names were among those that had endorsed the embargo. Nearly a quarter of the city's mercantile firms listed in business before secession thus still remained in operation after the occupation.[17]

The obverse of these figures, however, indicates that up to three-fourths of the city's merchants had left the city, and this exodus affected the demographic and political composition of the community that remained. In addition

---

[16] Corsan, *Two Months in the Confederate States*, 16–17 (emphases in original). According to Butler's most sympathetic biographer, after the general had publicly executed William Mumford on June 7 for tearing down the Union flag, "no further disturbance occurred while he was in command"; Trefousse, *Ben Butler*, 115.

[17] The data in the text were compiled by comparing the Gardner's 1861 New Orleans city directory (HTML-Tulane) with the July 1861 embargo circular as published in the New Orleans *Price-Current*, July 27, 1861 (circular dated July 17), and "Schedule B" as attached to Butler's General Orders No. 55, August 4, 1862, in *Official Records*, Ser. I, Vol. 15, pp. 538–42. The departure of many merchants for military service is noted in Corsan, *Two Months in the Confederate States*, 17; on their pre-occupation exodus and its effects see George W. Cable, "New Orleans before the Capture," in Johnson and Buel, eds., *Battles and Leaders*, II, 16–17.

to those who had gone off to fight the war, the first round of self-imposed exiles from New Orleans included merchants who were opposed to secession and the Confederacy. Some "conditional" Unionists had decamped the city prior to secession, such as banker and railroad promoter James Robb, who waited out the war in Chicago, but many other moderates departed later. The overall effect of these departures was to leave behind a smaller but more homogeneous mercantile community – one that was significantly older, considerably more foreign, and less inclined to support either restoration of the Union or the efforts of its occupying authorities.[18]

New Orleans businessmen also withheld support from U.S. authorities due to their concerns over slave emancipation, which they believed to be a likely outcome of Union control. Despite the Lincoln administration's cautious official stance, the suspicions ("paranoias" is probably not too strong a word) of those merchants who remained in occupied New Orleans were fueled by General Butler's outspoken advocacy of emancipation. Former U.S. senator Reverdy Johnson, sent to investigate conditions under Butler's command in the summer of 1862, reported back such widespread fears. Even a Unionist and Quaker like Jacob Barker harbored racial anxieties about how emancipation might unfold in a crowded urban environment. Seeking reassurance in a letter to President Lincoln that July, Barker described "the present frightful alarm" due to "agitations about slavery," but he asserted that citizens "were generally willing to return to the union ... provided they can be satisfied on the slave question." Of course, in addition to racial fears, New Orleans merchants had self-interested reasons to be worried. Barring any possible compensation schemes, emancipation would immediately negate most of what had served as regional capital stock, thereby threatening the credit structures on which they and their clients had long depended. Moreover, many merchants owned slaves themselves.[19]

[18] Denison to Salmon P. Chase, June 28, 1862, in *Chase Correspondence*, 307. On James Robb see Harry Howard Evans, "James Robb, Banker and Pioneer Railroad Builder of Ante-Bellum Louisiana," *Louisiana Historical Quarterly* 23 (January 1940), 249–53; and New Orleans *Times*, November 2 and 29, 1865.

[19] For figures on slaveholding in antebellum New Orleans derived from the 1860 census see Shugg, *Origins of Class Struggle in Louisiana*, 24–5, and Appendix, Tables 3 and 4 (pp. 318–19). On the importance of slave property as collateral in the antebellum southern financial system, see Richard H. Kilbourne Jr., *Debt, Investment, Slaves: Credit Relations in East Feliciana Parish, Louisiana, 1825–1885* (Tuscaloosa and London, 1995). Jacob Barker to Abraham Lincoln, July 16, 1862; and Reverdy Johnson to Abraham Lincoln, July 16, 1862, both in Abraham Lincoln Papers, Series 1, General Correspondence 1833–1916, Library of Congress, Washington, DC (available online at http://memory.loc.gov/ammem/alhtml/alser.html). For beliefs similar to Barker's from another local Unionist see W. Mitthoff to Butler, May 29, 1862, in *Butler Correspondence*, I, 525–7. James Robb laid out the basis of his conditional Unionism in correspondence with an unnamed "American in Paris" (who was probably the Confederate legatee to France, Louisianian John Slidell), which he then published in pamphlet form; see Robb, *A Southern Confederacy: Letters from James Robb, Late a Citizen of New Orleans, to an*

In fact, since emancipation was not yet official Federal policy, many merchants continued to hold slaves in the city even after the occupation. Unsurprisingly, this was not to General Butler's liking, and he purposely freed some slaves as part of his confiscations of Confederate sympathizers' property. On one occasion, as related in his self-serving 1864 campaign biography, Butler's officers brought to headquarters a light-skinned slave woman who had recently suffered a whipping. The general summoned her owner, "a respectable merchant" named Landry, and established that the injured woman was not only the gentleman's slave – but also his daughter. Aghast at both Landry's cruelty and his "insolent nonchalance" as to her parentage, Butler had the Creole merchant arrested. Landry's family, including his wife, then descended on the general to plead for clemency, explaining that "the war had half-ruined" the old business-man, making him "irritable of late." Butler penalized the merchant by ordering him to free his daughter and provide her with a thousand dollars.[20]

Regardless of our antislavery sympathies, this anecdote helps illustrate Butler's contempt for the resident merchants of New Orleans, Americans and foreign nationals alike. Not only did Butler fail to cultivate Unionism or collaborationism among the merchant community, but he repeatedly made that community the scapegoat for the city's woes. As historian Roger Shugg suggested, Butler's animosity toward city merchants was apparently part of his "aggressive design to separate the classes and court the good will of the majority." From the outset he directed invective against Crescent City commercial elites. On May 9, for example, Butler blamed "wealthy and influential" residents for suffering by the "working classes," and his tirade against bankers a few weeks later took a similar tack. However, this was not merely rhetoric for public consumption. Even in private, Butler stressed his belief in the prominent role played by the city's merchant and banking communities in the wider southern insurgency. He expounded this view in a May 1862 letter to Secretary of War Stanton, in which he further opined that "[to] a large degree the owners of the soil, planters and farmers, mechanics and small traders, have been passive rather than active in the rebellion."[21]

Butler was able to bring far more than harsh verbiage to bear in his campaign of class warfare. Using his sweeping powers under martial law, Butler implemented a wide range of policies that selectively targeted the objects of his

---

American in Paris, and Hon. Alexander H. Stephens, of Georgia (Chicago, 1862); and Evans, "James Robb," 250–3.

[20] Parton, *General Butler in New Orleans*, 143–4 (quotations); Caskey, *Secession and Restoration of Louisiana*, 53, 60–2. On staff dissension over contraband policies see Parton, *General Butler in New Orleans*, 132–4; and Capers, *Occupied City*, 95–6.

[21] Butler to Edwin P. Stanton, May 25, 1862, in *Butler Correspondence*, I, 517; George S. Denison to Jimmy, July 6, 1862, in Padgett, ed., "Some Letters of G. S. Denison," 1186; General Orders No. 30, May 19, 1862, in *Official Records*, Ser. I, Vol. 15, pp. 437–8; General Order No. 25, May 9, 1862, in *Butler Correspondence*, I, 457; Shugg, *Origins of Class Struggle in Louisiana*, 186–7.

wrath, often with scant legal justification. Despite his lip service to property rights, Butler (like the northern public) felt that southerners – the upper classes, in particular – had forfeited such rights by seceding and deserved to be punished in their pocketbooks. In fact, such policies had no statutory basis at that point, except as they could be arbitrarily justified under Butler's martial authority. On June 10 the general again ran in advance of his government's policy curve by mandating that the legitimacy of contracts and other legal protections would henceforth be extended only to those who had taken loyalty oaths. As historian Hans Trefousse argued, this order "in effect gave Confederate sympathizers the choice of abandoning their cause or going out of business." After Congress passed the Second Confiscation Act that summer, Butler relied on an overly broad interpretation to harass merchants as he saw fit. When all else failed, Butler simply seized the assets of firms he merely suspected of treachery, as he did with property belonging to those "most rabid rebels," the commission house of Wright & Allen. Such capricious property seizures generated enormous ill-will toward "Spoons" Butler, adding to his growing reputation for corruption and also fanning fears that emancipation was the next logical consequence of federal confiscation policies. Moreover, Butler had other tools in his arsenal to deploy against merchants. When he could not confiscate mercantile wealth, he formulated policies to redistribute it. In August he targeted the merchant community directly, assessing taxes to fund poor-relief programs on all firms that had supported the cotton embargo the previous summer. Defending this action to Secretary Stanton, Butler declared "there seemed to me to be no such fit subjects for taxation as the Cotton Brokers, who had brought distress upon the city by thus paralyzing commerce."[22]

Butler's resolute linkage of property rights with loyalty requirements, however, was probably his most effective weapon against New Orleans elites. Most merchants had indeed supported the Confederacy, in word even if not always in deed. But demonstrable neutrality was not an option, as Butler made clear in a curt reply to one banker's plea that fall. Furthermore, those who chose not to take loyalty oaths were required to register as enemies of the state, and as such, they were subject to physical expulsion from the city – a severe hardship for the many elderly merchants and their families who remained in New

[22] Butler to Stanton, October 12, 1862, in *Butler Correspondence*, II, 366; Butler to William H. Seward, September 19, 1862, in *Official Records*, Ser. III, Vol. 2, pp. 571–3 (quotation on p. 571); General Orders No. 55, August 4, 1862, in *Official Records*, Ser. I, Vol. 15, pp. 538–42; General Orders No. 48, July 9, 1862, in *Butler Correspondence*, II, 52–3; Parton, *General Butler in New Orleans*, 113; Butler, *Butler's Book*, 321. Thomas Ewing Dabney, "The Butler Regime in Louisiana," *Louisiana Historical Quarterly* 27 (April 1944), 31 (quotation); Trefousse, *Ben Butler*, 116 (quotation), 122–3; see also Caskey, *Secession and Restoration of Louisiana*, 60–63. General Orders No. 41, June 10, 1862, in *Butler Correspondence*, I, 574–6; Butler to Stanton, May 25, 1862, in ibid., 517. On the ambiguities of the Confiscation Acts and the Lincoln administration's conflicted attitudes toward them, see Silvana R. Siddali, *From Property to Person: Slavery and the Confiscation Acts, 1861–1862* (Baton Rouge, 2005). However, Siddali's discussion of occupied New Orleans, the prime site for enforcement of these acts, is surprisingly thin.

Orleans. Forced to take solace from the controversial doctrine that "a compulsory oath is not binding," the number who swore allegiance just in advance of the September deadline was ten times larger than that months earlier. But even by Butler's own generous estimate, only half of those who took the oath did so sincerely, and nearly 4,000 citizens held firm and registered as enemies instead. Butler-controlled newspapers nevertheless gleefully noted the prevalence of embarrassed merchants among the crowds of last-minute oath-takers:

These ... were of the plethoric sort of middle-aged gentlemen – old codgers, who have cavernous offices in Union, Gravier, and Perdido Streets – white-breasted cormorants, who own cotton planters, together with their plantations, and amass their tens of thousands a year by advancing on crops the money borrowed from banks. These are they who, by the mysterious operation of two and a half percent for accepting, two and a half for advancing – drayage, weighage, storage, brokerage, and stealage – manage to mortgage to their service the small cotton-planter, grow rich without effort, eat turkey and turtle, and swim in *Cliquot*.

The biting sarcasm of such reports emanating from the Butler camp clearly reveals the class tensions the general sought to exploit to Federal advantage. Such reports also show that Butler had little intention of cultivating either allies or Unionist sentiments among the city's influential gentlemen-merchants. Instead, the general sought his support mainly among the working class, especially immigrants – a strategy typical of the urban wing of the northern Democratic Party on which he had predicated his career. Over the long term, the Federals' emphasis on encouraging Unionism among "laboring men" during the occupation helped fuel political factionalism in the city, especially given elites' long-standing fears of "mob rule."[23]

Ironically, Butler's aggressive policies toward the city's Atlantic merchant community finally prompted his recall from New Orleans in December 1862. For it was not just recalcitrant southern elites that the imperious Yankee incited;

---

[23] George S. Denison to Mother, August 25, 1862, in Padgett, ed., "Some Letters of G. S. Denison," 1193–4; see also Parton, *General Butler in New Orleans*, 64–5, for a lengthy, revealing statement of Butler's view of Crescent City politics, particularly the old alliance "between the Spoiler and the Banker." On elites' fears of "mob rule," see William Howard Russell, *My Diary North and South* (Boston, 1863), 252; and John M. Sacher, *A Perfect War of Politics: Parties, Politicians, and Democracy in Louisiana, 1824–1861* (Baton Rouge, 2003), chap. 6. The undated [ca. late September 1862] account from the New Orleans press – almost certainly published by Butler's house organ, the *Daily Delta* – is reprinted along with two others similar in tone by Marion Southwood in *Beauty and Booty*, 128–37 (block quotation on pp. 132–3). Caskey, *Secession and Restoration in Louisiana*, 60; Howard Palmer Johnson, "New Orleans Under General Butler," *Louisiana Historical Quarterly* 24 (April 1941), 500–1. The doctrine that "a compulsory oath is not binding" is discussed in Southwood, *Beauty and Booty*, 159; and was opposed from exile by the influential New Orleans Presbyterian minister Benjamin M. Palmer in his 1863 pamphlet, *Oath of Allegiance to the United States*. General Orders No. 76, September 24, 1862, in *Official Records*, Ser. I, Vol. 15, pp. 575–6; Trefousse, *Ben Butler*, 116; Butler to W. N. Mercer, September 27, 1862, in *Butler Correspondence*, II, 332–3; General Orders No. 73, September 18, 1862, in *Official Records*, Ser. I, Vol. 15, 572–3.

resident foreign nationals were a special target of Butler's as well. Beginning
with his "woman order" in May, Butler's actions had repeatedly provoked
unwelcome European attentions, to the mounting chagrin of Secretary of State
William Seward, who had pinned high diplomatic hopes on the occupation
of New Orleans. "The President regards the renewal of commerce at New
Orleans ... as a most effective means of bringing this unhappy civil strife to an
end," Seward wrote in July, and it "is also calculated to deprive foreign powers
of all excuse for sympathy with the insurgents." Butler, however, did not take
such hints to go easy on foreign merchants; instead, his continued confiscations
embroiled him – and by extension, the State Department – in a series of controversies with the governments of Spain, Holland, Prussia, France, and Great
Britain. In particular, the brouhaha that resulted from his seizure of $800,000
in specie from the Dutch consul, money belonging to the European banking
houses of Baring Brothers and Hope & Company, brought Butler into conflict with international merchant capital at its highest echelons. His attempt to
extend oath-taking requirements to non-American citizens constituted another
dubious move under international law, which was further evidence that the
general was swimming in political waters well beyond his depth. Despite his
rationalizations that foreign merchants had actively aided the rebellion, Butler's
stubborn provocations finally led President Lincoln to bow to Seward's pressure and relieve the politically popular general of his eight-month command
over New Orleans.[24]

In a farewell address to the city on Christmas Eve 1862, Butler could not
resist getting in some final digs at the merchant community. He insisted that his

[24] Butler's elaborate justifications of his actions against foreign-born merchants and their diplomatic representatives in New Orleans are typified in his lengthy letter to Secretary of War Edwin
M. Stanton, October 12, 1862, in *Butler Correspondence*, II, 361–8; see also the post facto
accounts in his authorized biography; Parton, *General Butler in New Orleans*, 64, 94–105, and
119–26. William H. Seward to Reverdy Johnson, June 27, 1862, in *Official Records*, Ser. III,
Vol. 2, p. 179 (quotations). Scattered throughout this same volume of the *Official Records* is
much of the diplomatic correspondence concerning Butler's provocations; see esp. ibid., 423–9,
551–61, 566–9, 580–2, 710–12, and 716–20. A State Department internal memorandum of
May 30, 1862, noted that the British ambassador, Lord Lyons, had recently expressed his government's view that "the capture of New Orleans, which was expected by Mr. Seward to be
a relief in the relations between the United States and other countries, on the contrary was
attended ... by new causes of uneasiness" due to Butler's administration of the city; ibid., 130–1.
The definitive incident among many, however, was Butler's May seizure of funds that had been
transferred by Forstall's Citizens Bank to the Dutch consul at New Orleans, Amedie Couturie,
who was also a liquor merchant in the city; see ibid., 115–24, 132–42, 266–7, 488–91, and
497–505. For the European prominence of Hope & Co. of Amsterdam and Baring Brothers of
London, as well as the decades-long connections of both banking houses to global mercantile
operations centered on New Orleans, see Vincent Nolte, *The Memoirs of Vincent Nolte, or Fifty
Years in Both Hemispheres* (1854; repr., New York, 1934), esp. chaps. 4, 11, and 15; Ralph W.
Hidy, *The House of Baring in American Trade and Finance: English Merchant Bankers at Work,
1763–1861* (Cambridge, MA, 1949), 330–7, 346–8, and 436–55; and Sidney Pollard, *European
Economic Integration, 1815–1970* (London, 1974), 56.

rule over New Orleans had not been overly harsh. "It is true," he continued, "that I have levied upon the wealthy rebels ... nearly half a million of dollars to feed forty thousand of the starving poor," but only because:

I saw that this Rebellion was a war of the aristocrats against the middling men, of the rich against the poor.... I therefore felt no hesitation in taking the substance of the wealthy, who had caused the war.... and so am quite content to incur the sneers of the salon, or the curses of the rich.

Butler thus maintained the posture of heroic class warrior to the bitter end of his "reign" over the Crescent City. Again, while it is true that Butler was on what most would regard as the "side of angels" during his political career – emancipationist, women's suffragist, anti-monopolist, and labor advocate – his attempt to don the mantle of modern-day Robin Hood might ring less hollow were it not for the enormous personal profits he and his brother made during their stay in New Orleans. (Similarly, some historians have praised Butler for cleaning up the notoriously filthy city and providing it with "the most efficient municipal administration it had ever had" – but here one might also recall how remarkably prompt the train schedules were in pre–World War II Italy.)[25]

His successor in New Orleans, General Nathaniel Banks, was among those who believed the rumors of widespread depredations under Butler's command. Writing to his wife within a month of his arrival, Banks reported that residents had been "robbed" of their property under Butler, "not for the benefit of the government but for individual plunder." Although cotton speculation would increase markedly during his time in Louisiana, Banks himself steered free from charges of personal gain, and he strongly deplored his predecessor for not having done so. "This State could have been made and ought now to be thoroughly for the Union & against the Confederate States," he averred, but instead "they are terribly bitter against a [government] that permits such things." A city resident agreed with this assessment nearly simultaneously in her diary. Butler's unfortunate legacy to General Banks, she wrote, was a "sullen and dangerous hostility born of deep distrust and passionate alienation," because Butler had "abused the commerce of this city to his own profit" rather than using it to

[25] "Farewell Address by General Butler," December 24, 1862, in *Butler Correspondence*, II, 554–7 (quotations on p. 555); Edward Bacon, *Among the Cotton Thieves* (Detroit, 1867), 26. Even the pro-emancipation novelist George Washington Cable, who was in New Orleans during the occupation, later wrote that "the popular idea that a sudden revolution in the sanitary affairs of the Creole city was effected by General B. F. Butler in 1862 is erroneous"; Cable, *The Creoles of Louisiana* (1884; repr., New York, 1970), 305–6 (quotation on p. 305). For favorable revisionist views of Butler's administration in New Orleans, see Capers, *Occupied City*, 71–6 (quotation on p. 72); and Trefousse, *Ben Butler*, 118–21, 133–4. The sympathetic Trefousse admits that Butler's reformist commitments were "frequently those of a self-seeking politician" and "demagogue"; ibid., 256. In *Stormy Ben Butler* (New York, 1954), Robert S. Holzman approvingly cites estimates of the augmentation of Butler's wealth from about $150,000 before his stay in New Orleans to around $3 million by 1868; cf. Trefousse's mixed assessment in *Ben Butler*, 290 n. 89.

"foster and develop the great and permanent interests by which alone the loyalty of New Orleans could have been fortified and secured."[26]

To be sure, pro-Confederate sentiments were already prevalent in New
Orleans, but General Banks was right to recognize the political ramifications
of Butler's maladministration, which were arguably most serious with regard
to his relentless efforts to vilify, penalize, and alienate the city's mercantile
community. In this sense, the Butler regime may well have represented a lost
opportunity to successfully launch federal reconstruction efforts in the South.
A more sensible politician would have couched subtle appeals to businessmen's
conservative sensibilities and patiently cultivated relationships with the moderates among them. Economically, he might have encouraged a carefully supervised restoration of old trade patterns under local auspices, allowing some
profits to accrue, as before, to both rural producers and their urban agents.
Of course, it remains uncertain whether a more accommodationist approach
toward the New Orleans business community would have yielded different
results. The point, however, is that such a hypothetical "good faith" effort
to elicit mercantile support contrasts sharply with the punitive policies and
antagonistic posturing that actually occurred under Butler, all of which helped
set the stage for what occurred afterward. Butler did not leave behind a viable
Unionist movement in the city, partly because he had pushed the most likely
candidates to lead it, city merchants, deeper into the embrace of the South's
most reactionary elements, even as his arbitrary property confiscations helped
delegitimate their ability to provide effective political leadership. Moreover,
Butler's enforced disruption of business patterns, compounded by his attacks
on New Orleans banks, helped initiate processes of commercial erosion that
would ultimately replace the earlier modus vivendi between countryside and
city with a decentralized and undercapitalized agricultural system in the lower
Mississippi Valley.[27]

If all of this blame seems too much to foist off onto Ben Butler's (literally
hunched) back, then perhaps some of that responsibility ought to be shifted
onto the stooped shoulders of the indisputably more heroic man who had

---

[26] Southwood, *Beauty and Booty*, 268; Nathaniel P. Banks to his wife, January 15, 1863, quoted
in Ludwell H. Johnson, *Red River Campaign: Politics and Cotton in the Civil War* (1958; repr.,
Kent, OH, and London, 1993), 51. The U.S. naval commander David D. Porter, among many
others, was similarly convinced of (and appalled by) Butler-sanctioned corruption in New
Orleans; see Trefousse, *Ben Butler*, 123–4.

[27] Butler himself later admitted (through his biographical mouthpiece, James Parton) that he was
"baffled" by his inability to coax much cotton from the southern plantation interior, which is
borne out by the statistics on crop receipts at New Orleans in 1862. Products valued at $51
million were received at New Orleans that year, down from $155 million the previous season
(despite the advent of the war). Furthermore, more than 60 percent ($31.7 million) of the 1862
receipts were sugar products, most of which had been confiscated or otherwise cajoled from
planters in nearby parishes then under Union control. Parton, *General Butler in New Orleans*,
109. Crop-receipt totals are from *Appleton's Cyclopedia for 1862*, p. 229; and *Appleton's
Cyclopedia for 1861*, p. 113.

appointed him. Abraham Lincoln presided over a federal government that was, as historian Ludwell H. Johnson put it, "hagridden with men [who were] eager to make money" by trading with the enemy. (Other instances of Loretta Velazquez's "secret history" of wartime profiteering, fairly blatant under the Butler regime, will be elaborated in the next chapter.) Lincoln never made much effort to clamp down on such behaviors; perhaps he considered it politically expedient to allow them to continue unchecked, another means of juggling the competing egos in his beleaguered administration, for which he has been rightly admired. Similarly, however, it seems more than coincidental that he chose to bury not one but two of his most popular potential rivals – both of whom were from the nation's most cotton-dependent state – in distant New Orleans, which served as both proverbial cookie jar (for General Butler) and hornet's nest (for General Banks). In so doing, Lincoln again demonstrated that his priority was restoring the Union, and thus he sought to remove any obstacles to that goal. Scholars often assume that Reconstruction would have gone more smoothly had Lincoln remained in charge – and admittedly, things could hardly have turned out much worse than they did. (Or perhaps they could have, since Lincoln later unsuccessfully approached Butler about serving as his running mate in 1864.) But in the instance of Butler's appointment, Lincoln's political judgment seems questionable, with serious consequences over both the short and long terms. Surely the president was aware of the enormous value that a Unionist Crescent City would have represented, yet by selecting the contentious, self-serving Butler to administrate the early occupation of New Orleans, Lincoln seems to have displayed greater concern with despatching a noisome political opponent than with appointing the best-qualified leader to successfully launch federal Reconstruction policy in the South's largest city.[28]

[28] Ludwell H. Johnson, "Northern Profits and Profiteers: The Cotton Rings of 1864–1865," *Civil War History* 12.2 (1966), 109.

PART III

RECONSTRUCTION

6

New Orleans Merchants and the Political Economy of Reconstruction

In the summer of 1865 Whitelaw Reid, a journalist and aspiring Republican Party stalwart, was part of an entourage that accompanied his fellow Ohioan, U.S. Supreme Court Chief Justice Salmon P. Chase, on a whirlwind tour of the recently surrendered southern states. After visiting Mobile, Alabama, which had suffered significant devastation under Union naval bombardment, the group proceeded to New Orleans, where Reid found, to his evident surprise, that "the city itself showed no traces of war." "Even the levee began to be crowded again," he reported, "and business seemed quite as active as could be expected in June." (In fact, business still remained dull by prewar standards.) Reid also tried to give his readers a sense of the Crescent City's character and importance. "New Orleans," he wrote,

is a town where half the inhabitants think of Paris as their home ... [and] of the other half, the most are cotton factors or commercial men of some sort, with principles not infrequently on sale with their goods; that is, it is at once the most luxurious, the most unprincipled, the most extravagant, and, to many, the most fascinating city in the Union....

"What Boston is to the North, Charleston and Mobile are, in a diminished sense, to the South," Reid analogized, and "what New York is to the North, New Orleans is, in an exaggerated sense, to the South."[1]

Reid also compared New Orleans with Mobile, which had held out against Union forces until nearly the end of the war. Because New Orleans had been controlled by "national authorities" since 1862, he wrote, it "had been changing under the operation of Northern influences." As a result, Reid felt that

---

[1] Reid's press accounts from this journey (and a subsequent one in 1865–6) were edited and published as Whitelaw Reid, *After the War: A Tour of the Southern States, 1865–1866* (1866; repr., New York, 1965); quotations on pp. 234–5.

the Crescent City faced the postwar era not only in good physical condition, but also with a much-improved attitude among its citizenry as well. "Mobile showed us the last of the old South," the young journalist assured his readers, and "New Orleans the first of the new."[2]

During the late nineteenth century, this idea of a "new" South – one more open to "Northern influences," especially in commerce – gained wide popularity. In the hands of propagandists such as the Atlanta newspaper editor Henry C. Grady, the notion of a "New South" became the economic corollary to the sectional reconciliation implied by the "Lost Cause" myth, whereby the momentous differences that had prompted four years of armed conflict were buried beneath an avalanche of upbeat rhetoric about a fratricidal "brothers' war" now in the past. As later historians have shown, such ideas helped many Americans to start putting the war behind them. But as with most belief systems, the gap between idea and reality was often enormous. In postbellum New Orleans, events would soon cast doubt on Reid's sanguine estimate of the city's prospects. Far from epitomizing the New South, Reconstruction-era New Orleans constituted one of the region's foremost sites of revanchist sentiment and counterrevolutionary resistance. Moreover, commercial fortunes in the antebellum South's premier metropolis suffered a steep decline after the war, which helps dispel other myths about postbellum southern economic development that many scholars have been prone to accept at face value.[3]

Although New Orleans never reverted to Confederate control after its May 1862 surrender, the eight-month tenure of Benjamin F. Butler over the city had represented in many ways the war's continuation by political fiat. Only after Butler was replaced by General Nathaniel P. Banks did the process of federal reconstruction in New Orleans and its surrounding parishes begin in earnest. From the outset of Banks's administration, which lasted for the duration of the war, greater efforts were made to secure the cooperation of city residents still sympathetic to the Confederacy, as well as to cultivate and organize citizens loyal to the federal government. Under the supervisory gaze of President Lincoln and his cabinet (especially the ambitious Salmon P. Chase, then still serving as Secretary of the Treasury), New Orleans and its environs became a working laboratory for policies that sought to reintegrate the seceded states back into the Union. As would be true for the entire Reconstruction period, such federal efforts emphasized the political. In a nutshell, the problem was how to resume southern "home rule" while ensuring that local authorities acknowledged the inviolability, legitimacy, and authority of the national government. Balancing this equation proved enormously difficult, however, and was complicated by divisions within the federal government itself. Differences over Reconstruction

[2] Ibid., 227 (quotations).
[3] On the New South ideology see Paul M. Gaston, *The New South Creed: A Study in Southern Mythmaking* (Baton Rouge, 1970); on the Lost Cause see Gaines M. Foster, *Ghosts of the Confederacy: Defeat, the Lost Cause, and the Emergence of the New South* (New York, 1987).

policies were reflected in congressional factionalism between "radicals" and moderates, which became especially bitter after the accession of the incompetent southern Democrat Andrew Johnson to the presidency. Federal administrators also had to grapple with residual pro-Confederate sentiment, which fueled resistance in forms that varied from state to state.[4]

With byzantine politics at all levels driving events during these years, economic considerations may seem to have taken a backseat. Yet such factors were never far below the surface, and in fact, they lend special force to the term *political economy* during Reconstruction. This is most obvious with regard to the demise of slavery, which had been the dominant mode of production in the antebellum South. The South's "peculiar [economic] institution" had gradually become the defining issue of the still-young nation, and the inability to resolve its status within the federal framework had prompted secession and civil war. The advent of Reconstruction raised new sets of questions regarding the former bondspeople of the South. General Banks was still unpacking his bags in January 1863 when the cautious provisos of Lincoln's Emancipation Proclamation served notice that the southern labor system and blacks' role in it were likely to remain highly politicized for years to come. Indeed, this remained the case long after the Union victory and the Thirteenth Amendment (1865) ostensibly made slavery's abolition fait accompli. Although emancipation's meanings were contested on many fronts, the southern Black Codes of 1865–66 and the short-lived Freedmen's Bureau demonstrated that the constitutional negation of slavery did not itself sufficiently address former slaves' new status as "free laborers." Fashioning such a consensus was fundamentally a problem of political economy.[5]

In New Orleans, these and other struggles over the political economy of Reconstruction took place against a unique social backdrop. Beginning during General Butler's tenure, a large influx of refugees from the plantation districts had swelled the number of blacks in the city, which had long been home to the largest community of free blacks in the South. The ex-slaves' presence ratcheted

---

[4] The standard modern treatment of the period is Eric Foner, *Reconstruction: America's Unfinished Revolution, 1863–1877* (New York, 1988). Also still valuable are John Hope Franklin, *Reconstruction after the Civil War* (Chicago and London, 1961); and W. R. Brock, *An American Crisis: Congress and Reconstruction, 1865–1867* (New York, 1963). State-by-state reviews of the Reconstruction-era South can be found in W. E. B. Du Bois, *Black Reconstruction in America, 1860–1880* (1935; repr., New York, 1992); and Otto H. Olsen, ed., *Reconstruction and Redemption in the South* (Baton Rouge, 1980). On the Banks administration see Peyton McCrary, *Abraham Lincoln and Reconstruction: The Louisiana Experiment* (Princeton, NJ, 1978); and James G. Hollandsworth Jr., *Pretense of Glory: The Life of Nathaniel P. Banks* (Baton Rouge, 1998), chaps. 7–15.

[5] On the contested meanings of emancipation and free labor, see Foner, *Reconstruction*, chap. 3. Recent scholarship has emphasized the active role of ex-slaves themselves in negotiating and shaping the terms of their newly won freedoms; see, for example, Steven Hahn, *A Nation under Their Feet: Black Political Struggles in the Rural South from Slavery to the Great Migration* (Cambridge, MA, 2003).

up tensions in the city, especially after disgruntled working-class whites began straggling back from Confederate military service. The ongoing Union military presence in New Orleans was another thorn in the side of these Confederate States of America (CSA) veterans, who were particularly incensed by members of the U.S. Colored Troops (USCT). As state and municipal politics began to revolve around electoral franchisement (both its denial to Confederate loyalists and its extension to ex-slaves), these veterans assumed an enormous role in Crescent City affairs. Politics in Reconstruction-era New Orleans came to be characterized by well-armed factions with a proclivity to violence, earning the city national attention on two occasions: the race "riot" of late July 1866 and the short-lived coup against a Republican state government in 1874.

Although many New Orleans businessmen offered support to one faction or another, for the most part, the dramatic events of Reconstruction confirmed that their influence had been greatly weakened. The Treasury Department's sanctioning of interbelligerent trade encouraged large numbers of northern speculators to swarm into the city during the Banks regime, and even though it was widely condemned, cross-lines commerce helped entrench a culture of corruption centered on the federal Custom-house, one that favored Union loyalists and Republican Party supporters. To some degree, New Orleans merchants were reaping bitter oats they had helped to sow before the war. Their aloof attitudes toward politics during the late antebellum era had left them ill positioned to assume leadership during Reconstruction, and thus they were largely reduced to carping from the sidelines.

Although the notion of political economy is particularly apt for postwar New Orleans, this chapter focuses mainly on the political side of that equation. But just as crucial to New Orleans's rapidly declining postwar fortunes were a variety of interconnected economic changes during the period, such as the severe regional capital shortage, which was reflected in the failure of the city's banking sector to recover its prewar strength. Although some of these trends had originated during the antebellum years, the city's commercial shortcomings were greatly exacerbated in the wake of the Civil War. New Orleans merchants continued to rely on the river to deliver agricultural commodities to their doorsteps, even as their market share of that trade plummeted in the face of competition from more aggressive cities located around the perimeter of their former plantation hinterlands. A closely associated development was the shift of cotton marketing and its credit-provisioning functions into the hands of rural and small-town merchants in the interior. Although reinforced by the regional capital shortage, this trend was chiefly a consequence of the dispersal of plantation production among smaller farm units after emancipation. As a result, the New Orleans–based factorage system that had anchored southern merchant capitalism for decades was effectively destroyed in the aftermath of the Civil War.

These economic developments will be discussed mainly in the chapters that follow. Taken together, however, they all show how the Crescent City was demoted to a secondary and highly dependent role in the American urban system after the Civil War. Indeed, many roots of the city's long-term impoverishment (and the state's as well) can be found amidst the drift and chaos of the Reconstruction era. In the case of New Orleans, not until the late twentieth-century shift of industrial capital from urban centers in the "Rust Belt" can a comparably rapid decline of a formerly prosperous first-rank U.S. city be found. The "New South" asserted by Whitelaw Reid during his early postwar visit proved chimerical in New Orleans, whose merchants would never recover their prominence to the U.S. and transatlantic economies.

Like Benjamin Butler, Nathaniel P. Banks was a "political general" from Massachusetts, a state whose textile factories depended on the raw material that made them possible, southern cotton. Also like Butler, Banks's presidential ambitions were not much of a secret, which may have had something to do with Abraham Lincoln's decision to place him in charge of the distant southern city after Butler's command was no longer diplomatically tenable. From the beginning of his tenure in New Orleans, however, General Banks exhibited a sharply different style of governing, which was noted by local observers on both sides soon after his arrival in late 1862. On December 17, George S. Denison, a U.S. revenue collector in New Orleans, informed his patron, Treasury Secretary Salmon P. Chase, that public sentiment toward Banks's assumption of command was initially "one of satisfaction," particularly since the "extensive commercial proceedings which were tolerated (to say the least)" by Butler had left behind a residue of "general disgust." A few days later, Confederate partisan Julia LeGrand noted in her diary that the new commander "has so far commanded the respect of his enemies." Unlike Butler, she wrote, Banks did not seem to act as if "every rich man is his especial foe, to be robbed for his benefit." Attempts to solicit the cooperation, if not the active support, of the remaining residents from New Orleans's quondam elite would be a hallmark of Banks's administration. As one of his staff later put it, "[S]ince Butler had stroked the cat from the tail to head, and found her full of yawl and scratch, [Banks] was determined to stroke her from head to tail, and see if she would hide her claws, and commence to purr."[6]

Banks, however, usually left most of the day-to-day details of administrating the city to his subordinates. Denison was quick to note this proclivity, reporting that General Banks "seems disposed to occupy himself more with military and less with political and commercial affairs than General Butler did." Banks, eager to establish his reputation on the battlefield, spent much of 1863-4

---

[6] George H. Hepworth, *The Whip, Hoe, and Sword; or, The Gulf-department in '63* (Boston, 1864), 27–8; Diary entry, December 20, 1862, in Kate Mason Rowland and Mrs. Morris L. Croxall, eds., *The Journal of Julia LeGrand: New Orleans, 1862–1863* (Richmond, Va., 1911), 55–6; George S. Denison to Salmon P. Chase, December 17, 1862, in *Annual Report of the American Historical Association for the Year 1902* (2 vols., Washington, DC, 1903), II, 340 (hereinafter cited as *Chase Correspondence*).

conducting unimpressive yet destructive campaigns in the Louisiana interior. Only gradually did he seem to realize that he might be able to earn political capital by managing the formation of a new state government, especially if it could be packed with men favorable to his ambitions. But such self-interested meddling by Banks and others (e.g., Chase loyalists such as Denison), as well as Lincoln's own occasional interference, provoked bitter factionalism among the tiny pro-Unionist movement in the city from the outset, all of which further complicated the already difficult process of political Reconstruction in Louisiana.[7]

Denison also informed Chase that General Banks evinced little interest in commercial affairs. The general was angered by reports of "individual plunder" that occurred during Butler's administration, which he believed had left the local population "terribly bitter." However, he did sustain Butler's cotton tax on mercantile firms in 1863 and 1864, and much like his predecessor, he continued to harass the New Orleans banking sector. But for the most part, Banks delegated commercial matters to his officers, which thereby effectively ceded the formulation and implementation of trade policies to the Treasury Secretary and his minions.[8]

From the outset of the war, federal policies toward interbelligerent trade were characterized by a high degree of vacillation. Initially fearful of alienating border states like Kentucky and Missouri that he was desperate to keep in the Union, President Lincoln had waited until the late summer of 1861 before prohibiting further commercial intercourse with the seceded states. But almost as soon as this policy was announced, exceptions to it became the rule. For one thing, at the ground level, the supplies available through cross-lines trading were frequently a matter of survival for noncombatants in isolated communities affected by the war. But more importantly, high-ranking federal cabinet officials, especially Secretary of State William H. Seward and Treasury Secretary Chase, found themselves under pressure from manufacturing interests both at home and abroad to secure supplies of southern cotton, and they sought to shape military priorities accordingly. The occupation of New Orleans, for example, had been welcomed by Seward as a means of liberating the staple from Confederate control, but General Butler had produced disappointing

[7] Ted Tunnell, *Crucible of Reconstruction: War, Radicalism, and Race in Louisiana, 1862–1877* (Baton Rouge and London, 1984), 29, 43; Jefferson Davis Bragg, *Louisiana in the Confederacy* (1941; repr., Baton Rouge, 1997), 148–52; see also Ludwell H. Johnson, *Red River Campaign: Politics and Cotton in the Civil War* (1958; repr., Kent, OH, and London, 1993). Denison to Chase, January 2, 1863, in *Chase Correspondence*, II, 344.

[8] Gerald M. Capers, *Occupied City: New Orleans under the Federals, 1861–1865* (Lexington, KY, 1965), 158–60; Special Orders No. 202, August 17, 1863, signed original in Box 7, Folder 20, Kuntz Collection (Mss 600; Howard-Tilton Memorial Library, Tulane University; hereinafter cited as HTML-Tulane); Elisabeth Joan Doyle, "Civilian Life in Occupied New Orleans, 1862–65" (Ph.D. diss., Louisiana State University, 1955), 153–4; Banks to his wife, January 15, 1863, as cited in Johnson, *Red River Campaign*, 51 (quotations).

results in this regard, despite the notorious speculations of his brother Andrew. For his part, Secretary Chase was keen to renew the flow of cotton because of the customs revenues it could generate for federal coffers, so with the help of his field agents and less-than-enthusiastic War Department officials, he instituted a complex system of permits that promoted interbelligerent trading.[9]

After General Banks's arrival in New Orleans, efforts to obtain cotton from the hinterlands intensified among federal officials – both military and non-military – and private interests. The ships carrying Banks's expeditionary force had actually been financed by New York–based capitalists, and unbeknownst to the general, a bevy of northern cotton speculators (many of whom thought they were headed to Texas, not New Orleans) had been packed in alongside his troops during the journey southward. George Denison was led to complain to Chase in February that "a host of speculators, Jews, and camp-followers came hither in the wake of Banks's expedition" and that "every steamer brings an addition to the number." Denison was particularly incensed by Dr. Isachar Zacharie, a New York cotton merchant who enjoyed connections with both President Lincoln and General Banks, and whose brother James ran a commission firm in New Orleans. When Banks began making military incursions deep into the Louisiana countryside during the spring of 1863, many of these speculators tagged along behind his forces. At first, city business remained stagnant, with one local newspaper reporting in April on the "dull and cheerless aspect" of the commercial district, where "the great staple cotton may be deemed as an obsolete question at this time." But General Banks's forays into the interior prompted Dr. Zacharie to inform the president that he expected Louisiana's plantation regions would soon "again [be] opened to the commercial world."[10]

Signs of revival in New Orleans commerce became more apparent later that year, especially after Union military victories on the lower Mississippi River. Beginning in the late spring of 1863, Banks's forces besieged Confederate fortifications at Port Hudson above Baton Rouge, which finally fell in July, but only after General Ulysses S. Grant had captured Vicksburg less than 200 miles upriver, thereby depriving Banks of the military credit he so desperately sought. Regardless, with the great interior highway of commerce now entirely under Union control, Banks issued an order in early September declaring the river

[9] E. Merton Coulter, "Commercial Intercourse with the Confederacy in the Mississippi Valley, 1861–1865," *Mississippi Valley Historical Review* 5 (March 1919), 378–80; [Appleton's] *American Annual Cyclopedia and Register of Important Events of the Year 1862* (New York, 1865), 227–8, 387–8; Coulter, "The Effects of Secession Upon the Commerce of the Mississippi Valley," *Mississippi Valley Historical Review* 3 (December 1916), 289–90.

[10] Isachar Zacharie to Abraham Lincoln, April 25, 1863, in the Abraham Lincoln Papers, Library of Congress (available online at http://lcweb2.loc.gov/ammem/alhtml/malhome.html); "Things in General," New Orleans *Daily Picayune*, April 19, 1863; Denison to Chase, February 1, 5, and 12, 1863, in *Chase Correspondence*, II, 353, 355, 359–60 (quotations on p. 359); Johnson, *Red River Campaign*, 24–8.

TABLE 6.1. *Value of Products Received in New Orleans, 1860–1865*

Year	Value of Products
1860–1	$155,863,564
1861–2	$51,510,940
1862–3	$29,766,454
1863–4	$79,233,985
1864–5	$111,013,293

Source: De Bow's Review, New Series, Vol. I (January 1866), 49.

trade between New Orleans and the upper Mississippi, Ohio, and Missouri Valleys to be "free of any military restrictions whatsoever." Steamboat traffic between New Orleans and St. Louis was restored during the fall of 1863, and increased receipts on the city's long-dormant levees and wharves, according to Denison, began to give the city "somewhat the appearance of former times."[11]

Some historians have agreed with Denison by emphasizing the Crescent City's economic recovery after the river's reopening in 1863. But although trade in New Orleans did improve after mid-1863, especially compared with the near-total standstill over the previous two years, the city still had to recoup an enormous amount of lost ground in order to approximate its prewar vigor. In terms of total value (Table 6.1), much of the revival between 1863 and 1865 was a result of wartime inflation, especially in the price of cotton. Furthermore, the city's import sector benefited during these years from the need to transport most civilian goods inland via the river, since the northern and western rail systems were mostly devoted to military purposes. However, in terms of physical bulk, commercial statistics reveal that receipts from the interior continued to lag far below antebellum levels through the end of the war (Table 6.2). Western foodstuffs, especially flour, made the best recovery, but corn and pork receipts were but a fraction of their prewar totals by 1865. The decline in New Orleans's receipts of cotton, sugar, and tobacco – the chief staple crops of regional agriculture and long the city's lifeblood – was far more pronounced and illustrated the war's disastrous effects on southern commerce.[12]

However, even as lower Mississippi Valley commerce began to recover during the final years of the war, this revival carried with it several deleterious

[11] Denison to Chase, October 23, 1863, in *Chase Correspondence*, II, 412; Coulter, "Commercial Intercourse," 384 n. 22 (Banks quotation); Hollandsworth, *Pretense of Glory*, 120–33.

[12] Commercial statistics for New Orleans before, during, and immediately after the Civil War can be found in *De Bow's Review*, 2d ser., 1 (January 1866), 49; ibid. (February 1866), 202–3; and *De Bow's Review*, 2d ser., 2 (November 1866), 413–20. The city's "economic revival" during 1863–5 is emphasized by Capers, *Occupied City*, 152–3 (quotation on p. 152); see also Roger W. Shugg, *Origins of Class Struggle in Louisiana* (1939; repr., Baton Rouge, 1968), 188–9.

TABLE 6.2. *Receipts of Selected Interior Products in New Orleans, 1860–1865*

	Corn	Cotton	Flour	Pork	Sugar	Tobacco
1860–61	3,388,011	1,849,312	1,009,201	213,988	174,637	34,892
1861–62	315,652	38,880	281,645	11,452	225,356	1,063
1862–63	165,220	22,078	264,601	50,327	85,531	155
1863–64	410,138	131,044	399,897	67,022	75,153	1,363
1864–65	553,273	271,015	790,824	41,705	9,345	2,410

Source: De Bow's Review, New Series, Vol. I (February 1866), 202–3. Products are measured as follows: Corn, sacks; cotton, bales; flour and pork, barrels; sugar and tobacco, hogsheads.

consequences for New Orleans and its hinterlands. Just as most of the white population of New Orleans were still excluded from the incipient political processes of Reconstruction because of their Confederate allegiances, most Crescent City merchants found themselves frozen out of the nascent commercial revival. Under the permit system being run under the overlapping auspices of the Treasury and War Departments, licenses to do business across Union lines were generally reserved for the unimpeachably loyal, both past and present, conditions that relatively few resident merchants could meet. "There is no chance for a man here now unless he is identified with the Yankees and Bostonians," grumbled one local businessman in 1863. Moreover, when permits did become available, they were usually granted only after negotiating a bureaucratic maze that frequently involved the paying of bribes, sometimes to multiple officials.[13]

By vastly increasing the opportunities for official pettifoggery at all levels, the confusing welter of regulations and taxes imposed on cross-lines trading helped entrench a culture of corruption that revolved around the federal Custom-house, one that would plague business in New Orleans for years to come. Even though General Banks had condemned the high-level "plunder" that had occurred under his predecessor and would himself manage to stay surprisingly free of any taint of impropriety, his "hands-off" approach to commercial matters encouraged a diffusion of corruption throughout the Gulf Department that was, if anything, more serious than that during the Butler regime. Nor were these problems mere grousing by disgruntled Confederate sympathizers; in fact, pro-Union sources provided some of the most eloquent testimony as to their existence. George Denison, who would himself later stand accused of extorting bribes, complained to Secretary Chase as early as March 1863 that "there is a great deal more corruption here now than ever under

[13] Coulter, "Commercial Intercourse," 382–4, 390–3; Thomas H. Shields to Arthur W. Hyatt, August 15, 1863, quoted in Elisabeth Joan Doyle, "Greenbacks, Car Tickets, and the Pot of Gold: The Effects of Wartime Occupation on the Business Life of New Orleans, 1861–1865," *Civil War History* 5 (December 1959), 352.

Butler...." The following year Cuthbert Bullitt, a local Union loyalist who had been appointed U.S. customs collector, reported to President Lincoln that the "commercial condition of this department" demands "the most rigid & immediate action ... to put an end to the gross system of swindling & favoritism going on here, by unprincipled agents."[14]

Some high-ranking Union military officers, such as Admiral David D. Porter, were even more outspoken about the demoralizing and disruptive effects of cross-lines trading in the lower Mississippi Valley during the war's final years. General Banks's ill-fated Red River campaign of 1864, which probably put the nail in the coffin of his presidential ambitions, was marked by the prevalence of cotton-mad "camp-followers," and this mania spread among his troops as well, much to the detriment of discipline, which later led Admiral Porter to publicly declare, "Cotton killed that expedition, in my opinion." But interbelligerent commerce also had demoralizing consequences among civilians in the southern countryside. It tended to fan the flames of anti-mercantile sentiment against both New Orleans merchants and Yankee tradesmen, many of whom later settled in the region as landowners and storekeepers. It also fueled resentment toward Confederate authorities who encouraged trading with the enemy, thereby tacitly admitting their inability to provision their citizenry. Although deeply cynical attitudes toward government that would flourish among rural white southerners during and after Reconstruction were harvested on the field of politics, such feelings may have first taken root in the murky moral thickets of interbelligerent trading during the war's closing years.[15]

The wartime scramble for cotton in the lower Mississippi Valley, deplored by so many contemporary observers, was akin to another "gold rush," a frenzy

[14] Cuthbert Bullitt to Abraham Lincoln, April 29, 1864, in Lincoln Papers, Library of Congress; Denison to Chase, March 29, 1863, in *Chase Correspondence*, II, 373–4. For the accusations of corruption against Denison, see the testimony of New Orleans commission merchant George F. Brott in "Report of the Special Commission," September 23, 1865, Old Army Records (RG-94) Vol. 737, p. 59 (microfilm, National Archives; hereinafter cited as Smith-Brady Report). This report also catalogues a wide variety of other instances of wartime corruption in the New Orleans–based Gulf Department, as does the *Report of the Joint Committee on the Conduct of the War*, 38 Cong., 2 Sess. (3 vols., Washington, DC, 1865), esp. Vol. II ("The Red River Expedition") and Vol. III, pp. 26–44. A close associate of Benjamin Butler's brother Andrew sought unsuccessfully to bribe General Banks soon after his arrival to New Orleans for his aid in their continued interbelligerent trading; Ludwell H. Johnson, "Northern Profits and Profiteers: The Cotton Rings of 1864–1865," *Civil War History* 12.2 (1966), 109.

[15] Samuel C. Hyde Jr., *Pistols and Politics: The Dilemma of Democracy in Louisiana's Florida Parishes, 1810–1899* (Baton Rouge, 1996), 125; Bragg, *Louisiana in the Confederacy*, 260–1; and David G. Surdam, *Northern Naval Superiority and the Economics of the Civil War* (Columbia, SC, 2001), 182–6. Johnson, *Red River Campaign*, 71–8, 250–4, 285–8 (Admiral Porter quote on p. 285); Coulter, "Commercial Intercourse," 389–93. Although he neglects to discuss merchants, Armstead L. Robinson brilliantly analyzes the ways that growing intrasouthern class conflicts during the war contributed to the Confederacy's defeat; Robinson, *Bitter Fruits of Bondage: The Demise of Slavery and the Collapse of the Confederacy, 1861–1865* (Charlottesville, VA, 2005).

TABLE 6.3. *Cotton Prices and New Orleans Receipts, 1860–1865*

Crop Year	Price per lb. (cents)	Price per bale (dollars)	New Orleans Receipts (bales)	Total Value (dollars)
1860–1	0.11	$50.00	1,849,312	$92,465,600
1861–2	0.10	$45.50	38,880	$1,769,040
1862–3	0.56	$231.32	22,078	$15,107,082
1863–4	0.85	$356.20	131,044	$46,677,872
1864–5	0.69	$270.54	271,015	$73,326,398

Source: De Bow's Review, New Series, Vol. I (February 1866), 202–3; De Bow's Review, New Series, Vol. II (November 1866), 415. Minor discrepancies, probably attributable to typographical errors, have been corrected by comparing and extrapolating from the figures compiled in these issues.

that was provoked by several years of radically higher prices for the staple crop (Table 6.3). With a single bale of cotton now worth more than most men had previously earned in a year (the monthly salary for enlisted Union troops was only sixteen dollars at war's end), it is perhaps less surprising that so many northerners, civilian and military alike, were able to overcome whatever scruples they may have had about how their self-interested behaviors might damage the ongoing war effort. The upward spike in cotton prices during the Civil War had long-term economic consequences as well. For example, historian Sven Beckert has recently argued that this period of inordinately high market prices helped agricultural producers in other countries such as India and Egypt to overcome their competitive disadvantages with regard to cheaper, slave-produced cotton from the U.S. South. Increasing supplies from such sources began to break the long-standing southern monopoly on the staple, and they also contributed to keeping the price of cotton well below previous median levels in global commodities markets during the closing decades of the nineteenth century.[16]

The wartime cotton trade in the lower Mississippi Valley also established or reinforced patterns that would have more immediate consequences for New Orleans–based commerce during and after Reconstruction. Although the combined value of cotton receipts at New Orleans in 1864–5 represented more than three-quarters of the value of the last prewar crop, physical receipts barely reached 15 percent of the 1860–1 total. Furthermore, most of the profits from these wartime sales went into either federal coffers or the pockets of northern speculators; the old resident merchant community of New Orleans was

[16] Sven Beckert, "Emancipation and Empire: Reconstructing the Worldwide Web of Cotton Production in the Age of the American Civil War," *American Historical Review* 109 (December 2004), 1405–38; Lawrence N. Powell and Michael S. Wayne, "Self-Interest and the Decline of Confederate Nationalism," in *The Old South in the Crucible of War*, eds. Harry P. Owens and James J. Cooke (Jackson, MS, 1983), 39–43.

largely excluded from this lucrative trade. Even more important, the amount of cotton exported under federal auspices during the war totaled only 444,095 bales. Of this "legal" cotton, 310,931 bales were shipped out via the occupied port of New Orleans, a total that seemed to maintain the city's proportionally dominant share of cotton exports during the late antebellum era. But according to recent estimates, the amount of southern cotton shipped to northern and foreign markets illegally (which is to say, smuggled) during the war was far greater than this: between 1 to 1.5 million bales, or at least double the amount exported with official permission. It is unlikely that much of this smuggled cotton exited via the tightly controlled federal port of New Orleans; most was probably transported covertly along interior land and lake routes to northeastern markets, especially in New York and Boston.[17]

In this sense, the sharp reduction in physical receipts of cotton at New Orleans reflected two related trends that interbelligerent commerce helped accelerate: the marketing of cotton in interior urban markets, and its transportation to end-users via overland routes rather than circuitous river and coastal ones. The wartime isolation of New Orleans on the southwestern coastal periphery helped make previously cumbersome overland routes more cost-efficient, as did the expenses entailed in dealing with federal officials, from excise and customs taxes to bribery. In a fall 1863 letter to Secretary Chase, George Denison predicted that such disadvantages were likely to prompt a shift of the cotton trade to interior cities such as Memphis, and he was right. As historian E. Merton Coulter noted, Memphis became "the center of a truly gigantic traffic directly with the Confederacy" during the final years of the war, and contemporary observers also reported the growth of northern-backed commission houses in other interior towns like Vicksburg and Natchez. Border cities such as Louisville and St. Louis became increasingly involved with the southern cotton trade toward the end of the war as well. Merchants in these cities sought to boost their fortunes by end-running the old river-to-coastwise routes that had long directed so much commercial traffic southward to the Crescent City. During the war, the port of New Orleans added further disadvantages to its already lengthy list of institutional and infrastructural shortcomings, and its expensive facilities proved to be a point of last resort for cross-lines trading in cotton, particularly for those who sought to do so without federal sanction. Ironically, the very "legality" of New Orleans–based commerce during the occupation years helped suppress its current and future economic prospects, as did its island-like location near the Gulf Coast. Because the process of federal

---

[17] The data in the text are drawn from David G. Surdam's recent extensive economic analysis of the wartime cotton trade; Surdam, *Northern Naval Superiority*, 154–60. Surdam's conclusions about the extent of the "illegal" cotton trade are roughly the same as those in Stanley Lebergott, "Through the Blockade: The Profitability and Extent of Cotton Smuggling, 1861–1865," *Journal of Economic History* 41 (December 1981), 867–88; see also Thomas H. O'Connor, "Lincoln and the Cotton Trade," *Civil War History* 7 (March 1961), 32.

Reconstruction had begun three years earlier in the Crescent City than it did in most of the South, its merchants only received a head start toward losing their formerly dominant market share of the regional cotton trade.[18]

Upon the end of the war in April 1865, however, many of these trends were not fully apparent. At first, New Orleans continued to act as a magnet for hundreds of men on the make, northerners and southerners alike. In particular, veterans of both armies flocked into the city to seek their postwar fortunes. Charles Winder Squires, for example, had served as a young colonel in Louisiana's Washington Artillery, and he later remembered the situation at war's end:

The war was over and, like myself, many of my soldier friends were in New Orleans. The issue of the hour was the Almighty Dollar. The question with all of us then ... was, How to get it? Nearly twenty-three years old and my occupation gone. What was I to do?

Squires was soon introduced to an old resident merchant, William Witherell, who dispatched the young ex-officer to Shreveport with $10,000 in gold and instructions to buy up all the cotton he could lay his hands on. After his return to New Orleans, the young ex-Confederate officer continued to benefit from such patronage as he entered the wholesale grocery business. Local correspondents for the R. G. Dun & Co. credit agency noted that Squires, although "of limited means" himself, reputedly enjoyed financial backing from "good, strong friends." On the Union side, Bruno Trombly, a former peddler from Clinton County, New York, who had served as a lieutenant in the 20th U.S. Colored Troops Regiment in Louisiana, initially sought to establish a store in rural Pointe Coupee Parish northwest of Baton Rouge at the conclusion of the war. By January 1866, however, Trombly was forced to admit that his "first trial in business has been a total failure," so he made his way down to New Orleans to begin anew.[19]

Merchants based in New Orleans, whether northern arrivistes or long-time residents, moved quickly to reestablish relationships with the southern countryside after the war. Some, such as William Witherell, had apparently managed to hoard some capital during the occupation years, and they now wasted little

[18] Reid, *After the War*, 481; *Report of the Joint Committee on the Conduct of the War*, III, 26–44; Coulter, "Commercial Intercourse," 386; Johnson, "Northern Profits and Profiteers," 110–13; Surdam, *Northern Naval Superiority*, 190–1; Denison to Chase, September 12, 1863, in *Chase Correspondence*, II, 404.

[19] Diary entry, January 14, 1866, in Bruno Trombly Diary and Papers (Mss 4033-Z, Southern Historical Collection, Wilson Library, University of North Carolina at Chapel Hill; hereinafter cited as SHC); report dated July 1867, in Louisiana, Vol. XIII, 89, in R. G. Dun & Co. Credit Reports Collection (Baker Library Historical Collections, Harvard Business School); autobiographical manuscript of Charles Winder Squires (3 vols.), III, 11–12, in W. H. T. Squires Papers (Mss 1644-Z, SHC). On the postwar experiences of ex-Union soldiers and other northerners in the Mississippi Valley see Lawrence N. Powell, *New Masters: Northern Planters during the Civil War and Reconstruction* (New Haven, CT, and London, 1980).

time using it to secure a share of the cotton rumored to be stashed around the former plantation districts. Although the extent of these reserves soon proved considerably less than expected, interior river towns were thronged with buyers and sellers hoping to take advantage of still-high cotton prices. Serving as Witherell's agent in northwestern Louisiana in the summer of 1865, Charles Squires described how "from all the country round wagons loaded with the staple were daily driven into Shreveport." "The buyers would jump on the bales as the wagons stood in the mud and make their bids," he recalled. Some planters, however, reflexively reached out to their former New Orleans factors to exchange their long-hoarded cotton. "So wedded are most of the old residents to their old ways of doing business," reported Whitelaw Reid from Mississippi's river districts in January 1866, "that they see all these supplies steadily carried past their doors ... but wait until they reach New Orleans, pass through the hands of their old commission merchant, and thus return with double freights and double commissions, to be landed at the very places they passed the week before."[20]

This was a familiar pattern, perhaps even a depressing one, to observers like Reid. But changes were in the wind, and many of them centered on the rural and small-town stores of the interior. Again, Squires reported from Shreveport that "all of the dry-goods, groceries, hardware, saddlery, & c. had been used up" during the war, and what remained of many inventories had been plundered in a spate of store looting that occurred throughout Louisiana during the closing months of the conflict. After greater order prevailed, many country store owners sought to replenish their stocks as quickly as possible by ordering goods from New Orleans. One rural citizen later recounted "how new arrival after new arrival was greedily absorbed" when local stores began reopening with freshly stocked shelves during the summer of 1865, which confirmed a Crescent City newspaper's report that purchases by country merchants prompted "unprecedented activity [in] most branches of our wholesale trade" during the year after the war's conclusion.[21]

The winds of change also carried storm clouds, however, many of which bode ill for New Orleans's commercial prospects. (Indeed, inordinately bad weather would itself contribute to low crop output during the first full growing season after the war.) Although cotton prices remained high by prewar standards in 1865–6, when they averaged just over thirty-nine cents per pound, this

---

[20] Reid, *After the War*, 475; Squires autobiography, III, 13–14. For an overly sanguine estimate that 4 million bales of cotton remained "hidden in remote places or buried in underground caches throughout the South," see "Commercial Chronicle and Review," *Hunt's Merchants' Magazine* 53 (September 1865), 225.

[21] New Orleans *Times*, September 1, 1866; "Times in the Confederacy," *De Bow's Review*, 2d ser., II (November 1866), 573; Squires autobiography, III, 13–14 (quotation). On 1865 store looting in Louisiana see ibid., III, 1; and Sarah A. Dorsey, *Recollections of Henry Watkins Allen, Brigadier-General Confederate States Army [and] Ex-Governor of Louisiana* (New York and New Orleans, 1866), 294–5.

still represented a steep drop from the previous two years, during which market prices for the staple had already fallen from eighty-five to sixty-nine cents per pound. One rural diarist wrote that her family initially "had little trouble getting advances in New Orleans to plant" with "cotton so high," but when prices began creeping downward under peacetime conditions, easy credit from Crescent City merchants became much harder to obtain. Complaining about this lack of financial support in a January 1866 letter to the New Orleans *Daily Crescent*, an Arkansas planter sternly admonished "your merchants to make exertions to secure the next crop." Coyly alluding to business he had recently transacted with firms in Memphis and St. Louis, the planter lamented the absence of the usual visits to his region by New Orleans factors. "We are loyal to New Orleans," he claimed, but we "wish them ... to give us at least one nod of recognition."[22]

Most New Orleans merchants would have liked to oblige such planters, but their ability to resume their erstwhile relations with the southern countryside was hindered by numerous problems. Not least among them was the unsettled condition of labor in the former plantation districts. The New Orleans *Price-Current*, the organ of the city's mercantile elites, took a grim view of the issue at the outset, declaring in September 1865 that it could see "no other sure resort than a new labor system to be proscribed and enforced by the State." However, efforts to reinstitute compulsory labor were usually quashed by agents of the newly established Freedmen's Bureau. Direct compulsion being barred, the terms under which former slaves would resume working in cotton fields remained an ongoing negotiation between landowners and freedpeople for the first few years following the war. Despite considerable give-and-take, forms of contract labor featuring deferred payment in crop shares became widespread in Louisiana's cotton parishes as early as 1866, though the precise form of the labor units still varied widely. Most planters would have preferred to employ their former slaves en masse as gang labor, but freedpeople successfully resisted this; instead, they entered into share contracts with planters in smaller, self-associated groups. At first, "squads" of roughly six to twenty-five laborers were most common, but the sharecropping system soon came to be organized mainly around smaller, kin-based, household units of production.[23]

The full ramifications of the emergent sharecropping system in cotton production only became clear gradually to Crescent City merchants over the next several years. From their perspective, the most salient immediate problems were

[22] Letter signed "Euclid," New Orleans *Daily Crescent*, January 10, 1866; Kate Stone, *Brokenburn: The Journal of Kate Stone, 1861–1868*, ed. John Q. Anderson (Baton Rouge, 1955), 368. On declining cotton prices and poor weather conditions in 1865–66, see *De Bow's Review*, 2d ser., II (November 1866), 415–16.

[23] New Orleans *Price-Current*, September 1, 1865; Joe Gray Taylor, *Louisiana Reconstructed, 1863–1877* (Baton Rouge, 1974), 374–5. On the squad system and the rapid evolution of sharecropping in the postbellum South, see Gerald David Jaynes, *Branches without Roots: Genesis of the Black Working Class in the American South, 1862–1882* (New York, 1986).

the profound consequences that the downsizing of production units had for their ability to provide seasonal agricultural credit without exposure to inordinately high risk. Under the antebellum system, city merchants had extended credit directly to individual land- and slave-owning planters, with whom they usually had close personal relationships and whose capital assets served as collateral against possible defaults – say, in the instance of crop failure. But under sharecropping's newly dispersed system of cotton production, merchants could no longer rely on the close supervision and responsibility of landowners as sufficient security for credit extension. Sharecropping added a vast number of extra links to the production chain, thereby placing city factors at a crucial further remove from the cotton crops they were financing. By contrast, in Louisiana's sugar parishes, where the reconstruction of the slave-labor system had proceeded under federal supervision since at least 1863, the small farming units of sharecropping quickly proved unworkable. As a result, forms of wage payment, mainly to individual workers, soon became the norm in cane production, with enormous consequences for its economic structure and particularly for local merchants' role within it. (Chapter 8 provides a sustained comparison of postemancipation labor systems and mercantile development in cotton and sugar parishes.)[24]

Furthermore, the Louisiana sugar sector had suffered greater wartime devastation to its more capital-intensive aspects, such as processing and refining, which caused production to take longer to recover a semblance of its antebellum output. It eventually did so, in large part because of heavy infusions of northern capital, but this calls attention to another factor inhibiting the resumption of old commercial patterns by New Orleans merchants: the severe capital shortage in the postbellum South. In contrast to what one local newspaper in 1866 called the "state of incertitude and general chaos" surrounding evolving production arrangements in the countryside and merchants' role in them, the problem of regional capital shortage was viewed in postwar New Orleans as an immediate threat to the city's former dominance of staple-crop marketing in the lower Mississippi Valley. Still, it was difficult to completely distinguish between these problems. Slaves had previously not only served as the labor force for plantation agriculture, but along with land, they had also represented one of the primary forms of capital underpinning the antebellum southern financial system. In this latter sense, economic historians Roger L. Ransom and Richard Sutch have calculated that emancipation wiped out nearly half the aggregate wealth of the cotton-growing states of the South. A. P. Dostie, a Republican official in Louisiana during early Reconstruction, acknowledged

[24] John C. Rodrigue, *Reconstruction in the Cane Fields: From Slavery to Free Labor in Louisiana's Sugar Parishes, 1862–1880* (Baton Rouge, 2001), 73–7, 132–3, 150–3; Taylor, *Louisiana Reconstructed*, 367; Richard H. Kilbourne Jr., *Debt, Investment, Slaves: Credit Relations in East Feliciana Parish, Louisiana, 1825–1885* (Tuscaloosa, Ala., and London, 1995); Jaynes, *Branches without Roots*, 36–41.

this point in 1864 even while probably underestimating its full magnitude. "$170,000,000 [worth] of property has been stricken from among the objects of taxation," he declared, "and raised to the condition of citizens."[25]

Dostie's comment calls our attention to the fact that emancipation actually transferred the capitalized value of bonded labor to the control of its rightful owners – the ex-slaves themselves. Nevertheless, the abolition of slavery represented a staggering blow to the financial status quo antebellum, and the postwar depression of land values throughout the South both reflected and exacerbated this upheaval in regional capital markets. In New Orleans, these problems were epitomized by the condition of the city's banks, which had been devastated by the Civil War. In 1861 there had been some thirteen banks in the city, with a combined stock of about $24 million, which was by far the greatest concentration of banking capital in the South. As was discussed in Chapter 5, New Orleans banks had collectively shipped out several million dollars' worth of specie for safekeeping prior to May 1862, most of which had been promptly confiscated by the Confederate government for the war effort. Matters worsened during the early occupation, when Federal authorities not only forced the banks to relinquish their Confederate bonds and deposits, but also required them to do so in the form of gold or federally recognized notes. When the aptly named General Banks assumed control of the city in 1863, seven New Orleans banks had already gone into liquidation, and the rest were barely solvent. As of 1865 the combined capital stock of the city's banks had plummeted to only $7.67 million, a drop of more than two-thirds from four years earlier. "By the end of the war," two historians have recently concluded, "the New Orleans banking system was but a shadow of what it had been before the Union occupation."[26]

The situation faced by New Orleans bankers during early Reconstruction was made even more difficult by national financial developments. The federal government had expanded the nation's money supply during the war by

[25] A. P. Dostie (1864), as quoted in Shugg, *Origins of Class Struggle in Louisiana*, 192; Roger L. Ransom and Richard Sutch, *One Kind of Freedom: The Economic Consequences of Emancipation* (2nd ed.; New York and other cities, 2001), 52; New Orleans *Times*, September 1, 1866. On devastation and slow recovery in the Louisiana sugar industry, see Charles P. Roland, "Difficulties of Civil War Sugar Planting in Louisiana," *Louisiana Historical Quarterly* 38 (October 1955), 58–9; Rodrigue, *Reconstruction in the Cane Fields*, 56–9, 111–12; and John A. Heitmann, *The Modernization of the Louisiana Sugar Industry, 1830–1910* (Baton Rouge, 1987), 68–90.

[26] John B. Legler and Richard Sylla, "Integration of U.S. Capital Markets: Southern Stock Markets and the Case of New Orleans, 1871–1913," in *Finance, Intermediaries, and Economic Development*, eds. Stanley L. Engerman et al. (New York, 2003), 148–51 (quotation on p. 151); Stephen A. Caldwell, *A Banking History of Louisiana* (Baton Rouge, 1935), chap. 7 and p. 128. Census data show that the aggregate value of real estate in the South declined by 48 percent between 1860 and 1870, and other evidence indicates that the drop in Louisiana may have been even greater; see James L. Sellers, "The Economic Incidence of the Civil War in the South," in *The Economic Impact of the Civil War*, ed. Ralph Andreano (Cambridge, MA, 1962), 82.

creating a new circulating medium (commonly referred to as "greenbacks"), but afterward, the U.S. Treasury Department made no effort to balance the uneven regional apportionment of this currency. In 1866, almost twenty times more currency per capita was in circulation in New York and New England than in the southern states, and as late as 1876 a New Orleans factor informed a client that even "small bills ... are very hard to get and we have to buy them at about 1/4 premium most of the time...." Even more harmful to the South were provisions of the National Banking Act of 1863 that prohibited the use of real estate mortgages as collateral by chartered banks. After being deprived of both slaves and land as a basis for capital augmentation, the financial community of New Orleans was never able to recover its former prominence. Aggregate bank capitalization in Louisiana dropped to only $3.73 million by 1875 and continued to decline through the end of the century.[27]

Crescent City merchants were quick to recognize that the state of the city's banks was not just a local concern but instead threatened the entire southern cotton sector. These institutions had long stood at the apex of the pyramidal structure of regional credit, with city factors serving as intermediaries between them and rural planters. But merchants could no longer rely on these banks, and their own resources were too limited to finance crop production. In 1866 the New Orleans *Price-Current*, voice of the city's business interests, advanced a possible solution: federally backed agricultural credit. The *Price-Current* urged that "cotton banks" be established in "Southern cities to aid the planter," including one in New Orleans that would be capitalized at $20 million. Such largesse was not forthcoming from Congress, however, especially after hostile Radical Republicans assumed control of Reconstruction policy in 1867. But if the federal government would not help, perhaps private interests could be persuaded to do so. "What the South now needs is capital," *De Bow's Review* editorialized in January 1866, "and if the immense accumulations of the North could be only diverted in that channel, something like the old days of prosperity would be revived...." Forgetful of its routine antebellum condemnations of dependence on extraregional investment, the South's premier business journal now pleaded, "Will not these rich capitalists pause and consider?"[28]

[27] Figures on Louisiana bank capitalization are from Caldwell, *Banking History of Louisiana*, Appendix II (p. 128). Letter from J. H. Allen to Col. J. Robins, December 15, 1876, document no. 2007.257.53 in Louisiana Manuscripts Collection (Mss 579), Williams Research Center, Historic New Orleans Collection, New Orleans, LA. For a contemporary objection to the National Banking Act's real estate mortgage lending prohibitions, see Lysander Spooner, "Proposed Banking System for the South," *De Bow's Review*, 2d ser., II (August 1866), 150–9. On the disastrous effects of the 1863 act on the South in general, see Robert P. Sharkey, *Money, Class, and Party: An Economic Study of the Civil War and Reconstruction* (Baltimore, 1959), 229–36 (1866 regional per capita circulation data on p. 235); Ransom and Sutch, *One Kind of Freedom*, 110–13; and William G. Roy, *Socializing Capital: The Rise of the Large Industrial Corporation in America* (Princeton, NJ, 1997) 131–2.
[28] *De Bow's Review*, 2d ser., I (January 1866), 108; New Orleans *Price-Current*, reprinted as "What the Cotton Industry Requires," in *De Bow's Review*, 2d ser., I (February 1866), 197–8 (quotation on p. 198).

Some northerners did heed such calls, although ones who could be described as "rich capitalists" were relatively few. Most were men of modest means who had originally come to the region in capacities related to the Union occupation and then stayed on to advance their personal fortunes. These men ran the gamut from aspiring petit-bourgeois like former USCT officer Bruno Trombly, who returned to New Orleans in 1866 to become a clerk in a small sutlery, to George S. Denison, who exploited his connections as a U.S. Treasury Department official to help organize the city's only national bank in late 1863. Denison kept Secretary Chase closely apprised as to the progress of the First National Bank. Sensitive as always to his patron's keen interest in shifting political winds, he informed Chase that most of the new bank's paid-in capital "is owned by men of unconditional loyalty." "You may be assured that whatever political influence it has," Denison continued, "will be upon the right side." Although Trombly and Denison were perched on very different rungs of postwar Louisiana's rickety commercial ladder, both men soon grew frustrated with their endeavors and returned to the North. Admitting that "Southern feelings were not very good just now" toward Yankee entrepreneurs like himself, Trombly rejected an offer to become a partner in a new mercantile firm and left for his home state of New York in late 1866. For his part, Denison found his local influence considerably diminished after President Lincoln's shrewd elevation of Chase to the Supreme Court in 1864. Despite what he described in a June 1865 letter as the "continual & bitter antagonisms" between "Rebels" and "Union men" on the playing field of the regional political economy, Denison persisted in his money-making efforts by becoming a co-lessee of three nearby sugar plantations that year. "Eventually we shall lick them in business," he vowed, "but it will be a hard fight." However, he soon became disillusioned with this continuation of the war by other means, only to die suddenly while en route back to the North in the summer of 1866.[29]

Many contemporary observers described the large influx of northerners to New Orleans during early Reconstruction. According to Whitelaw Reid, "New Orleans had proved a rich harvest-field to a crowd of new men and miscellaneous adventurers from the North." "Hundreds had accumulated fortunes since the occupation of the city," he wrote in 1865. Similarly, Thomas W. Knox declared that "New Orleans could boast of more cotton factors than cotton" during the Banks regime, when most business fell into "the hands of merchants from the North, who had established themselves in the city" after the occupation. These "new and enterprising merchants monopolized the cotton traffic," Knox later recalled, "and left the slavery-worshiping factors of the olden

---

[29] George S. Denison to his uncle [D. C. Denison], June 2, 1865, in "Some Letters of George Stanton Denison, 1854–1866: Observations of a Yankee on Conditions in Louisiana and Texas," ed. James A. Padgett, *Louisiana Historical Quarterly* 23 (October 1940), 1224–5 (quotations on p. 1225); see also ibid., 1137–8; Diary entries, February 22 (quotation), November 13, and December 11–12, 1866, Trombly Diary and Papers (SHC); Denison to Chase, November 6, 1863, in *Chase Correspondence*, 416.

time to mourn the loss of their occupation." The rush of speculators continued after the war's conclusion. One traveler reported that his southbound steamer from St. Louis in late 1865 was packed with "a crowd of Northern men" who intended to "establish new firms ... or merely to 'prospect a little' with a view to future settlement."[30]

The influx of northerners gradually began to slow once it became clear that the supplies of cotton stashed throughout the interior had dried up. As trade began to depend more on newly harvested or impending crops, the scales of commercial power in the Crescent City gradually began to tilt back in favor of older resident merchants. Reid disparaged what he called a surge of north-ern "toadyism" in 1866 as newly arrived entrepreneurs sought to curry favor with local merchants who had reestablished their relationships with planters in the countryside. Nonetheless, most of the city's prewar firms faced an uphill battle to reclaim their dominance of the cotton trade. Their capital shortfalls were exacerbated by a rising tide of legal difficulties, some of which pitted them against their quondam plantation clientele. Northern firms were eager to recoup some of the estimated $150 million in prewar debts owed to them by southern houses, but to meet those obligations, Crescent City factors first had to settle outstanding accounts and notes from planters before the war. Before the conflict had even ended, for example, the Creole firm of P. J. Pavy & Co. hired an attorney to help collect overdue debts from the Louisiana country-side. Yet doing so sometimes meant that city merchants had to initiate forced sales of plantation properties by their ex-clients, and with parish courts usually controlled by appointees disinclined to look kindly on their straitened circum-stances, many commission houses found themselves on the losing end of such lawsuits. Their inability to collect prewar debts caused numerous old firms to declare insolvency, as did the long-established Crescent City houses of R. C. Cummings and Walter Cox in 1866.[31]

[30] J. E. Hilary Skinner, *After the Storm; or, Jonathan and His Neighbours in 1865–6* (2 vols., London, 1866), I, 308; Thomas W. Knox, *Camp-Fire and Cotton-Field: Southern Adventure in Time of War* (New York, 1865), 396; Reid, *After the War*, 240.

[31] On the dissolution of Cummings & Co., see New Orleans *Daily Crescent*, January 1, 1866; on W. Cox & Co. see New Orleans *Daily Picayune*, January 10, 1866. Nevertheless, Cox's firm was still held liable for over $30,000 in prewar obligations in five suits decided against him during 1866–7; see Docket Nos. 16184, 16819, 17380, 18609, and 19677, Fourth U.S. District Court, New Orleans (microfilm, New Orleans Public Library). Thus bankrupted, Cox died soon thereafter; New Orleans *Daily Picayune*, May 14, 1868. On P. J. Pavy & Co. see their bill col-lection authorization with L. J. Gary, March 19, 1865 (Folder 60) and their 1868 co-agreement with Mrs. Phoebe Pierce (Folder 89), both in Box 7, Kuntz Collection (HTML-Tulane). See also Richard H. Kilbourne Jr., "The Ongoing Agricultural Credit Crisis in the Florida Parishes of Louisiana, 1865–1890," in *A Fierce and Fractious Frontier: The Curious Development of Louisiana's Florida Parishes, 1699–2000*, ed. Samuel C. Hyde Jr. (Baton Rouge, 2004), 128–30. On prewar debts to northern firms see Harold D. Woodman, *King Cotton and His Retainers: Financing and Marketing the Cotton Crop of the South, 1800–1925* (Lexington, KY, 1968), 203. Reid, *After the War*, 449–51 (quotation on p. 451).

Most contemporary reports agree that New Orleans experienced a large, sudden influx of new businessmen after the city's occupation, and also that many resident merchants either deserted the city or failed during or just after the war. It would be useful, however, to have some quantitative evidence to substantiate these accounts, especially given the highly politicized contexts in which they were often advanced. In Chapter 5, a comparison of firms listed in the 1861 Gardner's city directory with those in subsequent wartime sources showed that nearly a quarter of the city's pre-secession mercantile houses remained in operation after the occupation and the rush to vacate the city that preceded it. For data on persisting and new firms after 1865, listings in pre- and postwar sources were similarly compared. As of 1866, the number of firms in the New Orleans cotton trade had decreased to 403 from 467 in 1861. To estimate the persistence of antebellum mercantile firms in New Orleans after the war, an effort was made to identify firms that were reorganized during the interim while retaining one or more partners from the original house. With their inclusion understood, comparative evidence indicates that 149 firms in New Orleans in 1866 (32 percent) had been in operation prior to the war, more than half of which (79 firms) had persisted without any reorganization. Thus, despite the war, one-third of antebellum mercantile firms remained in business, even if reorganized, five years later.[32]

It is hard to be as precise about the number of New Orleans firms established by newcomers during early Reconstruction. The obverse of the above data shows that new firms comprised 68 percent of those listed in 1866, indicating a significant amount of wartime turnover in the city's commercial houses. However, this figure should be adjusted downward to account for still-extant resident firms not included in directories, as well as others that had been reorganized but were not easily identifiable as such. Yet even after such adjustments, a conservative estimate still indicates that at least half the firms in the New Orleans commodities trade in 1866 were new establishments. These comparative aggregate data, however imperfect, thus confirm the copious anecdotal evidence about the large numbers of newcomers, mainly northerners, to the city's business circles after the occupation.[33]

---

[32] The data that follow in the text were compiled using Gardner's New Orleans city directories for 1861 and 1866 (HTML-Tulane). Unfortunately there are no other comparably complete sources for the number of businesses as the municipal census of merchants conducted in 1854 (which was discussed in Chapter 1). Nevertheless, city directories at least provide a listing of merchants that, while incomplete, can be used to obtain minimum baseline data. One could also reasonably estimate that the directories undercounted the actual number of firms by 20 percent or so, especially if the relatively consistent percentages of firms that appeared in the embargo circulars or Butler's Schedule B but *not* in the 1861 directory are an accurate guide. It is also interesting to note that, despite whatever punitive treatment may have been directed toward them by Federal authorities, over 40 percent of the 149 persisting firms had been signatories to the July 1861 embargo circular. This may indicate a correlation between larger, more stable firms with sufficient financial resources to withstand the war and those that had publicly backed the Confederacy.

[33] In order to identify older firms that had been reorganized, city directories were used to cross-reference partnerships featuring fairly unique surnames and/or unchanged addresses. This is

For the cotton merchants of New Orleans, this influx of northern speculators had important consequences for their ability to resume business. During the first five years after the war, as cotton production struggled to regain a semblance of antebellum levels, the presence of well-financed newcomers made it more difficult to secure shares of a shrunken commercial pie. Moreover, competition from northerners was not limited to private interests. The role of the federal government in the cotton trade had increased during the war and remained extensive for several years afterward. Military officials, including the Freedmen's Bureau, and Treasury Department agents were now deeply insinuated into commercial relationships, usually in unwelcome ways. The continuation of federal excise taxes imposed on cotton during the war, which represented up to 40 percent of crops' market value, prompted complaints from northern and southern merchants alike. The New York Chamber of Commerce protested to Congress that these taxes were slowing the resumption of cotton production and helping producers overseas to maintain their newfound price advantages, all to the detriment of the U.S. domestic economy.[34]

The New York petition tapped into long-standing American disdain for excise taxes to buttress its arguments, but Crescent City merchant-banker Jacob Barker expounded on this point in light of the South's continued exclusion from the federal government, declaring that "to tax us without representation is a terrible outrage...." However, other New Orleans merchants seemed surprisingly inclined to accept such taxes as inevitable. In one lengthy 1866 petition directed to the Treasury Department, they limited their complaints to "the oppressiveness of the system for collecting the Direct Tax upon Cotton." Composed by a committee of eight long-time city factors including A. H. May, John Watt, S. B. Buckner, and Aristide Miltenberger, this memorial did not seek

not always possible, however, when such identifying characteristics are not obvious. (W. Cox & Co., for example, was reorganized in 1866 under the auspices of Cox's son-in-law to become Johnson, Denegre & Penn, even though neither firm is listed in the 1866 directory; see New Orleans *Times*, January 10, 1866.) But if earlier evidence indicating that many firms had dissolved or left the city by 1862 is considered in conjunction with the percentage of quondam firms that are clearly identifiable as persisting through 1866 (32 percent), then it would seem that any downward revision of the number of "brand-new" firms in the city should be fairly limited. It is unlikely, for example, that "unidentifiable" reorganized firms were equal in number to those that can be identified (whether reorganized or not); if that were the case, then the proportion of older firms still in operation as of 1866 would rise to 64 percent. A more conservative adjustment might assume that unidentifiable reorganized older firms amounted to half the total number of identifiable ones. By that measure, the number of persisting antebellum firms in New Orleans would have constituted just under half (48 percent) of the 403 total firms listed in the 1866 directory – although in the author's judgment, that revised estimate probably errs on the high side.

[34] New York Chamber of Commerce (1866), repr. as "A Tax on Cotton; or, How to Kill the Goose that Lays the Golden Egg," *De Bow's Review* 2d ser., 2 (July 1866), 76–9. On federal cotton taxes see aslo Surdam, *Northern Naval Superiority*, 190–1; and Dan T. Carter, *When the War Was Over: The Failure of Self-Reconstruction in the South, 1865–1867* (Baton Rouge, 1985), 98–9.

the abolition of excise taxes on cotton, as had the New York petition; instead, it focused on the dispersed manner by which they were collected. As matters stood, taxes were assessed by federal agents at points all along the production and distribution chain, which created "a strong temptation for Government agents" to commit "extensive frauds" during the revenue-collection process. The prevalence of petty corruption among federal authorities in the Louisiana countryside had been noted by Charles Squires from Shreveport the previous year. "A more perfect and outrageous swindle was never concocted," he later recalled of one scheme.[35]

Such pervasive corruption demonstrates the interwoven nature of complaints about the influx of so-called carpetbaggers to New Orleans and its hinterlands during early Reconstruction. As the city-directory data seem to show, such grievances were not merely another excuse for anti-federal sentiment in the city and state. But even if New Orleans merchants' complaints about northern speculators and their governmental cohorts were exaggerated, the perception that they were true made an enormous difference. "Dominance [that] originates in the market," according to sociologist Max Weber, is often considered "much more oppressive" because of its diffuse, less formalized character, and in this sense, anxieties about 'carpetbaggers' and the cronyism favoring their interests formed another strand in the web of racial prejudices and anti-federal resentments that began elevating the hostilities felt by most Crescent City whites to pathological proportions. When conservative governor James Madison Wells declared in 1865 that "no miserable thieving Yankee shall rob us with impunity," he typified the animosity toward northern businessmen that became a staple of reactionary rhetoric in postwar Louisiana.[36]

Such statements reveal how economic developments during Reconstruction were inseparable from – and in some ways, subordinate to – conditions in the unstable political realm. To be sure, Crescent City merchants did not always speak with one voice about state and local politics, which can make generalizations difficult. Some New Orleans merchants sought to collaborate with federal authorities after the war, and while some did so for reasons of self-aggrandizement, others apparently hoped to help smooth the transition to a post-Confederate regime. Factor Aristide Miltenberger, for example, agreed to serve on a commission organized by General Banks to oversee the reorganization of the city's financial institutions, but he soon became frustrated by

[35] Squires autobiography, III, 12; New Orleans merchants' memorial to the U.S. Secretary of the Treasury, repr. as "The Southern Cotton Trade and the Excise Laws," *De Bow's Review* 2d ser., 2 (November 1866), 527–30 (quotations on p. 527); Jacob Barker to William A. Baker, October 2, 1866, in Jacob Barker Letters (Mss 183, HTML-Tulane).

[36] Governor Wells, as quoted in Ted Tunnell, *Crucible of Reconstruction: War, Radicalism, and Race in Louisiana, 1862–1877* (Baton Rouge, 1984), 98; Max Weber, *Economy and Society*, eds. Guenther Roth and Claus Wittich (2 vols.; Berkeley, CA, and other cities, 1978), II, 946. Interestingly, Weber was discussing the example of commercial New York's disproportionate influence over U.S. national politics.

policies that seemed designed to force most into liquidation. Private banker Jacob Barker, whose outspoken moderation had made him a target of mob violence in early 1862, participated in city politics during the occupation years, but despite his Unionist loyalties and support for factions beholden to the ambitions of Treasury Secretary Chase, the fiercely independent financier proved to be as much of a thorn in the side of Union authorities as he had to Confederate partisans.[37]

Still, such grudging cooperation by businessmen like Barker and Miltenberger was exceptional. Most merchants withheld active support for early federal efforts to reconstruct local government along pro-Union, much less pro-Republican, lines. George Denison admitted as much in 1864 when he informed Chase that Benjamin Flanders, recently installed as the Unionist mayor of New Orleans, had few allies "among the business men of this city." The paucity of mercantile support is also revealed in two recent studies of early Reconstruction in Louisiana. Historian Ted Tunnell identified 172 of the most prominent Reconstruction-era Unionists in the state by occupation; only 16 of them (9 percent) were merchants. Similarly, although Peyton McCrary characterized the background of delegates to the 1864 state constitutional convention as "strictly bourgeois," his own data show that mercantile participants in the convention were mainly small shopkeepers; out of ninety-six delegates, only four were commission merchants.[38]

For the most part, then, men who had been prominent in the New Orleans cotton trade before the war proved reluctant to publicly ally themselves with federal Reconstruction efforts. At the same time, however, few merchants assumed leadership roles in the growing resistance to these efforts, since doing so probably would have antagonized the officials who now exercised authority over regional commerce. During the period of reaction after the accession of J. Madison Wells to the governorship in 1865, which culminated with the riot of late July 1866, a handful of merchants who had backed the local secession movement served briefly in municipal government, among them long-time city factor Glendy Burke and banker Hugh Kennedy. But although such men were still respected, they represented the rather quixotic hopes for a revival of staid old Whig "government by gentlemen," like that which Kennedy described in a September 1865 letter to President Johnson. It was far too late for all that, however. Instead, the most serious resistance to federal authority in New Orleans flourished underground in the form of secret societies, "neighborhood protection associations," and other loosely organized paramilitary units.

---

[37] On Jacob Barker see Reid, *After the War*, 230–1; and Denison to Chase, February 5, 1864, in *Chase Correspondence*, II, 431. On Aristide Miltenberger see Capers, *Occupied City*, 159; and Johnson, *Red River Campaign*, 77.

[38] McCrary, *Abraham Lincoln and Reconstruction*, 245–8 (quotation on p. 245) and Appendix B (pp. 370–1); Tunnell, *Crucible of Reconstruction*, Appendix I (pp. 219–28). Attorneys were the most common occupational group among the Louisiana Unionists identified by Tunnell. Denison to Chase, October 8, 1864, in *Chase Correspondence*, II, 448.

The authorities were quite aware of these groupscules: in late 1865 President Johnson was advised of their growing influence by Thomas W. Conway, former head of the state's Freedmen's Bureau, and even Governor Wells publicly condemned their extralegal activities. It had been rumored for years that city merchants played a significant behind-the-scenes role in funding such covert groups. In 1865, a Union captain warned northern reporter John R. Dennett about the power of "secret societies" in New Orleans and insisted their membership "ain't your rapscallions either." "Some of the first merchants in town belong" to them, he claimed.[39]

Some probably did, especially when their support could be channeled through innocuous forms like private social clubs; the Pickwick Club would remain a particular hotbed of political resistance throughout Reconstruction. But for the most part, the old merchant-elites who still remained from antebellum days did not participate in local splinter groups such as the "Southern Cross Association No. 9"; most preferred to remain firmly ensconced on the fence of political moderation, at least publicly. Despite the Union officer's report, for example, Dennett reported that "all the men of wealth and influence" he had met in New Orleans were "disposed to be loyal, and to behave like good citizens." Despite the sympathies they may have felt for extremist goals, considerations of self-interest probably led many merchants to keep their distance from such elements. Moreover, just as when municipal politics had passed through a similar period of violence during the 1850s, most gentleman-merchants reflexively tended to reject manifestations of "mob rule," for which they had little but high-minded Whiggish disdain.[40]

Thus was the torch of political leadership in Reconstruction-era New Orleans passed off to a younger generation composed mainly of battle-hardened and highly racist Confederate veterans. "Everywhere one observed the same signs of reaction," Whitelaw Reid reported from New Orleans in the summer of 1865. "The returning Rebel soldiers," he wrote, "called into active utterance all the hostility to Northerners that for nearly four years had laid latent." Edward Atkinson also described the leadership of ex-CSA officers among those now

[39] John Richard Dennett, *The South As It Is, 1865–1866*, ed. Henry M. Christman (Athens, GA, and London, 1986), 308; Governor Wells's message to the legislature (November 23, 1865), repr. in New Orleans *Daily Picayune*, November 30, 1865; testimony of Thomas W. Conway, January 26, 1867, in *Report of the [House] Select Committee on the New Orleans Riots* (Washington, DC, 1867), 528; Hugh Kennedy to President Andrew Johnson, September 16, 1865, cited in Tunnell, *Crucible of Reconstruction*, 99; George S. Denison to Salmon P. Chase, March 21, 1865, in *Chase Correspondence*, II, 456–7; New Orleans *Times*, June 10, 1865; Capers, *Occupied City*, 143.

[40] Dennett, *South As It Is*, 307; Augusto P. Miceli, *The Pickwick Club of New Orleans* (New Orleans, 1964), 55–71. On the Southern Cross Association No. 9, see *Report of the [House] Select Committee*, 520–1; the group's membership roster as reprinted therein is dominated by men identified as gamblers, clerks, butchers, and firemen – and one "cotton sampler." On merchants and "mob rule" in prewar New Orleans politics see William Howard Russell, *My Diary North and South* (Boston, 1863), 252.

inclined to "molest Northern settlers" and freedpeople. Paramilitary groups often posed as veterans' mutual-aid societies, as did the Hays Brigade Relief Society led by Orleans Parish sheriff and Pickwick Club member Harry T. Hays, a former Confederate brigadier general. Of course, some merchants were Civil War veterans as well. Among the Louisiana merchants listed in one late nineteenth-century source, for example, 72 percent of those who were eligible had served in the Confederate military. But many merchants, both rural and urban, had availed themselves of the controversial practice of paying substitutes to serve in their stead; and furthermore, the most prominent Crescent City factors had simply been too old for military service when the war began. After the war, young Charles W. Squires became a junior partner in a New Orleans wholesale grocery firm, but it was his service as an officer in the Washington Artillery rather than his mercantile connections that caused him to be pressed into leadership of a local citizens' militia in 1867.[41]

As politics in New Orleans during Reconstruction devolved into an armed truce punctuated by outbreaks of well-organized, racially motivated violence, many merchant-elites grew increasingly concerned by the deterioration of civic order. Their political moderation in the face of escalating racial violence led by extremist CSA veterans was first made clear in the wake of the riot of July 30, 1866, in which at least forty-eight persons were killed and hundreds wounded, most of them African Americans. Several prominent city merchants were subsequently called to testify before a House committee investigating the incident, which had provoked national outrage and thereby helped set the stage for the advent of Radical Reconstruction. Few of them sought to make excuses for the violence, and most condemned it. Jacob Barker, for example, claimed that New Orleans citizens had deplored the riot "almost unanimously." "I do not drink and smoke with the rebels," he also testified. In private, however, the independent-minded Barker sang a different tune. In an October 1866 letter, the octogenarian banker blamed "a few designing men" for inciting "their colored brethren" to seek "control of the affairs of the State by force" – plans that were only "quashed by the prompt interference of the Mayor and police."[42]

[41] Squires autobiography, III, 19–20; George W. Cable, "New Orleans Before the Capture," in *Battles and Leaders of the Civil War*, eds. Robert U. Johnson and Clarence C. Buel (4 vols., 1887; repr., New York, 1956), II, 18. For West Feliciana Parish storekeeper Felix V. Leake's use of a substitute, see the letter from Evan to "Sister," December 22, 1863, in Box 7, Folder 31, Kuntz Collection (HTML-Tulane). The data sample on Louisiana merchants' CSA service was collected from *Biographical and Historical Memoirs of Louisiana* (2 vols.; Chicago, 1892), I, passim. James G. Hollandsworth Jr., *An Absolute Massacre: The New Orleans Race Riot of July 30, 1866* (Baton Rouge, 2001), 74; Miceli, *Pickwick Club of New Orleans*, 48–50; Edward Atkinson, "The Cotton Resources of the South, Present and Future," *De Bow's Review* 2d ser., 2 (August 1866), 139; Reid, *After the War*, 237.

[42] Jacob Barker to William A. Baker, October 2, 1866, in Barker Letters (HTML-Tulane); Barker testimony, in *Report of the [House] Committee*, 227–32 (first quotation on p. 229; second on p. 230); Hollandsworth, *Absolute Massacre*, 140–1, 148–50.

In many ways, Jacob Barker's two-faced stance typified how New Orleans merchants found themselves trapped between the proverbial "rock and a hard place" in the highly charged local political atmosphere during Reconstruction. Many realized that the city's growing notoriety did not present a very attractive climate for doing business. But rather than taking the lead in confronting the city's violent political milieu, they instead chose to aid and abet white extremism in private while piously preaching the need for good, orderly government in public. Indeed, the chief issue on which most New Orleans merchants proved willing to take a firm political stand during Reconstruction was corruption, which directly affected them in their pocketbooks. They especially condemned the growth of a Republican political machine in Louisiana centered on the city's federal Custom-house, which they felt was staffed by "inexperienced and incompetent men" who had only obtained their positions "as a reward for partisan services." To a large degree, this was probably an accurate assessment – yet when the beleaguered Republican governor Henry C. Warmoth, the bête noire of the Custom-house faction, sought to form a pro-business, reform coalition with old resident Whigs during the late 1860s and early 1870s, few businessmen proved willing to lend him support. Disenchanted with fractious municipal affairs and struggling to stay afloat commercially, many Crescent City merchants began to consider themselves above the fray of politics, a stance for which they were chided by the New Orleans *Picayune* in 1875. "The real cause of our misfortunes is the stolid indifference with which the educated classes have regarded the progress of the corruption which they so loudly bewail," the conservative newspaper editorialized. In searching for the reasons why their political "influence ... has declined," it continued, New Orleans businessmen should first take full responsibility for their own "persistent inaction."[43]

To be fair, the *Picayune*'s editors here displayed a conveniently short memory, for their own support had been late and lukewarm when, only two summers before, city businessmen had been the prime movers behind a remarkable but short-lived "Unification Movement" in Louisiana. This group had sought a biracial solution to the state's growing political stalemate after the controversial elections of late 1872 resulted in the accession to power of the Custom-house ring led by the despised "carpetbagging" governor William Pitt Kellogg – a result obtained only after federal intervention authorized by President Ulysses S. Grant, whose brother-in-law James F. Casey was a prominent member of the faction. Although fraud and intimidation had been rampant on both sides

---

[43] "The Business Man in Politics," New Orleans *Daily Picayune*, June 6, 1875; H. C. Warmoth, *War, Politics and Reconstruction: Stormy Days in Louisiana* (New York, 1930), 81; Michael A. Ross, "Resisting the New South: Commercial Crisis and Decline in New Orleans, 1865–85," *American Nineteenth-Century History* 4 (Spring 2003), 63–4. For complaints about Custom-house corruption see "Transit of Goods to and from the Interior, via New Orleans," *De Bow's Review* 2d ser., 5 (November 1868), 1031–41 (first quotation on p. 1031); and "Report to the [New Orleans] Chamber of Commerce on the Appointments of Inspectors," *De Bow's Review* 2d ser., 5 (October 1868), 970–1 (second quotation on p. 971).

during the election, a broad-based coalition of Liberal Republicans, conservative Democrats, and other assorted reformers was widely believed to have "won," and for several months afterward, defeated gubernatorial candidate John D. McEnery led a rump legislature that claimed legitimate authority over Louisiana.[44]

The divisive effects of this competition for power were most pronounced in New Orleans, which served as the state capital for both governments. Building on the discontent with politics-as-usual that had been reflected in the "Reform Party" in 1872 (one of several such ephemeral business-led parties in late nineteenth-century New Orleans), long-time resident wholesale merchant Isaac N. Marks began organizing a new coalition during the spring of 1873. In mid-June a committee of a hundred prominent local citizens – fifty members each from the black and white communities – presented a lengthy document to the public whose provisions were intended as "a basis of co-operation for the redemption of the state." In summary, they proposed that equal rights for blacks be immediately and fully recognized by white citizens – not only suffrage rights but also in education, property-ownership, and public accommodations. The quid pro quo was that the state's black majority would then join with the mass of reform-minded whites in restoring able, honest, and native government to Louisiana. But although the movement soon gained many more endorsements from community leaders, as well as most of the city's newspapers (including the grudging support of the conservative *Picayune*), it proved extremely unpopular among whites in the country parishes in the northern parts of the state, where racism was especially virulent. Their opposition helped cause the fragile biracial coalition to fall apart even more suddenly than it had sprung into being. During a mass meeting in mid-July, several black speakers made speeches that were regarded as overly assertive and insufficiently deferential by most whites, even ones who supported the Unification Movement, and thus what historian T. Harry Williams later recognized as "a bold new departure" from the usual reactionary fare of Louisiana politics during Reconstruction came to an ignominious end.[45]

Williams also pointed out that the Unification Movement was led by "another group whose importance has not been recognized" by historians:

[44] Taylor, *Louisiana Reconstructed*, 255–76; Tunnell, *Crucible of Reconstruction*, 170–2.

[45] T. Harry Williams, *Romance and Realism in Southern Politics* (1961; repr., Baton Rouge, 1966), 22 (quotation); see also Williams, "The Louisiana Unification Movement of 1873," *Journal of Southern History* 11 (August 1945), 349–69. Surprisingly, the movement merits only a paragraph in Eric Foner's monumental history of the period; see Foner, *Reconstruction*, 547. The original manifesto of the movement was published in the New Orleans *Daily Picayune*, June 17, 1873 (quotation); see also the extensive coverage of the July meeting and its aftermath in ibid., July 15, 16, and 18, 1873. On businessmen's short-lived and mostly unsuccessful reform party efforts in late nineteenth-century New Orleans, see Joy J. Jackson, *New Orleans in the Gilded Age: Politics and Urban Progress, 1880–1896*, 2d ed. (Lafayette, LA, 1997), 18–30; and Eric Arnesen, *Waterfront Workers of New Orleans: Race, Class, and Politics, 1863–1923* (Urbana and Chicago, 1991), 79–80.

businessmen, who comprised most of the signatories to the original document. Even so, banking, insurance, legal, and real-estate interests seemed overrepresented on the "Committee of 100" compared with those from the commodities trades. Furthermore, in keeping with the tendency for Civil War veterans to provide political leadership, by far the best-known public face of the Unification Movement was the popular ex-Confederate general P. G. T. Beauregard. The dashing Creole engineer had successfully established himself in New Orleans after the war as a railroad executive, among other interests, and his counsel on all matters affecting Louisiana (whether solicited or not) became a staple of the city's postbellum political culture. (However, Beauregard himself would never hold elective office, having lost a bitter mayoral election to the Know-Nothings in 1858.) But although he had been presented as chairman of the group in its June debut, Beauregard perhaps sensed the impending disaster and opted to steer clear of the July 15 mass meeting that put the nail in the movement's coffin.[46]

General Beauregard's successful business career provides an interesting counterpoint to that of another famous ex-Confederate general in postbellum New Orleans: James Longstreet, the "scalawag" whose outspoken postwar alliance with the Republican Party was responsible, or so he felt, for his failure to become securely established in the city's cotton trade. More important, the public's embrace of Beauregard reflected another trend in New Orleans commercial circles during Reconstruction: the further attenuation of long-standing rivalries between Creole and American businessmen. Their reconciliation, which had already become apparent during the 1850s, had been strengthened in the cauldron of war, and this solidarity was further engendered during the occupation years and, after the war, by the common foe of carpetbaggery. By 1868 *De Bow's Review* could praise Creole businessmen, formerly scorned for their ostensible indolence, as "invaluable allies" who were "temperate, steady, and polite," although the journal also noted that they had lost greatly from the recent decimation of their sugar and banking interests. Although many Creoles had been among the most vociferous defenders of southern slavery, their own multiethnic heritages had also long made them more racially tolerant, and their influence in this regard may have helped to convince some Anglo-American businessmen to join them in support of the brief-lived Unification Movement.[47]

---

[46] T. Harry Williams, *P. G. T. Beauregard: Napoleon in Gray* (1955; repr., Baton Rouge, 1995), 43–4, 268–71, and chap. 17. Beauregard's name was conspicuously absent among both the speakers and the vice presidents of the group seated on the platform at the July 15 meeting, which was chaired by Isaac N. Marks; see New Orleans *Daily Picayune*, July 16, 1873. Williams, "Louisiana Unification Movement," 356–7, 369 (quotation).

[47] "Transit of Goods to and from the Interior, via New Orleans," 1038–9 (quotations). For an example of a famous Creole complaining to a fellow American resident about their common postwar foe, the "stinking puritan" of the North, see Charles Gayarre to J. D. B. De Bow, July 4, 1866, quoted in Joseph G. Tregle Jr., "Creoles and Americans," in *Creole New Orleans: Race*

The family and business associations of cotton factor Michel Musson illustrates this evolution of Anglo-Creole relationships in mid-nineteenth-century New Orleans. Musson, as was discussed in the introduction, was the subject of two 1873 paintings by his nephew Edgar Degas; although Musson is the most prominent figure in both, in the more famous of the two, *A Cotton Office in New Orleans* (Plate 1), he is seated in the left foreground pensively inspecting cotton. Musson had come to New Orleans from France sometime in the 1840s, and in the 1850s the Creole émigré became a partner in John Watt & Co., an American firm linked to Glendy Burke, one of the best-known cotton factors in what George Washington Cable called "a city of merchants." Musson assimilated easily and fully into the city's Anglo-American commercial milieu. He built a mansion in the American district before the war, and his son-in-law William A. Bell was an American merchant, as was his later partner James A. Prestidge, both of whom would join Musson in the cotton firm he formed after John Watt's death in 1867.[48]

Upon the outbreak of the Civil War, Musson enlisted in the Confederate army and served locally as a quartermaster's assistant until the occupation. He and his family were also heavily invested in the southern cause in other ways – literally. Musson not only purchased large quantities of Confederate bonds himself during the war, but he also convinced his brother Auguste, a private banker back in France (and Edgar Degas's father), to do likewise, which was eventually the cause of great financial loss to them all. His family's investments in slavery were similarly literal but figurative as well. Michel Musson owned seven slaves in 1860, and another brother, Eugène Musson, who had lived in New Orleans for years but was back on the Continent during the Civil War, published a passionate 1862 letter in support of southern slavery

and Americanization, eds. Arnold R. Hirsch and Joseph Logsdon (Baton Rouge, 1992), 170. George Washington Cable, however, must have never gotten the memo rehabilitating Creoles' reputations, for he continued to heap scorn on them in his fictional and historical works about New Orleans during the late nineteenth century; see esp. Cable, *The Creoles of Louisiana* (1884; repr., New York, 1970). In this book, Cable argued that "the two types [had] lost some of their points of difference" during the 1850s, by which time the Americans of New Orleans also "had learned some of the Creole's lethargy" (262). On the other hand, Cable was rather unusual himself, insofar as he was basically run out of town due to his own outspoken support of civic equality for blacks. On General James Longstreet's career in postbellum New Orleans see his memoir, *From Manassas to Appomattox: Memoirs of the Civil War in America* (1896; repr., Bloomington, Ind., 1960), chap. 44, esp. 637; and William L. Richter, "James Longstreet: From Rebel to Scalawag," *Louisiana History* 11 (Spring 1970), 215–30.

[48] Marilyn R. Brown, *Degas and the Business of Art: A Cotton Office in New Orleans* (University Park, PA, 1994), 28–33; Christopher Benfey, *Degas in New Orleans: Encounters in the Creole World of Kate Chopin and George Washington Cable* (Berkeley, CA, and other cities, 1997). See also Gail Feigenbaum [ed.], *Degas and New Orleans: A French Impressionist in America* (New Orleans, 1999), which includes two essays by Brown and one by Benfey. John Watt's antebellum business connections with Glendy Burke are indicated in letters in the folders devoted to G. Burke & Co., Cotton Trade Series, No. 1 (HTML-Tulane).

addressed to the French monarch Napoleon III, which he subtitled "from a Creole of Louisiana."[49]

At the very moment that his nephew was painting the portrait of his office in late January 1873, Michel Musson's cotton factorage firm was facing insolvency. On February 1 the New Orleans *Picayune* published a notice that the firm was dissolved and its business would now be conducted under the management of a new house headed by Musson's former American partner, James A. Prestidge. Fortunately, the old Creole merchant still had other interests to sustain him. Ancillary services that Musson had offered as a cotton factor became his primary occupation for the next several years, during which he acted as an agent for the New Orleans Mutual Insurance Association. Even so, his personal fortunes generally continued to decline over the next decade.[50]

Even as his firm was being dissolved that February, Musson may have been able to take solace from the impending Mardi Gras season, whose festivities had become another source of growing reconciliation between Creoles and Americans in New Orleans since the late antebellum era. Mardi Gras was also celebrated in other southern cities with sizable Catholic communities, but "Carnivale" was associated with New Orleans more than anywhere else in the United States. However, although the boisterous festival season preceding the advent of Lent was an occasion for a great deal of interclass and even crossracial revelry, there was always a strong elite component to the celebrations as well. This aspect was clearest in the exclusive, invitation-only galas and balls thrown by the various "krewes" during Mardi Gras, which represented the

---

[49] [Eugène Musson], *Letter to Napoleon III on Slavery in the Southern States, by a Creole of Louisiana* (London, 1862); Marilyn R. Brown, "A Tale of Two Families: The De Gas–Musson Correspondence at Tulane University," in Feigenbaum [ed.], *Degas and New Orleans*, 78–81; Brown, *Degas and the Business of Art*, 28; George Washington Cable, "Madame Delphine," in *Old Creole Days* (1885 ed.; repr., New York, 1979), 15.

[50] Marilyn R. Brown, "Franco-American Aspects of Degas's *A Cotton Office in New Orleans*," in Feigenbaum [ed.], *Degas and New Orleans*, 55–6, and 63 n. 38. (The notice from the New Orleans *Daily Picayune*, February 1, 1873, is reproduced on p. 56.) Here it is worth applauding the extensive primary research done by the art historian Brown in order to reconstruct Musson's business interests. Furthermore, her discussions of the wider context of the postbellum decline of New Orleans's factorage sector are usually accurate and well-grounded. One minor exception is her suggestion that the formation of the New Orleans Cotton Exchange in 1871 represented "the most immediate economic challenge to the old factorage system"; see Brown, *Degas and the Business of Art*, 34–5 (quotation on p. 34). However, Michel Musson's increasing postwar involvement with insurance services may suggest another trend perhaps more directly related to the decline of city-based factorage. The number of insurance companies and their agents seems to have greatly multiplied in postwar New Orleans. As will be discussed at greater length in Chapter 7, cotton increasingly arrived to the Crescent City not for marketing but solely for trans-shipment elsewhere on through bills of lading. With their ability to derive profits from the actual sale of cotton thus suppressed, former factors such as Musson (and Joseph Slemmons Copes, whose activities in this field also grew after the war; see his collected papers at HTML-Tulane) may have begun to rely more heavily on insurance commissions for their income.

climax of the social season in caste-conscious New Orleans. Moreover, then as now, Mardi Gras was big business. Although natives like Crescent City historian Henry Rightor emphasized the "genuine emotion" that lay behind the celebrations, even he admitted that Mardi Gras "sets in motion powerful commercial activities." Another contemporary historian described "the material profit of mystic mummery" in more detail. Mardi Gras, wrote T. C. DeLeon, prompts an "influx ... of smaller merchants and business men" from the hinterlands, and "these classes spend money liberally, to the advantage of caterers, retailers, and the petty trades." Enticing visitors to combine business with pleasure presaged the synergy between professional conventions and tourist debauchery that became a mainstay of New Orleans's economy in the twentieth century.[51]

Regardless, not only did Mardi Gras depend on the backing of "the solid financial element," according to DeLeon, but the changing themes of annual pageants, which were planned for months in advance, always reflected the "culture and taste" of their wealthy sponsors. This latter point was especially significant for celebrations of Mardi Gras in New Orleans during the Reconstruction era. With federal military authorities still close at hand and the usual political channels dominated by opposing cliques of corrupt outsiders and violent youths, the latent function of carnival pageants as a barometer of upper-class opinion became all the more important. A few examples will suffice. When Comus, the "king" of Mardi Gras, first reemerged from four years of wartime exile to great popular interest in 1866, the theme of his initial reappearance was an elaborate paean to peace and sectional reconciliation. Like other newspapers, the *Picayune* praised this "Beautiful Allegory" and emphasized that its sentiments were those held by "a large number of our best citizens," including many who were recently "identified with the unsuccessful struggle of an independent South."[52]

Perhaps so, yet such optimistic demonstrations of incipient New South consciousness on the part of Comus and his retinue would not soon be repeated. By 1868 local authorities were so concerned that the King's appearance would

[51] T. C. DeLeon, *Our Creole Carnivals: Their Origin, History, Progress, and Results* (Mobile, AL, 1890), 33; Henry Rightor, "The Carnival of New Orleans," in Rightor, ed., *Standard History of New Orleans* (Chicago, 1900), 629. On the growth of tourism in New Orleans's economy during the twentieth century, see Anthony J. Stanonis, *Creating the Big Easy: New Orleans and the Emergence of Modern Tourism, 1918–1945* (Athens, GA, 2006).

[52] Perry Young, *The Mistick Krewe: Chronicles of Comus and His Kin* (New Orleans, 1931), 82–4 (New Orleans *Daily Picayune* [n.d., February 1866], as quoted on p. 84), 87; DeLeon, *Our Creole Carnivals*, 33. Several scholars have fruitfully explored the rich iconography of carnival pageantry in late nineteenth-century New Orleans; see Reid Mitchell, *All on a Mardi Gras Day: Episodes in the History of New Orleans Carnival* (Cambridge, MA, 1995), chaps. 4–7; James Gill, *Lords of Misrule: Mardi Gras and the Politics of Race in New Orleans* (Jackson, Ms., 1997), 76–165; Samuel Kinser, *Carnival, American Style: Mardi Gras at New Orleans and Mobile* (Chicago and London, 1990), 97–118; and Justin A. Nystrom, *New Orleans after the Civil War: Race, Politics, and a New Birth of Freedom* (Baltimore, 2010), 94–8, 133–5.

spark widespread rebellion that they banned the wearing of masks on the streets after sunset. Although similar concerns abounded in the spring of 1873 during the crisis of legitimacy between the dueling Kellogg and McEnery governments, that season's most noteworthy political agitation proved to be its Comus pageant. Taking their cue from ongoing controversies over Darwin's *Origin of Species*, the Mystick Krewe of Comus paraded various "Missing Links" that lampooned political bogeymen: President Grant was a tobacco grub; their old scourge Ben Butler, a hyena; the carpetbagger, a fox; and, sadly but somewhat inevitably, the freedman was caricatured as half-human, half-ape. One of Michel Musson's other nephews, René De Gas (the slouched, rather slothful looking man perusing the *Picayune* in his brother Edgar's cotton-office painting), was closely involved with this provocative production by the Comus Krewe, which was an offshoot of the Pickwick Club to which he belonged. A few years later, the Krewe of Momus further upped the ante of sedition by portraying many of the same figures, including Grant, as citizens of hell. But even though such iconography may appear heavy-handed from the standpoint of our more sophisticated visual culture today, Crescent City elites were then engaging in what was still an effective and popular form of public theatre, one that subversively signaled their contempt for federal authority and its perceived offshoots, and in terms no less scathing for being peaceably expressed. On the other hand, the reduction of elite opposition to such culturally performative types of protest helps confirm the essential powerlessness of the city's gentleman-merchants during Reconstruction, when their economic dominance was clearly on the wane and their political prospects otherwise circumscribed.[53]

In the summer of 1873, a few months after Mardi Gras, Michel Musson's name appeared near the top of the list of the "Committee of 100" among the many prominent Creole businessmen who backed the nascent Louisiana Unification Movement. But despite his support for biracial cooperation, Musson seemed to have little problem executing an apparent ideological *volte face* with regard to "the race question" in the wake of the movement's rapid demise. Musson, along with his nephew René De Gas and his son-in-law William A. Bell, became supporters of the White League, a resistance group that had grown out of the Crescent City Democratic Club, one of the city's many all-white vigilante factions during the late 1860s. After the controversial accession of Governor Kellogg in 1873, the White League had formed as an umbrella paramilitary organization to encompass all of the white splinter groups in New Orleans. On September 14, 1874, political tensions exploded into violence after the White League called for a public assembly at the statue of Henry Clay

---

[53] Kinser, *Carnival, American Style*, 93–9, 100–1; Benfey, *Degas in New Orleans*, 171–9; Miceli, *Pickwick Club of New Orleans*, 62–66 and Appendix H; Mitchell, *All in a Mardi Gras Day*, 65–80. Edgar Degas's two brothers in New Orleans, René and Achille, were in partnership together as cotton buyers, and both spelled their surname "De Gas"; see Brown, *Degas and the Business of Art*, 30–1.

on Canal Street. Thousands turned out, and the first speaker called to address the crowd was none other than Michel Musson. Well-disciplined White League units commanded by the charismatic general Fred N. Ogden, who was also associated in the cotton bagging business with Bell, then fanned out to success-fully seize the seat of government from the Metropolitans, a police militia led by the scalawag ex-Confederate general James Longstreet. Dozens from both sides were killed, but although their victory was short-lived, the White League had made its point: puppet regimes like Kellogg's that enjoyed no popular back-ing could only be maintained by outside military force. And once again, New Orleans played a decisive role in the evolution of federal Reconstruction policy. Just as the race riots of 1866 had helped bring about Radical Reconstruction, less than a decade later, the street battles of 1874 prompted northern opinion to coalesce against continued support for federally backed regimes throughout the South. As the *Nation*, a New York–based reformist journal, declared on September 24, "the insurgents had more plainly the right on their side." The White League remained an organized if latent presence in the city until, just over two years later, it helped direct Louisiana's transition to a "redeemed" Democratic Party–led government after the Compromise of 1877 had been brokered by an extraconstitutional national commission.[54]

Given the broad extent of whites' support for the coup against Kellogg, it is less surprising that businessmen such as Musson figured more prominently in these events than they had in previous mob-like actions. At least two White League fatalities on September 14 were from the merchant community: factor E. A. Toledano and S. B. Newman Jr., son of one of the city's most powerful cotton brokers. The New Orleans Cotton Exchange closed early the follow-ing day as "a mark of sympathy" with the insurgency, and in two telegrams that week, leaders from the financial and commercial sectors (Michel Musson among them) collectively sought to reassure President Grant that "business men [were] greatly encouraged" by the outcome. Nevertheless, as historian James K. Hogue has recently shown, both the White League's leadership and its rank-and-file were composed mainly of CSA veterans. During the post-Re-construction era, the primary political beneficiaries of the armed skirmishes of 1874 were General Ogden, whose role in the cotton trade seems to have been confined to his bagging business with William Bell, and General William J. Behan, a petit-bourgeois grocer who was elected mayor in 1882.[55]

[54] *Nation*, September 24, 1874, quoted in Foner, *Reconstruction*, 551; Taylor, *Louisiana Reconstructed*, 283–4, 291–6; Benfey, *Degas in New Orleans*, 184–92; Walter Prichard, ed., "The Origin and Activities of the 'White League' in New Orleans (Reminiscences of a Participant in the Movement), *Louisiana Historical Quarterly* 23 (April 1940), 525–43.
[55] Jackson, *New Orleans in the Gilded Age*, 58; Prichard, ed., "Origin and Activities of the White League," 528; James K. Hogue, *Uncivil Wars: Five New Orleans Street Battles and the Rise and fall of Radical Reconstruction* (Baton Rouge, 2006), 129–31; Stuart Omer Landry, *The Battle of Liberty Place: The Overthrow of Carpet-Bag Rule in New Orleans, September 14, 1874* (New Orleans, 1955), 140–1 (quotations), 201–3, 232–40. See also Lawrence N. Powell, "Reinventing

The events of late Reconstruction thus continued to show that political leadership in postwar New Orleans was in the hands of a younger generation, one for whom the Crescent City's days of commercial glory were fast becoming a distant memory. Many older resident merchants, broken up financially (and perhaps spiritually, too), began passing away during these years: John Watt and Walter Cox in 1868, Glendy Burke in 1879, and Joseph Slemmons Copes in 1885 – the same year that Michel Musson died, insolvent. But although such merchant-elites had often collaborated with the new generation in making late nineteenth-century New Orleans into what historian Michael A. Ross has called "a national byword for reactionary upheaval," most of them tended to follow the conservative drift of public opinion rather than shaping it during Reconstruction. Their noisome opposition to corruption often served to obscure the advent of race-based politics in much the same ways that secession was now being defended as a dispute over state sovereignty rather than as a means of preserving slavery. That they generally resisted the advent of a "New South," however, was clear in their support for groups like the White League, as well as in their lavish Mardi Gras theatrics.[56]

Indeed, the resistance of Crescent City elites to the much-heralded sectional reconciliation being promoted in other southern cities was still on display during carnival season in 1881. John F. Cowan, an officer who had led his New York regiment to New Orleans for a half-hearted celebration of fraternal unity among Civil War veterans, later described that year's Comus parade, whose theme was "Myths of the Northland." Among the tableaux derived from Norse mythology were "The Workshop of the Dwarves" and "The Hell of the Northland," with the fall of the Niblung dramatically depicted as "The Twilight of the Gods." The political allegory must have seemed clear to most Crescent City residents, but, perhaps distracted amid all the pomp and circumstance, Comus's barbed arrows flew unnoticed past the naive Yankee captain. On the other hand, when not staging such elaborate insults toward the "Northland" of the reunited nation, New Orleans merchants were preoccupied with the economic Götterdämmerung they had suffered during the Civil War and its aftermath. Their city's rapid fall from commercial grace and its unfolding consequences during and after Reconstruction are the subject of the next chapter.[57]

Tradition: Liberty Place, Historical Memory, and Silk-Stocking Vigilantism in New Orleans Politics," *Slavery & Abolition* 20 (April 1999), 127–49.

[56] Ross, "Resisting the New South," 65 (quotation).

[57] John F. Cowan, *A New Invasion of the South: Being a Narrative of the Expedition of the Seventy-First Infantry, National Guard, Through the Southern States to New Orleans* (New York, 1881), 68–9; cf. Mitchell, *All in a Mardi Gras Day*, 82–5.

7

The Economic Decline of Postbellum New Orleans

During Reconstruction, as endemic violence and cronyism cemented Louisiana's growing reputation as what one New York–based journal scornfully termed "a South American republic," New Orleans merchants found themselves relegated to the political sidelines. The predicament faced by the city's "most substantial citizens" was sympathetically noted by Charles Nordhoff, a Republican journalist who visited in 1875. With the Whig Party long since defunct and Republicans discredited by their northern and federal associations, pious pleas for "good government" by businessmen suffered from the absence of a stable party to call their own. The default option was the Democratic Party (as was true for most white southerners after the war), but in New Orleans, that party was firmly controlled by "Ring" politicians, who cultivated support from the working classes, not from hard-pressed gentleman-merchants – a trend toward urban machine politics that had begun during the late antebellum era and continued for several decades after the war. Moreover, when reform-minded businessmen did try to intervene in state and municipal politics, they could not avoid being drawn onto the unforgiving terrain of "the race question." The promising but short-lived biracial Louisiana Unification Movement was thus initially endorsed in 1873 by many of the same merchants who, only a year later, were involved with the "lily-white" counterrevolution that briefly overthrew the federally backed regime of Governor William Kellogg.[1]

---

[1] T. Harry Williams, "The Louisiana Unification Movement of 1873," *Journal of Southern History* 11 (August 1945), 349–69; Joe Gray Taylor, *Louisiana Reconstructed, 1863–1877* (Baton Rouge, 1974), 283–4, 291–6. On machine politics in postbellum New Orleans, see Joy J. Jackson, *New Orleans in the Gilded Age: Politics and Urban Progress, 1880–1896*, 2d ed. (Lafayette, LA, 1997); and Eric Arnesen, *Waterfront Workers of New Orleans: Race, Class, and Politics, 1863–1923* (Urbana and Chicago, 1991), chap. 3. Charles Nordhoff, *The Cotton States in the Spring and Summer of 1875* (1876; repr., New York, 1971), 41–4 (quotation on p. 42); *The Nation*, April 24, 1873.

Such dramatic, well-documented events have inclined most scholars to follow the lead of historian Joe Gray Taylor, who argued that "the problem of race overrode all other Louisiana problems, political or economic," during Reconstruction. There is a great deal of truth in Taylor's assessment, but it should be acknowledged that "the problem of race" in the postbellum South was at once both political *and* economic in nature, and clearly, such issues cannot be neatly compartmentalized. Furthermore, despite the overwhelming attention paid to the racial strife of Reconstruction politics by contemporaries and historians alike, some New Orleans merchants discerned other bewildering changes that were undermining their business prospects and forcing the quondam "Queen City of the South" ever further down the dependent lower rungs of the American urban system.[2]

Without unduly seeking to separate political and economic developments, this chapter focuses on New Orleans's deteriorating commercial conditions during the late nineteenth century. It examines some of the structural reasons for that decline, but at the same time, a measure of contingency is preserved by emphasizing the human volition behind many of these unfolding changes. For example, many residents believed that outsiders were orchestrating the state's political chaos to their economic advantage. Typical in this regard was an article from the Memphis *Appeal* reprinted locally in the summer of 1873. Titled "Why New Orleans Was Destroyed," it fixed responsibility for Louisiana's political turmoil on "adventurers" sent at "the instigation of Eastern monopolists" who sought to make the Crescent City "so repulsive ... that commerce will be driven away forever." Other observers, however, took a less conspiratorial view and placed greater blame on New Orleans's own citizenry. In 1869 long-time resident Durant Daponte bluntly reproached businessmen for the city's declining prospects, singling out their failure to provide the "improved methods which the commercial necessities of the times demand" – most notably, railroads. A few years later, a visitor reported that Crescent City merchants had resumed their long-standing reliance on the river to deliver trade to their doorsteps. Yet "so busily has the Mississippi been working out the fortune of New Orleans," he added, that these same men "may not have been turning it all to the best account." For their part, city merchants defended themselves in the face of circumstances they neither fully understood nor controlled. In 1868, for example, *De Bow's Review* described how planters were beseeching their former factors for credit, but it also noted that "here ... the most serious obstacles intervene." Because city merchants were no longer able to secure sufficient

[2] Taylor, *Louisiana Reconstructed*, 279. The historiographical dominance of racially focused political narratives is manifest in the works by Hollandsworth and Hogue cited above, but see also Ted Tunnell, *Crucible of Reconstruction: War, Radicalism, and Race in Louisiana, 1862–1877* (Baton Rouge and London, 1984); and Peyton McCrary, *Abraham Lincoln and Reconstruction: The Louisiana Experiment* (Princeton, NJ, 1978). A valuable recent exception is Michael A. Ross, "Resisting the New South: Commercial Crisis and Decline in New Orleans, 1865–85," *American Nineteenth-Century History* 4 (Spring 2003), 59–76.

credit from banks, the South's premier commercial journal argued that their ability to furnish rural clients – not to mention, invest in capital-intensive projects like railroads – was severely circumscribed.[3]

Such interwoven problems led the New Orleans–based journal to conclude that "our commerce must still be regarded as in a transition state." Exactly what it was "in transition" toward, however, no one was quite able to foresee. To some degree, all of these observers gave valid, important reasons for what Daponte recognized in 1869 as "the relative decrease of the commerce of New Orleans" – a situation that would worsen over the decades ahead. But even though some of the city's developmental failures had roots in the late antebellum period, historians who assert the postbellum ascendance of a "New South" have been slow to recognize how the Civil War greatly exacerbated such problems, with new ones added to the mix during Reconstruction. State and municipal government was indeed bankrupt, literally and sometimes ethically – and partly in consequence, politics was faction-ridden and prone to demagoguery. Modern commercial institutions remained slow to develop, and postwar corruption reached heights that made the inbred "gentlemanly capitalism" of old seem like a golden age. Tangible support for improvements to the port's ramshackle infrastructure was grudging, sporadic, and stymied by factionalism, while industrial development continued to generate little more than lip service from local investors. Such projects now also suffered from a pronounced regional capital shortage, which was largely a consequence of the prewar New Orleans–based banking system's destruction. Finally, Crescent City merchants still complacently relied on the river for commerce, as was revealed not only in their continued dependence on cotton, but also by their desperate efforts to resecure the midwestern grain trade they had ceded decades before. As a result, over a century before Hurricane Katrina, New Orleans was pummeled by the economic equivalent of a "perfect storm": a deadly combination of shortsighted commercial hubris, corrupt and reactionary government, and overarching changes to both the internal structure of southern agriculture and the broad, external trade flows that constituted the American urban system.[4]

[3] "Annual Review of the New Orleans Market," De Bow's Review 2d ser., 5 (September 1868), 877; for a similar view by a former New Orleans bank president, see Robert M. Davis, The Southern Planter, the Factor, and the Banker (New Orleans, 1871). Durant Daponte, "New Orleans and Ship Island Ship Canal," De Bow's Review, 2d ser., 6 (January 1869), 21–2; Robert Somers, The Southern States Since the War, 1870–71 (1871; repr., University, AL, 1965), 191–2 (quotation on p. 192); "Why New Orleans Was Destroyed," New Orleans Daily Picayune, July 16, 1873; see also the letter from "B.J.S." (Opelousas, LA), in ibid., July 19, 1873.

[4] Daponte, "New Orleans and Ship Island Canal," 22; "Annual Review of the New Orleans Market," 877. The historiography on antebellum New Orleans's economy is more extensive than that on the post–Civil War era, although it is not as well-developed as one might expect given its importance to the Old South; see, for example, John G. Clark, "New Orleans and the River: A Study in Attitudes and Responses," Louisiana History 8 (Winter 1967), 117–35; Lawrence H. Larsen, "New Orleans and the River Trade: Reinterpreting the Role of the Business Community," Wisconsin Magazine of History 61 (Winter 1977–78), 112–24; Merl E. Reed, New Orleans

The state of Louisiana had never enjoyed a reputation for thrift or efficiency in its political affairs, but these conditions worsened during Reconstruction. In October 1873 the New Orleans *Daily Picayune* informed its readers that "bad government is the sole cause of the universal wretchedness of the people of Louisiana." Given that paper's staunch opposition to the successive federally backed administrations that ruled the state, their hyperbolic stance was unsurprising. Still, even the Republican governor Henry C. Warmoth later admitted that "corruption [was] the fashion" in postwar Louisiana politics, and most observers agreed. After his 1875 visit to New Orleans, which was then the state capital (it would be moved back to Baton Rouge in 1882), Charles Nordhoff catalogued a litany of citizens' complaints, most of which centered on patronage, bribery, and other abuses of power by government officials. He also noted that the city suffered woefully inadequate municipal services, from the crumbling riverfront to drainage and sanitation problems, despite the fact that tax rates in New Orleans were particularly high. Nevertheless, apparently believing the adage that things had to get worse before they could get better, conservative whites often obstructed Republican efforts to clean up the notoriously filthy city, thereby contributing to a yellow-fever epidemic in 1878 that helped frighten away potential investors in post-"Redemption" New Orleans. Moreover, a large portion of government revenue was devoted to paying off the enormous state and municipal bonded debt, and elite bankers, fearing the wrath of northern and foreign bondholders, successfully resisted calls to scale back or repudiate this debt to free up funds for improved city services.[5]

The globally connected New Orleans banking community had been especially devastated by the Civil War. In 1861 there had been some thirteen banks in the city, and their combined capital stock of about $24 million had easily represented the greatest concentration of banking capital in the antebellum South. As of 1865 this figure had plummeted to only $7.67 million, a drop of more than two-thirds from its level four years earlier. With much of their dwindling capital tied up in government debt instruments, these banks had a direct stake in avoiding their repudiation. In the meantime, New Orleans banks

and the Railroads: The Struggle for Commercial Empire, 1830–1860 (Baton Rouge, 1966); and Robert Earl Roeder, "New Orleans Merchants, 1800–1837" (Ph.D. diss., Harvard University, 1959).

5 William Ivy Hair, *Bourbonism and Agrarian Protest: Louisiana Politics, 1877–1900* (Baton Rouge, 1969), 99–101; J. Mills Thornton, "Fiscal Policy and the Failure of Radical Reconstruction in the Lower South," in *Region, Race, and Reconstruction: Essays in Honor of C. Vann Woodward*, eds. J. Morgan Kousser and James M. McPherson (New York, 1982), 351, 383–4; Ross, "Resisting the New South," 67; Nordhoff, *Cotton States in 1875*, pp. 59–61. See also Edward King, *The Great South*, eds. W. Magruder Drake and Robert R. Jones (1875; repr. Baton Rouge, 1972), chaps. 1–8. H. C. Warmoth, *War, Politics and Reconstruction: Stormy Days in Louisiana* (New York, 1930), 79–80; New Orleans *Daily Picayune*, October 29, 1873. In 1881 the *Picayune* published statistics showing that New Orleans ranked last in municipal services compared with five other U.S. cities; see the chart compiled from these data in Jackson, *New Orleans in the Gilded Age*, 97–98.

sought to establish new institutional safeguards against the periodic financial crises that made the regional economy all the more precarious. The ripple effect of such problems had again become apparent during the national financial panic of 1873, which quickly squelched the moderate economic recovery the city had enjoyed over the previous few years. After years of negotiations, in 1875 city banks finally managed to create the New Orleans Clearing House Association, a centralized institution that offered a degree of mutual protection for their financial operations.[6]

Other private-sector groups in New Orleans also formed badly needed trade associations and exchanges during the late nineteenth century: the Produce Exchange (1880); the Mechanics, Dealers, and Lumbermen's Exchange (1881); the Mexican and South American Exchange (1882); and the Louisiana Sugar Exchange (1883). However, the most significant new association was undoubtedly the New Orleans Cotton Exchange, which was established in 1871. During the antebellum era, New Orleans had lagged far behind other commercial cities like New York and Chicago in the creation of commodities exchanges, and despite scattered efforts, cotton merchants' failure to fashion an institutional mechanism to help smooth the uneven flows of commerce had been widely deplored. These criticisms resumed after the war. In 1866 one writer complained to a local paper that "business must be got through in a lame and halting ... style totally unworthy of a city that aspires to be the metropolis of the Mississippi Valley." He blamed the absence of a cotton exchange on some "unexplained idiosyncrasy in the character of our mercantile population," a comment that highlighted the fragmented, incohesive nature of this most important "class" of local businessmen. But despite reports of an impending convention of cotton factors to discuss the formation of an exchange, several years passed before the long-delayed institution was finally established.[7]

Under the stewardship of a young newspaperman-turned-statistician named Henry G. Hester, the Exchange quickly filled a long-standing need for a central

---

[6] Andrew Morrison, *The Industries of New Orleans ... Historical, Descriptive, Statistical* (New Orleans, 1885), 27–29; Taylor, *Louisiana Reconstructed*, 358–61; Davis, *Southern Planter, Factor, and Banker*, 5–6; "Annual Review of the New Orleans Market" [1868], 889; John B. Legler and Richard Sylla, "Integration of U.S. Capital Markets: Southern Stock Markets and the Case of New Orleans, 1871–1913," in *Finance, Intermediaries, and Economic Development*, eds. Stanley L. Engerman et al. (New York, 2003), 148–51. Aggregate bank capitalization in Louisiana continued to drop through the end of the century; it stood at only $3.73 million in 1875 and was less than $2.5 million in 1897; Stephen A. Caldwell, *A Banking History of Louisiana* (Baton Rouge, 1935), chap. 7 and Appendix II (p. 128).

[7] New Orleans *Daily Crescent*, January 6 and 10 (quotations), March 13, 1866; James E. Boyle, *Cotton and the New Orleans Cotton Exchange: A Century of Commercial Evolution* (Garden City, NY, 1934), 68–71; Morrison, *Industries of New Orleans*, 27–9. See also L. Tuffly Ellis, "The New Orleans Cotton Exchange: The Formative Years, 1871–1880," *Journal of Southern History* 39 (November 1973), 545–64. For antebellum merchants' failure to establish a cotton exchange see "Cotton at New Orleans," *Hunt's Merchants' Magazine* 42 (January 1860), 105–6.

authority to standardize weighing, baling, and grading procedures. But the most immediate effect of the new cotton exchange was to systematically organize and synthesize the hundreds of crop reports that came in from the southern hinterlands, which were vital to forecasting the production trends on which prices depended. It proved more difficult for the Exchange to establish reliable, adequate communications with northern and European buyers at the other end of the commodity chain, since northern-controlled telegraph monopolies initially preferred to maintain the higher volume of business they enjoyed with hundreds of individual firms in the Crescent City rather than having them mediated under the auspices of a single institution.[8]

It took more time, however, to inculcate habits of collective discipline among New Orleans cotton merchants, who were accustomed to highly individuated market behaviors. The steady contraction of port trade during the 1870s made it difficult to cultivate the cooperative tendencies evident among urban capitalists elsewhere. In 1875, for example, Exchange members squabbled over a minor increase to the per-bale charges assessed to cover its operations – a measure that had only been proposed because revenues were proving "insufficient ... in consequence of the great falling off in [New Orleans] receipts of cotton." In other instances, the Exchange was unable to correct abuses and irregularities associated with crop marketing because of its limited enforcement power as a private-sector institution. Although complaints about falsely packed cotton were a matter of grave concern, for example, the practice was already prohibited by existing laws that fell under the jurisdiction of civil authorities, and thus the Exchange could only "earnestly call upon each planter and country merchant to aid in stopping this criminal practice." (The Exchange did take some comfort by noting that similar abuses occurred in New York.) The political toothlessness of the Exchange was sometimes revealed even in its seemingly innocuous information-gathering functions. When significant discrepancies in the port's statistics came to light in 1876, the Exchange criticized "the unreliability of Customhouse official records," but beyond chastising the responsible federal authorities, it could not do much else.[9]

Problems with the corruption-ridden U.S. Custom-house were among the many issues that plagued the port of New Orleans during Reconstruction. There was no unified administration over the chaotic system of wharves, levees, and warehouses that comprised the riverfront until the formation of the New Orleans Dock Board in 1896. Until then, the city typically parceled

---

[8] Ellis, "New Orleans Cotton Exchange," 548–51.

[9] Minute Book B [April–May 1875], pp. 142–51, 205 (first quotation on p. 143); August 1873 circular in ibid., p. 43 (second quotation); Ibid. (November 29, 1876), p. 292 (third quotation); all in New Orleans Cotton Exchange Collection (Howard-Tilton Memorial Library, Tulane University; cited hereinafter as NOCEX Records, HTML-Tulane). In November 1876 Exchange president William C. Black noted "how far from peculiar to New Orleans were the irregularities" in the cotton trade; Ibid., pp. 311–12. The New Orleans *Daily Picayune*, June 25 and 27, 1879, also waxed smug about cotton thievery in New York markets.

out riverfront sections on short-term leases to private concerns. Such companies lacked incentives to invest in improvements, especially when concessions were often little more than patronage grants subject to shifting political tides. Between such dubious private interests (there were others too, such as the tugboat monopoly) and the numerous municipal, state, and federal agencies that jealously guarded their stakes in various riverfront operations, it was no wonder that late nineteenth-century New Orleans maintained its long-standing reputation as one of the most expensive and inefficient commercial ports in the nation. According to an 1869 estimate, it cost more than three times as much to ship 100 tons of seagoing freight from New Orleans as it did from New York or Boston. Making a bad situation worse, from a commercial perspective, was the steady rise in conflicts with organized labor on New Orleans docks during the post–Civil War decades. Northern-born shipping magnate Charles Morgan, who had run extensive operations out of New Orleans since the 1840s, finally grew so frustrated with surcharges and other chicanery during Reconstruction that he built a port of his own near Atchafalaya Bay southwest of New Orleans, using it to siphon off trade from the Crescent City by means of a short-line railroad.[10]

Port development in late nineteenth-century New Orleans was further stymied by intense political struggles over regional infrastructure – most notably, levee and railroad systems. The New Orleans Cotton Exchange took a keen interest in river development, often lobbying local officials to remove obstructions and maintain the city's riverfront. The Exchange also sought to influence federal policy toward levee construction all along the Mississippi River, as did state and municipal authorities. Prominent citizens, especially the ubiquitous former engineer and ex-Confederate general P. G. T. Beauregard, became closely involved with levees and associated projects such as canal-dredging. But in turn, Reconstruction-era levee construction itself became the subject of bitter infighting among officials from the U.S. Army Corps of Engineers, with controversies raging around their dual purposes as a means of flood control and for scouring deeper channels in the Mississippi River. Jetties built below New Orleans during the late 1870s soon proved effective at removing natural obstructions that had long impeded port access by deep-draft oceangoing ships, which was a considerable boon for commerce. But Corps' policies along the Mississippi remained oriented toward levee rather than spillway construction,

[10] Arnesen, *Waterfront Workers of New Orleans*, 42–73; James P. Baughman, *Charles Morgan and the Development of Southern Transportation* (Nashville, 1968), 172–7; Taylor, *Louisiana Reconstructed*, 353. The comparative estimate of shipping costs is from Daponte, "New Orleans and the Ship Island Ship Canal," 26–7. For similar postwar complaints about port costs and operations see "Through Freights and Close Connections," *De Bow's Review*, 2d ser., 6 (July 1869), 571–4; and New Orleans *Daily Crescent*, January 6, 1866. On the tugboat monopoly see the critical article from the Chicago *Tribune* reprinted in New Orleans *Daily Picayune*, July 22, 1873. Raymond J. Martinez, *The Story of the River Front at New Orleans* (New Orleans, 1955), 33–6.

a misguided preference that would produce disastrous results during the great flood of 1927.[11]

Corruption and cronyism were even more rife in post–Civil War railroad development in Louisiana. The state had ranked last in the South in rail mileage before the war, and afterward, it mainly had a plethora of unconsolidated and often uncompleted short-line roads, most of them in poor condition and heavily encumbered with debt. Compared with other parts of the country, even with other southern states, officials in postbellum Louisiana seemed especially reluctant to cede control over railroad development to private capitalists, perhaps because doing so might have decreased their opportunities for ill-gotten gains. By rebuilding and extending a troubled line that had been constructed to Jackson, Mississippi, during the 1850s, the city enjoyed some long-term success in securing access to the burgeoning plantation districts of the Mississippi Delta. Yet even these efforts were beleaguered by political shenanigans, such as the 1870 arrest of prominent railroad developer Henry McComb in New Orleans. At the same time, Crescent City merchants were quick to recognize the importance of bringing the fast-expanding cotton production of Texas firmly into their commercial orbit, but after the Exchange's directors resolved that such east–west lines should be "owned and controlled in Louisiana," rail development efforts by Yankee transportation tycoons such as Morgan, McComb, and Thomas Scott were blocked by litigation and legislative obstructionism. Consequently, by the mid-1870s the vast Texas market had been lost by New Orleans. The inability of city elites to agree on a central railroad terminus further illustrates the responsibility of shortsighted, self-interested politicians for these failures. Although rail connections with the hinterlands would improve by the early twentieth century, by then New Orleans had ceded enormous commercial ground to its competitors that it would never recover.[12]

[11] George S. Pabis, "Delaying the Deluge: The Engineering Debate over Flood Control on the Lower Mississippi River, 1846–1861," *Journal of Southern History* 64 (August 1998), 423–5, 450–4; John M. Barry, *Rising Tide: The Great Mississippi Flood of 1927 and How It Changed America* (New York, 1997), chaps. 1–6; Nordhoff, *Cotton States in 1875*, pp. 58–9. For examples of General Beauregard's high-profile meddling with river policies see New Orleans *Daily Picayune*, June 15, 1873, and June 28, 1879; see also T. Harry Williams, *P. G. T. Beauregard: Napoleon in Gray* (1955; repr., Baton Rouge, 1995), 288–90. On the New Orleans Cotton Exchange and levees see Minute Book B, pp. 19–20, 70, NOCEX Records (HTML-Tulane).
[12] Peirce F. Lewis, *New Orleans: The Making of an Urban Landscape* (2nd ed., Santa Fe, NM, and Harrisonburg, VA, 2003), 55–6 and Figure 11; Jackson, *New Orleans in the Gilded Age*, 149; James P. Baughman, "The Evolution of Rail-Water Transportation Systems in the Gulf Southwest, 1836–1890," *Journal of Southern History* 34 (August 1968), 372–3; Minute Book B, pp. 9–10, 88 (quotation), 122–3, NOCEX Records (HTML-Tulane); King, *Great South*, 51; Ross, "Resisting the New South," 65–7; Warmoth, *War, Politics and Reconstruction*, 81–4; "Railroad Policy for the South," *De Bow's Review* 2d ser., 5 (July 1868), 607–11; New Orleans *Daily True Delta*, December 3, 1865; Nordhoff, *Cotton States in 1875*, p. 58. See also Mark W. Summers, *Railroads, Reconstruction, and the Gospel of Prosperity: Aid under the Radical Republicans, 1865–1877* (Princeton, NJ, 1984). For a brief, acerbic account of state railroad

Weak railroad development not only reflected merchants' continued over-reliance on river-generated commerce, but also their related failure to diversify the city's economic base after the Civil War. Economic historians John B. Legler and Richard Sylla have recently argued that "a broad range of stocks tied to the local economy" were traded on the New Orleans Stock Exchange during the late nineteenth century, yet their own data shows that two-thirds of the stocks offered prior to 1900 were clustered in the financial sector (banking and insurance), and moreover, all six "railroads" traded were actually only city streetcar lines. Perhaps most significantly, not a single manufacturing concern was among the stocks listed – an absence consistent with earlier listings they compiled from the New Orleans and Charleston exchanges. In 1865–6 the New Orleans exchange had also been dominated by financial institutions, two of the three listed railroads were urban short-lines, and no manufacturing firms were traded. By contrast, the Charleston exchange already listed fourteen rail-roads from throughout the Southeast, as well as six manufacturing and mining companies.[13]

Although it goes unacknowledged by Legler and Sylla, their data provides a fine illustration of the widely neglected difference between postwar economic growth in the "New South" states of the Atlantic seaboard and the far slower, even regressive, pace of development in the Deep South region centered on New Orleans. In particular, the much-ballyhooed cotton-mill craze that swept the Southeast beginning in the late nineteenth century never generated much more than a few small establishments and several notable failures in postbellum New Orleans. Exchange statistician Henry G. Hester reported that Louisiana textile mills consumed only 16,420 bales of cotton in 1900; the state itself harvested 625,000 bales that same year. Overall, as historian Joy J. Jackson noted, "most of the major industries in [New Orleans] were adjuncts of some commercial interest" at the turn of the century, and as had long been the case, such firms typically engaged in low value–added, first-stage agricultural processing. Between 1890 and 1900, both the number of manufacturing concerns in the city and the workers they employed actually fell.[14]

development in the nineteenth century, see George Washington Cable, *The Creoles of Louisiana* (1884; repr., New York, 1970), 246–52.

[13] Legler and Sylla, "Integration of U.S. Capital Markets," 136–9 and Appendix 5.1 (quotation on p. 139).

[14] Jackson, *New Orleans in the Gilded Age*, 157; New Orleans Cotton Exchange report appended to Henry G. Hester to Alcee Fortier, October 4, 1900, in Series 5, Cotton Trade Series (Mss 537; HTML-Tulane); Norman Walker, "Manufactures," in Rightor, ed., *Standard History of New Orleans* (Chicago, 1900), 532–3. In fact, the overall pace of cotton mill growth in the late nineteenth-century "New South" has been overstated by some historians, as is reflected in regional data on cotton retained for domestic consumption. Compared to late antebellum figures, the total crop retained in the South actually fell in proportion to that used by the North during Reconstruction, when the ratio was about 10:1 in the North's favor. At the end of the century southern consumption of cotton was still less than half that used by northern mills; see *Statistical Abstract of the United States*, No. 22 (1899; repr., New York, 1964), Table 72 (p. 331).

Any survey of New Orleans's postbellum political economy would be incomplete without mentioning what was easily the biggest nonagricultural business in the city and state during the late nineteenth century: the Louisiana State Lottery Company. Incorporated by the Republican-dominated state legislature in 1868, this company was the brainchild of a group of New Yorkers closely connected with Tammany Hall. Although tickets for its monthly drawings were sold by mail throughout the nation (in fact, 90 percent of its sales came from out of state), the Lottery Company's rapidly growing political influence was most pronounced in Louisiana, especially its home base of New Orleans. The Company sought to cover its controversial tracks by making a wide variety of charitable and other contributions – not least among them, the dollars with which it lined the pockets of politicians from both parties. In addition to cultivating such "bipartisan" support, the Company burnished its public relations aura by employing local Confederate hero P. G. T. Beauregard to conduct its prize drawings for a salary of $30,000; the co-sponsorship of its activities by the city's leading banks lent it a further measure of legitimacy as well. At its height during the 1880s, the Lottery Company, by its own account, was generating an incredible $29 million in annual income, a figure that represented more than triple the total capital invested in manufacturing in Orleans Parish. Over a quarter of this revenue was pure profit, most of which left the state to be distributed among its national shareholders and New York–based officers. After years of growing controversy, Congress finally took successful aim at the "Lottery Trust" in the early 1890s by prohibiting the use of interstate mails for the Company's purposes. In the meantime, however, a great deal of political capital had been squandered on anti-Lottery reform efforts in Louisiana. A harbinger of the casino interests that would play an enormous and similarly controversial role in the state's economy a century later, this emblematic Gilded Age institution successfully tapped into the speculative currents that had long characterized the commodity-based business culture of nineteenth-century New Orleans.[15]

The long-playing scandals over the Lottery Company helped solidify the state's growing notoriety as what would soon be termed a "banana republic," a reputation reinforced by New Orleans's well-known Creole community, as well as its frequent entanglements in Latin American affairs. (Indeed, after the Lottery Company was finally banished from the city, it sought refuge in Honduras, from which it attempted unsuccessfully to resuscitate its fortunes.)

---

[15] A detailed account of the history of the Louisiana Lottery Company by a contemporary "muck-raking" journalist is Clarence C. Buel, "The Degradation of a State; or, The Charitable Career of the Louisiana Lottery," *The Century Magazine* 43 (February 1892), 618–33. See also Berthold C. Alwes, "The History of the Louisiana State Lottery Company," *Louisiana Historical Quarterly* 27 (October 1944), 933–1118, esp. 1020–3; and Williams, *P. G. T. Beauregard*, 291–303. Data on the total capital invested in Orleans Parish manufacturing is from the 1880 U.S. census, as available through the University of Virginia Libraries' Historical Census Browser, located online at http://fisher.lib.virginia.edu/collections/stats/histcensus/ (accessed September 23, 2009).

Just as before (and even during) the Civil War, the city's underdeveloped trading potential with Latin America remained a popular refrain among globally ambitious Crescent City businessmen. Although even the New Orleans Cotton Exchange lent its imprimatur to such efforts during the 1870s, the best-known champion of increased Latin American trade during and after Reconstruction was the shady Ring politico "Major" Edward A. Burke. His New Orleans *Times-Democrat* tirelessly promoted the Crescent City's opportunities for enrichment from the many countries on the Gulf of Mexico rim. In fact, New Orleans would increase its commercial ties to Latin America during the late nineteenth century, but although imports of bananas and coffee were highly lucrative for emergent trusts like the United and Standard Fruit Companies, they hardly proved a panacea for the city's many economic woes. As for Major Burke, who had first established his reputation as one of the "heroes" of the anti-Kellogg resistance in 1874, his fortunes ended up linked rather more ignominiously to Latin America. After serving for several years as state treasurer and then playing a key role in that spectacular failure, the New Orleans World Cotton Exposition of 1884, it came to light in 1889 that Burke had embezzled hundreds of thousands of dollars from the Louisiana treasury by means of an ongoing fraudulent bond scheme. Like the Louisiana Lottery Company, Burke took refuge in Honduras, where he evaded U.S. justice and lived out his years as a landowning grandee.[16]

In the stifling local political atmosphere during Reconstruction, many New Orleans businessmen may have taken solace from grandiose commercial visions like Burke's, which offered them hope of renewed importance in the postwar global economic order. But such dreams notwithstanding, the Mississippi River long remained "the axis on which all the whirl of life in the city of New Orleans revolves," as visitor Robert Somers put it. As they had during the prosperous antebellum decades, Crescent City merchants expected the river to continue delivering the products of the sprawling Mississippi Valley to their doorsteps, and their apparent complacency in the face of worsening economic conditions drew increasing criticism. "The larger part of our old Southern business is now done outside New Orleans instead of inside," observed the New Orleans *Picayune* in the summer of 1873. Although the

---

[16] Jackson, *New Orleans in the Gilded Age*, 19, 25–7; Ellis, "New Orleans Cotton Exchange," 559; Ross, "Resisting the New South," 68. See also [Illinois Central Railroad], *The Commercial, Industrial, and Financial Outlook for New Orleans* (Cedar Rapids, Iowa, 1894), 10; Morrison, *Industries of New Orleans*, 13–15; and typescript history (c. 1966), in Folder 1, Box 1, Standard Fruit & Steamship Company Papers (Mss 653; HTML-Tulane). Ironically, the term *banana republic* was coined by the writer O. Henry in the 1890s, after he had fled first to New Orleans, then to Honduras, after his own indictment on embezzlement charges. On New Orleans merchants' efforts to establish themselves in the cotton trade from Mexico during the Civil War, see *Report of the Joint Committee on the Conduct of the War*, 38 Cong., 2 Sess. (3 vols., Washington, DC, 1865), III, 17–19; and James W. Daddysman, *The Matamoros Trade: Confederate Commerce, Diplomacy, and Intrigue* (Newark, DE, 1984), 61–3.

paper conceded several legitimate excuses for the drop in commercial traffic, it nevertheless argued:

While giving full weight to these influences, we are convinced that many of our own folk are at fault. They will not properly work for prosperity; they lack that driving energy that goes out into the highways of the land and compels business to come in; they wait for it, instead of going for it, and the result is that less advantageous markets and inferior men, by sheer brass and impudent assertion, combined with astonishing enterprise, carry the day.

It was an all-too-familiar theme, one that echoed James Robb's complaints of 1851 and that probably inclined some Creole residents to sigh, "Plus ça change, plus c'est la même chose."[17]

These cynics might have been forgiven if the sudden surge of postwar interest in reclaiming the midwestern grain trade for New Orleans also provoked a sense of déjà vu. Another extension of the Crescent City's habitual dependence on the river, the depressed state of southern cotton production immediately following the war prompted many merchants to again cast a covetous gaze toward the farm products of the upper Mississippi and Ohio Valleys – even though they had willingly abandoned this trade to new lake-canal and east-west railroad routes during the cotton boom of the 1850s. Western discontent with emergent rail monopolies had already been growing before the war, when some believed those grievances might serve as a basis for uniting the two great agricultural sections of the U.S. against a common northeastern foe. Even during the war, Confederate general Braxton Bragg had declared in Kentucky that "a community of interest will force a commercial and social coalition between the great grain and stock-growing states ... and the cotton, tobacco, and sugar regions of the South." In 1869 *De Bow's Review* chose to reprint Bragg's speech as part of a general barrage of publicity about the mutual advantages of river transport for midwestern farmers and Crescent City merchants. Although there was still a tendency to fall back on the tired old saw that New Orleans was the upper valley's "natural depot and outlet to the markets of the world," grain producers were now also assured that shipping their products downriver would offer them price relief from "elevator and railroad rings." At a commercial convention held in New Orleans in May 1869, some westerners seemed intrigued by this new antimonopolistic tack. However, they made it clear that they expected greater benefits from trading with Crescent City merchants, who were urged to offer a greater range of imported goods at more competitive prices, which they could do by establishing direct ocean connections with European markets. Still, delegates from both sections easily reached agreement that the federal government should be pressed to undertake extensive improvements to make the river more suitable for increased two-way traffic.[18]

---

[17] "New Orleans at Rest," New Orleans *Daily Picayune*, July 14, 1873; Somers, *Southern States in 1870–71*, p. 191; see also Larsen, "New Orleans and the River Trade."

[18] "An Abstract of ... the New Orleans Commercial Convention, May 1869," *De Bow's Review* 2d ser., 6 (August 1869), 688–95; see also "The Bulk Grain Trade," *De Bow's Review* 2d ser., 6

The renewed interest of New Orleans merchants in the western grain trade necessarily brought them into greater contact with the commercial community of their upriver sister city, St. Louis. The border state of Missouri had been badly divided during the Civil War, and although the Lincoln administration had managed to keep it in the Union camp, pro-Confederate sentiment had always remained high, particularly in St. Louis. Indeed, by the end of the war, the majority of the state's white citizens seemed more aligned than ever with their neighbors to the south, a tilt that was already apparent among St. Louis business interests during the late antebellum period. Their city had been steadily losing ground to its rapidly expanding urban rival to the north, Chicago, whose growth had been aided by its closer connections with New York–based capital. St. Louis's relationship with the Crescent City ran deeper than just the extensive commercial ties promoted by steamboat traffic between the two cities. Nearly half of St. Louis's population were Catholics, and as one visiting journalist observed in 1867, "the languor and carelessness induced" by slaveholding still remained apparent among the city's "old and wealthy families," whose influential (and formerly pro-secessionist) French Creole presence lent the town "something of the style of New Orleans."[19]

The resumption of steamboat connections between St. Louis and New Orleans during the late occupation period continued to provide the most consistent source of port traffic during the years immediately after the war, and with the concomitant slowdown in cotton receipts, many Crescent City businessmen began aggressively touting St. Louis as an upriver ally in their efforts to resecure the still-booming grain trade. With the southern plantation trade facing an uncertain future due to unsettled labor arrangements in the countryside and the influx of politically favored northern speculators to New Orleans, some former cotton factors now reoriented their operations partly or entirely toward the western produce business, as did the firms of S. H. Kennedy,

(May 1869), 837–45. "Chicago and the Mississippi Outlet," *De Bow's Review* 2d. ser., 6 (March 1869), 251–6 (quotations on pp. 252–3); Braxton Bragg, "The South and the Northwest" [1862], *De Bow's Review* 2d ser., 6 (August 1869), 696–9 (quotation on p. 698).
[19] James Parton, "The City of St. Louis," *Atlantic Monthly* 19 (June 1867), 658 (quotations), 662, 670–1. Parton was familiar with Civil War–era New Orleans due to his recent collaboration with Benjamin F. Butler on a highly sympathetic account of the general's eight-month rule over the city; see Parton, *General Butler in New Orleans; Being a History of the Administration of the Department of the Gulf in the Year 1862* (New York, 1864). On pro-southern sympathizers in St. Louis and Missouri, see also Knox, *Camp-Fire and Cotton-Field*, 23–34, 55–6; and Christopher Phillips, *Missouri's Confederate Governor: Claiborne Fox Jackson and the Creation of Southern Identity in the Border West* (Columbia, MO, 2000), esp. 290–4. On St. Louis businessmen's late antebellum competition with Chicago and their tilt toward the South, see Jeffrey S. Adler, *Yankee Merchants and the Making of the Urban West* (New York and other cities, 1991), 172–4; Wyatt W. Belcher, *The Economic Rivalry between St. Louis and Chicago, 1850–1880* (New York, 1947), 101–25; William Cronon, *Nature's Metropolis: Chicago and the Great West* (New York, 1991), 295–309; and Timothy R. Mahoney, *River Towns in the Great West: The Structure of Provincial Urbanization in the American Midwest, 1820–1870* (New York and other cities, 1990), 213–19, 239–42.

E. K. Converse, and Aristide Miltenberger. After a brief postwar foray as a purchasing agent for a New Orleans cotton merchant, young Charles W. Squires
became a junior partner in a new wholesale grocery business established in
1866 by former cotton factor James Cammack Sr. "In New Orleans," he later
recalled, "I met with signal success at selling pork and bacon," but as economic and political conditions in the city went "from bad to worse" during
Reconstruction, Squires took the skills and connections he had established and
moved to St. Louis, where he "opened up a produce house" in late 1873.[20]

Squires's example helps show how the city's attempt to cultivate a closer
relationship with postbellum St. Louis was a double-edged sword. For one
thing, it fostered the same sort of dangerous dependency on external capital
that New Orleans businessmen had frequently condemned with regard to New
York City before the war. Moreover, locked into their own intense commercial rivalry with Chicago, St. Louis merchants were just as likely to encroach
on New Orleans's hinterlands as they were to serve as allies in a resuscitated
river trade. By the 1880s, for example, St. Louis's greater willingness to accommodate northern railroad investors had gained its markets the lucrative East
Texas cotton trade coveted by the Crescent City. Finally, most New Orleans
merchants' plans for resecuring the grain trade centered on steamboats (which,
despite an early postwar surge, soon became an outmoded form of transport),
thereby further delaying their pursuit of rail development. Significant upgrades
to riverfront warehousing would also be required to prevent the spoilage of
foodstuffs in the city's damp climate, which had been a problem long before
the war. Finally, the full benefits of a revived grain trade still largely depended
on improved conditions in the southern countryside, a dilemma that led one St.
Louis merchant to remind his Crescent City brethren at the 1869 commercial
convention that "cotton and wheat go hand in hand." The New Orleans *Price
Current* had noted in 1865 that "the ability of the Southern planter to pay for
Western produce must depend upon the degree of his success in the culture of
cotton and sugar." However, when cotton prices began their steady postwar

---

[20] Autobiographical manuscript of Charles Winder Squires (3 vols.), III, 19–20, 23–5 (quotations
on pp. 23 and 25), in W. H. T. Squires Papers (Mss 1644-Z, Southern Historical Collection,
Wilson Library, University of North Carolina at Chapel Hill; hereinafter cited as SHC). For the
shift of other New Orleans cotton factors into the western trade, see the signatories to the notice
published by "Western Produce Merchants," New Orleans *Daily Picayune*, June 15, 1873. On
the rapid postwar resumption of river trade between St. Louis and New Orleans, see J. E. Hilary
Skinner, *After the Storm; or, Jonathan and His Neighbours in 1865-6* (2 vols., London, 1866),
I, 299–300; and Oscar O. Winther, *The Transportation Frontier: Trans-Mississippi West, 1865–
1890* (New York and other cities, 1964), 74–5. Examples of New Orleans's sudden infatuation
with the possibilities of trade with St. Louis are "St. Louis, a Port of Entry," *De Bow's Review*
2d ser., 1 (March 1866), 309–10; S. Waterhouse, "St. Louis, the Future Capital of the United
States," *De Bow's Review* 2d ser., 5 (December 1868), 1096–1100; "The Grain Movement," *De
Bow's Review* 2d ser., 6 (May 1869), 440; and William M. Burwell, "Plan of Through Trade
between St. Louis and Liverpool by Way of New Orleans," *De Bow's Review* 2d ser., 6 (August
1869), 633–42.

decline, many planters sought greater self-sufficiency by laying in more food crops, thus obviating their need to purchase from urban markets – and if New Orleans were to serve mainly as a mere transshipping point for exports of western produce, then the advantages it could derive from an increased share of the grain trade would be severely limited.[21]

Yet despite such dabbling with the upper Mississippi Valley trade, New Orleans merchants' hopes for a commercial revival during Reconstruction continued to rest largely on the recovery of their old southern plantation markets. There were some encouraging signs of growth in cotton production by the early 1870s, when sharecropping contracts between white landowners and ex-slaves became entrenched as the preferred mode of resuming staple-crop production, finally lending a measure of stability to labor conditions after several years of uncertainty and stagnation in the southern countryside. Charles Nordhoff reported in 1875 that the freedpeople he encountered in Louisiana were "mak[ing] handsome returns" as croppers, and he also noted that they had earned a reputation with "petty shopkeepers, of whom the country is full," as better debtors than their white neighbors. Further boosting regional output of cotton were these white yeoman households, many of whom had begun concentrating more on staple-crop production after being initially attracted by temporarily inflated prices during the early postwar years. Whitelaw Reid described this trend from Mississippi in 1866, writing that these "tobacco-chewing, muddy-footed men from the hills were among the best customers the Natchez merchants had."[22]

Postwar visitors to the lower Mississippi Valley, perhaps overly impressed by superficial appearances, often seemed slow to grasp the damaging changes that the war and its aftermath had already wrought on the city's commerce. Robert Somers believed that he had witnessed the "rapid re-establishment"

---

[21] New Orleans *Price Current*, September 1, 1865, quoted in William E. Highsmith, "Louisiana Landholding during War and Reconstruction," *Louisiana Historical Quarterly* 38 (January 1955), 43; see also "Annual Review of the Mobile Cotton Market," *De Bow's Review* 2d ser., 5 (October 1868), 972. "Abstract of the New Orleans Commercial Convention," 692 (quotation). On postbellum St. Louis's commercial ambitions, see George Ruble Woolfolk, *The Cotton Regency: The Northern Merchants and Reconstruction, 1865–1880* (New York, 1958), 156–63; Belcher, *Economic Rivalry between St. Louis and Chicago*, 101–2; Winther, *Transportation Frontier*, 84–5; Ross, "Resisting the New South," 61–2.

[22] Reid, *After the War*, 482; Nordhoff, *Cotton States in 1875*, pp. 70–1; Taylor, *Louisiana Reconstructed*, 374–80. On the emergence of sharecropping as the dominant mode of production in the South during Reconstruction, see Gerald David Jaynes, *Branches without Roots: Genesis of the Black Working Class in the American South, 1862–1882* (New York, 1986); and Scott P. Marler, "Labor Systems," in *Encyclopedia of the Reconstruction Era*, ed. Richard Zuczek (2 vols., Westport, CT, 2006), I, 367–70. The embrace of cotton production by white yeoman farmers after the war is described in Steven Hahn, *The Roots of Southern Populism: Yeoman Farmers and the Transformation of the Georgia Upcountry, 1850–1890* (New York and other cities, 1983); for the similar but more gradual trend in Louisiana see Roger W. Shugg, *Origins of Class Struggle in Louisiana* (1939; repr., Baton Rouge, 1968), 269–73.

of the cotton business in New Orleans, which he felt "had all the more probability of continuing" in light of the "natural" advantages of river transport. Edwin De Leon chose to highlight the Crescent City in his optimistic account of "the New South" for *Harper's Magazine* in 1874. "The wonder is that [New Orleans] ... has so rapidly recovered lost ground, commercially," De Leon declared. However, local merchants, particularly those who had been around before the war, knew better. While Somers waxed enthusiastically over the fact that the city handled "about one-third" of the South's cotton output in 1870–1, more seasoned observers realized that the port's receipts had averaged over half of total production during the 1850s. Many New Orleans merchants saw other disturbing signs that commercial conditions remained poor and might never return to "normal," regardless of whether regional agriculture continued its gradual revival. Cotton prices were trending downward, and they were rightly concerned that the entrance of new foreign suppliers into global markets bode continuing ills in this regard. Also deeply worrisome to New Orleans businessmen during the early 1870s was the persistent shortfall of capital in the city's crucial banking sector, which had been the rock of the South's antebellum financial system.[23]

Incidentally, though, both Charles Nordhoff and Whitelaw Reid had called attention to what was the most troubling development of all from the perspective of New Orleans cotton merchants: the newly enhanced economic role of the "country store" in the former plantation districts. Some rural and small-town stores in Louisiana had begun purchasing and consolidating small farmers' staple-crop production for resale in Crescent City markets during the late antebellum era. But the vast majority of cotton was then still produced on slave plantations, whose owners were the primary clientele for hundreds of New Orleans–based factorage firms. Although big planters had often complained about high prices, interest charges, and other aspects of the factorage system, city merchants had thrived for decades by handling their crop sales and supplying them with foodstuffs and a wide range of other goods. For the most part, then, antebellum factorage had been a comfortable arrangement for both parties, but slave emancipation and its aftermath profoundly altered the terms of this long-balanced commercial equation. For one thing, the abolition of property rights in human beings essentially wiped out what had served, along with land, as one of the twin pillars of southern capital stock before the war, and the rolling annual loans that had been routinely extended by factors to their planter-clients had depended on bank credit that was collateralized mainly by this slave property. At the same time, land could not replace this

[23] Davis, *Southern Planter, Factor, and Banker*; "Monthly Markets," *De Bow's Review* 2d ser., 6 (May 1869), 442; Edwin De Leon, "The New South," *Harper's New Monthly Magazine* 49 (September 1874), 557; Somers, *Southern States in 1870-71*, p. 197. Data on New Orleans receipts as a proportion of total antebellum cotton production are compiled from E. J. Donnell, *Chronological and Statistical History of Cotton* (1872; repr., Wilmington, DE, 1973).

sudden capital deficit. New federal statutes severely restricted the use of real estate mortgages as a form of bank capital creation, and postwar land values were greatly depressed in any case.[24]

Even apart from this severe regional capital shortage, the dispersal of postemancipation agricultural production among thousands of individual small-farming units under sharecropping now made it nearly impossible for distant city factors to furnish supplies on credit as they had before, not only from the standpoint of prudent risk management, but also because of the insurmountable logistical difficulties involved. Into this breach stepped rural storekeepers, whose linchpin role in postbellum crop production and marketing gradually became apparent to New Orleans merchants during Reconstruction. In 1871, for example, long-time city banker Robert M. Davis argued that "the difficulty of collecting in the country is so great that credit to planters is refused in the city unless some tangible city security" could be offered as collateral. That same year, the New Orleans *Price Current*, the semi-weekly organ of the mercantile elite, offered a similar analysis of how business relationships between bankers, factors, and planters had "materially changed" since the war. Although landowners were still seeking supplies on credit from their former factors to help their tenants lay in crops, such arrangements were now deemed "too precarious" by city merchants and their banker allies. The risks involved in extending loans guaranteed solely by future crops, whose production and value were themselves subject to numerous contingencies, were no longer justifiable from the standpoint of factors, who, after all, only stood to earn 2.5 percent commission from their eventual sale.[25]

On the other hand, the *Price Current* continued, "the advance of merchandize on account" prior to the harvest and marketing season could be made instead "by the country merchant, who is taking somewhat the place of the factor, with superior facilities of saving himself by watching the crop growing and gathered." With this in mind, a few Crescent City merchants with sufficient foresight (and capital) bankrolled subsidiary stores under the management of kinfolk or close associates at strategic points throughout the countryside. Such was the relationship, for example, between Moses Mann and the Fischer

---

[24] For the impact of emancipation and sharecropping on the postbellum southern financial system, see Roger L. Ransom and Richard Sutch, *One Kind of Freedom: The Economic Consequences of Emancipation* (2nd ed.; New York and other cities, 2001), 51–2, 87–113; and John A. James, "Financial Underdevelopment in the Postbellum South," *Journal of Interdisciplinary History* 11 (Winter 1981), 443–54. Richard H. Kilbourne Jr. emphasizes the role of slave collateral in his *Debt, Investment, Slaves: Credit Relations in East Feliciana Parish, Louisiana, 1825–1885* (Tuscaloosa, AL, and London, 1995).

[25] Davis, *Southern Planter, Factor, and Banker*, 10; "The Factor and the Planter," New Orleans *Price Current*, March 15, 1871. See also Somers, *Southern States in 1870–71*, p. 198; Richard H. Kilbourne Jr., "The Ongoing Agricultural Credit Crisis in the Florida Parishes of Louisiana, 1865–1890," in *A Fierce and Fractious Frontier: The Curious Development of Louisiana's Florida Parishes, 1699–2000*, ed. Samuel C. Hyde Jr. (Baton Rouge, 2004), 128–30; Ransom and Sutch, *One Kind of Freedom*, 117–28; and Harold D. Woodman, *King Cotton and His Retainers: Financing and Marketing the Cotton Crop of the South, 1800–1925* (Lexington, KY, 1968), 296–303.

Brothers of West Feliciana Parish during the early 1870s. Conversely, some wealthier landowners, occasionally with support from their former city factors, established "plantation stores" to furnish their tenants and gather their crops. In both instances, at least some of the quondam functions of New Orleans merchants could be preserved largely intact.[26]

Such relationships were the exception, however, not the rule. Most interior stores were independent operations, and their owners were free to make whatever arrangements would net them the most profit. In light of the many disadvantages of New Orleans as a marketing center – conditions that worsened during Reconstruction – rural and small-town merchants began exploiting new alternatives that allowed them to boost their own bottom lines without the need to share profits with Crescent City intermediaries. To avoid the high costs associated with New Orleans, rural merchants started taking greater control of crop processing and marketing. By ginning, pressing, baling, and weighing cotton either at their own on-site facilities or ones nearby, they no longer needed to pay for such expensive processing in the Crescent City. Interior storekeepers also began availing themselves of improved telegraphic connections that allowed them to market cotton directly to buyers in distant markets like New York and Boston; similarly, they were able to sell it to the manufacturers' agents who started appearing more frequently in the southern countryside during the late nineteenth century. In 1873 the New Orleans *Picayune* confirmed the changed state of commercial affairs that now favored country merchants. Since the end of the war, the paper noted, "This class of dealers have become the 'middle-men' between the crop raiser and the final purchaser," and as a result, rural merchants were now doing an "astonishing" volume of business that earned them "very large" profits. Ironically, the advent of futures trading under New Orleans Cotton Exchange auspices only hastened the growth of direct sales from the interior. Although Crescent City merchants initially resisted the practice as "mere gambling," by the early 1880s the majority of southern crop production was marketed through futures contracts. Since this cotton had already been sold in advance, it could then be shipped via New Orleans on through bills of lading, thereby circumventing city merchants' commission fees and many other port surcharges as well.[27]

[26] On the Mann–Fischer Brothers relationship see Mann, Fischer & Co. Account Books, 1869–1880 (Mss 896, Louisiana and Lower Mississippi Valley Collection, Hill Memorial Library, Louisiana State University, Baton Rouge, LA); see the similar arrangements in East Feliciana Parish described in Kilbourne, *Debt, Investment, Slaves*, 110–29, 141–51; and Elliott Ashkenazi, *The Business of Jews in Louisiana, 1840–1875* (Tuscaloosa and London, 1988), 67–91. "Plantation stores" seem to have been most common in the rich alluvial parishes that bordered the Natchez District; see Michael Wayne, *The Reshaping of Plantation Society: The Natchez District, 1860–1880* (1983; repr., Urbana and Chicago, 1990), 186–91. New Orleans *Price Current*, March 15, 1871.

[27] Boyle, *Cotton and the New Orleans Cotton Exchange*, 99–100 (quotation on p. 100), 104–9, 164; New Orleans *Daily Picayune*, July 14, 1873; M. B. Hammond, *The Cotton Industry: An Essay in American Economic History. Part I: The Cotton Culture and the Cotton Trade* (New York, 1897), 291–9; Woodman, *King Cotton and His Retainers*, 273–7.

The easiest way to avoid New Orleans's drawbacks, however, was simply not to ship cotton there at all. For many years, the "natural advantages" of downriver transport and the relative lack of cost- and time-efficient alternatives had made New Orleans the default option when it came to crop marketing in the Southwest. Although the city had seen its trading territory shrink before the Civil War, most notably in its loss of upper Mississippi Valley commerce, it had made up for it through an increased volume of trade with its southern plantation hinterlands, especially during the boom years of the 1850s. But as historians John Legler and Richard Sylla recently noted, "after 1870, the volume of trade in [New Orleans's] remaining territory also began to decrease" – a trend whose outlines could actually be traced to the Civil War years themselves. With occupied New Orleans and its federal Custom-house a fount of bureaucracy, toll-taking, and corruption, overland shipments direct to East Coast markets became a more attractive and common option, and semi-sanctioned interbelligerent trading helped spur the growth of interior cities such as Memphis and Louisville. During Reconstruction, overland transportation networks became more extensive and efficient. With massive aid from northern capital, the southern railroad system, which had still been in its infancy before the war (except in South Carolina and Georgia), was rapidly refurbished and further extended throughout much of the interior. New east-west lines especially altered the previous flows of commercial traffic. Such direct rail connections to seaboard markets caused one observer in 1875 to declare "the diversion of trade from old routes" throughout the lower South as "among the many striking changes wrought by the war."[28]

Railroad development not only prompted the growth of small interior market towns during and after Reconstruction, but it also helped larger cities around the southern periphery to begin successfully encroaching on New Orleans's former plantation hinterlands. To the east, the rival port of Mobile was fighting its own battle for commercial survival as railroads based in South Carolina and Georgia extended into the cotton districts of northern Alabama, Tennessee, and eastern Mississippi. To the west, the port of Galveston Island, which enjoyed considerable support from New York–based capital and extensive rail connections centered on Houston to its north, thrived on Texas's burgeoning cotton and sugar production. To the immediate north, along the east bank of the Mississippi, the towns of Natchez, Vicksburg, and Greenville became important cotton marketing centers in their own right; and further north, in Tennessee, Nashville joined Memphis in rapid rail-fostered commercial growth, as did Louisville, Kentucky. Even erstwhile upriver ally St. Louis

[28] De Leon, "New South," 558; John F. Stover, *The Railroads of the South, 1865–1890: A Study in Finance and Control* (Chapel Hill, 1955), 190–3; Hammond, *Cotton Industry*, 298–300; E. Merton Coulter, "Commercial Intercourse with the Confederacy in the Mississippi Valley, 1861–1865," *Mississippi Valley Historical Review* 5 (March 1919), 385–7; Legler and Sylla, "Integration of U.S. Capital Markets," 151.

became "an aggressive competitor" for the Crescent City's southern trade during Reconstruction. Rail connections between St. Louis and the cotton regions of Arkansas and eastern Texas, which were completed by 1873, put the nail in the coffin of New Orleans's hopes of holding onto the Red River Valley trade. By 1880 St. Louis was the third largest cotton market in the nation, which prompted Crescent City business refugee Charles Squires to abandon western produce and hurry back into the cotton trade.[29]

In 1885 a comprehensive federal government report confirmed how interior marketing, new transportation outlets, and competition from other cities had reshaped postwar trade patterns to the Crescent City's disadvantage. Only 14,000 bales of cotton had been transported to market via overland routes in 1860; just two decades later, over a million bales were moved overland. This growth was attributed mainly to the expansion of cotton production in Texas and Arkansas, most of which was shipped by rail to points on the Ohio and upper Mississippi Rivers. The report also noted that "a large percentage of the shipments overland consists of purchases at interior points in the Southern States by agents of northern mills or by agents in eastern cities," because "local charges at many interior towns are lower than those at southern seaports...." Not all southern seaports were suffering, however. Although "there has been a considerable falling off in the receipts of cotton at the Gulf ports," improved east–west rail connections with the southern interior had prompted "a very large increase in the receipts at the South Atlantic ports," such as Savannah, Charleston, and Norfolk. If not for the steadily increasing commerce of Galveston, the decline in cotton receipts at Gulf Coast ports would have been even greater, although the report failed to explicitly recognize this fact.[30]

With the help of data furnished by cotton statistician Henry G. Hester, the federal report took special note of the steep proportional decline of cotton

---

[29] Squires autobiographical manuscript, III, 25; Ross, "Resisting the New South," 61–2 (quotation on p. 62), 67. For early Crescent City expressions of concern over St. Louis's designs on the Red River Valley trade, see "Railroad Connections between Texas and Missouri," *De Bow's Review* 2d ser., 1 (March 1866), 319–20; and "Trade between St. Louis and Arkansas," *De Bow's Review* 2d ser., 1 (April 1866), 424–5. On urban and commercial growth in postbellum Mississippi, see John C. Willis, *Forgotten Time: The Yazoo-Mississippi Delta after the Civil War* (Charlottesville, VA, 2000), 80–113; on Tennessee and Alabama see Don H. Doyle, *New Men, New Cities, New South: Atlanta, Nashville, Charleston, Mobile, 1860–1910* (Chapel Hill and London, 1990), 76–110. On Galveston, Houston, and the Texas trade see Baughman, *Charles Morgan and the Development of Southern Transportation*, 191–7; see also New Orleans *Daily True Delta*, December 3, 1865. Woodman, *King Cotton and His Retainers*, 274–5.

[30] Joseph Nimmo Jr., *Report on the Internal Commerce of the United States*, 48 Cong., 2d Sess., Ex.Doc. 7, Part 3 (Washington, DC, 1885), 77–85 (first and second quotations on p. 79; third quotation on p. 82). See also Emory R. Johnson et al., *History of the Domestic and Foreign Commerce of the United States* (2 vols.; Washington, DC, 1915), I, 278–81. Cotton receipts at Galveston roughly doubled every decade between 1870 and 1900. In 1899, its cotton exports surpassed those of New Orleans for the first time, but after the island port was laid flat by a hurricane in September 1900, its commerce never fully recovered; see *Statistical Abstract of the U.S.* (1899), Table 57 (p. 282).

receipts at New Orleans – a drop it claimed was "mainly attributable to the diversion overland of the crops of Mississippi and Arkansas." During the 1860–1 crop season, the last before the war, New Orleans had received 53.8 percent of the South's aggregate cotton production of 3.66 million bales, a figure consistent with the previous decade, when the city's annual receipts had averaged just over half of total regional output. A quarter-century later, the South was producing around six million bales of cotton per year, but now less than a third of those crops passed through New Orleans. Not until 1889 did New Orleans cotton receipts equal their previous record set during the 1859–60 season. Furthermore, this decline was even worse than it appeared at first glance, since an increasing share of the crops still received at New Orleans arrived on through bills of lading. Between 1881 and 1884 alone, the percentage of total New Orleans cotton receipts designated "in transit" rose from 24.7 percent to 35.5 percent. These crops had already been sold, and stripped of the modest multiplier effects that came from being marketed locally, they contributed relatively little to the city's economy. Such receipts certainly contributed almost nothing to local merchants, for whom this trend marked the final blow to the formerly lucrative dual functions of cotton factorage. First, New Orleans merchants had been forced to cede their role as plantation furnishing agents to country storekeepers after the war. Now, with less than 20 percent of the region's cotton actually being marketed in New Orleans, few could rely on income from the diminishing amount of unsold crops that still passed through their city. In any case, during a period when cotton prices were routinely struggling to reach ten cents per pound, merchants' standard 2.5 percent commission looked paltry indeed. This fact, along with the growth of futures trading, caused the remaining business to be increasingly consolidated in the hands of larger brokerage firms. The city's former stranglehold on the southern cotton trade had been broken, and with it, the glory days of the independent commodities speculator in New Orleans came to an end.[31]

Yet despite declining prices, the southern cotton sector had "recovered" by 1880, at least in the limited sense of surpassing antebellum production levels, and it would continue to grow for several decades to come. Interestingly, however, this late nineteenth-century recovery held true everywhere in the South – except in Louisiana (Table 7.1). Indeed, the 1885 federal report had partly blamed declining New Orleans cotton receipts on "reduced production in Louisiana." Even though the southern portion of the state was mostly devoted to sugar or livestock raising, Louisiana had still been the fourth-ranked producer of cotton in 1860. But alone among the southern states that accounted for nearly all of U.S. production during the late nineteenth century, Louisiana's cotton output in 1900 failed to surpass its 1860 levels (although it did briefly

[31] Nimmo, *Report on Internal Commerce*, 79–80, 85 (quotation on p. 85); Woodman, *King Cotton and His Retainers*, 288–94. The 1860–1 crop figures are from Donnell, *Chronological and Statistical History of Cotton*, 503–5.

TABLE 7.1. *Cotton Production (in Hundred Thousand Bales) by State, Ten-Year Intervals, 1860–1900*

State	1860	1870	1880	1890	1900
Alabama	990	429	700	915	1,104
Arkansas	367	248	608	691	719
Georgia	702	438	814	1,192	1,297
Louisiana	778	351	509	659	709
Mississippi	1,203	565	963	1,155	1,264
N. Carolina	146	145	390	336	473
S. Carolina	353	225	523	747	877
Tennesssee	296	182	331	191	215
Texas	431	351	805	1,471	2,659
TOTAL U.S.	5,387	3,012	5,755	7,473	9,436

Source: Data derived from James L. Watkins, *King Cotton: A Historical and Statistical Review, 1790 to 1908* (1908; repr., New York, 1969). The nine states listed never accounted for less than 97 percent of total U.S. production during the period. The drop in Tennessee's production in 1890 was anomalous; state cotton production averaged about 300,000 bales annually during both the 1880s and 1890s.

pass that level once, just barely, in 1898). Had Louisiana matched the 77 percent combined growth rate of the nine major cotton-producing states during the period, its production would have increased to 1.38 million bales in 1900; and if it had only kept pace with the other four "cotton states" of the lower South (Alabama, Georgia, Mississippi, and South Carolina), its production would have grown 40 percent by 1900 to 1.09 million bales.[32]

In light of this uniquely poor agricultural recovery during the late nineteenth century (the state's sugar sector was just as slow to recuperate), it is reasonable to ask what relationship existed between Louisiana's performance and the commercial decline of postbellum New Orleans. Before the war, New Orleans had exerted a profound gravitational pull on its Louisiana plantation hinterlands, especially with regard to the financial support it offered in the form of agricultural credit, even though these developmental linkages were weaker than the self-sustaining forms of economic growth they promoted between city and countryside elsewhere (e.g., in the case of nineteenth-century Chicago). In this sense, the devastation to capital stock represented by emancipation had far worse consequences in Louisiana than in Texas, where slavery had not been as entrenched before the war, which helps explain the Lone Star State's impressive postwar growth. Partly as a result of emancipation, New Orleans suffered the near-total destruction of its crucial banking sector, which had underpinned

[32] All figures are calculated from the data in Table 7.1. The "five cotton states" are those identified as such in Ransom and Sutch, *One Kind of Freedom.* Nimmo, *Report on Internal Commerce,* 85 (quotation).

the prewar factorage system. The elimination of slave property as a basis for capital augmentation also affected other southern states, but to a greater extent than in neighboring Mississippi or states along the eastern seaboard, Louisiana failed to rebuild its financial or agricultural sectors after the war with the aid of outside capital. Not only did the state's notorious political instability frighten off many potential investors during Reconstruction, but even after Redemption, New Orleans elites continued to resist the importation of northern capital. As the *Picayune* stubbornly insisted in 1878, Louisiana "can save herself, and stand alone, without a dollar of capital from other states." But such attitudes were belied by the facts: between 1860 and 1880, the state plummeted from second to thirty-seventh in the nation in per capita wealth. The lack of local enthusiasm for the incipient New South movement was further demonstrated during the disappointing World Cotton Exposition mounted by the city in 1884. Although "many northern capitalists" visited New Orleans during the Exposition, even one later boosterist pamphlet admitted that the city's poor condition "did not leave a good impression as to the business character and enterprise" of its citizens.[33]

In sum, as the postbellum South gradually developed a network of towns and cities better linked to the interdependent American urban system during the late nineteenth century, the Crescent City was left by the wayside in the process. It is perhaps a measure of the oft-overstated success of this "New South" that New Orleans would remain the Deep South's most populous city through World War II, yet even its "real" increases in population only served to disguise low growth rates that were out of step with the rest of the urbanizing

---

[33] [Illinois Central Railroad], *Commercial, Industrial, and Financial Outlook for New Orleans*, 4; Ross, "Resisting the New South," 71–3; New Orleans *Daily Picayune*, January 6, 1878, quoted in ibid., 67; Caldwell, *Banking History of Louisiana*, 111. On devastation and slow recovery in the Louisiana sugar industry, see Charles P. Roland, "Difficulties of Civil War Sugar Planting in Louisiana," *Louisiana Historical Quarterly* 38 (October 1955), 58–9; and John A. Heitmann, *The Modernization of the Louisiana Sugar Industry, 1830–1910* (Baton Rouge, 1987), 68–90. On the participation of outside capital in the postwar southern agricultural sector, see C. Vann Woodward, *Origins of the New South, 1877–1913* (1951; repr., Baton Rouge, 1971), 118–20. As Woodward notes, development of the lumber industry in western Louisiana during the late nineteenth century was sponsored by outside capital, and most profits were siphoned off to Texas-based interests backed by English investors. Much the same was true of the nascent rice industry concentrated in the sparsely populated coastal plains of southwestern Louisiana. Moreover, like the slow-recovering Louisiana sugar sector, rice production faced stout competition from neighboring states after the turn of the century; by 1910, both Arkansas and Texas produced more rice than Louisiana, and in terms of value, the staple accounted for less than a third of the state's agricultural output at its proportional peak through World War II; see Edward Hake Phillips, "The Gulf Coast Rice Industry," *Agricultural History* 25 (April 1951), 91–6. The postwar economic trajectories of Louisiana and Texas are suggestively compared in Linda Kay Murphy, "The Shifting Economic Relationships of the Cotton South: A Study of the Financial Relationships of the South During Its Industrial Development, 1864–1913" (Ph.D. diss., Texas A&M University, 1999), 76–8. On the developmental symbiosis between nineteenth-century Chicago and its hinterlands see Cronon, *Nature's Metropolis*.

South. Reactionary and counterproductive attitudes among its business elites certainly played a role in the city's regressive development, but the wartime destruction of its financial sector proved especially damaging to New Orleans's fortunes. In this regard, the final blow to the city's hopes of regaining its prominence as a banking center came in 1914, when New Orleans, despite an intensive lobbying effort, was passed over in favor of Dallas as a location for one of the new Federal Reserve System's twelve regional banks. In the typically reserved manner of economic historians, John Legler and Richard Sylla have concluded that New Orleans was "slow" to attract outside investment and "not well integrated" with national markets during the half-century following the Civil War, but this is an understatement. The sundering of the city's financial ties with large swaths of its former plantation hinterlands led historian Joy J. Jackson to declare more emphatically that "no other major [U.S.] port showed such a radical change in trade patterns" during the late nineteenth century as did New Orleans.[34]

The gradual revivification of the midwestern grain trade in New Orleans exemplified the limited commercial benefits it derived from serving as a mere waystation for commodities produced and marketed elsewhere. The city's role in the postbellum grain trade, which has been overemphasized by some recent historians, occurred mainly after a series of extensive port reforms during the twentieth century; at the turn of the century, New Orleans's share of national grain receipts barely reached 20 percent of those destined for northern ports. Instead, cotton long remained "king" among the commodities the city handled, with sugar, rice, and low-value bulk agricultural imports from Latin America bringing up the rear. Ultimately, merchants' failure to maintain the city's position in the fast-expanding grain trade during the antebellum era had long-term effects, since the durable linkages that this trade established with the northeastern financial sector proved crucial to the economic development of cities such as Chicago and St. Louis.[35]

---

[34] Jackson, *New Orleans in the Gilded Age*, 150–1 (quotation on p. 150); Legler and Sylla, "Integration of U.S. Capital Markets," 153. New Orleans's rapid descent from a first-order U.S. banking center to third-rank status is described in James, "Financial Underdevelopment in the Postbellum South," 446–7, 453–4; and Michael P. Conzen, "The Maturing Urban System of the United States, 1840–1910," *Annals of the Association of American Geographers* 67 (March 1977), 88–108. The reinscribed map of regional banking imposed by the Federal Reserve not only assigned northern Louisiana's cotton parishes to the Dallas bank's supervision, but also added insult to injury by relegating New Orleans itself to the administration of Atlanta's. For other insights into New Orleans's anomalous status in the gradually urbanizing New South, see Lawrence H. Larsen, *The Rise of the Urban South* (Lexington, KY, 1985), 148–52; Morton J. Rothstein, "The New South and the International Economy," *Agricultural History* 57 (Fall 1983), 385–402; and David Goldfield, "A Regional Framework for the Urban South," in Goldfield, *Region, Race, and Cities: Interpreting the Urban South* (Baton Rouge, 1997), 45–9.

[35] For data on the composition of New Orleans commerce and its relative position compared with other ports at the turn of the century, see *Statistical Abstract of the U.S.* (1899), 136, 145, 364, 366; on the grain trade see also U.S. Treasury Department, Bureau of Statistics, *Monthly*

In the integrated national marketplace consolidated during the late nineteenth century, interregional flows of capital were becoming more important than the physical movement of commodities themselves. However, this was a lesson that New Orleans businessmen were painfully slow to learn. As late as World War II, an ironically named local reformer, Henry Grady Meador, lamented the Crescent City's lack of industrial development, yet he and others continued to champion expanded ties with the Midwest and Latin America as a solution to the city's economic woes. Any port in a storm, as it were – but at least Meador recognized that New Orleans's failure to diversify its economic base resulted from its persistent reliance on a southern "trade territory" that was "just beginning to emerge from the thrall of the plantation system." "Surely it does not suffice," Meador argued in 1942, "that we take a toll on this traffic, produce nothing ourselves, and add nothing to the value of the raw materials which we handle through the Port." Again, it was a depressingly familiar refrain. In 1869 long-time Creole resident Durant Daponte had lambasted merchants' renewed commitment to the river-borne commodities trade. Their complacency, he insisted, was turning New Orleans into "a monument to commercial isolation." It was already clear to Daponte, only four years after Appomattox, that the Crescent City's ability to draw sustenance from its agricultural hinterlands had been profoundly altered by a series of interwoven, mutually reinforcing changes that occurred during and after the Civil War. More than a century and a half later, it seems safe to conclude that no first-rank American city's fortunes have ever collapsed as quickly as did those of New Orleans after 1860.[36]

Summary of Commerce and Finance of the United States, January 1900 (Washington, DC, 1900), 1981–3. Historian Ari Kelman places questionable emphasis on the postbellum grain trade as a spur to local economic development in *A River and Its City: The Nature of Landscape in New Orleans* (Berkeley, CA, and other cities, 2003), esp. pp. 135–6; cf. Larsen, "New Orleans and the River Trade," 124. On port reforms after the mid-1890s see Boyle, *Cotton and the New Orleans Cotton Exchange*, 135–6; and Jackson, *New Orleans in the Gilded Age*, 153–7.
[36] Daponte, "New Orleans and Ship Island Ship Canal," 26; H[enry] Grady Meador, "Port Commerce and the Industrial Development of New Orleans," *Port Record* 1 (September 1942), 17; see also Richard Tate, "Latin American Trade Will Help Unify New Orleans and the Mid-West," *Port Record* 1 (April 1943), 28.

8

Rural Merchants and the Reconstruction of Louisiana Agriculture

After the Civil War, some white southerners were quick to recognize that the Union's victory would have wide-ranging ramifications for the region's political economy. Most obvious was emancipation, which forced them to reorganize the slave-labor system that had underpinned plantation agriculture for generations. George Fitzhugh, one of the most influential pro-slavery ideologists before the war, mixed sarcasm and realism in an 1866 *De Bow's Review* article on the subject. Because "the abolition of the relation of master and slave begets the relation of debtor and creditor," wrote the acidulous critic of northern free labor, "let us accept as true, humane, and Christian, what all the world says is so, and apply the lash of capital or debt to the negro, just as strenuously as it is applied elsewhere to the white laboring man."[1]

Like most former slaveholders, commercial elites in New Orleans initially hoped to replace slavery with a strict "new labor system to be proscribed and enforced by the State," but federal authorities soon made it clear that draconian measures such as the Black Codes of 1865-6 would not be tolerated. Who, then, would wield the whip that administered "the lash of capital"? The severe shortage of money among southern landowners and merchants made a system of wage payments impractical, so instead, makeshift arrangements based on dividing crop-sale proceeds rapidly became the norm in cotton-growing regions of the South. But even forms of farm tenancy like sharecropping required capitalists who could furnish farmers with supplies and credit prior to the harvest and marketing season. Most city merchants were unable to fill this role, not only because of their own depleted finances, but also because

---

[1] [George Fitzhugh], "National Debt a National Blessing," *De Bow's Review* 2d ser., II (October 1866), 399-402 (quotations on pp. 399-400). On Fitzhugh's pro-slavery, anticapitalist thought see Eugene D. Genovese, *The World the Slaveholders Made: Two Essays in Interpretation* (1969; repr., Middletown, CT, 1988), 165-234.

of logistical difficulties and the higher risks inherent to decentralized production arrangements. And for the same reasons that landowners were incapable
of paying wages, neither could most furnish their tenants. As a result, as one
Crescent City newspaper put it in 1873, "a new era began" with the end of the
Civil War, when "the cross-road country store commenced its mission."[2]

Other contemporaries realized the "lash of capital" was now in the hands
of rural and small-town storekeepers, and some foresaw serious consequences
for the New Orleans–based factorage system. In 1871 the New Orleans *Price-
Current* noted that the rural merchant "is taking ... the place of the factor,
with superior facilities of saving himself by watching the crop growing and
gathered." Some of the foundations for these changes had been laid before the
war, when increasing numbers of Louisiana store owners had begun tailor-
ing their operations toward yeoman households whose output did not earn
much attention from New Orleans merchants. As discussed in Chapter 3, these
rural storekeepers had not only sold goods on credit to small farmers, but they
had also marketed their growing staple-crop production. As a result, many
rural and small-town storekeepers were already well-positioned to step into
the postwar credit-provisioning breach created by the dispersal of crop production under sharecropping and other forms of tenancy. However, their own
lack of access to bank capital, as well as defaults caused by crop failures and
absconding debtors, prompted many to charge excessively high interest for
supply advances. By the closing decades of the nineteenth century, when credit-
furnishing merchants had become a ubiquitous presence in the everyday lives
of black and white southern farmers alike, their practices helped provoke the
outburst of southern agrarian discontent known as the Populist movement.[3]

Most later historians acknowledged these merchants' importance to the
economy of the post–Civil War South. Although monographic treatments of
country stores have been scarce, scholars such as C. Vann Woodward and
Harold D. Woodman emphasized rural and small-town merchants' provision of
seasonal credit, especially in cotton-growing regions, which was secured via the
legal mechanism of the crop lien. Both Woodman and Woodward condemned
the cycle of debt that the crop-lien system fostered among sharecroppers and
other small farmers, yet they were reasonably temperate in their criticisms of
southern storekeepers. Woodward, for example, concluded that it "would be a

---

[2] New Orleans *Daily Picayune*, July 14, 1873; New Orleans *Price-Current*, September 1, 1865
(first quotation). On the Black Codes of 1865–6, see William Cohen, *At Freedom's Edge: Black
Mobility and the Southern White Quest for Racial Control, 1861–1915* (Baton Rouge, 1991),
28–43.

[3] New Orleans *Price-Current*, March 15, 1871; see also Robert Somers, *The Southern States Since
the War, 1870–71* (1871; repr., University, AL., 1965), 198. For two late nineteenth-century critical views of rural furnishing merchants in the South, see Charles H. Otken, *The Ills of the South*
(New York and London, 1894), 12–57; and M. B. Hammond, *The Cotton Industry: An Essay
in American Economic History*. Part I: *The Cotton Culture and the Cotton Trade* (New York,
1897), 141–65.

mistake to make the supply merchant the villain in the piece," because he was "only a bucket on an endless chain by which the agricultural well of a tributary region was drained of its flow." Such views became less common with the advent of the new social history in the 1970s, whose class-oriented studies cast rural merchants among the late nineteenth-century South's primary villains.[4]

Woodward seemed to understand that furnishing merchants operated under numerous disadvantages, some of which were related to their standing as small businesses. The small-business sector has long presented a challenge for economic historians. While most agree that small businesses have been a significant presence in American life, their ephemeral nature (most, it has been noted, fail in their first year) makes attempts to specify their economic contributions seem nearly oxymoronic. Moreover, the scarcity of records left behind by such nineteenth-century firms is exacerbated by the lack of "transparency" most displayed. Small businesses were usually family-owned enterprises or partnerships, and only rarely were they incorporated.[5]

The consequences of the failure to accord small business greater historical significance are most pronounced in the distribution and marketing sector. In his classic study of nineteenth-century American business development, Alfred D. Chandler explicitly linked the consolidation of mass production to evolving marketing structures, but his insights have rarely been pursued with regard to small retailers. Historians still have much to learn about the thousands of independently owned stores that remained a dominant presence in consumers' lives

[4] C. Vann Woodward, *Origins of the New South, 1877–1913* (Baton Rouge, 1951), chap. 7 (quotation on pp. 184–5); Harold D. Woodman, *King Cotton and His Retainers: Financing and Marketing the Cotton Crop of the South, 1800–1925* (Lexington, KY, 1968), 295–314. See also Jacqueline P. Bull, "The General Merchant in the Economic History of the New South," *Journal of Southern History* 18 (February 1952), 37–59. The only monograph on postbellum southern merchants remains Thomas D. Clark, *Pills, Petticoats, and Plows: The Southern Country Store* (1944; repr. Norman, Ok., 1989). Examples of "new social histories" that emphasized rural merchants are Michael Schwartz, *Radical Protest and Social Structure: The Southern Farmers' Alliance and Cotton Tenancy, 1880–1890* (New York, 1976); Lawrence Goodwyn, *Democratic Promise: The Populist Moment in America* (New York and Oxford, 1976); Michael Wayne, *The Reshaping of Plantation Society: The Natchez District, 1860–1880* (1980; repr., Urbana and Chicago, 1990); and Jonathan M. Wiener, *Social Origins of the New South: Alabama, 1860–1885* (Baton Rouge and London, 1978); see also Wiener, "Class Structure and Economic Development in the American South, 1865–1955," *American Historical Review* 84 (October 1979), 970–1006, which includes a rebuttal by Woodman (ibid., 997–1001). In *"Man Over Money": The Southern Populist Critique of American Capitalism* (Chapel Hill, 1980), Bruce Palmer carefully examined some of the ambiguities of Populist ideology, such as their attitudes toward merchants as fellow independent proprietors; see esp. pp. 172–3, 208–15.

[5] William A. Brock and David S. Evans try to specify the economic contributions of the small-business sector in *The Economics of Small Businesses: Their Role and Regulation in the American Economy* (New York, 1986). See also Mansel G. Blackford, *A History of Small Business in America* (New York, 1991); and Stuart Bruchey, ed., *Small Business in American Life* (New York, 1980). On the lack of "transparency" among small firms, see Rowena Olegario, "'That Mysterious People': Jewish Merchants, Transparency, and Community in Mid-Nineteenth-Century America," *Business History Review* 73 (Summer 1999), 161–89.

deep into the twentieth century, especially in rural regions, where the majority of the U.S. population continued to reside through 1920. With few exceptions, however, economic historians have neglected distribution in favor of production-oriented topics, with the small-business sector barely on their radar.[6]

The most sophisticated analysis of rural and small-town merchants in the post–Civil War South has been Roger L. Ransom and Richard Sutch's 1977 study *One Kind of Freedom* – or, as the popular shorthand refers to it, "1KF." Like the new social historians with whom their book was contemporaneous, the two economic historians assigned a great deal of responsibility to furnishing merchants for regional poverty after emancipation. For example, they confirmed long-standing claims that the interest rates charged by rural storeowners were unjustifiably high. But the crux of their arguments about country stores was their insistence that the South was "partitioned ... into literally thousands of separate territorial monopolies, each one dominated by a local merchant" (1KF, p. 137). Absent the competitive conditions that would have restrained their behavior, storekeepers were free to charge as much interest as their consciences would bear. But despite their criticisms of merchants' business practices, Ransom and Sutch neither endorsed nor engaged with class-conflict models in their study. Instead, they couched their analysis in the discourse of mainstream economics: condemning stores as "flawed economic institutions" (1KF, p. 2) rather than as sites of class-based exploitation.[7]

---

[6] Alfred D. Chandler Jr., *The Visible Hand: The Managerial Revolution in American Business* (Cambridge, MA, 1977), esp. chap. 7. The most valuable history of American distribution remains Glenn Porter and Harold C. Livesay, *Merchants and Manufacturers: Studies in the Changing Structure of Nineteenth-Century Marketing* (Baltimore, 1971; repr. Chicago, 1989); see also George L. Mehren, "Market Organization and Economic Development," *Journal of Farm Economics* 41 (1959), 1307–15; Harold Barger, *Distribution's Place in the American Economy since 1869*, National Bureau of Economic Research, General Series No. 58 (Princeton, NJ, 1955); Lance E. Davis and Douglass C. North, *Institutional Change and American Economic Growth* (New York and London, 1971), esp. chap. 9. To the extent that recent historians have focused on marketing developments, their attention has been mostly on the creation of American consumer culture from the late nineteenth century forward, with the result being a plethora of studies that usually pay little heed to small businesses, instead tending to focus on emergent, often-incorporated organizational forms such as department stores and mail-order houses; see, for example, Richard S. Tedlow, *New and Improved: The Story of Mass Marketing in America* (New York, 1990) and Susan Strasser, *Satisfaction Guaranteed: The Making of the American Mass Market* (New York, 1989).

[7] Roger L. Ransom and Richard Sutch, *One Kind of Freedom: The Economic Consequences of Emancipation* (2nd ed.; New York and other cities, 2001), esp. chaps. 6–8 (quotation on p. 137). This work will be cited parenthetically in the text hereinafter as 1KF. Although Ransom and Sutch eschewed class-conflict frameworks – nor did they discuss such approaches at all – they provided insight into their rationale in a footnote buried in a rejoinder to their critics. Commenting on a citation of Jonathan Wiener's work against 1KF's characterization of "a coincidence of interest between landlords and merchants," Ransom and Sutch wrote, "[W]e interpret the conflict which Wiener focuses on as being political and social rather than economic in nature." This is a good example of the walls that economic historians often erect between quantitative data and "political and social" factors. Ransom and Sutch, "Credit Merchandising in the Post-Emancipation

One Kind of Freedom provoked polite scholarly controversy after its release, some of which continues to this day. In particular, their thesis that postbellum merchants in the Cotton South owed their powerful positions to the establishment of localized "territorial monopolies" over agricultural credit has come under close scrutiny. Ransom and Sutch reached their conclusions about southern country stores during Reconstruction using evidence from the records of the R. G. Dun & Co. credit-reporting agency and complex spatial modeling techniques derived from economic anthropology. Their conclusions were based on a sample of stores in twenty-two counties of the five-state region they identified as the "Cotton South" (Alabama, Georgia, Louisiana, Mississippi, and South Carolina), with several key contentions actually predicated on an even smaller subset comprised of only six counties.[8]

Conceding that the importance of merchants' credit-provisioning role in the postbellum South is well-established, this chapter analyzes state- and parish-level data on Louisiana stores similar to that compiled by Ransom and Sutch. Using an evidentiary base also drawn mainly from the Dun records, two discrete sets of county-level data on stores in Reconstruction-era Louisiana are described and compared. By contrasting the numbers, persistence rates, spatial density, and capital invested in general stores in two carefully selected parishes, it will describe how the merchants' experiences in these rural localities were shaped by the very divergent market environments in which their stores were embedded. Data from these two parishes – one devoted to cotton production, the other to sugar – are supplemented by state- and parish-level data from others. Ultimately, the evidence presented on mercantile development in postemancipation Louisiana will call into question key aspects of Ransom and Sutch's study, especially the spatial-density estimates behind their "territorial monopoly" thesis. However, these data will also cast a dubious light on other conventional understandings of southern country stores, suggesting that

South: Structure, Conduct, and Performance," in *Market Institutions and Economic Progress in the New South, 1865–1900*, eds. Gary M. Walton and James F. Shepherd (New York, 1981), 62 n. 10. Ironically, though, Ransom and Sutch's conclusions about "the trap of debt peonage" (1KF chap. 8) and sharecropping as a form of tenancy (chap. 5) were largely congruent with those of the new social historians. Even so, such characterizations have been replaced in more recent scholarship, which tends to view sharecroppers as mobile, wage-earning free laborers in a "New South" permeated by capitalist institutions and mentalités. For a critique of this historiographical trend see my article "Fables of the Reconstruction: Reconstruction of the Fables," *Journal of the Historical Society* 4 (Winter 2004), 113–37.

[8] For a more detailed discussion of 1KF and its methodology, see an earlier version of this chapter published as "Two Kinds of Freedom: Mercantile Development and Labor Systems in Louisiana Cotton and Sugar Parishes during Reconstruction," *Agricultural History* 85 (Spring 2011), 225–51. See also Walton and Shepherd, eds., *Market Institutions and Economic Progress in the New South*; and Gavin Wright, *Old South, New South: Revolutions in the Southern Economy since the Civil War* (New York, 1986), 110–15. A 1999 symposium on the mostly unrevised second edition of 1KF featured contributions by Wright, Peter Coclanis, Harold Woodman, Stanley Engerman, and Ransom and Sutch; see the special issue of *Explorations in Economic History* 38 (January 2001).

previous historiography has overgeneralized the significance of merchants in disparate agricultural regions of the postemancipation South, and sometimes misrepresented them as well. Although aggregate analysis undergirds most of these findings, individual examples will also be provided to help "thicken" the quantitative data.[9]

As new systems of agricultural production took shape in postemancipation Louisiana, differences between cotton- and sugar-producing parishes became increasingly pronounced. This chapter analyzes such differences by comparing Ascension and West Feliciana Parishes, which were only about fifty miles apart and connected by the Mississippi River, with the town of Baton Rouge lying roughly equidistant between them (Ascension to its southeast, West Feliciana to its northwest). These parishes are well-suited for purposes of comparison. Both were almost exactly the same size (373 and 370 square miles, respectively); each contained a population of about 11,000 people in 1870, a majority of whom were ex-slaves; and each featured a riverside burg of about 2,000 inhabitants (Donaldsonville in Ascension Parish, and the twin towns of Bayou Sara/ St. Francisville in West Feliciana). In addition, plantation agriculture had long been the fulcrum of each parish's economy and had made both among antebellum Louisiana's wealthiest, most politically influential parishes. After the war, cotton planters in West Feliciana Parish adopted (or acceded to) a share-tenancy system of decentralized production units composed mainly of freedpeople's households. In Ascension Parish, by contrast, sugar was the dominant staple crop. Since growing and processing cane was not well-suited to production on small tenant farms, plantation owners were obliged to come to terms with free laborers – not just as "non-slaves" but as wage-earning workers.[10]

Looking at some basic data on the numbers of stores should begin demonstrating how such differences in the organization of agricultural production affected mercantile development. Table 8.1 shows the number of general stores reported in each parish from the late antebellum period through 1878. Obviously, the number of general stores in each parish increased sharply after

---

[9] As defined in this study, the Reconstruction period in Louisiana extends from 1863 (after which most of the state was effectively under Union control) to about 1879 (two years after the final withdrawal of Federal troops and also the year when the most complete records of the Dun agency end). On the history of Reconstruction-era Louisiana in general, see Joe Gray Taylor, *Louisiana Reconstructed, 1863–1877* (Baton Rouge, 1974).

[10] The economic history of postbellum Louisiana has been surprisingly neglected. A good overview is Taylor, *Louisiana Reconstructed*, chaps. 8–9. Particularly lacking has been a focus on cotton production in the state, although the Natchez district, comprised of cotton-growing areas on both the Louisiana and Mississippi sides of the river, was examined in Wayne, *Reshaping of Plantation Society*. Louisiana's sugar-growing regions have received more attention; see, for example, J. Carlyle Sitterson, *Sugar Country: The Cane-Sugar Industry in the South, 1753–1950* (Lexington, KY, 1953); and John A. Heitmann, *The Modernization of the Louisiana Sugar Industry, 1830–1910* (Baton Rouge, 1987). On the consequences of the shift to wage labor in postwar sugar production, see John C. Rodrigue, *Reconstruction in the Cane Fields: From Slavery to Free Labor in Louisiana's Sugar Parishes, 1862–1880* (Baton Rouge, 2001).

the war. In West Feliciana there were twenty-three general stores reported in 1860, with seventy-two new ones established in the fifteen years after the war. In 1860 there were thirty-four stores in Ascension Parish, and 138 new ones were established between 1863 and 1878. These figures confirm the conventional wisdom about the rapid postwar proliferation of such establishments, but on the other hand, they also represent a puzzle. Given that rural and small-town furnishing merchants were structurally essential to the resumption of cotton production, one might have expected store growth in West Feliciana Parish, *ceteris paribus* (population, size, resources), to have outpaced the sugar parish, where stores were not relied on for seasonal credit. But instead, the number of general stores established in Ascension Parish during Reconstruction was nearly double that in West Feliciana.[11]

A closer look at the antebellum period, when there were already more than 50 percent more stores in Ascension Parish, may help begin solving that riddle. Since the personal wealth of Ascension Parish's free population was lower in both real and per-capita terms in 1860, one might again have predicted more stores to be located in West Feliciana Parish. Ascension Parish was also closer to New Orleans, which could have drained off more local spending. However, the higher number of stores in prewar Ascension Parish is probably attributable to the greater number of free households, almost twice as many as West Feliciana (823 to 454), which formed a larger local market for retailers. Moreover, wealth distribution among those households was less concentrated in Ascension Parish, which had more small, owner-operated farms than did West Feliciana. Because they had neither the collateral nor the credit to participate in the New Orleans–based factorage system on which large planters relied for housewares and plantation supplies, these yeoman households had to buy or barter goods locally; hence, there were more stores in antebellum Ascension Parish.[12]

[11] "General stores" are categorized herein not only as those referred to specifically as such by the local reporters for the Dun agency, whose practices were wildly – often frustratingly – not standardized. Like Ransom and Sutch (1KF, 416 n. 45), this study includes grocers and dry-goods merchants under the rubric of general stores. Also like them, it does not include specialized retail stores; for example, booksellers and drugstores, even though some of these (especially drugstores, the progenitor elsewhere of the "five-and-dime") may have been more akin to "general stores" than some small groceries *qua* produce stands.

[12] *Eighth Census of the United States*, 1860, Vol. I: *Population*, 303, 344. On small farms in Ascension Parish see Samuel H. Lockett, *Louisiana As It Is: A Geographical and Topographical Description of the State*, ed. Lauren C. Post (orig. ms. 1869–72; repr., Baton Rouge, 1969); and Shugg, *Origins of Class Struggle in Louisiana*, 266. The concentrated landholdings of West Feliciana Parish are discussed in Samuel C. Hyde Jr., *Pistols and Politics: The Dilemma of Democracy in Louisiana's Florida Parishes, 1810–1899* (Baton Rouge, 1996), 26–8; and Floyd M. Clay, "Economic Survival of the Plantation System within the Feliciana Parishes, 1865–1880" (M.A. thesis, Louisiana State University, 1962). For mercantile development in yeoman-dominated regions, see Scott P. Marler, "Merchants in the Transition to a New South: Central Louisiana, 1840–1880," *Louisiana History* 42 (Spring 2001), 165–92; and Steven Hahn, *The Roots of Southern Populism: Yeoman Farmers and the Transformation of the Georgia Upcountry, 1850–1890* (New York, 1983), chap. 5.

Like studies that demonstrate "planter persistence" after the war, many rural stores in postbellum Louisiana were operated by the same men as before the war. Ransom and Sutch claimed that "few" antebellum stores "survive[d]" the war (1KF, p. 117), but in 1866, when the Dun agency resumed compiling reports from the South, twelve of Ascension Parish's thirty-four stores from 1860 were still in business. Among them was John Dominque's riverfront store about ten miles north of Donaldsonville, which had been the subject of an idyllic painting by the noted artist Marie Adrien Persac in 1857. After his death, Dominque's store remained in business under his son's management through at least the mid-1880s. Similarly, Victor Maurin had been one of the parish's most prosperous merchants since the 1840s, but despite some "destruction of his property during the war," he had rebuilt his business, which was carried on by his son after his death in 1875. Marks Israel, who had purchased Henry Pforzheimer's store in 1859 after serving as his clerk for several years, became one of the town's "leading merchants" after the war, with inventory estimated at $40,000 in 1873. Jacob Lemann had sold out his Donaldsonville store in 1856 but continued to hold notes and real estate interests in the parish after departing for New York and Europe. Lemann returned with his family in 1866 to manage his newly obtained sugar plantations, and he also financed his son Bernard in reacquiring his riverfront store. By the mid-1870s the younger Lemann was doing the "largest business in the place," with an in-store capital estimated at over $30,000. Solomon Weinschenck (who would serve as Donaldsonville's mayor), J. H. Gondrau, Emile Collin, and J. B. Rodrigue were among other merchants of lesser means who managed to maintain stores first established during the 1840s and 1850s until at least the end of Reconstruction.[13]

The situation was similar in West Feliciana Parish, where nearly half of the twenty-three antebellum stores resumed business after the war, although the going could be precarious. For example, the French immigrant Peter Lebret had been in the merchandising trade in Bayou Sara since 1837, but he had increasingly attended to his plantation's affairs during the mid-1850s, leaving his wife Elise largely in charge of the family store. After the war, the financially besieged Lebrets steadily sold off their real estate holdings while trying to regroup their fortunes behind the more stable income provided by their Bayou Sara store. In 1859 they had pledged two thousand acres of land and sixty slaves to wholesalers Bellocq, Nobblom & Co. of New Orleans in lieu

[13] On Bernard Lemann, see Louisiana, Vol. II, 21, 35, 58, in R. G. Dun & Co. Credit Report Collections (Baker Library Historical Collections, Harvard Business School; cited hereinafter as Dun & Co., Louisiana, with appropriate volume and page numbers); Elliott Ashkenazi, *The Business of Jews in Louisiana, 1840–1875* (Tuscaloosa, AL, 1988), 46 and *passim*; and Leslie A. Lovett, "From Merchant to Sugar Planter: The Rise and Success of Jacob Lemann and Son" (unpublished B.A. thesis, Tulane University, 1990). On Dominque's store, see Dun & Co., Louisiana, II, 57; and H. Parrott Bacot et al., *Marie Adrien Persac: Louisiana Artist* (Baton Rouge, 2000), 38–9. On Maurin, see Dun & Co., Louisiana, II, 5, 31; Israel, ibid., 19, 31; Weinschenck, ibid., 2, 31, 34; Gondrau, ibid., 18, 19, 30, 63; Collin, ibid., 15, 30; and Rodrigue, ibid., 6.

of a \$35,000 debt, a mortgage they finally managed to pay off in 1868. After Peter's death in the early 1870s, his son tried to manage the firm in conjunction with his mother, but by 1875 they were forced to rely on friends to obtain credit to stock their shrinking business. Not long thereafter, the Lebrets' store failed, after nearly forty years in business.[14]

In spite of sometimes frequent partnership and intrafamilial reorganizations, however, some antebellum West Feliciana merchants and their kin avoided the fate of the Lebrets and stayed prominent in parish affairs for many years – men such as Conrad Bockel and the Farrelly brothers (both of whose businesses persisted through century's end), or the Wolf brothers, who ran several country stores in the northern part of the parish. The Whitemans were another West Feliciana Parish family that steered its mercantile interests across the Civil War. John Whiteman went into merchandising in Bayou Sara during the mid-1850s and he was succeeded after the war by his sons Charles and Henry, then by sons Edwin and Theodore, who bought out their siblings in 1868. A family often deemed "too extravagant" for their means (at least in the view of the conservative reporters for the Dun agency), the Whitemans were aggressive entrepreneurs nonetheless. Edwin and Theo, who bought much of their inventory from wholesalers in St. Louis and Cincinnati rather than New Orleans, were known to directly beseech planters for their cotton business – a form of "cold-calling" that may have struck some as untoward behavior.[15]

Probably the most prominent persisting antebellum merchant of West Feliciana was John F. Irvine. Having begun as a grocer prior to the war, Irvine branched out his mercantile interests into real estate afterward, and soon became a major landlord in the parish's reviving cotton economy. Yet he also expanded his store operations, adding a lucrative saw mill to his "extensive commissioning and forwarding business" in the late 1870s. Later the mayor of St. Francisville, Irvine enhanced his burgeoning real estate holdings in 1885 by purchasing nine town lots in Bayou Sara from the elderly widow Elise Lebret, who continued to liquidate her family's landholdings for what seems an inordinately low price of \$45, or a mere \$5 a lot.[16]

[14] On the Lebrets' fortunes see Dun & Co., Louisiana, XXII, 240, 254, 267; Lebret & Hearsey Record Books, 1838–1875 (Special Collections, Hill Memorial Library, Louisiana State University, Baton Rouge, LA); and West Feliciana Mortgage Records, Vol. 9, pp. 378–81, Vol. 15, pp. 12–13 (West Feliciana Parish Courthouse, St. Francisville, LA).

[15] On the Whitemans see Dun & Co., Louisiana, XXII, 243, 268, 291; and Whiteman Bros. to Henry McKowen, October 20, 1868, in John McKowen Papers, 1830–1898 (Mss 1353, Louisiana and Lower Mississippi Valley Collection, Hill Memorial Library, Louisiana State University; hereinafter cited as LLMVC); [St. Francisville, La.] *West Feliciana Sentinel*, August 30, 1876, p. 3. On Bockel see Dun & Co., Louisiana, XXII, 249, 271; on the Farrellys, see ibid., 259, 268; and for the persistence of each into the 1890s, see [R. G. Dun & Co.], *Mercantile Agency Reference Book*, January 1890, Louisiana (Hill Memorial Library, Louisiana State University). On the Wolfs, see Dun & Co., Louisiana, XXII, 247, 278.

[16] On John F. Irvine see Dun & Co., Louisiana, XXII, 258, 261, 264; and the permanent display on Irvine as a local "captain of industry," West Feliciana Historical Society, St. Francisville,

The relatively good chances that Ascension and West Feliciana Parish merchants had for resuming business after the war were typical in other parishes as well. For example, of twenty-seven stores in large, mixed-farming Avoyelles Parish in 1867, sixteen had been in operation before the war. Several of those stores continued to thrive through the end of Reconstruction, which was also true in Ascension and West Feliciana Parishes, where over half of the antebellum stores that made it across the war were still afloat in 1878 – a strong showing for firms that Ransom and Sutch described as "exist[ing] only on the fringe of the plantation economy" before the war (1KF, p. 117). It was probably easier for such storekeepers to revive their fortunes because, unlike planters, the bulk of their prewar capital had not been tied up in slaves (whose property value was negated by emancipation) or land (the value of which plummeted after the war). In addition, retailing had always been a fairly low-capital vocation, which made recovery somewhat less difficult.[17]

Particularly for small businesses, the ability to survive over time is a key measure of success, in some ways even more basic than profit-and-loss. Although conventional wisdom maintains that conditions in the South favored rural merchants in cotton-growing regions, the persistence rates of the stores in Table 8.1 that were established after 1863 belie that claim. Not only were nearly twice as many stores established in non-sharecropped Ascension Parish after the war, but despite operating in a more crowded market environment, they stayed in business longer than their counterparts in West Feliciana Parish. More than half of the stores established in Ascension Parish after 1863 persisted through 1878 (72 of 138), compared with a survival rate of only 35 percent in its cotton-parish counterpart (25 of 72). Put another way, a newly established store in sugar-growing Ascension Parish after the Civil War had roughly double the chance of surviving Reconstruction as did one in West Feliciana Parish.

Although most new stores established after the war in West Feliciana Parish soon failed, there were notable exceptions. Most prominent was that of Julius Freyhan, a former clerk and small shopkeeper who had left the parish during the war. He returned in 1869, opening a small store with a modest $3,000 in stock the following year. But his fortunes improved rapidly: by 1874 Freyhan had added a steam gin and was "doing a very large business, perhaps the largest

LA. On the sale of nine Bayou Sara lots (nos. 535–46) by Lebret to Irvine on July 29, 1885, see West Feliciana Conveyance Books, Vol. 46, p. 4 (West Feliciana Parish Courthouse, St. Francisville, LA).

[17] On the microeconomics of retailing see Harold Barger, "Income Originating in Trade, 1869–1929," in National Bureau of Economic Research, *Trends in the American Economy in the Nineteenth Century* (Princeton, NJ, 1960), esp. 329. Historian Lewis E. Atherton pointed out long ago that adaptations to business practices significantly improved the strength of southern stores during the 1850s – improvements too often attributed to post–Civil War conditions; see Atherton, *The Southern Country Store, 1800–1860* (Baton Rouge, 1949), 175–6. Avoyelles Parish figures compiled from R. G. Dun & Co., *The Mercantile Agency Reference Book*, 1867–1878 (July volumes) (Library of Congress, Washington, DC).

TABLE 8.1. *Total Number of General Stores Reported, with Persistence Rates: Ascension and West Feliciana Parishes, Louisiana, 1860–1878*

Timeframe	Number of General Stores Reported in:	
	Ascension [sugar]	West Feliciana [cotton]
ANTEBELLUM STORES[a]	34	23
Persisted through 1863	12 (35%)	11 (48%)
POSTBELLUM STORES[b]	138	72
Persisted through 1878	72 (52%)	25 (35%)
Plus antebellum survivors	150	83
Persisted through 1878	79 (53%)	31 (37%)

Notes

[a] Antebellum stores are those reported by the Dun Agency to have been in operation as of 1860.

[b] The term *postbellum* refers to stores established after mid-1863, when most of Louisiana reverted to Union control, and 1878, when the ledger-based Dun credit reports end.

Sources: Louisiana, Vol. II, pp. 1–77 (Ascension Parish), and Vol. XXII, pp. 240–92 (West Feliciana Parish), both in R. G. Dun & Co. Collection, Baker Library, Harvard Business School, Boston, Mass.; R. G. Dun & Co., *The Mercantile Agency Reference Book*, 1867–1878 (July volumes), Library of Congress, Washington, DC.

in this parish." By 1878 his estimated worth was over $50,000, "clear" of any debts or claims, and he would prosper even further through the turn of the century. Freyhan reportedly enjoyed financial backing from the East Feliciana Parish firm of Levi & Adler, which was itself closely linked to interests in New Orleans and New York. Similarly, Moses Mann, a resident of New Orleans allied with the Crescent City wholesale firm of Katz & Barnett, managed or maintained interests in several West Feliciana stores. Among them was a store established in 1869 that he held in absentee partnership with brothers Max and August Fischer. The external connections of stores like Freyhan & Co. and the Fischer Brothers, as well as others elsewhere in Louisiana, offer another contrast to Ransom and Sutch's study, in which they encountered "only a single case where a firm was controlled or backed by other than local individuals" (1KF, p. 140).[18]

Despite success stories like Freyhan's, the lower overall persistence rates for cotton-parish stores complicates the usual portrayals of mercantile growth in the postbellum Black Belt. (Here one might also note that if the territorial-monopoly thesis were broadly true, persistence rates in cotton regions ought to

[18] On Freyhan see Dun & Co., Louisiana, XXII, 258–9, 282; see also the listing for J. Freyhan and Co. in [R. G. Dun & Co.], *Mercantile Agency Reference Book*, January 1890. On the Fischer brothers see Dun & Co., Louisiana, XXII, 282; on Mann see ibid., 276; and Mann, Fischer, & Co. Account Books, 1869–80 (Mss 896, LLMVC). On Katz & Barnett of New Orleans, as well as their connections to Ascension Parish storeowner Jacob Lemann, see Ashkenazi, *Business of Jews in Louisiana*, 63.

approximate nearly 100 percent, given the absence of competition that inheres to monopolistic power.) By the end of the ten-year period that began in 1869 (when Dun coverage of the region had fully recovered), West Feliciana Parish had managed a net gain of only two stores: twenty-nine were in operation in 1869 and thirty-one in 1878. The figures for Ascension Parish during the same years reflect a stronger business climate. The parish had seventy-nine stores in 1878, a net increase of twenty-five (or 46 percent) over the fifty-four in 1869, averaging eighty-one stores annually during the decade. Clearly, what business historians refer to as "conditions of entry and exit" were superior in the sugar parish.[19]

Such conditions are also reflected in the lower number of reorganized firms reported in Ascension Parish during Reconstruction. Like Ransom and Sutch, this study counted stores that took on or jettisoned partners, sold out to a new owner, or (a fairly common occurrence) revived their fortunes by declaring bankruptcy while remaining in business under their wives' names, as "reorganized" – not as new. In West Feliciana Parish, over a third of the stores in operation after 1863 underwent one or more reorganizations (30 of 83), which is consistent with the number of reorganized firms in Ransom and Sutch's six-county sample of Cotton South stores from 1870–80 (1KF, Table 7.8, p. 143). In Ascension Parish, however, only sixteen stores – roughly one in ten – reported modifications to their original ownership status during the same time span.[20]

Ascension Parish's stores were thus demonstrably more stable in terms of their persistence rates and ownership characteristics, and the sugar parish also managed to support over twice as many general stores as did West Feliciana – all despite the highly similar demographic and geographic characteristics of the two parishes. In terms of population, there was one store for every 449 inhabitants (including slaves) in West Feliciana Parish on the eve of the Civil War, and one store for every 261 people in Ascension. By the end of 1878 (but using 1880 population data), West Feliciana had only one store for every 400 residents, whereas Ascension Parish, despite experiencing a greater real and proportionate population increase, had improved to one store for every 186 residents. Despite incongruities in the ways the census bureau counted individual farm units under the tenancy system during this period, Ransom and Sutch expressed such per-capita density figures in terms of stores per farm, calculating that "there averaged less than seventy farms per rural general store in 1880" (p. 137). Reservations about the census's farm count notwithstanding, the equivalent figures for the two Louisiana parishes are significantly different.

[19] Donald McCloskey specifically uses the example of southern country stores to typify the importance of "entry and exit" conditions to economic analysis; McCloskey, "The Economics of Choice," in *Economics and the Historian*, eds. Thomas G. Rawski et al. (Berkeley, 1996), 131–3.
[20] Data compiled from the ledger reports in Dun & Co., Louisiana, II, 1–77 (Ascension Parish); Ibid., XXII, 240–92 (West Feliciana Parish); and cross-referenced with R. G. Dun & Co., *The Mercantile Agency Reference Book*, 1867–1878 (July volumes), Library of Congress.

In West Feliciana Parish, there was one store for every thirty-two "farms." But in Ascension Parish, where landholdings rapidly became concentrated after the war, there was one store for every four farm units. While this figure confirms that census-defined farm units are not the best yardstick for per-capita measurements during Reconstruction, it does suggest, on the other hand, the greater mercantile benefits of having a customer base comprised mainly of wage laborers, as opposed to one made up of cash-poor sharecroppers.[21]

Most important for Ransom and Sutch's territorial-monopoly thesis is the geographic density of these stores. The duo calculated that there was at least one store location for every 70.3 square miles of the Cotton South, a figure they used to extrapolate a hypothetical "minimum average distance" between evenly spaced store locations of 5.5 to 9.0 miles, arguing that the latter estimate was not only more accurate but probably even "too low" (p. 136). Oddly, Ransom and Sutch chose to base their highly localized estimates of spatial density, so essential to their territorial-monopoly thesis, on a total count of nearly 8,000 stores scattered over 200,000-plus square miles of the Cotton South in 1880 (p. 132). At no point did they test or refine these crucial estimates by comparison with more detailed county-level store data. As Table 8.2 shows, the two rural Louisiana parishes reveal a far greater spatial density of stores through the end of 1878 than do Ransom and Sutch's estimates. In West Feliciana Parish, there was one store for every 11.9 square miles in 1878; in Ascension, one for every 4.7 square miles. Using Ransom and Sutch's formula, this results in a hypothetical minimum average distance between evenly spaced store locations of 3.7 miles in West Feliciana Parish, and 2.3 miles in Ascension Parish – both of which are considerably less than Ransom and Sutch's preferred estimate of 9 miles or more.[22]

Parishes and counties are not closed territories, however; markets usually pay little heed to such political subdivisions unless they are somehow enforced. An Ascension Parish consumer in 1878 – say, one who resided along Bayou LaFourche about five miles south of the parish seat of Donaldsonville and its thirty-seven stores – was under no obligation to shop within his own parish. He might choose to patronize a store in Paincourtville (three miles south; seven general stores) or Napoleonville (six miles; twelve general stores), both of which were towns located in neighboring Assumption Parish. The point is

[21] These numbers are subject to the provision that the end date for my store sample is 1878 rather than 1880, but mitigated by the fact some of the Tenth Census data was gathered in 1879. Ransom and Sutch wrote that field reports in the Dun ledgers (from which the *Reference Books* were compiled) were transcribed until "around 1880" (1KF, p. 309). This author found no transcribed reports from Louisiana parishes in the Dun ledgers after the summer of 1879, with February 1879 the last date for the vast majority.

[22] The formula used for spatial-density estimates is to divide the given area's square mileage by the number of stores, with the result being (A); the square root of the product of 1.1547 multiplied by (A) then gives the hypothetical minimum average distance between evenly spaced stores. See 1KF, pp. 136 and 389 n. 19.

TABLE 8.2. *Spatial Density of General Stores, 1878–1880[a]: Ascension and West Feliciana Parishes, Louisiana, Compared with Ransom and Sutch's "Cotton South" Estimates[b]*

Geographic Area	Number of Stores	Sq. Miles per Store	Avg. Minimum Distance between Stores (miles)[c]
ASCENSION PARISH (373 sq. miles)[a]	79	4.7	2.3
WEST FELICIANA PARISH (370 sq. miles)[a]	31	11.9	3.7
"COTTON SOUTH" [1KF] (206,419 sq. miles)[b]	7,977[d]	25.9	5.5
	2,937[e]	70.3	9.0

Notes

[a] West Feliciana and Ascension Parish figures represent the total number of general stores in operation as of the end of 1878 and were compiled from cross-comparison of both the Dun *Reference Books* and ledgers; Ransom and Sutch's Cotton South estimates are based on a total count of stores in the 1880 *Reference Book*, excluding those in thirty-one Class I and II urban centers of the Cotton South (Ransom and Sutch, *One Kind of Freedom* [hereinafter, 1KF], p. 132; and Appendix G, Table G-16 and p. 300).

[b] 1KF, pp. 132–37. The "Cotton South" is defined by Ransom and Sutch as the five states of South Carolina, Georgia, Alabama, Mississippi, and Louisiana.

[c] Estimated minimum average distance in miles between hypothetically evenly dispersed store locations. For the formula on which these estimates are based, see 1KF, pp. 136 and 389 n. 19.

[d] Total number of general stores, Cotton South, 1880 (1KF, p. 132).

[e] Total number of locations reporting one or more general stores, Cotton South, 1880 (1KF, p. 132).

Sources: Louisiana, Vol. II, pp. 1–77 (Ascension Parish); Vol. XXII, pp. 240–92 (West Feliciana Parish), both in R. G. Dun & Co. Collection, Baker Library, Harvard Business School, Boston, MA.; R. G. Dun & Co., *The Mercantile Agency Reference Book*, July 1878; Roger L. Ransom and Richard Sutch; *One Kind of Freedom: The Economic Consequences of Emancipation* (2nd ed.; New York, 2001), 132–37 [hereinafter, 1KF].

obvious: there were more stores in a given geographic area than those in a consumer's parish of residence. Table 8.3 shows the spatial-density results of drawing a hypothetical thirty-mile square roughly centered on each parish seat to add non-parish stores located on the same side of the river in three selected town clusters within each territory. (However, with a nod to Ransom and Sutch's questionable decision to exclude second- and third-rank towns from their store samples, this expanded hypothetical square does not include Baton Rouge, even though the town and its sixty-one stores in 1878 was only about twenty-five miles along the river from either parish seat.) For West Feliciana Parish, this expanded territory adds twenty-two more stores to the thirty-one in the parish in 1878; and by pushing this hypothetical square slightly eastward (a reasonable adjustment for several reasons), it adds twenty general

TABLE 8.3. *Spatial Density of General Stores, 1878: Ascension and West Feliciana Parishes, Louisiana, Including Selected Contiguous-Parish Towns*

Parish	Number of Stores	Sq. Miles per Store[a]	Avg. Minimum Distance between Stores (miles)
ASCENSION[b]	134	6.7	2.8
WEST FELICIANA[c]	73	12.3	3.8

Notes

[a] Calculated for a hypothetical thirty-mile square roughly centered on each parish seat, consisting of 900 total square miles. See text and note 23 for further description.

[b] The selected towns in contiguous parishes for which 55 general stores were added to Ascension Parish totals as of the end of 1878 (79 stores) are: Paincourtville and Napoleonville (8 and 10 miles south of Donaldsonville, in Assumption Parish; 7 and 12 stores, respectively); Cantrelle (10 miles southwest in St. James Parish; 7 stores); and Plaquemine (19 miles northwest in Iberville Parish; 29 stores).

[c] The selected towns in contiguous parishes for which 42 general stores were added to West Feliciana Parish totals as of the end of 1878 (31 stores) are: Port Hudson (9 miles southeast of St. Francisville in East Baton Rouge Parish; 10 stores); Jackson and Clinton (11 and 21 miles northeast in East Feliciana Parish; 12 and 20 stores, respectively).

Sources: Louisiana, Vol. II, pp. 1–77 (Ascension Parish); Vol. XXII, pp. 240–92 (West Feliciana Parish), both in R. G. Dun & Co. Collection, Baker Library, Harvard Business School, Boston, MA; R. G. Dun & Co., *The Mercantile Agency Reference Book*, July 1878.

stores in Clinton, which was connected to Bayou Sara/St. Francisville by a well-travelled road, for a total of seventy-three. In Ascension Parish – where there were even closer, more accessible towns in contiguous parishes – placing Donaldsonville at the center of a similar hypothetical square resulted in fifty-five more stores added to Ascension's seventy-nine, for an 1878 total of 134 stores. (Although Convent was only ten miles to the southeast, its thirty-two stores were not added since the town was on the opposite bank of the river from Donaldsonville.) Using Ransom and Sutch's formula again, but this time within territories over twice as large, and undercounting stores by sampling only those in a few nearby towns, the resulting spatial-density figures remain steady for each parish. For West Feliciana Parish, adding stores in selected contiguous-parish towns results in an average minimum distance of 3.8 miles between evenly spaced stores, compared to 3.7 miles in the parish alone. For Ascension Parish, the average minimum distance between stores rises from 2.3 to 2.8 miles. For both parishes, however, this more realistic inclusion of stores across parish lines still results in hypothetical spatial-density estimates that are well below Ransom and Sutch's Cotton South–wide estimates of 5.5 to 9 miles (or more) between evenly spaced stores.[23]

[23] The exercise reflected in Table 8.3 tries to account for geographic reality to some degree by counting stores only on the river side of the parish seat, since the river was surely a significant

To be sure, these spatial-density estimates, which were created using the same evidence and procedures as Ransom and Sutch, contrast sharply with those in 1KF. But it is important to emphasize the questionable nature of the assumptions that underlie their hypothetical exercise in evenly distributed rural monopolies, which are derived from the central-place theory of markets, a useful but nondefinitive approach that can yield widely variant results according to specific geographic and economic contexts. In particular, there are strong grounds for doubting that there was any inherent reason for merchants to disperse themselves in rough equidistance over the southern countryside. Other scholars of small-firm competition have argued that "[a]s more and more sellers ... arise, the tendency is not to become distributed in the socially optimum manner but to cluster unduly." In a recent quantitative analysis of mercantile development in postbellum Alabama, Louis M. Kyriakoudes has provided empirical confirmation of this "store-clustering" thesis. Taking exception to Ransom and Sutch's arguments, Kyriakoudes describes how stores in the postwar southern interior tended to group together in the growing number of small towns and hamlets, many of which began as railroad depots.[24]

The Louisiana data indicate a similar tendency toward store-clustering, especially in cotton-producing parishes. In 1872, the Dun Reference Book listed only five of thirty-two West Feliciana general stores outside the twin towns of Bayou Sara/St. Francisville; but in contrast, thirty-four of Ascension Parish's seventy-eight stores were located outside the parish seat of Donaldsonville. The higher concentration of town-clustered stores in the cotton parish not

barrier to store accessibility). However, Bayou Sara/St. Francisville's riverside location on the southern boundary of West Feliciana Parish would have immediately eliminated about one-third of this hypothetical expanded territory. If this seems to be unfairly tweaking the geographic sample, it should be noted that Woodville, Mississippi, is *not* included in this revised market area. Twenty-five miles from St. Francisville and connected to it by rail since the 1830s, Woodville was an integrated part of market life in West Feliciana Parish, especially its northern portions.

[24] Louis M. Kyriakoudes, "Lower-Order Urbanization and Territorial Monopoly in the Southern Furnishing Trade: Alabama, 1871–1890," *Social Science History* 26 (Spring 2002), 179–98 (quotation on p. 192); see also Aaron D. Anderson, *Builders of a New South: Merchants, Capital, and the Remaking of Natchez, 1865–1914* (Jackson, MS, 2013); and Peter W. FitzRandolph, "The Rural Furnishing Merchant in the Postbellum United States: A Study in Spatial Economics" (Ph.D. diss., Tufts University, 1979). Harold Hotelling, "Stability in Competition," *Economic Journal* 39 (1929), repr. in *The Collected Economics Articles of Harold Hotelling*, ed. Adrian C. Darnell (New York and other cities, 1990), 50–63 (quotation on p. 61). I am grateful to Gavin Wright for calling my attention to Hotelling's work. The hexagonal modeling used by Ransom and Sutch as the basis of their hypothetical store-dispersal estimates (1KF, Fig. 7.1, p. 136) features prominently in central-place theory; see, for example, Stuart Plattner, "Markets and Marketplaces," in Plattner, ed., *Economic Anthropology* (Stanford, CA, 1989), esp. 182–90. Examples of central-place theory applied to historical changes in U.S. distributional networks are Brian J. L. Berry, *The Geography of Market Centers and Retail Distribution* (Englewood Cliffs, NJ, 1967); and James E. Vance Jr., *The Merchant's World: The Geography of Wholesaling* (Englewood Cliffs, NJ, 1970); see also William Cronon's provisional revisions to central-place theory in *Nature's Metropolis: Chicago and the Great West* (New York, 1991).

only flatly contradicts the territorial-monopoly thesis, but it also suggests another interesting comparison with the sugar-producing one. If generalizable, the sugar-parish data suggest a possible inverse relationship between cluster- ing tendencies and market development. In other words, as improved business conditions prompted greater competition in towns like Donaldsonville, propri- etors were gradually driven into the countryside in order to prosper – and once established, these stores probably helped initiate new cycles of clustering and small-town development.[25]

The data for both Louisiana parishes also indicate that the better capitalized the store, the more likely it was to be located "in town." Probably the most important function of local reporters for the Dun agency was their provision of assessments of merchants' net worth, which were based on their investments in inventory, real estate, and other fixed expenses (such as steam-powered cotton gins). While Ransom and Sutch did not calculate an average in-store capital for their sample of stores in the Cotton South, they believed that "optimally sized firms" were capitalized between $5,000 and $10,000, even as they also endorsed the conventional wisdom that most country stores in the Cotton South had inventories in the range of a thousand dollars or less (pp. 137–40). In Louisiana, the average pecuniary strength of general stores in 1878 (exclud- ing those in urban Orleans Parish) was $4,088 in 1878 (see Table 8.6). That same year, the average merchant's capital in Ascension Parish was about $5,050 per store. West Feliciana Parish, despite having less combined capital among all its merchants, still ranked well ahead of Ascension with an average capital of $6,016 per store in 1878. The hypothetical average merchant in West Feliciana Parish thus had 75 percent more capital than her counterpart in Ascension at Reconstruction's end. While the total combined capital of Ascension Parish's merchants was more than double that of West Feliciana's, a much greater pro- portion of that wealth was distributed among small- to mid-sized firms, ones with less than $10,000 in capital.[26]

Such differences in the distribution of store capital within the two parishes were already visible several years earlier. Tables 8.4 and 8.5 display the capi- talization of parish stores in 1872, Reconstruction's midpoint (and before the economic depression that began in 1873). The first table shows the number of stores sorted into upper-, mid-, and low-capital ranges, as well as the per- centage of stores comprising each category. In Table 8.5, the capital of the individual stores in each range was added together to arrive at an estimate of the combined store capital in each parish in 1872. The second table shows that, with three of its thirty-two stores estimated at over $25,000 in capital

[25] Store locations were collected and tabulated from [R. G. Dun & Co.], *Mercantile Agency Reference Book* (July 1872).

[26] The numbers of stores and capitalization figures were calculated from a cross-comparison of the 1878 ledger reports in Dun & Co., Louisiana, II, 1–77 (Ascension Parish); Ibid., XXII, 240–92 (West Feliciana Parish); and the published listings in R. G. Dun & Co., *The Mercantile Agency Reference Book* (July 1878).

TABLE 8.4. *Number and Percentage of General Stores by Range of Capital Invested, Ascension and West Feliciana Parishes, Louisiana, 1872*

Parish	Total Number of Stores	Number of Stores $25–50m	Number of Stores $10–25m	Per Cent	Number of Stores $2–10m	Per Cent	Number of Stores Under $2m	Per Cent
ASCENSION	78	3	3	8%	23	29%	49	63%
W. FELICIANA	32	3	3	20%	11	35%	15	47%

Note: m = thousands of dollars

Source: R. G. Dun & Co., *Mercantile Agency Reference Book* (July 1872), Library of Congress, Washington, DC. The Dun Agency assigned stores a letter code for their estimated capitalization, which was based on a range of dollar values: K = under $2,000; H = $2,000–$5,000; G = $5,000–$10,000; F = $10,000–$25,000; and E = $25,000–$50,000. For the purpose of adding these figures and thereby producing estimates of combined capital (Table 3-B), the capital of each store in these categories was counted at the midpoint of these ranges—thus having, respectively, $1,000; $3,500; $7,500; $17,500; and $37,500 in capital.

TABLE 8.5. *Combined General Store Capital by Range and Percentage of Estimated Value, Ascension and West Feliciana Parishes, Louisiana, 1872*

Parish	Total Capital	Capital $25–50m	Capital $10–25m	Per Cent	Capital $2–10m	Per Cent	Capital under $2m	Per Cent
ASCENSION	$326,500	$112,500	$52,500	51%	$112,500	34%	$49,000	15%
W. FELICIANA	$234,500	$112,500	$52,500	70%	$54,500	23%	$15,000	6%

Note: m = thousands of dollars

Source: R. G. Dun & Co., *Mercantile Agency Reference Book* (July 1872), Library of Congress, Washington, DC. The Dun Agency assigned stores a letter code for their estimated capitalization, which was based on a range of dollar values: K = under $2,000; H = $2,000–$5,000; G = $5,000–$10,000; F = $10,000–$25,000; and E = $25,000–$50,000. For the purpose of adding these figures and thereby producing estimates of combined capital (Table 3-B), the capital of each store in these categories was counted at the midpoint of these ranges—thus having, respectively, $1,000; $3,500; $7,500; $17,500; and $37,500 in capital.

and three others between $10,000 and $25,000, 70 percent of merchants' capital in cotton-producing West Feliciana Parish was invested in what should be considered large establishments. But while Ascension Parish also had a half-dozen firms in the same high-capital ranges, those stores accounted for a significantly lower proportion of the sugar parish's combined mercantile capital. In other words, small- to medium-sized firms comprised nearly half the combined store capital in sugar-producing Ascension Parish, but similarly sized stores accounted for less than a third of total mercantile investments in West Feliciana Parish.

Ransom and Sutch depicted a South characterized mainly by small, dispersed, yet powerful "country stores." However, the West Feliciana Parish data suggest not only that cotton-producing regions may have been dominated instead by capital-intensive, town-based establishments, but also that such firms made it more difficult for smaller stores to thrive alongside them. Furthermore, the very ways that merchants were typologized by Dun reporters highlights important differences between the business environments of the two parishes. In 1872 more than a third of the twenty-six West Feliciana storeowners with less than $10,000 in capital were listed by the Dun agency as carrying on a secondary trade. Apparently unable to generate sufficient income in the cotton parish by simply running "general stores," these small-scale proprietors were also described in the published Mercantile Agency volumes as hoteliers, saloonkeepers, bakers, and saddlemakers. In Ascension Parish, by contrast, only four of seventy-two general-store owners in the same range of estimated worth were listed with ancillary occupations. For storekeepers in the sugar parish, retailing alone seems to have provided enough of a revenue stream that they did not have to engage in artisanal or other side trades. Yet at the same time, the Dun records indicate that business conditions in Ascension Parish enabled more entrepreneurs to specialize in merchandise such as books, drugs, or jewelry. As historian Maunsel Blackford has noted, when competition increases over time in a stable market environment, the opportunities and incentives for small businesses to specialize grow as well. With thirty-six such "niche" firms in 1872, there was nearly one business offering specialized goods or services for every two general stores in Ascension Parish. In West Feliciana Parish that same year, by contrast, the ratio was less than 1:6.[27]

Although considerable data have been presented on the numbers of stores, their growth and persistence rates, geographic density, capitalization, and other characteristics, some might argue that these two parishes constitute too limited a geographic sample to refute Ransom and Sutch's conclusions. Two rejoinders – one conceptual, the other empirical – might help satisfy this objection. First, the intention herein is not so much to refute Ransom and Sutch's arguments as it is to test them. (It is also worth reiterating that many of their own conclusions about stores were based on a sample drawn from only six southern counties.) Examining and comparing data from two carefully selected parishes seemed especially appropriate to assess the possibility that, by relying on the Cotton South's total square mileage for localized store-density estimates, Ransom and Sutch had cast their geographic net too widely, and that a more confined territory might better reflect reality. While it is true that one should not overgeneralize from a limited sample, this example shows the terms of that criticism can be reversed; in other words, one should also be wary of data sets that are too broad to produce reliable microlevel results.

[27] Blackford, *History of Small Business in America*, 10; *Mercantile Agency Reference Book*, July 1872.

TABLE 8.6. *General Stores in Louisiana (Excluding Orleans Parish), 1878*

Number of Stores	Avg Stores per Parish[a]	Avg Total Store Capital	Avg Capital per Store	Avg Minimum Distance between Stores[b]
2,165	39	$157,982	$4,088	4.9 miles

Notes
[a] Reflects data aggregated from fifty-six Louisiana parishes (excluding only urban Orleans Parish).
[b] Estimated minimum average distance in miles between hypothetically evenly dispersed store locations. For the formula on which these estimates are based, 1KF, pp. 136 and 389 n.19.

Sources: Marler, "Merchants and the Political Economy of Nineteenth-Century Louisiana," 441–45; and Appendix B (pp. 507–9), which collates data from R. G. Dun & Co., *Mercantile Agency Reference Book* (July 1878), Library of Congress, Washington, DC; and *Tenth Census of the United States* (1880).

Apart from such considerations, however, Tables 8.6 and 8.7 provide a more empirical rejoinder to the limited-sample objection. In nearly every particular, these tables reveal that statewide and subregional data on stores are highly consistent with that from Ascension and West Feliciana Parishes. Perhaps most noteworthy in Table 8.6, which compiles data from all fifty-six parishes statewide (excluding urban Orleans Parish), is the average minimum distance of 4.9 miles between stores for Louisiana as a whole, a figure still well below Ransom and Sutch's preferred estimate of nine-plus miles for the entire Cotton South. Table 8.7 shows strong correlations between agricultural production and the number and capitalization of general stores in selected parish clusters. It is unsurprising that the state's poorest parishes, as measured by agricultural value produced in 1880, had fewer stores and far less capital invested in them. More interesting is the average minimum distance between stores in these most under-developed parishes: 7.6 miles – right at the midpoint of Ransom and Sutch's 5.5- to 9-mile spatial-density estimates. Measured by the same standard, the five wealthiest rural parishes supported, on average, over twice as many stores as the poorest ones, and these firms were better capitalized, roughly 25 percent higher than the statewide average of $4,088.00. The average minimum distance between stores in these wealthiest parishes, 3.7 miles, is also well below the estimates that underlie 1KF's territorial-monopoly thesis.

Further consistencies emerge when store data from Ascension and West Feliciana Parishes are compared with averages from stores in the top three sugar and cotton-producing parishes. The average store capital is again higher in cotton than sugar parishes, with a difference of less than 10 percent from the equivalent figures for West Feliciana and Ascension Parishes. Similarly, the combined store capital of the three top sugar parishes is again considerably greater than that of the cotton parishes, like that of Ascension Parish compared with West Feliciana. In terms of spatial density, the average minimum distance

TABLE 8.7. *General Stores in Selected Louisiana Parish Clusters, 1878–1880*

Parish Group	Number of Stores	Avg Stores per Parish	Avg Total Store Capital	Avg Capital per Store	Avg Minimum Distance between Stores[a]
Bottom 5 Agric Value Produced[b]	155	31	$91,000	$2,900	7.6 miles
Top 5 Agric Value Produced[c]	313	63	$308,000	$4,900	3.7 miles
Top 3 Cotton Parishes[d]	103	34	$198,000	$5,766	4.8 miles
Top 3 Sugar Parishes[e]	197	66	$312,000	$4,746	3.1 miles

Notes

[a] Estimated minimum average distance in miles between hypothetically evenly dispersed store locations. For the formula on which these estimates are based, see 1KF, pp. 136 and 389 n.19.

[b] Value of agricultural products as listed in the Tenth Census (1880). The five poorest parishes by this measure were (from lowest to highest) St. Tammany, Cameron, Livingston, Vermilion, and Calcasieu.

[c] Value of agricultural products as listed in the Tenth Census (1880). The five wealthiest parishes by this measure were (from highest to lowest) Terrebonne, Tensas, St. James, St. Mary, and Ascension.

[d] The top three cotton-producing parishes as listed in the Tenth Census (1880) were Tensas, Carroll, Concordia, Bossier, and Morehouse.

[e] The top three sugar-producing parishes as listed in the Tenth Census (1880) were St. Mary, Iberville, and St. James.

Sources: Marler, "Merchants and the Political Economy of Nineteenth-Century Louisiana," 441–45; and Appendix B (pp. 507–9), which collates data from R. G. Dun & Co., *Mercantile Agency Reference Book* (July 1878), Library of Congress, Washington, DC; and *Tenth Census of the United States* (1880).

between evenly spaced store locations in the three top cotton-producing parishes is 4.8 miles, and 3.1 miles in the top three sugar parishes. Although these are higher than the equivalent figures for West Feliciana and Ascension Parishes (3.7 and 2.3 miles, respectively), the differences are proportionally consistent – and all are still well below Ransom and Sutch's preferred estimates.[28]

[28] Some of the statewide data in the text are presented in more detailed form as Figures 9.5-A and 9.5-B in Scott P. Marler, "Merchants and the Political Economy of Nineteenth-Century Louisiana: New Orleans and Its Hinterlands" (Ph.D. diss., Rice University, 2007). The complete set of data from all fifty-six rural Louisiana parishes on store numbers and capitalization, agricultural production, and other relevant statistics are compiled in spreadsheet form in Ibid., Appendix B.

To understand why the various comparative barometers of mercantile health – numbers of stores, persistence rates, capitalization – tilted so heavily toward Ascension Parish during Reconstruction, it is first worth emphasizing that the "sugar bowl" was no postbellum economic powerhouse. Whether measured by price or crop production, the recovery of Louisiana's sugar industry was just as slow as in the cotton sector. Given that economic-growth differentials do not account for the superior commercial environment, and keeping in mind that the territorial size of the two parishes remained constant and equal, our attention is drawn to the very different ways that new systems of agricultural labor were organized in cotton and sugar districts.[29]

In West Feliciana Parish, as elsewhere in the Cotton South, forms of agricultural tenancy – most notably, sharecropping – quickly became the dominant mode of production after emancipation. To take advantage of economies of scale (not to mention, retaining control over labor in a manner akin to slavery), most landowners preferred their quondam plantations to be worked by gang labor. The majority of freedpeople, by contrast, hoped to work on plots of land that they owned. Since neither group was able to impose its preference on the other, tenancy arose as a compromise "solution," one that was not fully satisfactory to either party but that did allow cotton production to resume. At the same time, because sharecropping and other forms of tenancy tend to require financial intermediaries between landlords and laborers, the importance of furnishing merchants to postbellum southern cotton-production systems grew accordingly.[30]

Rural merchants' enhanced role as credit providers in the various forms of share-tenancy that arose in cotton regions during Reconstruction has long been well established in the historical literature. The implications of the crop-lien system are examined more closely in the epilogue, but at this point it is worth noting that records from cotton-producing West Feliciana Parish confirm the rapidity with which local merchants assumed pivotal functions in the postemancipation economy. During the 1869–70 crop season, 253 leases, liens, and mortgages of various sorts were recorded in the West Feliciana courthouse register. Of these, only sixteen lease or crop-division agreements were made directly between landlords and freedpeople; in two others, landowners pledged their own property to merchants as security for supplies then apparently distributed to laborers. But the overwhelming majority of these debt-security instruments were formal agreements between freedpeople – either as individuals, families, or in squads – and merchants. Of the 230 such contracts recorded

---

[29] On the slow recovery of the sugar industry in Louisiana, see Sitterson, *Sugar Country*, chap 14; and Mark D. Schmitz, "Postbellum Developments in the Louisiana Cane Sugar Industry," *Business and Economic History*, 2d ser., 5 (1976), 88–101.

[30] Ransom and Sutch carefully detail the development of sharecropping and its associated crop-lien system in 1KF, chaps. 4–8; see also Gerald David Jaynes, *Branches without Roots: Genesis of the Black Working Class in the American South, 1862–1882* (New York, 1986).

by merchants, most specified dollar amounts for supplies to be advanced to freedpeople during the year and repaid from crop proceeds at harvest-time. Moreover, 201 of these crop liens were registered by only eight parish firms, all of them located in Bayou Sara/St. Francisville – a figure that further demonstrates how postwar cotton marketing was being concentrated in the hands of town-based merchants rather than among smaller stores dispersed throughout the countryside.[31]

Credit-providing merchants in cotton parishes like West Feliciana suffered three interrelated disadvantages as a result of the newly structured local economy. First, most of their customers were extremely poor, as incomes were generally low among cotton farmers throughout the postwar South. Second, these customers were also cash-poor, since the share-tenancy system only paid off once annually after the harvest. Finally, customers' lack of regular cash on-hand forced merchants to accommodate them via credit sales. This was not only a de facto riskier practice than cash sales, but it forced merchants into an essential role in the ongoing functioning of the local economy, one that small businesses are not especially well equipped to handle. In this regard, Richard H. Kilbourne Jr. has recently described the "staggering" default rates faced by one postbellum mercantile firm that operated several stores in the Feliciana parishes. Nevertheless, many merchants, including ones who had been in business prior to the war, were able to adapt to their complex postwar roles as retailers, credit providers, and marketing agents. Some of them, though probably fewer than previously believed, prospered considerably.[32]

By contrast, the early adoption of a system of regularized cash wages to workers meant that none of these disadvantages applied in sugar-producing parishes such as Ascension. To be sure, sugar workers were still poor, but they were significantly less so than tenant farmers in cotton production. Gross annual earnings of wage laborers employed in sugar production were about $325 to $350 (compared to under $200 annually for share-tenant households

[31] All data in the text was compiled from agreements recorded between September 1, 1869 and August 31, 1870 in Mortgage Record Book, Vol. 11 (1867–71), pp. 175–441 (West Feliciana Parish Courthouse, St. Francisville, LA.). Interestingly, among the 253 agreements that season were five crop liens or mortgages recorded by New Orleans–based factorage firms, which indicates that some city merchants were still trying to find ways to involve themselves in the newly dispersed production arrangements taking hold throughout the former plantation districts of Louisiana. Cf. Aaron D. Anderson's impressive analysis of similar records from the Mississippi Delta in his *Builders of a New South*, which reveals enhanced activities by merchants from fast-growing interior marketing centers such as Natchez.

[32] Richard H. Kilbourne Jr., "The Ongoing Agricultural Credit Crisis in the Florida Parishes of Louisiana, 1865–1890," in *A Fierce and Fractious Frontier: The Curious Development of Louisiana's Florida Parishes, 1699–2000*, ed. Samuel C. Hyde Jr. (Baton Rouge, 2004), 125–39 (quotation on p. 135). See also Harold D. Woodman, *New South – New Law: The Legal Foundations of Credit and Labor Relations in the Postbellum Agricultural South* (Baton Rouge, 1995).

in cotton production [see 1KF, p. 216]), which was an income comparable to other segments of the American working class outside the South during the 1870s. Thus, as early as 1867, Jacob Lemann, the merchant and nascent sugar baron of Donaldsonville, exclaimed to an acquaintance in New York City that his "[b]usiness is better than it was before. All the negroes work and have money, which they spend in Donaldsonville." Lemann explicitly connected workers "having money" with flush times for storeowners like himself. His comment highlights the ways that a wage-labor economy, in which workers have a modicum of cash on hand at regular intervals, can promote a healthier economic environment, one in which production-derived dollars "trickle down" to subsidiary trades such as retailers. Although wages in the sugar region were sometimes partially deferred, at least some weekly or monthly payment was the norm. While a few sugar-parish stores sold goods on credit, this was less a structural imperative than a matter of individual merchant choice or circumstance. Until the advent of plantation stores in the sugar region during the 1880s, when attempts to make wage payments in company scrip became a flashpoint of labor rebellion, credit sales were simply not woven into the institutional fabric of local retailing.[33]

Furthermore, stores in the sugar region were not closely involved in the marketing of the crops produced. When historian Thomas D. Clark wrote that "it is doubtful that there was ever organized anywhere on the globe a system of merchandising so thoroughly integrated with the economy of the daily lives of the common everyday people as the southern country store," he clearly had in mind stores in cotton-growing areas of the South. Cotton was the dominant staple crop of the region as a whole, but this was not so much the case in Louisiana. Yet even though the economic role of stores in sugar parishes was generally restricted to retailing, their limited institutional functions seem to have considerably improved merchants' odds of surviving and prospering in the more stable regional market environment.[34]

These conclusions are less an example of what might be dismissed as crop determinism than they are an illustration of economic path-dependence. The long-standing focus of neoclassical economics on production as the proper measure of economic growth – based on assumptions common to both Marxists and orthodox economists – has long deflected attention from the importance of our own "nation of shopkeepers." Yet, as George Mehren pointed out long ago, "modern distribution systems do not graft to primitive production units, and vice versa." The reciprocal developmental tendencies at work between production and distribution, such as those in this chapter's comparative data on

---

[33] See Rodrigue, *Reconstruction in the Cane Fields*, 183–91, on the "sugar war" of 1887; and Ibid., 150, on the wages paid to sugar workers. See also Rebecca J. Scott, *Degrees of Freedom: Louisiana and Cuba after Slavery* (Cambridge, MA, 2005), chap. 2. Jacob Lemann letter book, November 24, 1867, as quoted in Ashkenazi, *Business of Jews in Louisiana*, 46.

[34] Thomas D. Clark, "The Post–Civil War Economy in the South," in *Jews in the South*, eds. Leonard Dinnerstein and Mary Dale Palsson (Baton Rouge, 1973), 161.

stores in cotton and sugar parishes, provide important clues to the underlying character of particular economies. In this case, the distribution and marketing networks that accompanied the forms of share-tenancy in the postbellum Cotton South reflected a makeshift, transitional form of production – one that represented, at best, a perverse type of capitalism; and at worst, a rickety and hastily conceived "solution" to postemancipation conditions that helped perpetuate regional poverty and inequality for decades to come. By contrast, even while admitting that there is no single normative path to capitalist development, it seems difficult not to view the superior performance of stores in Ascension Parish as commensurate with the Reconstruction-era sugar region's greater resemblance to other historical examples of agricultural systems that eventuated in self-sustaining economic growth.[35]

The parish-level comparisons presented in this chapter constitute empirical challenges to the similar data that Ransom and Sutch assembled on southern merchants. However, these findings do not fully disprove their arguments; in fact, the overall analysis herein tends to reinforce *One Kind of Freedom*'s characterizations of the underdeveloped postbellum cotton economy and merchants' role in it. Yet Ransom and Sutch's reluctance to explore how their conclusions meshed with the wider southern political economy (such as the apparent congruence of their findings with the class-conflict approaches of "new social historians") remains problematic. For example, Harold D. Woodman, whose *King Cotton and His Retainers* (1968) remains the best study of nineteenth-century southern merchants, recently described the New South's revivified agriculture as a capitalist "system ... that in its essential features replicated that of the North." While the data presented herein on the Louisiana sugar region seem to confirm this characterization, those conditions were fairly unique. Woodman's assertion seems less defensible when considered in light of the institutions, systems, and class structure of the wider postbellum South. Firms that played prominent structural roles comparable to those of stores in the Cotton South were not especially common in other U.S. regions, although in some instances (such as the "company stores" of western mining towns), fruitful analogies can be drawn.[36]

---

[35] Mehren, "Market Organization and Economic Development," 1311. See also the essays collected in Lou Ferleger, ed., *Agriculture and National Development: Views on the Nineteenth Century* (Ames, IA, 1990). Ferleger also persuasively documents sugar planters' "resistance to the institutionalization of capitalistic economic relations" in his article "The Problem of 'Labor' in the Post-Reconstruction Louisiana Sugar Industry," *Agricultural History* 72 (Spring 1998), 140–58 (quotation on p. 141). The productionist bias of contemporary economics is not limited to orthodox neoclassicists. Maurice Dobb, the influential Marxist economic historian, observed that classical economists through John Stuart Mill believed that "the theory of value rested on a theory of distribution." But, he added, "Modern economics [including Marx] ... has formally integrated distribution (i.e., the pricing of factors of production) into the structure of general price-equilibrium." Dobb, *Studies in the Development of Capitalism* (New York, 1947), 28 n. 1.

[36] Harold D. Woodman, "The Political Economy of the New South: Retrospects and Prospects," *Journal of Southern History* 67 (November 2001), 807. For Woodman's skepticism toward the

Despite its shortcomings, Ransom and Sutch generally deployed their evidence in *One Kind of Freedom* in ways that confirm this study's portrayal of a nineteenth-century southern political economy strongly influenced by the culture and practices of merchant capitalism. Whereas this chapter has focused on the structural factors that shaped and reflected rural and small-town storekeepers' enhanced roles in postbellum Louisiana, there is another dimension of merchants' contributions to the southern political economy: the intellectual principles, or "mentalités," that served as an overarching context for economic behavior and activity. In the post–Civil War South, many of these mentalités were simply not the sort generally associated with robust capitalist development. As a different historical duo described it, the "undynamic, even stodgy nature" of postbellum southern industrial development was both cause *and* effect of low regional investment levels, rightly concluding that a conservative commercial climate "materially shaped the character of southern entrepreneurship itself." Such symbiotic relationships between impersonal economic structures and internalized values and behaviors point us toward a better understanding of the headlong rush into low-capital retailing occupations in the South after the war. Considered alongside the structural and institutional data in this chapter, such insights help explain how the rural and small-town storeowner, the representative of merchant capital in its most primitive guise, soon became the archetypal figure of the New South. The world-historical roots and broader implications of the culture of southern merchant capitalism – an anachronistic form of wealth-accumulation strategy in an industrial age, but one that was deeply imbricated throughout the South in various forms during the entire nineteenth century – are explored more broadly in the epilogue that follows.[37]

new social history, see his "Response" to Jonathan M. Wiener, "Class Structure and Economic Development in the American South, 1865–1955," *American Historical Review* 84 (October 1979), 999. For a critique of Woodman's approach see Marler, "Fables of the Reconstruction."

[37] David L. Carlton and Peter A. Coclanis, "Capital Mobilization and Southern Industry, 1880–1905: The Case of the Carolina Piedmont," *Journal of Economic History* 49 (March 1989), 75. Although the complicated relationships between mentalités and marketplace practices have been insightfully traced in works by diverse and well-known scholars like Max Weber, C. B. MacPherson, and Fernand Braudel, most contemporary economic historians have steered even clearer of such "fuzzy" thinking than they have of class-oriented analysis. But just as the "new institutionalism" has seemed to herald a resurgence of interest in studies of the political economy, the recent acclaim for "behavioral economics" (for which psychologist Daniel Kahneman was awarded the Nobel Prize for Economics in 2002) – an approach that focuses on persistent market behaviors deemed irrational and self-destructive by neoclassical economists – may portend greater attention by historians to the interaction of subjective perceptions and objective conditions in economic life. See, for example, Andrei Shleifer, *Inefficient Markets: An Introduction to Behavioral Finance* (New York, 1999).

Epilogue

Merchant Capital and Economic Development in the Postbellum South

Historians have long agreed that the Civil War was followed by wide-ranging changes to the U.S. political economy. In the 1930s, progressive historians Charles and Mary Beard famously termed the consolidation of a new industrial class in the postwar North a "Second American Revolution." A few decades later, the influential British historian Eric Hobsbawm situated the origins and outcome of the Civil War within the epochal changes transforming the mid-nineteenth-century world, which he called "the Age of Capital." But although he agreed that "American capitalism developed with dramatic speed" after the war, Hobsbawm also argued that the South "remained agrarian, poor, backward, and resentful" for nearly a century, despite the abolition of slavery, mainly because the region quickly "reverted to the control of conservative white ... racists."[1]

While the fact of rapid American industrialization after the Civil War seems beyond dispute, the same cannot be said of Hobsbawm's assessment of the postbellum South. From C. Vann Woodward's neo-Beardian vision of a "new middle class" of pro-business southern elites to Harold D. Woodman's influential studies portraying the New South as an "emergent bourgeois society," most scholarship over the last half-century has tended to describe the South as being rapidly absorbed into the national and world economic order after the Civil War, with less attention paid to white southerners' continued resistance to capitalist values and practices. Behind this perspective lies a syllogistic logic that

[1] Eric Hobsbawm, *The Age of Capital, 1848–1875* (New York, 1974), 155–6 (quotations); Charles A. Beard and Mary R. Beard, *The Rise of American Civilization* (2 vols.; New York, 1927), II, chap. 18. For a similar view of the Civil War's outcome see Barrington Moore Jr.'s influential *Social Origins of Dictatorship and Democracy: Lord and Peasant in the Making of the Modern World* (New York, 1966), chap. 3. The Beards' "Second American Revolution" thesis is discussed in Peter A. Coclanis and Scott Marler, "The Economics of Reconstruction," in *A Companion to the Civil War and Reconstruction*, ed. Lacy K. Ford (Malden, MA, 2005), 344–52.

begins by describing sharecropping as a form of wage labor rather than tenancy. With sharecroppers thus considered a "rural proletariat," regional agriculture is declared a "free-labor" economy, and from there, it is but a short step to characterizing the post–Civil War South as a "bourgeois society." Although some have pointed out weak links in this argumentative chain, most recent scholars have deployed the idea of a new capitalist order in the postbellum South – too often, without interrogating its assumptions – as a background to their studies of important topics such as the freedpeople, the white yeomanry, women's status, urbanization, and the development of discrete subregions, states, and localities.[2]

In other words, there is now a historiographical consensus that considers the postbellum South as only a moderately peculiar example of the broader arc of social formations possible under modern capitalism. To a subtle degree, such perspectives shift responsibility for the vicious racism and endemic poverty in which the South was mired through World War II onto the muscular shoulders of industrial capitalism, whose unchecked excesses during the period of its late nineteenth-century consolidation are usually deplored. However, if Hobsbawm's assessment of the South was right, such blame seems misplaced. To paraphrase T. S. Eliot, the bang of the Civil War ended with the whimper of Reconstruction, after which ex-slaveholders and their allies were allowed to put their region's own house in order. Yet in light of "home rule" (also termed "Redemption" by white southerners – a revealing religious metaphor), it is difficult to view the social relations of dominance and subordinance that they created, which in some respects exceeded even slavery in cruelty, as primarily a result of the triumph of American industrial capitalism. In a nutshell, Jim Crow and Judge Lynch should be considered less as Yankee transplants to the region than as southerners born and bred.[3]

[2] C. Vann Woodward, *Origins of the New South, 1877–1913* (Baton Rouge, 1951). The characterization of a "bourgeois South" by Harold D. Woodman can be found most recently in his "The Political Economy of the New South: Retrospects and Prospects," *Journal of Southern History* 67 (November 2001), 789–810; but the evolution of his sophisticated viewpoint is well-worth tracing in his other works, most notably *King Cotton and His Retainers: Financing and Marketing the Cotton Crop of the South, 1800–1925* (Lexington, KY, 1968); "Sequel to Slavery: The New History Views the Postbellum South," *Journal of Southern History* 43 (November 1977), 523–54; "Post-Civil War Southern Agriculture and the Law," *Agricultural History* 53 (January 1979), 319–37; "Postbellum Social Change and Its Effects on Marketing the South's Cotton Crop," *Agricultural History* 56 (January 1982), 215–30; "The Reconstruction of the Cotton Plantation in the New South," in *Essays on the Postbellum Southern Economy*, eds. Thavolia Glymph and John J. Kushma (College Station, TX, 1985), 95–119; and *New South – New Law: The Legal Foundations of Credit and Labor Relations in the Postbellum Agricultural South* (Baton Rouge, 1995).

[3] Such views of the postbellum South were recently termed the new "conventional wisdom" by John C. Rodrigue in "More Souths?" *Reviews in American History* 30 (March 2002), 66–7. Two critiques of the "New [Capitalist] South" consensus are Alex Lichtenstein, "Proletarians or Peasants? Sharecroppers and the Politics of Protest in the Rural South, 1880–1940," *Plantation Society in the Americas* 5 (Fall 1998), 297–331; and Scott P. Marler, "Fables of the

This epilogue offers a framework for understanding the New South that acknowledges the persistence of residual economic, political, and cultural factors after the Civil War. Broadly congruent with interpretations of a precapitalist Old South also now out of fashion, this framework argues against the rather counterintuitive view of a submissive South suddenly converted to bourgeois social relations by emancipation. While in keeping with the preceding chapters, this epilogue broadens the historical lens, first discussing some theoretical and comparative aspects of merchant capital, then employing those insights to emphasize merchants' roles in helping establish and maintain what Hobsbawm rightly described as an "agrarian, poor, backward, and resentful" postbellum South. For example, to demonstrate how sharecropping, in which southern merchants played a linchpin role, deviated from capitalist techniques elsewhere during the late nineteenth century, it discusses some of the ways that this system was historically analogous to forms of household-based rural production spearheaded by merchants in early modern Europe.

While such comparative dimensions should advance our appreciation of the protracted, uneven, and contingent nature of transitions from one mode of production to another, it is first necessary to examine the concept of merchant capital that had been developed in classical political economy – not only in the fragmentary historical writings of Karl Marx, but also among canonical non-Marxists such as Adam Smith and Max Weber. During the twentieth century, historians such as Hobsbawm, Maurice Dobb, and Robert Brenner followed Marx in their reluctance to acknowledge the transformative roles often played by merchant capital, as well as its ability to adapt and persist in the face of changing conditions. At the same time, the intellectual heirs of Adam Smith, who can be broadly lumped under the rubric of neoclassical economics, have also been disinclined to give merchants much historical credit. Thus, another broad goal of this epilogue is to reassert merchant capital as a category of political economy, resulting in a perspective distinct from the more "orthodox" positions of Marx, Smith, and their successors. Although this discussion of merchant capital may strike some as too abstract, it will try to remain grounded in historically specific contexts – most notably, in the prolonged decline of feudalism in early modern Europe. Once our attention shifts to the late nineteenth-century South, it should become clearer why this discussion is relevant to understanding the significance of merchant capitalism's practices, mentalities, and habits after the Civil War, especially their detrimental regional economic effects in areas such as industrialization and urbanization.

A good place to begin is with the outspoken southern historian Eugene D. Genovese. For many years, the most consistent theme associated with

Reconstruction: Reconstruction of the Fables," *Journal of the Historical Society* IV (Winter 2004), 113–37. A more sympathetic view of the trend is offered by Joseph P. Reidy, "Economic Consequences of the Civil War and Reconstruction," in *A Companion to the American South*, ed. John B. Boles (Malden, MA, 2002), 303–17.

Genovese's work was his Marxist interpretation of the slaveholding regime of the Old South as essentially precapitalist and, in some respects, neo-feudal in character. First articulated in his studies of the "political economy of slavery" published in 1965, this notion took a cultural turn in *Roll, Jordan, Roll* (1974), a work that elucidated a complex dialectic of mutual dependence between masters and slaves, one that contrasted sharply with the individualist ethos undergirding the emerging free-labor society of the North. Over the ensuing decades, Genovese developed this notion mainly by elaborating the organicist worldview held by the proslavery planter classes of the Old South. This later work displayed Genovese's growing (and for some, disturbing) admiration for the traditionalist values and decidedly non-bourgeois "mind of the master class."[4]

Although Genovese and his wife, Elizabeth Fox-Genovese, were uncharacteristically silent about the postemancipation South, they briefly revisited the southern political economy in a 1983 collection of essays, *Fruits of Merchant Capital,* whose implications have long been neglected. Building explicitly on a long-standing series of influential debates over the protracted European transition from feudalism to capitalism, the Genoveses sought to specify the conditions that had shaped the Old South's slave-based mode of production. To do so, they considered the region in a global-comparative context that foreshadowed the emergent scholarly preoccupation with the Atlantic world. Most of the wide-ranging essays were tied together by the theme promised in the title: the role of merchant capital, a historically distinct form of deploying and exploiting economic resources based on commercial exchange, in the rise, development, and perpetuation of plantation slavery in the Americas, especially in the southern United States. As they put it in their introduction, merchant capital and the slave-based mode of production it fostered had served as "the breeding ground of an essentially hybrid system in the Old South, ... [which] developed as a noncapitalist society increasingly antagonistic to, but inseparable from, the bourgeois world" in which it was embedded. Yet there seemed to be tensions in their essays that pulled them in multiple, sometimes contradictory directions. For example, even though they gave numerous examples of merchant capital's contributions over the *longue durée,* from its patronage of Renaissance art

---

[4] Eugene D. Genovese and Elizabeth Fox-Genovese, *The Mind of the Master Class: History and Faith in the Southern Slaveholders' Worldview* (New York, 2005). For critiques of the Genoveses' later perspectives on southern slaveholders by scholars sympathetic to their earlier work, see Alex Lichtenstein, "Right Church, Wrong Pew: Eugene Genovese's Defense of Southern Conservatism," *New Politics,* n.s. 6 (Summer 1997), 59–68; and Manisha Sinha, "Eugene D. Genovese: The Mind of a Marxist Conservative," *Radical History Review,* No. 88 (Winter 2004), 4–29. Eugene D. Genovese, *The Political Economy of Slavery: Studies in the Economy and Society of the Slave South* (New York, 1965); Genovese, *Roll Jordan Roll: The World the Slaves Made* (New York, 1974). For a fine but lesser-known work that describes the "seigneurial" nature of antebellum southern society see Raimondo Luraghi, *The Rise and Fall of the Plantation South* (New York, 1978).

to its role as an "agent of primitive accumulation," the Genoveses nevertheless insisted that these "represented the great, if spectacular, exceptions to its common role throughout history" (p. 5). More common throughout the book were disparaging references to merchant capital as "conservative" and "parasitic." It might help to sort matters out by discussing precisely what is meant by "merchant capital." To do so, however, we must venture onto what may be unfamiliar terrain for many southern historians: early modern Europe and its prolonged "transition from feudalism to capitalism."[5]

The simplest way of defining merchant capital is conveyed by the old adage, "Buy cheap, sell dear." In other words, the merchant capitalist facilitates long-distance exchange processes and extracts profits from differentials in commodity values. Since such activities date back to antiquity, Marx referred to merchant capital as "the oldest historical mode in which capital has an independent existence" (*Capital* III, 442), though he resisted attempts by thinkers such as Adam Smith to consider such economic behavior "natural." Still, although Marx, like many other economists of his day, located the source of the surplus-value extracted under modern capitalism in production processes, he admitted that those expanded processes were necessarily predicated on market exchange. He therefore conceded that merchant capital was "a historical precondition for the development of the capitalist mode of production," insofar as the latter "presupposes production for trade" (*Capital* III, 444).[6]

5 Elizabeth Fox-Genovese and Eugene D. Genovese, *Fruits of Merchant Capital: Slavery and Bourgeois Property in the Rise and Expansion of Capitalism* (Oxford, UK, and other cities, 1983). References to this work will be cited parenthetically in the text. The starting point of modern discussion of the "transition problem" remains Maurice Dobb, *Studies in the Development of Capitalism* (1947; rev. ed., New York, 1963); and the ensuing debates prompted by Paul M. Sweezy's reply to Dobb collected in Rodney J. Hilton, ed., *The Transition from Feudalism to Capitalism* (London, 1976). On Dobb's enormous influence not only on a young generation of independent radical historians but on legitimizing Marxist scholarship in the Western academy, see Bill Schwartz, "'The People' in History: The Communist Party Historians Group, 1946–56," in *Making Histories: Studies in History-Writing and Politics*, eds. Richard Johnson et al. (Minneapolis, MN, 1982), esp. 46–53. Debates over the transition enjoyed a resurgence in the late 1970s and 1980s, with Robert Brenner playing Dobb's role to Immanuel Wallerstein's Sweezy; see the collection by T. H. Aston and C. H. E. Philpin, eds., *The Brenner Debate* (New York, 1985). To put these debates in a nutshell (though at the risk of oversimplification): Dobb, Brenner et al. emphasize the "internal" development of class conflict in the countryside as the "prime mover" in the transition from feudalism to capitalism. For Sweezy, Wallerstein et al., however, the dissolvent role of increasing town-based, export-oriented commerce – an "external" determinant – was the critical transformative factor. Both positions can find support in Marx, but as Rodney Hilton rightly pointed out, Marx's position evolved over the course of his lifetime toward the class-conflict interpretation later favored by Dobb and Brenner; see Hilton, "Introduction," *Transition*, 23 n.15.
6 Karl Marx, *Grundrisse: Foundations of the Critique of Political Economy*, trans. Martin Nicholas (New York, 1973), 856 ("buy cheap and sell dear"). Marx's most important writings on merchant capital are in the third volume of *Capital*, trans. David Fernbach (New York, 1981), esp. chap. 20 ("Historical Material on Merchant's Capital"), as well as in chaps. 16, 18, and 47. See also the sections of Marx's *Grundrisse* on "Pre-Capitalist Economic Formations," esp.

Another important aspect of merchant capital was its historical development into various gradations and types. Thus, whereas banking and finance represents merchant capitalism in its most highly developed form, the petty shopkeeper or itinerant trader represents it at its most primitive. Even more crucial, and consonant with Marx's valuable understanding of capital less as a static object than as a dynamic social process, merchant capital is defined empirically – that is, by reference to the *effects* it has displayed in disparate historical contexts. One such effect is that, when deployed successfully (not a given, due to the inherent risks of trade), merchant capital tends to promote increased concentrations of wealth. Although Marx reluctantly included this form of capital in the process of what he termed "primitive accumulation," he and Adam Smith both insisted that such wealth was generally either conspicuously consumed by merchants (who are perpetually insecure creatures obsessed with social prestige) or reinvested in more speculative, less productive economic activities. In either case, even in concentrated form, merchant capital tends to remain confined to the circulation sphere rather than deployed in organizing higher-order production processes. Still another by-product of merchant capital was the promotion of commodities' "exchange-values," which allowed them to be converted into other forms of wealth, such as money. Over time, as more commodities came to be produced for exchange than for use, mentalities and habits associated with the market began to replace more traditional relationships between means-and-ends in economic life. To paraphrase one recent scholar, the market in early modern Europe served as a "theater" in which nearly everyone performed – but directed and choreographed by merchant capitalists. As historians like Steven Hahn and Bruce Palmer have shown, the advent of such market-oriented, merchant-sponsored exchange relationships would create a great deal of psychological dissonance among white yeoman farmers in the nineteenth-century South, who had long been accustomed to production for self-sufficiency and its related preindustrial values.[7]

The exchange relations spearheaded by merchant capital forced Marx to concede that commercial trade "always has, to a greater or lesser degree, a solvent effect on the pre-existing organizations of production, which in all their various forms are principally oriented to use-value" (*Capital* III, 444). Even

502–13; and *Capital*, Vol. I, trans. Ben Fowkes (New York, 1976), esp. chaps. 4–5; and Part VIII ("So-Called Primitive Accumulation"), esp. chaps. 29–32. Citations to these works will be made parenthetically in the text. Adam Smith refers to "a certain propensity in human nature ... to truck, barter, and exchange" in *The Wealth of Nations* (1776; repr. New York, 2003), 22. Smith discussed merchants frequently throughout his classic work, but see esp. Book III, chaps. 3 and 4. While it is commonplace to regard these two giants of political economy as polar opposites, it is actually just as remarkable how many premises they shared.

[7] Steven Hahn, *The Roots of Southern Populism: Yeoman Farmers and the Transformation of the Georgia Upcountry, 1850–1890* (New York, 1982); Bruce Palmer, *"Man Over Money": The Southern Populist Critique of American Capitalism* (Chapel Hill, 1980). Jean-Christophe Agnew, *Worlds Apart: The Market and the Theater in Anglo-American Thought, 1550–1750* (Cambridge, UK, and other cities, 1986).

unsatisfyingly formulated as a context-free structural imperative, the admission of a "solvent effect" undermined Marx's refusal to acknowledge merchant capital's transformative powers. At the very least, the exchange relations promoted by merchant capital are indeed capable of "transforming," if only by means of weakening and undermining precapitalist modes of production. By extension, merchant capital's contribution to the transition from feudalism to capitalism constituted a necessary if not sufficient condition for the emergence of a new economic order; and moreover, had merchant capital not developed as it did in early modern Europe, more "advanced" forms of capitalism might have been different, delayed, or perhaps never occurred at all.[8]

The notion of a solvent effect is closely linked to another key aspect of merchant capital: its relatively greater power and influence in underdeveloped economies. As Marx put the point, merchant capital's level of dominance "stands in inverse proportion to the general economic development of society" (*Capital* III, 444–5). There seems to be wide agreement on this point. For example, despite approaching matters from the opposite causal direction (i.e., from mentalité-to-structure rather than vice versa), sociologist Max Weber also emphasized the qualitative changes that distinguished modern capitalism (which, like Smith and Marx, he also viewed as production based on free labor) from its predecessor and competitor forms, especially merchant capital. Weber's terminology differed – he tended to call merchant capital "speculatively oriented adventurous capitalism" (or, in a more anti-Semitic vein, "pariah capitalism") – but the result was the same. Weber, like Marx, described the extent and durability of merchant capital as "a specific characteristic of those countries whose bourgeois-capitalistic development ... has remained backward" – as was the case in the nineteenth-century South.[9]

There were also more positive transformative roles that merchant capital played during the long transition. For example, the institutional techniques that merchants pioneered in early modern Europe, from double-entry bookkeeping and joint-stock companies to commodity exchanges and international banking, would all later prove to be vital aspects of global industrial capitalism by the nineteenth century. Indeed, Marx credited such sophisticated, institutionally based techniques with promoting a "division of labor between capitals"

---

[8] See Jan Luiten van Zanden, "Do We Need a Theory of Merchant Capitalism?" *Review* 20 (Spring 1997), 255–67. In his recent book *Africans and the Industrial Revolution in England: A Study in International Trade and Economic Development* (Cambridge, UK, and other cities, 2002), Joseph E. Inikori links the transatlantic slave trade to the emergence of British industrialism; see also Robin Blackburn, *The Making of New World Slavery: From the Baroque to the Modern, 1492–1800* (New York, 1997).

[9] Max Weber, *The Protestant Ethic and the Spirit of Capitalism*, trans. Talcott Parsons (1904; repr. London and New York, 1992), 165–66 (first quotation), 57 (second quotation). Weber also anticipated the Genoveses' perspective on the Old South, claiming that "adventurers" arranged a plantation society that allowed them to "live like feudal lords," and whose underlying ethos he contrasted with the "specifically middle-class outlook" of the New England Puritans he admired; Ibid., 173–4.

(*Capital* III, 392–3), a distinction appreciated by Smith as well. In this sense, then, merchant capital provided industrial capital with an advantageous institutional framework that enabled exponential growth of the scale and scope of economic enterprise. The neglected notion of a "division of labor between capitals" highlights merchants' ability to persist by adapting to changing circumstances, and they also make merchant capital a more flexible, context-specific, and historically useful concept.[10]

The characterization of merchant capital as "parasitic" is most applicable to the political conditions of its existence. But even though merchants were often ingratiating and servile to established powers, this characterization underestimates their opportunism and adaptability. Moreover, to the extent that merchants did seek to coexist with various forms of state power, there is an important corollary effect. By frequently allying themselves with regimes founded on extra-economic forms of tributary extraction, merchants help ensure that transitions from one mode of production to another are protracted in nature. Outmoded structures thus often gain extended life from merchant capitalists, even while they simultaneously but unintentionally subvert (or, "dissolve") the non-bourgeois basis of surplus extraction on which precapitalist ruling classes routinely rely. The Genoveses referred to these contradictory impulses as "the Janus face of merchant capital" (p. 3).

Two related historical effects of merchant capital in transitional epochs are important to understanding its later role in the New South. The first is colonialism, particularly in the guise of New World slavery. Shrewd political alliances often lent much-needed protection and legitimacy to the investment consortiums formed by "adventurous" merchant capitalists in early modern Europe to exploit overseas territories. It is unnecessary to rehearse the details of the establishment of European colonies in the Americas beginning in the sixteenth century for the purpose of extracting precious metals and agricultural commodities, particularly tobacco and sugar, although it is worth noting that neither Marx, Smith, nor Weber paid much attention to slavery's contributions to colonial development. Most important for understanding the

[10] In *Capitalism Divided? The City and Industry in British Social Development* (New York, 1984), Geoffrey Ingham detailed the metamorphosis of merchant capital in England, the very heart of bourgeois-industrial capitalism. The evolution of financial and commercial capital centered in London between the sixteenth and nineteenth centuries, he writes, displayed "adaptation to changing and more favorable circumstances; it did not involve a radical break with the past." In many ways, Ingham's analysis builds on the cultural foundation of the similar argument persuasively articulated by Martin J. Wiener in *English Culture and the Decline of the Industrial Spirit, 1850–1980* (Cambridge, UK, and other cities, 1981), in which the English industrial bourgeoisie itself is shown to have never quite broken free of entrenched premodern values and habits – in fact, persistent City-based financial capitalists were "richer, more powerful, and ... enjoyed a social cachet that evaded industry" (p. 128). See also P. J. Cain and A. G. Hopkins, "Gentlemanly Capitalism and British Expansion Overseas I: The Old Colonial System, 1688–1850," *Economic History Review* 2d ser., 39 (November 1986), 501–5. For Adam Smith's version of the "division of labor between capitals," see *Wealth of Nations*, Book II, esp. chap. 1.

postemancipation South is the proclivity of merchant capitalists (in the vein of the parasite metaphor) to serve as intermediaries in colonial settings, lubricating and enforcing the terms of exchanges, however unequal, between different cultures. In this way, merchants in disparate settings often settle comfortably into the role of a comprador class, a satrapy – a role they would also assume in the "colonial economy" of the New South.[11]

An even more important effect that merchant capital had during the centuries-long, geographically uneven transition to modern capitalism was its establishment of domestic (or, "putting-out") forms of rural manufacturing – a system that bears a powerful resemblance, as will be shown, to the sharecropping system of the New South. The basic form of the putting-out system (also termed "proto-industrialization" by some economic historians), which first appeared in locations around Europe during the sixteenth century and persisted well into the nineteenth (even in the northern United States), was for the merchant to advance raw materials to rural households, where these supplies were converted into finished commodities that were then purchased and marketed by the merchant. Most frequently associated with early forms of textile production, this system of advances to small producers was also common in nascent industries from shoes to metal-working, and such household-based production was geared toward turning out commodities intended for exchange in distant markets.[12]

---

[11] Luraghi, *Rise and Fall of the Plantation South*, 37–9. Interestingly, Marx probably overstated merchant capital's involvement in the internal organization of colonial production by underestimating the extent to which such ventures often relied on state sponsorship; see, for example, *Capital* III, p. 446. See also Walter Johnson, "The Pedestal and the Veil: Rethinking the Capitalism/Slavery Question," *Journal of the Early Republic* 24 (Summer 2004), 299–308. Robert Brenner examines the crucial role of merchants in early English colonialism in *Merchants and Revolution: Commercial Change, Political Conflict, and London's Overseas Traders, 1550–1653* (Princeton, NJ, 1993).

[12] Dobb, *Studies*, 265–6, admits that domestic forms of industry remained important in England through the nineteenth century. For similar merchant capitalist involvement in production in the antebellum North, see Paul E. Johnson, *A Shopkeeper's Millenium: Society and Revivals in Rochester, New York, 1815–1837* (New York, 1978), 38–42. Immanuel Wallerstein, *The Modern World-System*. Vol. II: *Mercantilism and the Consolidation of the World Economy, 1600–1750* (San Diego and other cities, 1980), chap. 5; Wallerstein, *The Modern World-System*. Vol. III: *The Second Great Era of the Expansion of the Capitalist World-Economy, 1730–1840s* (San Diego and other cities, 1989), 153. Wallerstein's work is iconoclastic, to say the least. For example, although he drew the Genoveses' ire for being too prone to credit international trade with the transition to capitalism (*Fruits*, pp. 15, 36), John Merrington has pointed out that Wallerstein himself rejects "the key Marxist distinction between *merchant* and *industrial* capital ... as 'unfortunate terminology.'" Merrington, "Town and Country in the Transition to Capitalism," in Hilton, ed., *Transition from Feudalism to Capitalism*, 187 n. 42. But such odd conjunctures have their echoes on the more orthodox side of the debates over the transition as well. Robert Brenner, the most prominent recent advocate of an internalist, "class struggle in the countryside-as-prime mover" approach to the transition, has seemed to demonstrate precisely the opposite in his own studies of seventeenth-century English merchants. As Perry Anderson thus described Brenner's work, "the detractor of the significance of merchant capital in principle

Marx downplayed the significance of the putting-out system because of its incongruence with his overall schematic for the emergence of factory-style industrial production laid out in the first volume of *Capital*. But even so, his views were ambiguous and contradictory, as he simply could not seem to get around its importance. He admitted that "in the so-called domestic industries, this exploitation [of 'cheap and immature labour-power'] is still more shameless than in modern manufacture, because the workers' power of resistance declines with their dispersal; [and] because a whole range of plundering parasites insinuate themselves between the actual employer and the worker he employs" (*Capital* I, 591). Less orthodox thinkers, as well as many mainstream economic historians, have been more willing to insist on the importance and persistence of household forms of production organized under mercantile auspices to the long transition. Commensurate with other forms in which merchant capital had been deployed over time, the market insecurities that adhered to fickle international demand made the putting-out system well-suited to backward, precapitalist regions. Technologies were mostly rudimentary, thereby limiting fixed capital expenses. Overhead was kept even lower by externalizing labor costs – that is, by maintaining a relatively safe distance from the internal organization of the household production units themselves. (There were as yet few readily available opportunities to reduce costs by subdividing manufacturing processes.) Profits were further stabilized by "plundering" rural producers through the debt bondage built into the merchants' furnishing system for raw materials and other supplies.[13]

By means of the putting-out system, then, precapitalist societies in Western Europe were "incorporated into the reproduction and accumulation machinery of merchant capitalism," as historian Peter Kriedte has written. But since proto-industrialization "could only establish itself where the ties of the feudal system had either loosened or were in the process of full disintegration," it is not surprising that the "relations of production in proto-industrial regions" retained a "transitional character." Because merchants had yet to establish full authority over the dynamics of the production process, the profits attained from the commodities produced were still basically derived from their exchange-values rather than built into production itself, as would be the case later under fully developed industrial capitalism. This "transitional character" held true for both poles of production relations. As a result of their geographic dispersal, imbrication within persistent feudal relationships in the countryside, and maintenance of control over most aspects of production itself, producers did not yet form a "proletariat" under the putting-out system. At the same time, neither

---

has been the first to establish, in spellbinding detail, its role as demiurge in practice." Anderson, *Spectrum: From Left to Right in the World of Ideas* (New York, 2005), 251–2.
[13] Peter Kriedte, *Peasants, Landlords, and Merchant Capitalists: Europe and the World Economy, 1500–1800* (Warwickshire, UK, 1983). See also Barry Supple, "The Nature of Enterprise," in E. E. Rich and C. H. Wilson, eds., *The Cambridge Economic History of Europe*. Vol. V: *The Economic Organization of Early Modern Europe* (London and New York, 1977), 425.

did the protocapitalist merchant "putter-out" display the business practices or economic mindsets that accompanied later bourgeois-industrial capitalism. In this sense, Max Weber pointed out that although the putting-out system may have been forward-looking and "capitalistic" in orientation, it essentially remained "traditionalistic business, if one considers the spirit which animated the entrepreneur." The merchant's ethos still reflected a transitional system of production in which labor had not been fully alienated, either from itself as a commodity or from the means of production; in which traditional forms of social relations based on status rather than contract remained dominant; and in which work-discipline was not yet subject to the intense regulation later imposed under mature industrial capitalism.[14]

All of these conditions were also true of the nineteenth-century South, both before and after the Civil War. The Genoveses famously described the Old South's economy and society as precapitalist, akin to a neo-feudal order featuring a proud and "prebourgeois" slaveowning ruling class that was extremely hostile toward free-labor society (p. 16). In the same vein, the Genoveses also insisted that the slave-based mode of production, despite being entwined in international commodities markets, was not itself a form of bourgeois capitalism – an almost tautological truth that they defended with subtlety and wit against all comers.[15]

So as our attention now turns fully to the New South, there are two main points to bear in mind from such an understanding of the Old. First, it was the mediating role of merchant capital that provided southern slaveholders with the necessary social distance from the ongoing "market revolution" elsewhere to preside over the development of their aggressively non-bourgeois society. Second, if one accepts that precapitalist social relations were entrenched in the slave South, then it follows that the transition to a postemancipation regime would have been protracted and characterized by the persistence of reactionary

[14] Weber, *Protestant Ethic*, 66–7; E. P. Thompson, "Time, Work-Discipline, and Industrial Capitalism," *Past and Present* 38 (December 1967), 56–97; Peter Kriedte, Hans Medick, and Jurgen Schlumbohm, *Industrialization before Industrialization: Rural Industry in the Genesis of Capitalism* (Cambridge, UK, and other cities, 1981), 6; Kriedte, *Peasants, Landlords, and Merchant Capitalists*, 13–14 (quotation).

[15] Or, *nearly* all comers. As Larry McDonnell pointed out in an astute review of *Fruits*, the Genoveses failed to engage with what he called "the stunning neo-revisionist assault" on Marxist interpretations of the slave South that had just gotten underway in the early 1980s, in which scholars such as Harry Watson, Lacy Ford, and James Oakes emphasized the capitalist orientation of slaveholding planters and placed them in the context of what soon came to called the "market revolution" thesis. Lawrence T. McDonnell, "The Janus Face of *Fruits of Merchant Capital*," *Labour/Le Travail* 15 (Spring 1985), 185–90 (quotation on p. 188). Yet logically, for the "emergent bourgeois society" thesis regarding the New South to be broadly accurate, then the road to such an apparent ideological *volte-face* necessarily would have been paved well in advance. In this sense, then, the advocates of an Old South wing to the market revolution are more historiographically congruent with the post–Civil War interpretations of Harold Woodman et al. than would be the Genoveses'.

planters and merchants alike. As the Genoveses argued, "the penetration of the economy by merchant capital usually resulted in the reinforcement of feudal social relations and of obstacles to the emergence of bourgeois social relations, specifically, of free labor" (p. 8). In this sense, the elimination of slavery by force of arms certainly did not change the minds of either planters or their merchant allies as to the propriety of their quondam regime. Equally important, emancipation did not cause an economy whose global functions had been organized and run for two centuries under mercantile auspices to simply roll over in the face of nascent industrial hegemony – a hegemony, it should be pointed out, that remained the source of bitter conflicts in the late nineteenth-century North itself.

To assess the adaptation and persistence of merchant capital in the New South, the reorganization of cotton-plantation agriculture seems the best place to start, since it remained the motor of the southern economy for decades to come. Moreover, the cotton sector has provided the grist for the many recent interpretations that, in one way or another, assert the triumph of bourgeois capitalism in the post–Civil War South. Yet merchants served even more crucial functions in cotton production after the war than before, despite the breakup of the urban-based factorage system. Ultimately, the postbellum contributions of merchant capital offer a more satisfactory starting point for explaining under-developed regional conditions through the Great Depression than does Harold D. Woodman's insistence that "in its basic class structure and its organization, [the New South] resembled the North more than it differed."[16]

Let us begin with sharecropping, the closest approximation to a dominant mode of production that the region had for nearly a century after the Civil War. Of course, this system was not unique to the New South. As John Merrington has noted, sharecropping had a lengthy European pedigree (*metayage* in France, *mezzadria* in Italy) as a "transitional form" of agricultural lease that "associat[ed] merchant capital and peasant agriculture." Yet in its makeshift southern guise, this form of agricultural labor actually bore far greater structural resemblances to the rural putting-out system that had been organized by merchants during the early modern transition to capitalism than it did to the wage-labor economies of either the industrial North or the agricultural West.

---

[16] Woodman, "The Reconstruction of the Cotton Plantation," in Glymph and Kushma, eds., *Essays on the Postbellum Southern Economy*, 113. It is interesting to note that a much earlier generation of Marxists would have rejected Woodman's interpretation. W. E. B. Du Bois, for example, argued that the failure of the federal government to enforce any fundamental "reconstruction" of the South had locked regional agriculture into "a new feudalism." Du Bois, *Black Reconstruction in America, 1860–1880* (1935; repr., New York, 1992), 583–4. Also, in one of their rare comments on the nature of postbellum southern society, the Genoveses cited an obscure study of capitalism and agriculture in the United States. "[I]n the formerly slave-owning South," Vladimir Lenin had written in 1913, one should not "confuse the latifundia with large-scale capitalist farming" of the sort increasingly prevalent in midwestern U.S. agriculture. The Genoveses thus implicitly endorsed Lenin's view of the tenant-farmed plantations of the New South as "merely a survival of pre-capitalist relations" (Lenin, as quoted in *Fruits*, p. 24).

For example, rather than working in closely supervised gangs, tenant plantations relied on dispersed household units of production, as had the putting-out system. Such denucleated production not only mitigated against the intense supervision that accompanied "factories in the field"–types of agriculture, it also stifled the emergence of any incipient proletarian class-consciousness among croppers and other tenants since, as Marx had noted of household-based industry, "the workers' power of resistance declines with their dispersal" (*Capital* I, 591).[17]

Southern sharecropping displayed other broad similarities to precapitalist economic forms maintained by merchant capital. For example, production was geared toward commodities of practically no local utility; cotton's value derived, as it had under slavery, solely from its exchange value in long-distance markets. Also, merchants were notably averse to assuming any fixed capital costs in the production systems they sponsored, and sharecropping systems in particular had long displayed a tendency to repress investments in technological improvements by either landlords or producers. These traits were mirrored by the snail's pace of mechanization in southern cotton production after the war. It has often been argued that southern cotton production exhibited slow productivity growth due to the lack of incentives to develop or invest in new forms of machinery, which is most frequently explained by recourse to the ready availability of cheap labor. This was doubtless an important factor, but the South's failure to mechanize agricultural production should also be understood as reflecting merchants' usual desires to limit fixed capital expenses, thereby preserving flexibility in the face of both underdeveloped regional demand and fickle international markets. Although postbellum southern cotton output would outpace its pre-1860 levels fairly rapidly, like other proto-industrializing regimes, southern merchants and landlords were usually satisfied to confine their efforts to the "quantitative expansion of production," as opposed to seeking "qualitative change[s]" of the sort represented by capital-intensive technological improvements.[18]

[17] Merrington, "Town and Country," 185 (quotations); see also Richard Lachmann, *Capitalists in Spite of Themselves: Elite Conflict and Economic Transitions in Early Modern Europe* (New York and Oxford, 2000), 88–9. In *Branches Without Roots: The Genesis of the Black Working Class in the American South, 1862–1882* (New York, 1986), 26–8, Gerald David Jaynes made passing note of sharecropping's similarity to the putting-out system. Marx also analyzed sharecropping in various European contexts as a rent-based "transitional form" that antedated capitalist relations in agriculture (*Capital* III, p. 939), which raises the question of whether sharecroppers should be regarded as having paid rent in kind (tenants) or were "compensated" with a portion of the crop (wage laborers). The recent assertion of capitalist relations in New South agriculture in many ways hinges on this superficially innocuous distinction. For the complex issues involved, see esp. Woodman, *New South – New Law*; Marler, "Fables of the Reconstruction"; and Lichtenstein, "Proletarians or Peasants?"

[18] Kriedte et al., *Industrialization before Industrialization*, 136 (quotations), 146; Louis Ferleger, "Sharecropping Contracts in the Late-Nineteenth-Century South," *Agricultural History* 67 (Summer 1993), 31–46; Jay R. Mandle, *Not Slave, Not Free: The African American Economic*

The analogy to domestic systems of production is further supported by a rough similarity among the constellation of classes that characterized the revamped southern plantation system. Even though landownership remained concentrated in the hands of former slaveholders (thus affording them a more prominent role in southern sharecropping than European landed classes had in the putting-out system), household-based production units under sharecropping were vitally dependent on merchant capitalists to promote, perpetuate, and underwrite them. In this respect, the centrality of the southern 'country store' to the postbellum cotton sector has long been acknowledged by historians, even if it has been understudied and sometimes obscured by folk nostalgia. The number of such stores multiplied rapidly in the agricultural South after the war. Even excluding those in urban areas, economic historians Roger Ransom and Richard Sutch identified nearly 8,000 such stores in 1880 among the five states of the "Cotton South" alone. To be sure, most of these stores were small, family-run operations with assets valued under $5,000, which is unsurprising given that retail trades have historically required fairly low levels of capital input. But the small scale of these firms should not lead one to underestimate them as merely merchant capital at its most primitive, for despite their size and instability (although many did grow and persist), these stores served crucial functions belied by their cozy hot stoves, cracker barrels, and jugs of whiskey. What caused the explosive growth in such stores after the Civil War was the need for financial intermediaries between landowners and sharecroppers, and rural furnishing merchants alone proved able to advance seasonal credit to cash-poor farm households, loans that were secured by crop liens on future production.[19]

Given that few historians dispute the extent or significance of these stores in cotton production after the war, the adaptation, persistence, and importance of merchant capital to the postemancipation South should therefore be nearly self-evident. One might pause again to note that merchants' tactic of insinuating themselves into production processes via credit provisioning was not a new one. Immanuel Wallerstein has described how the export-minded merchant of early modern Europe frequently sought to "establish a dependency upon him on the part of a mass of small producers," which was most efficiently accomplished through "debt bondage." Furthermore, kin- and ethnoculturally based forms of enterprise were another long-standing hallmark of merchant capital. Not only did such firms avoid the more "transparent" forms of corporate

Experience since the Civil War (Durham, NC, 1992), 48–57; Warren Whatley, "Southern Agrarian Labor Contracts as Impediments to Cotton Mechanization," *Journal of Economic History* 47 (March 1987), 45–70.

[19] Roger L. Ransom and Richard Sutch, *One Kind of Freedom: The Economic Consequences of Emancipation* (2nd ed.; New York and other cities, 2001), 132–8; Harold Barger, "Income Originating in Trade, 1869–1929," in National Bureau of Economic Research, *Trends in the American Economy in the Nineteenth Century* (Princeton, NJ, 1960), 329; Louis M. Kyriakoudes, "Lower-Order Urbanization and Territorial Monopoly in the Southern Furnishing Trade: Alabama, 1871–1890," *Social Science History* 26 (Spring 2002), 186.

organization that would become the industrial standard, but the mutualism they displayed was characteristic of a more conservative type of business, one more limited in scope and concerned largely with maintaining and passing along wealth and status.[20]

To the degree that rural merchants have been the subject of recent studies in southern history, a great deal of energy has been expended on whether and how they merged, supplanted, or otherwise interacted with the planter classes. Often asserted but less adequately discussed have been questions associated with the class character of these merchants – specifically, whether or not they should be considered a "new bourgeoisie." The dubious aspects of this proposition are revealed through closer attention to the vocabulary of class that was initially developed and clarified by sociologists and historians. From such perspectives, a bourgeoisie is far more than the "nation of shopkeepers" famously skewered by Napoleon, and recent uses of the term as a mere synonym for "middle class" (an especially common lapse with reference to cultural norms) also significantly dilute the analytical specificity it long enjoyed in political economy. In the more rigorous and empirically based distinction accepted by Marx, Weber, and many contemporary sociologists, a bourgeoisie is an independent capitalist class defined by its fulfillment of two conditions: ownership of the means of production and employment of wage labor. Neither of those conditions are generally satisfied by merchant capitalists (even less so simultaneously) – not in theory, not in early modern Europe, and not in the New South.[21]

Recent scholarship often represents the gentleman-merchants of antebellum New Orleans and other southern cities as a bourgeoisie, but the fragmented nature of the speculative market culture in which those merchants were embedded, as well as their investments in plantation-based slavery, all mitigated against the cohesiveness that helps create independent classes that view their collective interests in opposition to those of other groups. Such

[20] On the relationship between kinship and merchant capitalism, see Johnson, *Shopkeeper's Millenium*, 16–42; David L. Carlton, *Mill and Town in South Carolina, 1880–1920* (Baton Rouge, 1982), 29; on the mutual-aid displayed by ethnic groups in mercantile enterprises, see Elliott Ashkenazi, *The Business of Jews in Louisiana, 1840–1875* (Tuscaloosa, AL, 1988), 33, 58; see also Scott P. Marler, "Merchants in the Transition to a New South: Central Louisiana, 1840–1880," *Louisiana History* 42 (Spring 2001), 182–7. Wallerstein, *Modern World-System*, III, 152–3 (quotation).

[21] Two examples of scholarship that present New South merchants as a "bourgeoisie" are Lacy K. Ford, "Rednecks and Merchants: Economic Development and Social Tensions in the South Carolina Upcountry, 1865–1900," *Journal of American History* 71 (September 1984), 294–318 (quotation on p. 317); and Michael D. Wayne, *The Reshaping of Plantation Society: The Natchez District, 1860–80* (Baton Rouge, 1983), 203–4. Though he assigned them an appropriate measure of significance, David Carlton was more cautious about characterizing this "new class of merchants" as a "bourgeoisie"; see Carlton, *Mill and Town*, 8–9, 26. Jonathan M. Wiener emphasized planter-merchant relations in his *Social Origins of the New South: Alabama, 1860–1885* (Baton Rouge, 1978). For a modern sociological analysis of bourgeois class formation and consciousness, see Anthony Giddens, *The Class Structure of the Advanced Societies* (1973; repr., New York, 1975), 26–45, 82–93.

distinctions become clearer when class (much like capital) is understood more as a relationship than as a static object. But there is another sense in which *bourgeois* is often employed to describe merchants in the Old South as well as the New: the word's etymological root in the word *burgher*, or "town-dweller." This usage also represents a slippage from its more specific meanings in socio-economic theory, but in the case of New South furnishing merchants, there are other reasons that it is of questionable utility, even according to its own logic. For example, to the extent that many "country stores" were literally scattered throughout the former plantation districts, class cohesion among their owners was suppressed for the same reasons that rurally dispersed sharecroppers were unable to regard themselves as a collective proletarian class. Admittedly, there is considerable evidence that stores, particularly more successful ones, tended to "cluster" in small towns. The number of these towns grew during the post-bellum decades, especially in the interior districts, with much of this growth prompted by railroad development. But in fact, most such "towns" were basically only tiny villages that consisted of a rail depot, a handful of stores (which frequently also served as processing stations for outgoing commodities), and perhaps a few ancillary service establishments.[22]

Ultimately, the post–Civil War South remained an overwhelmingly rural society through at least the New Deal. The social character of small towns continued to be shaped mainly within a decidedly agrarian context, and intense interfirm competition also diminished storekeepers' sense of the mutual interests that might have helped them form a distinct new "bourgeois" class. The stubbornly rural nature of the New South is also clear in demographic terms. One historian concluded that "by almost any statistical measurement, the South of about 1900 to 1920 occupied a weaker position in terms of urban development relative to the rest of the country than was true of the Old South." Although a few southern cities like Atlanta and Houston grew impressively during the period, the steady decay of coastal entrepôts such as New Orleans (even in the face of minimal "real" growth) largely offset these gains. Most small interior towns were little more than conservative enclaves of merchant capital (an apt description of New Orleans as well), and their dependence on often-tenuous political alliances with rural planters tended to help perpetuate more aspects of the old mode of production than they paved the way for the emergence of a new one.[23]

[22] Kyriakoudes, "Lower-Order Urbanization." See also Kenneth Weiher, "The Cotton Industry and Southern Urbanization, 1880–1930," *Explorations in Economic History* 14 (1977), 120–40; and David R. Meyer, "The Industrial Retardation of Southern Cities, 1860–1880," *Explorations in Economic History* 25 (1988), 366–86. For attempts to portray antebellum southern merchants as a bourgeoisie, see Jonathan Daniel Wells, *The Origins of the Southern Middle Class, 1800–1861* (Chapel Hill, 2004); and Frank J. Byrne, *Becoming Bourgeois: Merchant Culture in the South, 1820–1865* (Lexington, KY, 2006).
[23] Leonard P. Curry, "Urbanization and Urbanism in the Old South: A Comparative View," *Journal of Southern History* 40 (February 1974), 60 (quotation). On the decline of southern entrepôt

In this sense, it is also important to recognize that town growth does not always necessarily equate with capitalist development, especially of the self-sustaining industrial variety. Towns and cities in the nineteenth-century South, like most of those in early modern Europe, were still islands in the preindustrial stream. The absence of fully developed capitalist agriculture in the New South made its urban growth weaker and less stable than in the rest of the United States. Compared to the mutually reinforcive urban–rural development cycle in the Midwest, for example, the weak demand factors generated by the impoverished southern countryside were unable to provide much in the way of a "positive backward linkage effect" to sustain an urban network already stunted by its orientation toward commodity extraction under merchant capitalist auspices – a state of affairs first noticeable in the antebellum era. From railroads to banking, most of the region's urban centers served mainly as way-stations on the ever-lengthening global commodity chain that drained off the South's natural resources.[24]

Historians such as David L. Carlton have demonstrated the pivotal role that town merchants, especially commission houses with outside financial connections, played in the establishment of cotton textile mills on the mid-Atlantic seaboard. While their prominence in the community did sometimes translate into local political offices, less often were such small-town merchants able to match their ample boosterist rhetoric with an equivalent amount of investment capital from their own pockets. It is also unsurprising that the mill-village culture that these southern merchant capitalists–*cum*–would-be industrialists helped to establish was permeated with precisely the sorts of traditionalist economic behaviors – most notably, paternalism – that were usually scorned by the hardened bourgeoisie of laissez-faire capitalism. The mills themselves remained relatively undercapitalized, small-scale operations, evidenced by the fact that the aggregate regional value of finished textile exports barely reached 10 percent of its raw cotton exports before World War I. As Morton J. Rothstein

---

cities see Morton J. Rothstein, "The New South and the International Economy," *Agricultural History* 57 (Fall 1983), 385–402. On postbellum New Orleans see Michael A. Ross, "Resisting the New South: Commercial Crisis and Decline in New Orleans, 1865–85," *American Nineteenth-Century History* 4 (Spring 2003), 59–76.

[24] Morton J. Rothstein, "Antebellum Wheat and Cotton Exports: A Contrast in Marketing Organization and Economic Development," *Agricultural History* 40 (April 1966), 94 (quotation). See also David L. Carlton, "Antebellum Southern Urbanization," in Carlton and Peter A. Coclanis, *The South, the Nation, and the World: Perspectives on Southern Economic Development* (Charlottesville, VA, 2003), 35–48; and David Goldfield, "A Regional Framework for the Urban South," in Goldfield, *Region, Race, and Cities: Interpreting the Urban South* (Baton Rouge, 1997), 45–9. It is also worth reading William Cronon's *Nature's Metropolis: Chicago and the Great West* (New York, 1991) with the South in mind: the relationships between merchants and industrialists, towns and metropoles, and core and periphery that emerged in the nineteenth-century Midwest were very different from those in the South, both Old and New. See also Douglas F. Dowd, "A Comparative Analysis of Economic Development in the American West and South," *Journal of Economic History* 16 (December 1956), 558–74.

concluded, rather than providing evidence of incipient industrial capitalism in the New South, cotton mills were simply part of a "trend to put[ting] first-stage processing industries closer to the supply of raw materials."[25]

And this was in the South's largest industry – much the same could be said of steel, coal, and lumber. The most successful industries in the postbellum South were fairly late to develop and based on resource extraction rather than value-added enterprise; the Texas petroleum sector after 1900 was perhaps the most successful "pure" industry of this type. The restructuring of postbellum sugar production in the Southwest, however, provides an interesting example of the hybridity of agriculture and industry in the New South. Colonized by northern capital almost immediately after the war, both key aspects of Louisiana sugar production, cane growing and refining/processing, quickly became vertically integrated, and despite what Louis Ferleger has described as "resistance to the institutionalization of capitalistic economic relations" among planters and workers alike, the entire industry soon came to rely on wage labor. As a result, furnishing merchants never gained much of a credit-based foothold to establish the fundamental influence in the sugar region that they enjoyed in the Black Belt. By the early twentieth century, however, the industry began splitting off its corporate-controlled, capital-intensive processing components, where intensive factory-style mechanization led to impressive productivity gains, which caused the agricultural portion to devolve separately, in many cases, into smaller-scale, even sharecropped, production. Still, merchant capitalists sometimes played important roles even in this hybridized industry. Jacob Lemann of Ascension Parish, Louisiana, who had begun as a peddler in the 1840s, branched out after the war into cane production, but maintained his retail interests with a plantation store that accepted company scrip. The Kempners of Galveston, Texas, rose from similarly humble origins to become commission merchants and bankers during the late nineteenth century, and they ultimately founded Imperial Sugar on the Texas mainland.[26]

[25] Rothstein, "New South and the International Economy," 399–400. On mill villages see Carlton, *Mill and Town*; on merchants' role in organizing them, see ibid., esp. p. 58. Despite working within very different frameworks, similar conclusions about the significance of "market paternalism" to the New South are reached by Mandle, *Not Slave, Not Free*, esp. pp. 62–3 (quotation); and Lee J. Alston and Joseph P. Ferrie, *Southern Paternalism and the American Welfare State: Economics, Politics, and Institutions in the South, 1865–1965* (New York, 1999), esp. pp. 30–3; see also Jay Mandle, *The Roots of Black Poverty: The Southern Plantation Economy after the Civil War* (Durham, NC, 1978).

[26] On Lemann see Ashkenazi, *Business of Jews in Louisiana*, chap. 2, esp. 32–3; on the Kempners see Harold M. Hyman, *Oleander Odyssey: The Kempners of Galveston, Texas, 1854–1980s* (College Station, TX, 1990). On the shift to wage labor in Louisiana sugar see Louis Ferleger, "The Problem of 'Labor' in the Post-Reconstruction Louisiana Sugar Industry," *Agricultural History* 72 (Spring 1998), 140–58 (quotation on p. 141); and John C. Rodrigue, *Reconstruction in the Cane Fields: From Slavery to Free Labor in Louisiana's Sugar Parishes, 1862–1880* (Baton Rouge, 2001); on the role of stores in the sugar region, see ibid., 150–2, 189. For discussions of the effects of mechanization in the industry, see Ferleger, "Farm Mechanization in the Louisiana

Overall, however, despite such advances in a few subregional pockets and sectors, modern forms of capitalist industrialization were slow to take root in the post–Civil War South. The lack of a capital-goods sector was evidence of industrialization's shallow penetration of the region, and its absence also reflected continued resistance to achieving productivity growth through investments in technological innovation. Indeed, the preternaturally cautious investment mentality of merchant capitalism was deeply ingrained in the South. "The business environment of the postbellum South materially shaped the character of southern entrepreneurship itself," as two historians recently concluded. Local investors "enforced their own distinctly conservative financial goals on the enterprises they aided, contributing to the undynamic, even stodgy nature" of southern industry. Again, this state of affairs had its analogue in the long, uneven European transition to capitalism. Proto-industrializing rural areas beholden to merchant capitalists had also failed to see much in the way of so-called multiplier effects during the seventeenth and eighteenth centuries. Instead, given "the absence of subsidiary and service industries, which would have made possible external savings," such regions exhibited a mean tendency toward economic stagnation.[27]

The conservative nature of southern investment is visible in areas besides industry. The Genoveses noted how merchant capital siphoned off profits from the international cotton trade in the antebellum period, thereby inhibiting the minimal multiplier effects available for "investment in human capital" (p. 49), most notably in education – a situation that did not improve after emancipation. Also, the explosive growth of rural and small-town stores, apart from the structural vacuum they filled as financial intermediaries in staple-crop production, was prompted in part by low capital requirements, since historically, incomes derived from retailing have been relatively more stable in depressed or underdeveloped regions. Even when town-based storeowners did enjoy a measure of success, they most frequently favored investments in real estate (despite plummeting postwar land values), which reflected the oft-observed tendency of merchant capitalists to "refeudalize" themselves; that is, not only to spend their profits on forms of conspicuous consumption in pursuit of social prestige, but more important, also to invest their wealth in real estate in an attempt to

---

Sugar Sector after the Civil War," *Louisiana History* 23 (Winter 1982), 21–34; and Ferleger, "Productivity Change in the Post-Bellum Louisiana Sugar Industry," in *Time Series Analysis*, eds. O. D. Anderson and M. R. Perryman (New York, 1981), 147–61. Cf. John A. Heitmann's account of institutional change in *The Modernization of the Louisiana Sugar Industry, 1830–1910* (Baton Rouge, 1987).

[27] Kriedte et al., *Industrialization before Industrialization*, 124, 148 (quotation); David L. Carlton and Peter A. Coclanis, "Capital Mobilization and Southern Industry, 1880–1905: The Case of the Carolina Piedmont," *Journal of Economic History* 49 (March 1989), 75 (quotations); Carlton and Coclanis, "The Uninventive South? A Quantitative Look at Region and American Inventiveness," *Technology and Culture* 36 (April 1995), 302–26; Louis Ferleger, "Capital Goods and Southern Economic Development," *Journal of Economic History* 45 (June 1985), 411–17.

mimic the nobility and lesser gentry. By thus fusing mercantile interests with the sedentary lifestyle of landed property, many small-town southern merchants transformed themselves, at least partly, into a rentier class. Such conservative investment mentalities were duplicated at the upper end of the merchant capitalist scale as well. Despite the weak and dependent nature of postbellum southern banking, sociologist Rupert Vance estimated that nearly a third of the prime cotton land of the South was owned by banks and other advanced institutional forms of merchant capital (such as insurance companies) by 1930.[28]

As in banking, as in textile mills, as elsewhere, the New South was fundamentally what C. Vann Woodward long ago characterized as a "colonial economy." But this convenient label need not serve as a substitute for further analysis. David L. Carlton and Peter A. Coclanis have articulated a more sophisticated version of Woodward's assessment in their "quantitative look" at the dearth of technological innovation in the New South. They conclude that "southern entrepreneurs, the conservative legatees of a society deficient in business or technological skills, were perfectly willing to become, in effect, franchisees of the already developed ... manufacturing belt" of the northeastern "core." Even in cotton production, the Delta Pine & Land Company of Scott, Mississippi – an advanced "business plantation" sometimes used to exemplify the modern capitalistic tendencies of postbellum southern agriculture – was owned by a consortium of English investors. Such relationships lent many southern neo-plantation owner-operators the less-than-endearing character of what Barbara J. Fields has called "a decadent colonial ruling class." But even so, the New South still lagged well behind regions such as the West in attracting foreign investment dollars, perhaps because, as historian Douglas Dowd suggested, "inhibiting forms of economic and social organization were absent" in the West that might have constituted "significant institutional obstacles" to capitalist development. Instead, the trajectory of postbellum southern economic development remained low, largely due to the limited entrepreneurial horizons of a comprador class of merchants who favored essentially preindustrial, decidedly non-bourgeois, and frequently perverse forms of production relations for the New South – from sharecropping and tenancy to mill villages and convict labor.[29]

[28] Vance cited in Charles S. Johnson, Edwin R. Embree, and W. W. Alexander, *The Collapse of Cotton Tenancy: Summary of Field Studies and Statistical Surveys, 1933–35* (Chapel Hill, 1935), 33. Carlton and Coclanis, "Capital Mobilization," 86; Merrington, "Town and Country," 183–84. Adam Smith also noted that "merchants are frequently ambitious of becoming country gentlemen"; *Wealth of Nations*, Book III, chap. 4, pp. 519–20. Thomas S. Berry, "Comment," appended to Barger, "Income Originating in Trade," 334–5. A study of postbellum southern banking is still badly needed, but see Carlton and Coclanis, "Capital Mobilization"; Carlton, *Mill and Town*, 31–2; and John A. James, "Financial Underdevelopment in the Postbellum South," *Journal of Interdisciplinary History* 11 (Winter 1981), 443–54.

[29] Rothstein, "New South and the International Economy," 393–5; Dowd, "Comparative Analysis," 275 (quotations); Woodman, "Postbellum Social Change," 219–22; Woodman, "Political Economy of the New South," 800, 809–10; Barbara Jeanne Fields, "The Advent of Capitalist

The Genoveses argued that "to the extent that [merchant capital] escaped becoming an agent of industrial capital" in the Old South, "it eventually became an impediment to the capitalist mode of production" (p. 7). With a peculiar investment ethos that blended opportunistic market gambles and tight-fisted conservatism (in contradistinction to the sober and thrifty bourgeois industrialist), the typical southern merchant capitalist preferred to stick with the quick payoffs from the economic games he knew best and was therefore not particularly inclined to seek capitalist development on the northern or English model. Such forms of property and social relations were not only too unfamiliar; they were also potentially too confining. For example, rights-based bourgeois egalitarianism was somewhat less comfortable sanctioning the iron fist of institutionally condoned violence, a method of control to which precapitalist rulers frequently and shamelessly resorted. Yet at the same time, neither was the velvet glove of paternalism its preferred method of maintaining social hierarchy and privilege.[30]

However, despite their mutation from urban factorage to the dispersed institutional form of rural furnishing stores – a process that paralleled the decentralization of the plantation system itself – postbellum merchants did strongly favor the rapid revitalization of cotton production, the old regional lifeblood. In pursuit of this goal, most merchants were still symbiotically drawn toward alliances with their old friends among the rural planter elite. Yet by helping to perpetuate the old regime, merchants in the New South helped prolong the South's transition to a bourgeois society, one that would have been more consonant with national and global trends. The priorities and techniques of merchant capitalism thus remained a crucial prop to the postbellum southern political economy, although less as an entrenched mode of production than as a congeries of precapitalist practices and mentalities that staggered along until made thoroughly obsolete under the interrelated pressures of the Great Depression and the New Deal.[31]

Agriculture: The New South in a Bourgeois World," in Glymph and Kushma, eds., *Essays on the Postbellum Southern Economy*, 87 (quotation); Carlton and Coclanis, "The Uninventive South?" 325 (quotation); Woodward, *Origins of the New South*, chap. 11. For a recent analysis of "core vs. periphery" relationships in the postbellum United States, see Richard Franklin Bensel, *The Political Economy of American Industrialization, 1877–1900* (Cambridge, UK, and other cities, 2000). On the important role of convict labor in the New South, see Alex Lichtenstein, *Twice the Work of Free Labor: The Political Economy of Convict Labor in the New South* (London and New York, 1996).

[30] On institutional violence in proto-industrial regimes, see Kriedte et al., *Industrialization before Industrialization*, 126; on neopaternalism in the New South, see Mandle, *Not Slave, Not Free*, esp. 62–3.

[31] In her wide-ranging analysis of the postbellum South, historical sociologist Susan Archer Mann called attention to Harriet Friedmann's distinction between "forms" and "modes" of production, which may help us to understand "agrarian social classes as having an internal logic not entirely subsumed or defined by market relations"; Mann, *Agrarian Capitalism in Theory and Practice* (Chapel Hill and London, 1990), 24–5. By contrast, economist Jay R. Mandle has

A few caveats are now in order. Admittedly, economic development in the New South as a whole was uneven: cotton production shifted steadily westward, with consequent subregional differentiation within the Black Belt itself; other agricultural staples such as sugar, rice, and tobacco experienced their own unique path-dependencies; and there were indeed a few important pockets of industrialization and urbanization in the region. But if one focuses on any of these as representative of the New South, a case can be made for practically anything. The overarching role played by merchant capital, however, provides a stronger basis for understanding the postbellum region as a whole, one that does not short-shrift the deep roots laid down by the slave-based mode of production, and one that acknowledges how improbable it was that these roots were extracted with the stroke of a pen at Appomattox.

In terms of "continuity or change" – that tired old saw of southern history – it is not this epilogue's intention to pitch permanent camp with the former. (Indeed, one of the more intriguing aspects of the "New [Capitalist"] South" interpretation is its congruence with the rise of a wider historiographical paradigm that emphasizes global interconnections, thereby finessing problems such as "continuity vs. change" by focusing on convergence processes.) Nevertheless, it is difficult to dispute the wisdom of looking for elements of the old in the new. By contrast, the recent stress in southern history has been to emphasize the radical, all-encompassing break with the past that emancipation represented. But as historian Martin J. Wiener has pointed out, many socioeconomic explanations, whether Marxist or neoclassical, tend to neglect "residual factors." More specifically, Geoffrey Ingham has shown how Marxists have frequently "underestimated the efficacy of the *political* conditions of existence of non-productive forms" such as merchant capital, in particular by neglecting the persistence and metamorphosis of powerful London-based financial interests in Great Britain.[32]

Such arguments also hold true for the many more-or-less Marxist interpretations of the postemancipation South that downplay the persistence of older, prebourgeois forms of social relations in favor of schematic views that assume the abolition of slavery necessarily propelled the region forward toward liberal bourgeois capitalism. But a better understanding of southern sharecropping as a transitional, jerry-rigged form of production, neither feudal nor capitalist,

characterized the New South as having its own mode of production distinct from the rest of the U.S. based on its "decisively different" plantation economy; Mandle, *Not Slave, Not Free*, 65. See also the similar conclusions of historical geographer Charles H. Aiken in *The Cotton Plantation South since the Civil War* (Baltimore and London, 1998), chaps. 2 and 3.

[32] Wiener, *English Culture and the Decline of the Industrial Spirit*, 4; Ingham, *Capitalism Divided?* 38 (emphasis in original). See also the discussion of southern historiography set partly in the context of older debates over "continuity and change" in Lichtenstein, *Twice the Work of Free Labor*, 3–13. For an important example of the emergent "globalizing" paradigm in the historical profession, see Thomas Bender, *A Nation Among Nations: America's Place in World History* (New York, 2006).

should help make clear that a "bourgeois society" was not a normative or imperative outcome of emancipation. Indeed, just because one retrospectively posits an unstable transitional form, this should not presuppose the precise direction toward which a society is thus said to be "in transition." To give one important example, Barbara J. Fields emphasized hybridity in her sophisticated account of the "advent of capitalist agriculture" in the postbellum South, but she also insisted that emancipation "imposed a definite direction upon the ensuing period of transition." The global consolidation of capitalism in the late nineteenth century, she insisted, "[lent] unity to widely scattered events that superficially appeared each to follow its own idiosyncratic logic." Yet Fields's stance has a certain teleological quality, one in which cause-and-effect are not adequately established. Although she was right to argue that a fully developed capitalist economy in the South was delayed until roughly World War II, the cause of that development can arguably be attributed less to the gradual gestation of embryonic bourgeois social relations than to empirically observable changes such as mechanization, outmigration, and the collapse of sharecropping during the Depression. It is also historiographically ironic that the perspective promoted most effectively by Fields and Harold D. Woodman (but mimicked by many others) seems to assume an inherent momentum toward capitalist relations in the absence of slavery – a position those same scholars condemn when it is advanced by neoclassical proponents of "free-market" development.[33]

At his best, Karl Marx himself knew better. Even though he focused most of his energies on uncovering "the innermost secret" of modern capitalist development, which he thought was located in the relationship between bourgeoisie and proletariat, he admitted that there are "endless variations and gradations" that are "the result of innumerable different empirical circumstances, natural conditions, racial relations, [and] historical influences acting from outside, ... and these can only be understood by analyzing these empirically given conditions" (*Capital* III, 927). Historians, in this sense, should be more willing to combine theory and practice by comparing capitalist development in disparate periods and places, using concepts like proto-industrialization to synthesize long-standing "either/or" debates over transitional epochs.

The transnational dimensions of Marx's comment (like his understanding of capitalism in general) are also relevant to historians of the Atlantic world. It is not coincidental that the Atlantic paradigm has become what Peter Coclanis calls the "official establishment position" during the two decades since the Soviet Union's collapse, an event that many younger scholars wrongly believe to have thoroughly discredited Marxist historical practice. Regardless, while some Atlantic histories describe merchants in various contexts, fewer works

<hr/>

[33] Barbara J. Fields, "The Advent of Capitalist Agriculture: The New South in a Bourgeois World," in Glymph and Kushma, eds., *Essays on the Postbellum Southern Economy*, 73–94 (quotations on pp. 74 and 77).

are sufficiently explicit as to their theoretical assumptions, which makes their assessments of merchants' significance less convincing and suppresses their ability to provide useful comparisons.[34]

Indeed, this study's findings suggest that the notion of an "Atlantic world" is not only underconceptualized in theory but also unevenly applied in practice. Two interrelated examples will suffice. First is the lack of attention that New Orleans has received from Atlantic historians. A handful of works focus mainly on colonial-era New Orleans and the Louisiana Territory it anchored, yet the city barely merits an index entry in the two major textbooks on Atlantic history that have been published to date, and it was ignored in a collection of essays on Atlantic port cities. Despite its obvious credentials as a multiracial, transnational site of exchange, New Orleans has also been neglected in monographs focused on the Ibero-Catholic zone of the South Atlantic, on whose northern rim the city was perched.[35]

Explaining this neglect brings up the second point: the odd reluctance of Atlantic historians to venture into the nineteenth century – which was, of course, when New Orleans grew most rapidly. Atlanticists often frame the chronological boundaries of their heuristic construct around the African slave trade that began in the mid-fifteenth century, and rightly so, yet the vast majority of their works focus on the seventeenth and eighteenth centuries. Atlantic-themed studies that extend past the so-called Age of Revolutions, which culminated around 1820, are surprisingly exceptional, even though over 1.7 million more slaves are estimated to have been shipped to the Americas during the half-century afterward. This lack of attention to the nineteenth century, acknowledged by some, suggests that historians have not explored the conditions that constituted

---

[34] An important exception to this trend is Blackburn, *Making of New World Slavery*, a revisionist Marxist study that emphasizes the links between slavery and merchant capital in Atlantic development; see also Johnson, "Pedestal and the Veil." Peter Coclanis, "Beyond Atlantic History," in *Atlantic History: A Critical Appraisal*, eds. Jack P. Greene and Philip D. Morgan (New York, 2009), 337. Atlantic-themed histories centered on merchants begin with Bernard Bailyn, *The New England Merchants in the Seventeenth Century* (1955; repr., New York, 1964); see also the many contributions made by economic historian Jacob M. Price, such as *Capital and Credit in British Overseas Trade: The View from the Chesapeake, 1700–1776* (Cambridge, MA, 1980). See also David Hancock, *Citizens of the World: London Merchants and the Integration of the British Atlantic Community, 1735–1785* (New York, 1995); and Pierre Gervais, "Neither Imperial, Nor Atlantic: A Merchant Perspective on International Trade in the Eighteenth Century," *History of European Ideas* 34 (December 2008), 465–73.

[35] Douglas Egerton et al., *The Atlantic World: A History, 1400–1888* (Wheeling, IL, 2007) mentions New Orleans four times in passing; the city does not appear at all in Thomas Benjamin, *The Atlantic World: Europeans, Africans, and Their Shared History* (New York, 2009). Franklin W. Knight and Peggy K. Liss, eds., *Atlantic Port Cities: Economy, Culture, and Society in the Atlantic World, 1650–1850* (Knoxville, TN, 1991); Bradley G. Bond, ed., *French Colonial Louisiana and the Atlantic World* (Baton Rouge, 2005). New Orleans is mapped but otherwise ignored in two acclaimed recent monographs: Jeremy Adelman, *Sovereignty and Revolution in the Iberian Atlantic* (Princeton, NJ, 2006); and J. H. Elliott's monumental comparative study, *Empires of the Atlantic World: Britain and Spain in America, 1492–1830* (New Haven, 2006).

the Atlantic world's decline with the same vigor they have devoted to its origins and consolidation. The supercession of exchange-based economies – many of them grounded in networks of slave-produced commodities formed and maintained under merchant capital auspices – by industrial regimes driven by domestic consumer demand was an important factor in this decline. Certainly, that is suggested by the experience of nineteenth-century New Orleans – along with the wider South of which it was such a vital cog.[36]

As for southern historians, if they hope to move their accounts "beyond planters and industrialists" (as James C. Cobb admonished them a generation ago), then their analyses of the New South should pay greater heed to other groups, institutions, and structures; their adaptation to the changes that accompanied emancipation; and the various desperate and often successful attempts to preserve as much order and stability from the *ancien regime* as possible. And for their part, business and economic historians ought to devote more attention to the complexities introduced by what Marx described as the "division of labor between types of capital" – especially the role of distribution and exchange, the bailiwick of merchant capital, as more than a mere "factor of production" in Western economies that were becoming increasingly consumer-oriented and financially dominated beginning in the late nineteenth century. Ultimately, a greater appreciation of merchant capital's continuing role in the postbellum southern, American, and global economies might also help us trace the historical continuities that underlie the recent emergence of a small-town Arkansas retailer to its current position as the United States's largest employer and the world's largest multinational corporation – that is, to better understand how, over the last 150 years, the southern economy has gradually, but with relative consistency, shifted its foundation from whips to Wal-Marts.[37]

---

[36] On historians' neglect of the Atlantic world during the nineteenth century, see Alison Games, "Atlantic History: Definitions, Challenges, and Opportunities," *American Historical Review* 111 (June 2006), 747–8; and Donna Gabaccia, "A Long Atlantic in a Wider World," *Atlantic Studies* 1 No.1 (2004), 1–27. A crucial exception to this neglect is Rebecca J. Scott, *Degrees of Freedom: Louisiana and Cuba after Slavery* (Cambridge, MA, 2005). Figures on slave imports to the Americas after 1820 are derived from Herbert S. Klein, *The Atlantic Slave Trade* (New York, 1999), Appendix Table A.2 (pp. 210–11).

[37] Nelson Lichtenstein suggests historical links between merchant capitalism and Wal-Mart in "The Return of Merchant Capitalism," *International Labor and Working-Class History* 81 (March 2012), 8–27; I am grateful for an earlier version that he shared with me. James C. Cobb, "Beyond Planters and Industrialists: A New Perspective on the New South," *Journal of Southern History* 54 (February 1988), 45–68.

Bibliography

I. Archival Sources

Baker Library Historical Collections, Harvard Business School

R. G. Dun & Company Credit Report Collections

Library of Congress

Abraham Lincoln Papers
[R. G. Dun & Co.] Mercantile Agency Reference Books, 1866–1880 (semi-annual)

Louisiana and Lower Mississippi Valley Collection, Louisiana State University

J. M. Ellis Papers
Samuel Haas Letterpress Copybook, 1887
Lebret & Hearsey Record Books, 1838–1875
Lebret Diary, 1858–61
Mann, Fischer & Co. Account Books, 1869–1880
Mercantile Agency Reference Book, Louisiana, 1890
John McKowen Papers, 1830–1898

Louisiana Division, New Orleans Public Library

Administrations of the Mayors of New Orleans (typescript, 1931)
Census of Merchants, 1854, City of New Orleans, Treasurer's Office
Fourth U.S. District Court (New Orleans) Records
W[alter] Cox & Co. Letters, 1860–61

Howard-Tilton Memorial Library, Tulane University

Jacob Barker Letters

Mrs. Frank M. Besthoff Collection
Joseph Slemmons Copes Papers
Cotton Trade Series
John G. Dunlap Correspondence
Rosamonde E. and Emile Kuntz Collection
New Orleans Cotton Exchange Collection
Standard Fruit & Steamship Company Papers

Southern Historical Collection, Wilson Library, University of North Carolina at Chapel Hill

Jackson, Riddle & Company Papers
Wyche-Otey Family Papers
W. H. T. Squires Papers
Bruno Trombly Diary and Papers

West Feliciana Parish Courthouse, St. Francisville, LA

Mortgage Records, 1855–1878
Conveyance Books, 1868–1885

Williams Research Center, The Historic New Orleans Collection

Louisiana Manuscripts Collection (MSS 579)
Federal Occupation of New Orleans Collection (MSS 577)

Woodson Research Center, Rice University

Kuntz Civil War Collection
Charles P. Leverich Papers, 1833–1851

II. Contemporary Periodicals and Newspapers

Atlantic Monthly
Banker's Magazine
Century Illustrated Magazine
De Bow's Review
Harper's New Monthly Magazine
Hunt's Merchant's Magazine
Port Record
Southern Literary Messenger
[Appleton's] *American Annual Cyclopedia and Register of Important Events of the Year 1861* (New York, 1870)
[Appleton's] *American Annual Cyclopedia and Register of Important Events of the Year 1862* (New York, 1865)
Gardner's New Orleans City Directories, 1858–1878
[Alexandria] *Louisiana Democrat*
[Alexandria, LA] *Red River Whig*

Harrisonburg [LA] *Independent*
New Orleans *Daily Picayune*
New Orleans *Daily Crescent*
New Orleans *Daily Delta*
New Orleans *Daily True Delta*
New Orleans *News-Letter and General Weekly Review*
New Orleans *Price Current*
New Orleans *Times*
[St. Francisville, LA] *West Feliciana Sentinel*

III. Government Publications

[Israel D. Andrews], *Report of Israel D. Andrews on the Trade and Commerce of the British North American Colonies, and Upon the Trade of the Great Lakes and Rivers,* Senate Executive Document No. 112 (32 Cong., 1st Sess.) (Washington, DC, 1853).
Eighth Census of the United States *(1860),* Vol. I: *Population and Other Statistics* (Washington, DC, 1864).
Joseph Nimmo Jr., *Report on the Internal Commerce of the United States,* 48 Cong., 2d Sess., Ex.Doc. 7, Part 3 (Washington, DC, 1885).
Official Journal of the House of Representatives of the State of Louisiana, Session of November 1861 (Baton Rouge, 1861).
Official Records of the Union and Confederate Navies in the War of the Rebellion (Washington, DC, 1922).
Report of the [House] Select Committee on the New Orleans Riots (Washington, DC, 1867).
Statistical Abstract of the United States, No. 22 (1899; repr., New York, 1964).
Report of the Joint Committee on the Conduct of the War, 38 Cong., 2 Sess. (3 vols., Washington, DC, 1865).
"Report of the Special Commission" [Smith-Brady Report], September 23, 1865, Old Army Records (RG-94), Vol. 737 (microfilm, National Archives).
Raphael P. Thian, comp., *Reports of the Secretary of the Treasury of the Confederate States of America, 1861–65* (Washington, DC, 1878).
    Extracts from the Journals of the Provisional Congress and of the First and Second Congresses of the Confederate States of America on Legislation Affecting Finance, Revenue, and Commerce, 1861–65 (Washington, DC, 1880).
U.S. Manuscript Census, 1850, Schedule I, Free Inhabitants, Town of Bayou Sara, West Feliciana Parish, Louisiana.
U.S. Treasury Department, Bureau of Statistics, *Monthly Summary of Commerce and Finance of the United States, January 1900* (Washington, DC, 1900).
The War of the Rebellion: A Compilation of the Official Records of the Union and Confederate Armies (Washington, DC, 1900–).

IV. Published Primary Sources (Books and Articles)

Horace Adams, ed., "Arkansas Traveler, 1852–1853: The Diary of John W. Brown," *Journal of Southern History* 4 (August 1938).
[Anonymous], *New Orleans As It Is: Its Manners and Morals ...* (Utica, NY, 1849).

Thomas Ashe, *Travels in America Performed in the Year 1806* (London, 1809).

Elliott Ashkenazi, ed., *The Civil War Diary of Clara Solomon: Growing Up in New Orleans, 1861–1862* (Baton Rouge, 1995).

Edward Bacon, *Among the Cotton Thieves* (Detroit, 1867).

[Jacob Barker], *Incidents in the Life of Jacob Barker, of New Orleans ... from 1800 to 1855* (Washington, DC, 1855).

James Bennet, *The American System of Practical Book-Keeping....* (21st ed., 1842; repr., New York, 1976).

Biographical and Historical Memoirs of Louisiana (2 vols.; Chicago, 1892).

Biographical and Historical Memoirs of Northwestern Louisiana (Nashville and Chicago, 1890).

Julian P. Boyd et al., eds., *The Papers of Thomas Jefferson* (Princeton, NJ, 1965–).

James E. Boyle, *Cotton and the New Orleans Cotton Exchange: A Century of Commercial Evolution* (Garden City, NY, 1934).

John Crosby Brown, *A Hundred Years of Merchant Banking: A History of Brown Brothers and Company* (New York, 1909).

Stuart Bruchey, comp. and ed., *Cotton and the Growth of the American Economy, 1790–1860: Sources and Readings* (New York and other cities, 1967).

Clarence C. Buel, "The Degradation of a State; or, The Charitable Career of the Louisiana Lottery," *The Century Magazine* 43 (February 1892), 618–33.

Benjamin F. Butler, *Butler's Book: Autobiography and Personal Reminiscences of Major-General Benjamin F. Butler* (Boston, 1892).

George Washington Cable, *Old Creole Days* (1885 ed.; repr., New York, 1964).

The Creoles of Louisiana (1884; repr., New York, 1970).

John E. Cairnes, *The Slave Power: Its Character, Career, and Probable Designs* (1862; repr., Columbia, SC, 2003).

[Salmon P. Chase], "Diary and Correspondence of Salmon P. Chase," *Annual Report of the American Historical Association for the Year 1902* (2 vols., Washington, DC, 1903).

David Christy, *Cotton Is King: or, The Culture of Cotton ...* (1855; 2nd ed., New York, 1856).

Stephen Colwell, *The South: A Letter from a Friend in the North, with Special Reference to the Effects of Disunion upon Slavery* (Philadelphia, 1856).

The Five Cotton States and New York (Philadelphia, 1861).

W. C. Corsan, *Two Months in the Confederate States: An Englishman's Travels Through the South*, ed. Benjamin H. Trask (1863; repr., Baton Rouge and London, 1996).

John F. Cowan, *A New Invasion of the South: Being a Narrative of the Expedition of the Seventy-First Infantry, National Guard, Through the Southern States to New Orleans* (New York, 1881).

J. A. Dacus, *A Guide to Success, with Forms for Business and Society* (St. Louis, 1880).

Robert M. Davis, *The Southern Planter, the Factor, and the Banker* (New Orleans, 1871).

T. C. DeLeon, *Our Creole Carnivals: Their Origin, History, Progress, and Results* (Mobile, AL, 1890).

John Richard Dennett, *The South As It Is, 1865–1866*, ed. Henry M. Christman (Athens, Ga., and London, 1986).

E. J. Donnell, *Chronological and Statistical History of Cotton* (1872; repr., Wilmington, DE, 1973).

J. W. Dorr, "A Tourist's Description of Louisiana in 1860," ed. Walter Prichard, *Louisiana Historical Quarterly* 21 (October 1938), 1110–79.

Sarah A. Dorsey, *Recollections of Henry Watkins Allen, Brigadier-General Confederate States Army [and] Ex-Governor of Louisiana* (New York and New Orleans, 1866).

J[ohn] F. Entz, *Exchange and Cotton Trade between England and the United States* (New York, 1840).

Walter L. Fleming, ed., *General W. T. Sherman as College President ... 1859–1861* (Cleveland, OH, 1912).

Paul Leicester Ford, comp. and ed., *The Writings of Thomas Jefferson* (New York, 1897).

A. Oakey Hall, *The Manhattaner in New Orleans; or, Phases of Crescent City Life* (New York, 1851).

M[atthew] B. Hammond, *The Cotton Industry: An Essay in American Economic History*. Part I: The Cotton Culture and the Cotton Trade (New York, 1897).

Hinton Rowan Helper, *The Impending Crisis of the South: How to Meet It*, ed. George M. Fredrickson (1857; repr., Cambridge, MA, 1968).

George H. Hepworth, *The Whip, Hoe, and Sword; or, The Gulf-department in '63* (Boston, 1864).

Daniel R. Hundley, *Social Relations in Our Southern States* (New York, 1860).

[Illinois Central Railroad], *The Commercial, Industrial, and Financial Outlook for New Orleans* (Cedar Rapids, IA, 1894).

J. H. Ingraham, *The Sunny South; or, The Southerner at Home....* (Philadelphia, 1860).

Robert U. Johnson and Clarence C. Buel, eds., *Battles and Leaders of the Civil War* (4 vols., 1887; repr., New York, 1956).

Thomas Prentice Kettell, *Southern Wealth and Northern Profits* (New York, 1860).

Edward King, *The Great South*, eds. W. Magruder Drake and Robert R. Jones (1875; repr. Baton Rouge, 1972).

William Kingsford, *Impressions of the West and South during a Six Weeks' Holiday* (Toronto, 1858).

Thomas W. Knox, *Camp-Fire and Cotton-Field: Southern Adventure in Time of War* (New York, 1865).

Gazaway B. Lamar [ed.], *Proceedings of the Bank Convention of the Confederate States Held at Richmond, Va., July 24th, 25th, and 26th, 1861* (Charleston, SC, 1861).

Benjamin Henry Boneval Latrobe, *Impressions Respecting New Orleans: Diary and Sketches, 1818–1820*, ed. Samuel Wilson Jr. (New York, 1951).

Samuel H. Lockett, *Louisiana As It Is: A Geographical and Topographical Description of the State*, ed. Lauren C. Post (orig. ms. 1869–72; Baton Rouge, 1969).

James Longstreet, *From Manassas to Appomattox: Memoirs of the Civil War in America* (1896; repr., Bloomington, IN, 1960).

[Daniel Lord], *The Effect of Secession upon the Commercial Relations between the North and South, and upon Each Section* (New York, 1861).

Sidney A. Marchand, ed., *The Flight of a Century (1800–1900) in Ascension Parish, Louisiana* (Donaldsonville, LA, 1936).

Don C. Marler, ed., *The Carruth Journals, 1872–1902* (Woodville, TX, 1996).

Jessie Ames Marshall, comp., *Private and Official Correspondence of Gen. Benjamin F. Butler during the Period of the Civil War* (5 vols..; Norwood, MA, 1917).

Karl Marx, *On America and the Civil War*, ed. and trans. Saul K. Padover (New York, 1972).

Karl Marx and Frederick Engels, *The Civil War in the United States*, ed. Richard Enmale (2nd ed.; New York, 1940).

[John McDonogh], *The Last Will and Testament of John McDonogh....* (New Orleans, 1851).

Andrew Morrison, *The Industries of New Orleans ... Historical, Descriptive, Statistical* (New Orleans, 1885).

[William Mure], "Financial and Economic Disturbance in New Orleans on the Eve of Secession," ed. Milledge L. Bonham, *Louisiana Historical Quarterly* 13 (January 1930), 32–6.

[Eugène Musson], *Letter to Napoleon III on Slavery in the Southern States, by a Creole of Louisiana* (London, 1862).

Vincent Nolte, *The Memoirs of Vincent Nolte, or Fifty Years in Both Hemispheres*, trans. Burton Rascoe (1854; repr., New York, 1934).

Charles Nordhoff, *The Cotton States in the Spring and Summer of 1875* (1876; repr., New York, 1971).

Frederick Law Olmsted, *The Cotton Kingdom: A Traveller's Observations on Cotton and Slavery in the American Slave States*, ed. Arthur M. Schlesinger (New York, 1953).

Charles H. Otken, *The Ills of the South* (New York and London, 1894).

James A. Padgett, ed., "Some Letters of George Stanton Denison, 1854–1866: Observations of a Yankee on Conditions in Louisiana and Texas," *Louisiana Historical Quarterly* 23 (October 1940).

[Reverend] B. M. Palmer, *The Oath of Allegiance to the United States, Discussed in Its Moral and Political Bearings* (Richmond, VA, 1863).

James Parton, *General Butler in New Orleans; Being a History of the Administration of the Department of the Gulf in the Year 1862* (New York, 1864).

Samuel J. Peters, *An Address to the Legislature of Louisiana, Showing the Importance of the Credit System on the Prosperity of the United States, and Particularly Its Influence on the Agricultural, Commercial, and Manufacturing Interests of Louisiana* (New Orleans, 1837).

Edwards Pierrepont, *A Review by Judge Pierrepont of Gen. Butler's Defense Before the House of Representatives in Relation to the New Orleans Gold* (New York, 1865).

G. W. Pierson, [ed.], "Alexis de Tocqueville in New Orleans," *Franco-American Review* 1 (1936).

James M. Phillippo, *The United States and Cuba* (London, 1857).

Walter Prichard, ed., "The Origin and Activities of the 'White League' in New Orleans (Reminiscences of a Participant in the Movement)," *Louisiana Historical Quarterly* 23 (April 1940), 525–43.

Whitelaw Reid, *After the War: A Tour of the Southern States, 1865–1866* (1866; repr., New York, 1965).

Henry Rightor, ed., *Standard History of New Orleans* (Chicago, 1900).

James Robb, *A Southern Confederacy: Letters from James Robb, Late a Citizen of New Orleans, to an American in Paris, and Hon. Alexander H. Stephens, of Georgia* (Chicago, 1862).

James Robertson, *A Few Months in America* (London, 1855).

Clinton Rossiter, ed., *The Federalist Papers* (New York, 2003).

Kate Mason Rowland and Mrs. Morris L. Croxall, eds., *The Journal of Julia LeGrand: New Orleans, 1862–1863* (Richmond, VA, 1911).

Robert Russell, *North America: Its Agriculture and Climate* (Edinburgh, 1858).

William Howard Russell, *My Diary North and South* (Boston, 1863).

J. E. Hilary Skinner, *After the Storm; or, Jonathan and His Neighbours in 1865–6* (2 vols., London, 1866).

Adam Smith, *The Wealth of Nations*, ed. Andrew Skinner (1776; New York and other cities, 1986).

Robert Somers, *The Southern States Since the War, 1870–71* (1871; repr., University, AL, 1965).

Marion Southwood, *Beauty and Booty: The Watchword of New Orleans* (New York, 1867).

James Spence, *The American Union* (London, 1861).

Kate Stone, *Brokenburn: The Journal of Kate Stone, 1861–1868*, ed. John Q. Anderson (Baton Rouge, 1955).

James Stuart, *Three Years in North America* (2 vols., 1828; rev. ed., Edinburgh, 1833).

William Carter Stubbs, *Handbook of Louisiana, Giving Geographical and Agricultural Features....* (New Orleans, 1895).

Edward Sullivan, *Rambles and Scrambles in North and South America* (London, 1852).

Alexis de Tocqueville, *Democracy in America*, introduction by Alan Ryan (New York, 1994).

R. D. Turner, *The Conspiracy Trials of 1826 and 1827: A Chapter in the Life of Jacob Barker* (Philadelphia, 1864).

Loretta Janeta Velazquez, *The Woman in Battle: A Narrative of the Exploits, Adventures, and Travels of Madame Loretta Janeta Velazquez....* (Hartford, CT, 1876).

Jon L. Wakelyn, ed., *Southern Pamphlets on Secession, November 1860–April 1861* (Chapel Hill, 1996).

H. C. Warmoth, *War, Politics and Reconstruction: Stormy Days in Louisiana* (New York, 1930).

James L. Watkins, *King Cotton: A Historical and Statistical Review, 1790 to 1908* (1908; repr., New York, 1969).

Clyde N. Wilson and Shirley Bright Cook, eds., *The Papers of John C. Calhoun*, Vol. 26 (Columbia, SC, 2001)

V. Secondary Sources: Books

Jeffrey S. Adler, *Yankee Merchants and the Making of the Urban West* (New York and other cities, 1991).

Jean-Christophe Agnew, *Worlds Apart: The Market and the Theater in Anglo-American Thought, 1550–1750* (Cambridge, UK, and other cities, 1986).

Charles H. Aiken, *The Cotton Plantation South since the Civil War* (Baltimore and London, 1998).

Robert G. Albion, *The Rise of New York Port, 1815–1860* (1939; repr., Boston and New York, 1967).

Lee J. Alston and Joseph P. Ferrie, *Southern Paternalism and the American Welfare State: Economics, Politics, and Institutions in the South, 1865–1965* (New York, 1999).

Aaron D. Anderson, *Builders of a New South: Merchants, Capital, and the Remaking of Natchez, 1865–1914* (Jackson, MS, 2013).

O. D. Anderson and M. R. Perryman, eds., *Time Series Analysis* (New York, 1981).

Perry Anderson, *Spectrum: From Left to Right in the World of Ideas* (New York, 2005).

Ralph Andreano, ed., *The Economic Impact of the Civil War* (Cambridge, MA, 1962).

Eric Arnesen, *Waterfront Workers of New Orleans: Race, Class, and Politics, 1863–1923* (Urbana and Chicago, 1991).

Elliott Ashkenazi, *The Business of Jews in Louisiana, 1840–1875* (Tuscaloosa and London, 1988).

John Ashworth, *Slavery, Capitalism, and Politics in the Antebellum Republic*, Vol. 1: *Commerce and Compromise, 1820–1850* (New York, 1995).

Slavery, Capitalism, and Politics in the Antebellum Republic, Vol. 2: *The Coming of the Civil War, 1850–1861* (New York, 2007).

T. H. Aston and C. H. E. Philpin, eds., *The Brenner Debate* (New York, 1985).

Jeremy Atack and Peter Passell, *A New Economic View of American History from Colonial Times to 1940*, 2nd ed. (New York, 1994).

Lewis E. Atherton, *The Southern Country Store, 1800–1860* (Baton Rouge, 1949).

Edward L. Ayers, *The Promise of the New South: Life after Reconstruction* (New York and Oxford, 1992).

H. Parrott Bacot, Sally Kittredge Reeves, and John H. Lawrence, *Marie Adrien Persac: Louisiana Artist* (Baton Rouge, 2000).

Bernard Bailyn, *The New England Merchants in the Seventeenth Century* (1955; repr., New York, 1964).

Douglas B. Ball, *Financial Failure and Confederate Defeat* (Urbana and Chicago, 1991).

Edward J. Balleisen, *Navigating Failure: Bankruptcy and Commercial Society in Antebellum America* (Chapel Hill, NC, 2001).

Frederic Bancroft, *Slave-Trading in the Old South* (Baltimore, 1931).

Erik Banks, *The Rise and Decline of the Merchant Banks* (London, 1999).

Harold Barger, *Distribution's Place in the American Economy since 1869*. National Bureau of Economic Research, General Series No. 58 (Princeton, NJ, 1955).

L. Diane Barnes, Brian Schoen, and Frank Towers, eds., *The Old South's Modern Worlds: Slavery, Region, and Nation in the Age of Progress* (New York, 2011).

William L. Barney, *The Road to Secession: A New Perspective on the Old South* (New York, 1972).

The Secessionist Impulse: Alabama and Mississippi in 1860 (Princeton, NJ, 1974).

John M. Barry, *Rising Tide: The Great Mississippi Flood of 1927 and How It Changed America* (New York, 1997).

Fred Bateman and Thomas Weiss, *A Deplorable Scarcity: The Failure of Industrialization in the Slave Economy* (Chapel Hill, 1981).

James P. Baughman, *Charles Morgan and the Development of Southern Transportation* (Nashville, 1968).

Charles A. Beard and Mary R. Beard, *The Rise of American Civilization* (2 vols.; New York, 1927).

Sven Beckert, *The Monied Metropolis: New York City and the Consolidation of the American Bourgeoisie, 1850–1896* (New York, 2001).

Wyatt W. Belcher, *The Economic Rivalry between St. Louis and Chicago, 1850–1880* (New York, 1947).

Thomas Bender, ed., *The Antislavery Debate: Capitalism and Abolitionism as a Problem in Historical Interpretation* (Berkeley and Los Angeles, 1992).

Thomas Bender, *A Nation among Nations: America's Place in World History* (New York, 2006).

Christopher Benfey, *Degas in New Orleans: Encounters in the Creole World of Kate Chopin and George Washington Cable* (Berkeley, CA, and other cities, 1997).

Richard Franklin Bensel, *The Political Economy of American Industrialization, 1877–1900* (Cambridge, UK, and other cities, 2000).

Brian J. L. Berry, *Geography of Market Centers and Retail Distribution* (Englewood Cliffs, NJ, 1967).

Carolyn Earle Billingsley, *Communities of Kinship: Antebellum Families and the Settlement of the Cotton Frontier* (Athens, GA, 2004).

Robin Blackburn, *The Making of New World Slavery: From the Baroque to the Modern, 1492–1800* (2nd ed.; New York, 2010).

Mansel G. Blackford, *A History of Small Business in America* (New York, 1991).

DeAnne Blanton and Lauren M. Cook, *They Fought Like Demons: Women Soldiers in the American Civil War* (Baton Rouge, 2002).

Howard Bodenhorn, *A History of Banking in Antebellum America* (New York, 2000).

Jefferson Davis Bragg, *Louisiana in the Confederacy* (1941; repr., Baton Rouge, 1997).

Fernand Braudel, *Civilization and Capitalism, 15th–18th Century*, Vol. 2: *The Wheels of Commerce*, trans. Sian Reynolds (New York and other cities, 1982).

T. H. Breen, *Tobacco Culture: The Mentality of the Great Tidewater Planters on the Eve of Revolution* (Princeton, NJ, 1985).

Robert Brenner, *Merchants and Revolution: Commercial Change, Political Conflict, and London's Overseas Traders, 1550–1653* (Princeton, NJ, 1993).

W. R. Brock, *An American Crisis: Congress and Reconstruction, 1865–1867* (New York, 1963).

William A. Brock and David S. Evans, *The Economics of Small Businesses: Their Role and Regulation in the American Economy* (New York, 1986).

Marilyn R. Brown, *Degas and the Business of Art: A Cotton Office in New Orleans* (University Park, PA, 1994).

Stuart Bruchey, ed., *Small Business in American Life* (New York, 1980).

Steven C. Bullock, *Revolutionary Brotherhood: Freemasonry and the Transformation of the American Social Order, 1730–1840* (Chapel Hill and London, 1996).

Frank J. Byrne, *Becoming Bourgeois: Merchant Culture in the South, 1820–1865* (Lexington, KY, 2006).

T. J. Byres, ed., *Sharecropping and Sharecroppers* (London, 1983).

Stephen A. Caldwell, *A Banking History of Louisiana* (Baton Rouge, 1935).

Richard Campanella, *Time and Place in New Orleans: Past Geographies in the Present Day* (Gretna, LA, 2002).

Bienville's Dilemma: A Historical Geography of New Orleans (Lafayette, LA, 2008).

Gerald M. Capers, *Occupied City: New Orleans under the Federals, 1861–1865* (Lexington, KY, 1965).

David L. Carlton, *Mill and Town in South Carolina, 1880–1920* (Baton Rouge, 1982).

David L. Carlton and Peter A. Coclanis, *The South, the Nation, and the World: Perspectives on Southern Economic Development* (Charlottesville, VA, 2003).

Dan T. Carter, *When the War Was Over: The Failure of Self-Reconstruction in the South, 1865–1867* (Baton Rouge, 1985).

Willie Malvin Caskey, *Secession and Restoration of Louisiana* (Baton Rouge, 1938).

Youssef Cassis, *Capitals of Capital: A History of International Financial Centres, 1780–2005*, trans. Jacqueline Collier (New York, 2007).

Alfred D. Chandler Jr., *The Visible Hand: The Managerial Revolution in American Business* (Cambridge, MA, 1977).

David R. Chesnutt and Clyde N. Wilson. eds., *The Meaning of South Carolina History: Essays in Honor of George C. Rogers Jr.* (Columbia, SC, 1990).

Steven N. S. Cheung, *The Theory of Share Tenancy, with Special Application to Asian Agriculture and the First Phase of Taiwan Land Reform* (Chicago, 1969).

John G. Clark, *The Grain Trade of the Old Northwest* (Urbana, II, 1966).

     New Orleans, 1718–1812: An Economic History (Baton Rouge, 1970).

Thomas D. Clark, *Pills, Petticoats, and Plows: The Southern Country Store* (1944; repr., Norman, OK, 1989).

William Cohen, *At Freedom's Edge: Black Mobility and the Southern White Quest for Racial Control, 1861–1915* (Baton Rouge, 1991).

Arthur C. Cole, *Wholesale Commodity Prices in the United States, 1700–1861* (Cambridge, MA, 1938).

Harry A. Corbin, *The Men's Clothing Industry: Colonial through Modern Times* (New York, 1970).

E. Merton Coulter, *The Confederate States of America, 1861–1865* (Baton Rouge, 1950).

Ruth Schwartz Cowan, *A Social History of American Technology* (New York, 1997).

William Cronon, *Nature's Metropolis: Chicago and the Great West* (New York, 1991).

D. P. Crook, *The North, the South, and the Powers, 1861–1865* (New York and other cities, 1974).

James W. Daddysman, *The Matamoros Trade: Confederate Commerce, Diplomacy, and Intrigue* (Newark, DE, 1984).

Adrian C. Darnell, ed., *The Collected Economics Articles of Harold Hotelling* (New York and other cities, 1990).

Gene Dattel, *Cotton and Race in the Making of America: The Human Costs of Economic Power* (Chicago, 2009).

Paul A. David and Kenneth M. Stampp, eds., *Reckoning with Slavery: A Critical Study in the Quantitative History of American Negro Slavery* (New York, 1976).

Lance E. Davis and Douglass C. North, *Institutional Change and American Economic Growth* (Cambridge, UK, and New York, 1971).

William C. Davis, *The Pirates Laffite: The Treacherous World of the Corsairs of the Gulf* (Orlando, FL, and other cities, 2005).

Shannon Lee Dawdy, *Building the Devil's Empire: French Colonial New Orleans* (Chicago, 2008).

Steven Deyle, *Carry Me Back: The Domestic Slave Trade in American Life* (New York, 2005).

Charles B. Dew, *Bond of Iron: Master and Slave at Buffalo Forge* (New York, 1994).

Leonard Dinnerstein and Mary Dale Passon, eds., *Jews in the South* (Baton Rouge, 1973).

Maurice Dobb, *Studies in the Development of Capitalism* (1947; rev. ed., New York, 1963).

Don H. Doyle, *New Men, New Cities, New South: Atlanta, Nashville, Charleston, Mobile, 1860–1910* (Chapel Hill and London, 1990).

John N. Drobak and John V. C. Nye, eds., *The Frontiers of the New Institutional Economics* (San Diego and other cities, 1997).

W. E. B. Du Bois, *Black Reconstruction in America, 1860–1880* (1935; repr., New York, 1992).

John Duffy, *Sword of Pestilence: The New Orleans Yellow Fever Epidemic of 1853* (Baton Rouge, 1966).

Sue Eakin, *Rapides Parish: An Illustrated History* (Northridge, CA, 1987),

Clement Eaton, *The Mind of the Old South* (rev. ed., Baton Rouge, 1967).

Stanley Elkins and Eric McKitrick, *The Age of Federalism: The Early American Republic, 1788–1800* (New York and Oxford, 1993).

Stanley L. Engerman, Philip T. Hoffman, Jean-Laurent Rosenthal, and Kenneth L. Sokoloff, eds., *Finance, Intermediaries, and Economic Development* (New York, 2003).

D. A. Farnie, *The English Cotton Industry and the World Market, 1815–1896* (Oxford, 1979).

D. A. Farnie and D. J. Jeremy, eds., *The Fibre that Changed the World: The Cotton Industry in International Perspective, 1600–1990s* (Oxford and other cities, 2004).

Drew Gilpin Faust, *James Henry Hammond and the Old South: A Design for Mastery* (Baton Rouge, 1982).

Gail Feigenbaum [ed.], *Degas and New Orleans: A French Impressionist in America* (New Orleans, 1999).

Lou Ferleger, ed., *Agriculture and National Development: Views on the Nineteenth Century* (Ames, IA, 1990).

Albert Fishlow, *American Railroads and the Transformation of the Ante-Bellum Economy* (Cambridge, MA, 1965).

Robert William Fogel and Stanley L. Engerman, *Time on the Cross: The Economics of American Negro Slavery* (New York, 1974).

Fred E. Foldvary, ed., *Beyond Neoclassical Economics: Heterodox Approaches to Economic Theory* (Brookfield, VT, 1996).

Richard J. Follett, *The Sugar Masters: Planters and Slaves in Louisiana's Cane World, 1820–1860* (Baton Rouge, 2005).

Eric Foner, *Free Soil, Free Labor, Free Men: The Ideology of the Republican Party before the Civil War* (New York, 1970).

Reconstruction: America's Unfinished Revolution, 1863–1877 (New York, 1988).

Philip S. Foner, *Business and Slavery: The New York Merchants and the Irrepressible Conflict* (Chapel Hill, NC, 1941).

Lacy K. Ford, ed., *A Companion to the Civil War and Reconstruction* (Malden, MA, 2005).

Gaines M. Foster, *Ghosts of the Confederacy: Defeat, the Lost Cause, and the Emergence of the New South* (New York, 1987).

Ray A. Foulke, *The Sinews of American Commerce* (New York, 1941).

Elizabeth Fox-Genovese and Eugene D. Genovese, *Fruits of Merchant Capital: Slavery and Bourgeois Property in the Rise and Expansion of Capitalism* (Oxford and other cities, 1983).

The Mind of the Master Class: History and Faith in the Southern Slaveholders' Worldview (New York, 2005).

John Hope Franklin, *Reconstruction after the Civil War* (Chicago and London, 1961).

Walter J. Fraser Jr. and Winfred B. Moore Jr., eds., *The Southern Enigma: Essays on Race, Class, and Folk Culture*, eds. (Westport, CT, 1983).

William W. Freehling, *The Road to Disunion, Vol. I: Secessionists at Bay, 1776–1854* (New York, 1990).

  The Road to Disunion, Vol. II: Secessionists Triumphant, 1854–1861 (New York, 2007).

Paul M. Gaston, *The New South Creed: A Study in Southern Mythmaking* (Baton Rouge, 1970).

Eugene D. Genovese, *The Political Economy of Slavery: Studies in the Economy and Society of the Slave South* (New York, 1965).

  The World the Slaveholders Made: Two Essays in Interpretation (1969; repr., Middletown, CT, 1988).

Gary Gereffi and Miguel Korzeniewicz, eds., *Commodity Chains and Global Capitalism* (Westport, CT, and London, 1993).

David T. Gilchrist and W. David Lewis, eds., *Economic Change in the Civil War Era*, eds. (Greeneville, DE, 1965).

James Gill, *Lords of Misrule: Mardi Gras and the Politics of Race in New Orleans* (Jackson, MS, 1997).

Thavolia Glymph and John J. Kushma, eds., *Essays on the Postbellum Southern Economy* (College Station: Texas A&M University Press, 1985).

David Goldfield, *Region, Race, and Cities: Interpreting the Urban South* (Baton Rouge, 1997).

Lawrence Goodwyn, *Democratic Promise: The Populist Moment in America* (New York and Oxford, 1976).

N. S. B. Gras, *Business and Capitalism: An Introduction to Business History* (New York, 1939).

Lewis C. Gray, *History of Agriculture in the Southern United States to 1860* (2 vols., 1933; repr. Gloucester, MA, 1958).

George D. Green, *Finance and Economic Development in the Old South: Louisiana Banking, 1804–1861* (Stanford, CA, 1972).

Jack P. Greene and Philip D. Morgan, eds., *Atlantic History: A Critical Appraisal* (New York, 2009).

Robert H. Gudmestad, *A Troublesome Commerce: The Transformation of the Interstate Slave Trade* (Baton Rouge, 2003).

Matthew Pratt Guterl, *American Mediterranean: Southern Slaveholders in the Age of Emancipation* (Cambridge, MA, 2008).

Louis M. Hacker, *The Triumph of American Capitalism* (New York, 1940).

Steven Hahn, *The Roots of Southern Populism: Yeoman Farmers and the Transformation of the Georgia Upcountry, 1850–1890* (New York and Oxford, 1983).

  A Nation Under Their Feet: Black Political Struggles in the Rural South from Slavery to the Great Migration (Cambridge, MA, 2003).

William Ivy Hair, *Bourbonism and Agrarian Protest: Louisiana Politics, 1877–1900* (Baton Rouge, 1969).

Bray Hammond, *Banks and Politics in America from the Revolution to the Civil War* (Princeton, NJ, 1957).

  Sovereignty and an Empty Purse: Banks and Politics in the Civil War (Princeton, NJ, 1970).

David Hancock, *Citizens of the World: London Merchants and the Integration of the British Atlantic Community, 1735–1785* (New York, 1995).

J. Fair Hardin, *Northwestern Louisiana: A History* (3 vols.; Louisville, KY and Shreveport, LA, 1937).

Louis Hartz, *Economic Policy and Democratic Thought: Pennsylvania, 1776–1860* (1948; repr., Chicago, 1968).

Thomas L. Haskell and Richard F. Teichgraeber III, eds., *The Culture of the Market: Historical Essays* (New York, 1993).

John A. Heitmann, *The Modernization of the Louisiana Sugar Industry, 1830–1910* (Baton Rouge, 1987).

Ralph W. Hidy, *The House of Baring in American Trade and Finance: English Merchant Bankers at Work, 1763–1861* (Cambridge, MA, 1949).

Sam Bowers Hilliard, *Hog Meat and Hoecake: Food Supply in the Old South, 1840–1860* (Carbondale, IL, 1972).

Rodney J. Hilton, ed., *The Transition from Feudalism to Capitalism* (London, 1976).

Arnold R. Hirsch and Joseph Logsdon, eds., *Creole New Orleans: Race and Americanization* (Baton Rouge, 1992)

Eric Hobsbawm, *The Age of Capital, 1848–1875* (New York, 1974).

On History (New York, 1997).

James K. Hogue, *Uncivil Wars: Five New Orleans Street Battles and the Rise and Fall of Radical Reconstruction* (Baton Rouge, 2006).

James G. Hollandsworth Jr., *Pretense of Glory: The Life of Nathaniel P. Banks* (Baton Rouge, 1998).

An Absolute Massacre: The New Orleans Race Riot of July 30, 1866 (Baton Rouge, 2001).

Michael F. Holt, *The Rise and Fall of the Whig Party: Jacksonian Politics and the Onset of the Civil War* (New York, 1999).

Charles M. Hubbard, *The Burden of Confederate Diplomacy* (Knoxville, TN, 1998).

James L. Huston, *Calculating the Value of the Union: Slavery, Property Rights, and the Economic Origins of the Civil War* (Chapel Hill, 2003).

Samuel C. Hyde Jr., *Pistols and Politics: The Dilemma of Democracy in Louisiana's Florida Parishes, 1810–1899* (Baton Rouge, 1996).

Samuel C. Hyde Jr., ed., *A Fierce and Fractious Frontier: The Curious Development of Louisiana's Florida Parishes, 1699–2000* (Baton Rouge, 2004)

Harold M. Hyman, *Oleander Odyssey: The Kempners of Galveston, Texas, 1854–1980s* (College Station, TX, 1990).

Thomas N. Ingersoll, *Mammon and Manon in Early New Orleans: The First Slave Society in the Deep South, 1718–1819* (Knoxville, TN, 1999).

Geoffrey Ingham, *Capitalism Divided? The City and Industry in British Social Development* (New York, 1984).

Joseph E. Inikori, *Africans and the Industrial Revolution in England: A Study in International Trade and Economic Development* (Cambridge, UK, and other cities, 2002).

Joy J. Jackson, *New Orleans in the Gilded Age: Politics and Urban Progress, 1880–1896* (2nd ed.; Lafayette, LA, 1997).

Gerald David Jaynes, *Branches without Roots: Genesis of the Black Working Class in the American South, 1862–1882* (New York, 1986).

Leland Hamilton Jenks, *The Migration of British Capital to 1875* (New York, 1927).

Charles S. Johnson, Edwin R. Embree, and W. W. Alexander, *The Collapse of Cotton Tenancy: Summary of Field Studies and Statistical Surveys, 1933–35* (Chapel Hill, 1935).

Emory R. Johnson, T. W. Van Metre, Grover G. Huebner, David Scott Hanchett, and Henry W. Farnam, *History of the Domestic and Foreign Commerce of the United States* (2 vols.; Washington, DC, 1915).

Ludwell H. Johnson, *Red River Campaign: Politics and Cotton in the Civil War* (1958; repr., Kent, Ohio, and London, 1993).

Paul E. Johnson, *A Shopkeeper's Millenium: Society and Revivals in Rochester, New York, 1815–1837* (New York, 1978).

Richard Johnson, ed., *Making Histories: Studies in History-Writing and Politics* (Minneapolis, MN, 1982).

Walter Johnson, *Soul by Soul: Life Inside the Antebellum Slave Market* (Cambridge, MA, and London, 1999).

Fred Mitchell Jones, *Middlemen in the Domestic Trade of the United States, 1800–1860* (Urbana, IL, 1937).

Howard Jones, *Union in Peril: The Crisis over British Intervention in the Civil War* (Chapel Hill, 1992).

Ari Kelman, *A River and Its City: The Nature of Landscape in New Orleans* (Berkeley, CA, and other cities, 2003).

Richard H. Kilbourne Jr., *Debt, Investment, Slaves: Credit Relations in East Feliciana Parish, Louisiana, 1825–1885* (Tuscaloosa, AL, and London, 1995).

Samuel Kinser, *Carnival, American Style: Mardi Gras at New Orleans and Mobile* (Chicago and London, 1990).

Herbert S. Klein, *The Atlantic Slave Trade* (New York, 1999).

James T. Kloppenberg, *Uncertain Victory: Social Democracy and Progressivism in American and European Thought, 1870–1920* (New York, 1986).

Bertram Wallace Korn, *The Early Jews of New Orleans* (Waltham, MA, 1969).

J. Morgan Kousser and James M. McPherson, eds., *Region, Race, and Reconstruction: Essays in Honor of C. Vann Woodward* (New York, 1982).

Peter Kriedte, *Peasants, Landlords, and Merchant Capitalists: Europe and the World Economy, 1500–1800* (Warwickshire, UK, 1983).

Peter Kriedte, Hans Medick, and Jurgen Schlumbohm, *Industrialization before Industrialization: Rural Industry in the Genesis of Capitalism* (Cambridge, UK, and other cities, 1981).

Richard Lachmann, *Capitalists in Spite of Themselves: Elite Conflict and Economic Transitions in Early Modern Europe* (New York and Oxford, 2000).

Stuart O. Landry, *History of the Boston Club* (New Orleans, 1938).

   The Battle of Liberty Place: The Overthrow of Carpet-Bag Rule in New Orleans, September 14, 1874 (New Orleans, 1955).

Peirce F. Lewis, *New Orleans: The Making of an Urban Landscape* (2nd ed., Santa Fe, NM, and Harrisonburg, VA, 2003).

Alex Lichtenstein, *Twice the Work of Free Labor: The Political Economy of Convict Labor in the New South* (London and New York, 1996).

Raimondo Luraghi, *The Rise and Fall of the Plantation South* (New York, 1978).

Jay R. Mandle, *The Roots of Black Poverty: The Southern Plantation Economy after the Civil War* (Durham, NC, 1978).

Not Slave, Not Free: The African American Economic Experience since the Civil War (Durham, NC, 1992).

Susan Archer Mann, *Agrarian Capitalism in Theory and Practice* (Chapel Hill, 1990).

Raymond J. Martinez, *The Story of the River Front at New Orleans* (New Orleans, 1955).

Karl Marx, *Grundrisse: Foundations of the Critique of Political Economy*, trans. Martin Nicolaus (New York, 1973).

Capital, Vol. III, trans. David Fernbach (1981; repr., London, 1991).

Robert E. May, *The Southern Dream of a Caribbean Empire, 1854–1861* (Baton Rouge, 1973).

Manifest Destiny's Underworld: Filibustering in Antebellum America (Chapel Hill, 2002).

Peyton McCrary, *Abraham Lincoln and Reconstruction: The Louisiana Experiment* (Princeton, NJ, 1978).

Roderick A. McDonald, *The Economy and Material Culture of Slaves: Goods and Chattels on the Sugar Plantations of Jamaica and Louisiana* (Baton Rouge, 1993).

Robert D. Meade, *Judah P. Benjamin: Confederate Statesman* (New York, 1943).

Joseph Karl Menn, *The Large Slaveholders of Louisiana, 1860* (New Orleans, 1964).

Augusto P. Miceli, *The Pickwick Club of New Orleans* (New Orleans, 1964).

R. W. Michie, ed., *Commercial and Financial Services* (Oxford, 1994).

Graeme J. Milne, *Trade and Traders in Mid-Victorian Liverpool: Mercantile Business and the Making of a World Port* (Liverpool, 2000).

Reid Mitchell, *All on a Mardi Gras Day: Episodes in the History of New Orleans Carnival* (Cambridge, MA, 1995).

Barrington Moore Jr., *Social Origins of Dictatorship and Democracy: Lord and Peasant in the Making of the Modern World* (New York, 1966).

John Hebron Moore, *The Emergence of the Cotton Kingdom in the Old Southwest: Mississippi, 1770–1860* (Baton Rouge, 1988).

Phillip E. Myers, *Caution and Cooperation: The American Civil War in British-American Relations* (Kent, OH, 2008).

National Bureau of Economic Research, *Trends in the American Economy in the Nineteenth Century* (Princeton, NJ, 1960).

James D. Norris, *R. G. Dun & Co. 1841–1900: The Development of Credit-Reporting in the Nineteenth Century* (Westport, CT, 1978).

Douglass C. North, *The Economic Growth of the United States, 1790–1860* (1961; repr., New York, 1966).

Justin A. Nystrom, *New Orleans after the Civil War: Race, Politics, and a New Birth of Freedom* (Baltimore, 2010).

James Oakes, *The Ruling Race: A History of American Slaveholders* (New York, 1982).

Slavery and Freedom: An Interpretation of the Old South (New York, 1990).

Otto H. Olsen, ed., *Reconstruction and Redemption in the South* (Baton Rouge, 1980).

Harry P. Owens and James J. Cooke, eds., *The Old South in the Crucible of War* (Jackson, MS, 1983).

Ted Ownby, *American Dreams in Mississippi: Consumers, Poverty, and Culture, 1830–1998* (Chapel Hill, 1999).

Frank L. Owsley, *King Cotton Diplomacy: Foreign Relations of the Confederate States of America* (Chicago, 1931).

Bruce Palmer, *"Man Over Money": The Southern Populist Critique of American Capitalism* (Chapel Hill, 1980).

Edwin J. Perkins, *Financing Anglo-American Trade: The House of Brown, 1800–1880* (Cambridge, MA, and London, 1975).

Christopher Phillips, *Missouri's Confederate Governor: Claiborne Fox Jackson and the Creation of Southern Identity in the Border West* (Columbia, MO, 2000).

Stuart Plattner, ed., *Economic Anthropology* (Stanford, CA, 1989).

J. G. A. Pocock, *Virtue, Commerce, and History* (Cambridge, UK, and other cities, 1985).

Sidney Pollard, *European Economic Integration, 1815–1970* (London, 1974).

Glenn Porter and Harold C. Livesay, *Merchants and Manufacturers: Studies in the Changing Structure of Nineteenth-Century Marketing* (Baltimore, 1971).

David M. Potter, *The Impending Crisis, 1848–1861*, ed. Don E. Fehrenbacher (New York, 1976).

Lawrence N. Powell, *New Masters: Northern Planters during the Civil War and Reconstruction* (New Haven, CT, and London, 1980).

 The Accidental City: Improvising New Orleans (Cambridge, MA, 2012).

Allan Pred, *Urban Growth and City-Systems in the United States, 1840–1860* (Cambridge, MA, 1980).

Jacob M. Price, *Capital and Credit in British Overseas Trade: The View from the Chesapeake, 1700–1776* (Cambridge, MA, 1980).

Roger L. Ransom and Richard Sutch, *One Kind of Freedom: The Economic Consequences of Emancipation* (2nd ed.; New York and other cities, 2001).

Thomas G. Rawski, Jon S. Cohen, Susan B. Carter, Stephen Cullenberg, Donald N. McCloskey, Richard Sutch, Hugh Rockoff, and Peter H. Lindert, *Economics and the Historian* (Berkeley, CA, and other cities, 1996).

Marcus Rediker, *Between the Devil and the Deep Blue Sea: Merchant Seamen, Pirates, and the Anglo-American Maritime World, 1700–1750* (New York and other cities, 1987).

Merl E. Reed, *New Orleans and the Railroads: The Struggle for Commercial Empire, 1830–1860* (Baton Rouge, 1966).

Robert C. Reinders, *End of an Era, New Orleans 1850–1860* (New Orleans, 1964).

E. E. Rich and C. H. Wilson, eds., *The Cambridge Economic History of Europe*. Vol. V: *The Economic Organization of Early Modern Europe* (London and New York, 1977).

Armstead L. Robinson, *Bitter Fruits of Bondage: The Demise of Slavery and the Collapse of the Confederacy, 1861–1865* (Charlottesville, VA, 2005).

John C. Rodrigue, *Reconstruction in the Cane Fields: From Slavery to Free Labor in Louisiana's Sugar Parishes, 1862–1880* (Baton Rouge, 2001).

Charles P. Roland, *Louisiana Sugar Plantations during the American Civil War* (Leiden, Netherlands, 1957).

Adam Rothman, *Slave Country: American Expansion and the Origins of the Deep South* (Cambridge, MA, 2005).

Dennis Rousey, *Policing the Southern City: New Orleans, 1805–1889* (Baton Rouge, 1996).

William G. Roy, *Socializing Capital: The Rise of the Large Industrial Corporation in America* (Princeton, NJ, 1997).

Edward Royce, *The Origins of Southern Sharecropping* (Philadelphia, 1993).

Robert Royal Russel, *Economic Aspects of Southern Sectionalism, 1840–1861* (Urbana, IL, 1924).

Malcolm Rutherford, *Institutions in Economics: The Old and the New Institutionalism* (New York, 1994).

John M. Sacher, *A Perfect War of Politics: Parties, Politicians, and Democracy in Louisiana, 1824–1861* (Baton Rouge, 2003).

Robert Blair St. George, ed., *Material Life in America, 1600–1860* (Boston, 1988).

Warren J. Samuels, ed., *Institutional Economics* (3 vols.; Brookfield, Vt., 1988).

William Kauffman Scarborough, *Masters of the Big House: Elite Slaveholders of the Mid-Nineteenth Century South* (Baton Rouge, 2003).

Brian Schoen, *The Fragile Fabric of Union: Cotton, Federal Politics, and the Global Origins of the Civil War* (Baltimore, 2009).

John Christopher Schwab, *The Confederate States of America, 1861–1865: A Financial and Industrial History of the South during the Civil War* (New York and London, 1901).

Michael Schwartz, *Radical Protest and Social Structure: The Southern Farmers' Alliance and Cotton Tenancy, 1880–1890* (New York, 1976).

Larry Schweikart, *Banking in the American South from the Age of Jackson to Reconstruction* (Baton Rouge, 1987).

Larry E. Schweikart, ed., *Banking and Finance to 1913* (New York, 1990).

Loren Schweninger, *Black Property Owners in the South, 1790–1915* (Urbana, IL, 1990).

Rebecca J. Scott, *Degrees of Freedom: Louisiana and Cuba after Slavery* (Cambridge, MA, 2005).

Louis Martin Sears, *John Slidell* (Durham, NC, 1925).

Charles Sellers, *The Market Revolution: Jacksonian America, 1815–1846* (New York, 1991).

Robert P. Sharkey, *Money, Class, and Party: An Economic Study of the Civil War and Reconstruction* (Baltimore, 1959).

Andrei Shleifer, *Inefficient Markets: An Introduction to Behavioral Finance* (New York, 1999).

Roger W. Shugg, *Origins of Class Struggle in Louisiana: A Social History of White Farmers and Laborers during Slavery and After* (1939; repr., Baton Rouge, 1968).

Silvana R. Siddali, *From Property to Person: Slavery and the Confiscation Acts, 1861–1862* (Baton Rouge, 2005).

J. Carlyle Sitterson, *Sugar Country: The Cane Sugar Industry in the South, 1753–1950* (Louisville, KY, 1953).

Mark M. Smith, *Mastered by the Clock: Time, Slavery, and Freedom in the American South* (Chapel Hill, 1997).

Debating Slavery: Economy and Society in the American Antebellum South (New York, 1998).

Leon Cyprian Soulé, *The Know Nothing Party in New Orleans: A Reappraisal* (Baton Rouge, 1961).

Anthony J. Stanonis, *Creating the Big Easy: New Orleans and the Emergence of Modern Tourism, 1918–1945* (Athens, GA, 2006).

Wendell Holmes Stephenson, *Isaac Franklin: Slave Trader and Planter of the Old South, with Plantation Records* (Baton Rouge, 1938).

John F. Stover, *The Railroads of the South: A Study in Finance and Control* (Chapel Hill, 1955).

Susan Strasser, *Satisfaction Guaranteed: The Making of the American Mass Market* (New York, 1989).

Mark W. Summers, *Railroads, Reconstruction, and the Gospel of Prosperity: Aid under the Radical Republicans, 1865–1877* (Princeton, NJ, 1984).

David G. Surdam, *Northern Naval Superiority and the Economics of the Civil War* (Columbia, SC, 2001).

Michael Tadman, *Speculators and Slaves: Masters, Traders, and Slaves in the Old South* (Madison, WI, 1989).

George Rogers Taylor, *The Transportation Revolution, 1815–1860* (1951; repr., New York, 1968).

Joe Gray Taylor, *Louisiana Reconstructed, 1863–1877* (Baton Rouge, 1974).

Richard S. Tedlow, *New and Improved: The Story of Mass Marketing in America* (New York, 1990).

Richard Cecil Todd, *Confederate Finance* (Athens, GA., 1954).

Frank Towers, *The Urban South and the Coming of the Civil War* (Charlottesville, VA, 2004).

Hans L. Trefousse, *Ben Butler: The South Called Him Beast!* (New York, 1957).

Joseph G. Tregle Jr., *Louisiana in the Age of Jackson: A Clash of Cultures and Personalities* (Baton Rouge, 1999).

Ted Tunnell, *Crucible of Reconstruction: War, Radicalism, and Race in Louisiana, 1862–1877* (Baton Rouge and London, 1984).

Frederick Jackson Turner, *The United States, 1830–1860: The Nation and Its Sections* (1935; repr., New York, 1950).

James E. Vance Jr., *The Merchants' World: The Geography of Wholesaling* (Englewood Cliffs, NJ, 1970).

Thorstein Veblen, *The Theory of the Leisure Class: An Economic Study of Institutions* (1899; repr., New York, 1953).

Richard C. Wade, *Slavery in the Cities: The South, 1820–1860* (New York, 1964).

Immanuel Wallerstein, *The Modern World-System*. Vol. II: *Mercantilism and the Consolidation of the World Economy, 1600–1750* (San Diego and other cities, 1980).

The Modern World-System. Vol. III: *The Second Great Era of the Expansion of the Capitalist World-Economy, 1730–1840s* (San Diego and other cities, 1989).

Gary M. Walton and James F. Shepherd, eds., *Market Institutions and Economic Progress in the New South, 1865–1900* (New York and other cities, 1981).

Gary M. Walton and Hugh Rockoff, *History of the American Economy*, 9th ed. (Mason, OH, 2002).

Harry L. Watson, *Liberty and Power: The Politics of Jacksonian America* (New York, 1990).

Michael Wayne, *The Reshaping of Plantation Society: The Natchez District, 1860–1880* (1983; repr., Urbana and Chicago, 1990).

Max Weber, *The Protestant Ethic and the Spirit of Capitalism*, trans. Talcott Parsons (1904–5; repr., London and New York, 1992).

Economy and Society, eds. Guenther Roth and Claus Wittich (2 vols.; Berkeley, CA, and other cities, 1978).

Jonathan Daniel Wells, *The Origins of the Southern Middle Class, 1800–1861* (Chapel Hill, 2004).

Herbert Wender, *Southern Commercial Conventions, 1837–1859* (Baltimore, 1930).

Jonathan M. Wiener, *Social Origins of the New South: Alabama, 1860–1885* (Baton Rouge, 1978).

Martin J. Wiener, *English Culture and the Decline of the Industrial Spirit, 1850–1980* (Cambridge, UK, and other cities, 1981).

Eric Williams, *Capitalism and Slavery* (1944; repr., Chapel Hill and London, 1994).

T. Harry Williams, *P. G. T. Beauregard: Napoleon in Gray* (1955; repr., Baton Rouge, 1995).

Romance and Realism in Southern Politics (1961; repr., Baton Rouge, 1966).

John C. Willis, *Forgotten Time: The Yazoo-Mississippi Delta after the Civil War* (Charlottesville, VA, 2000).

John D. Winters, *The Civil War in Louisiana* (Baton Rouge, 1963).

Oscar O. Winther, *The Transportation Frontier: Trans-Mississippi West, 1865–1890* (New York and other cities, 1964).

Stephen R. Wise, *Lifeline of the Confederacy: Blockade Running during the Civil War* (Columbia, S.C., 1988).

Harold D. Woodman, *King Cotton and His Retainers: Financing and Marketing the Cotton Crop of the South, 1800–1925* (Lexington, KY, 1968).

New South – New Law: The Legal Foundations of Credit and Labor Relations in the Postbellum Agricultural South (Baton Rouge: Louisiana State University Press, 1995).

C. Vann Woodward, *Origins of the New South, 1877–1913* (1951; repr., Baton Rouge, 1971).

George Ruble Woolfolk, *The Cotton Regency: The Northern Merchants and Reconstruction, 1865–1880* (New York, 1958).

Gavin Wright, *The Political Economy of the Cotton South: Households, Markets, and Wealth in the Nineteenth Century* (New York, 1978).

Old South, New South: Revolutions in the Southern Economy Since the Civil War (New York, 1986).

Yuval P. Yonay, *The Struggle Over the Soul of Economics: Institutionalist and Neoclassical Economists in America between the Wars* (Princeton, NJ, 1998).

Perry Young, *The Mistick Krewe: Chronicles of Comus and His Kin* (New Orleans, 1931).

Nuala Zahedieh, *The Capital and the Colonies: London and the Atlantic Economy, 1660–1700* (Cambridge, UK, and other cities, 2010).

Richard Zuczek, ed., *Encyclopedia of the Reconstruction Era* (2 vols., Westport, CT, 2006).

VI. Secondary Sources: Articles

Berthold C. Alwes, "The History of the Louisiana State Lottery Company," *Louisiana Historical Quarterly* 27 (October 1944), 933–1118.

Lewis E. Atherton, "John McDonogh – New Orleans Mercantile Capitalist," *Journal of Southern History* 7 (November 1941), 451–81.

"John McDonogh and the Mississippi River Trade," *Louisiana Historical Quarterly* 26 (January 1943), 37–43.

"The Problem of Credit-Rating in the Antebellum South," *Journal of Southern History* 12 (November 1946), 534–6.

James P. Baughman. "The Evolution of Rail-Water Systems of Transportation in the Gulf Southwest, 1836–1890," *Journal of Southern History* 34 (August 1968), 357–81.

Sven Beckert, "Emancipation and Empire: Reconstructing the Worldwide Web of Cotton Production in the Age of the American Civil War," *American Historical Review* 109 (December 2004), 1405–38.

Henry Blumenthal, "Confederate Diplomacy: Popular Notions and International Realities," *Journal of Southern History* 32 (May 1966), 159–67.

Eugene A. Brady, "A Reconsideration of the Lancashire 'Cotton Famine'," *Agricultural History* 37 (October 1963), 156–62.

William W. Brown and Morgan O. Reynolds, "Debt Peonage Re-examined," *Journal of Economic History* 33 (December 1973), 862–71.

Jacqueline P. Bull, "The General Merchant in the Economic History of the New South," *Journal of Southern History* 18 (February 1952), 37–59.

P. J. Cain and A. G. Hopkins, "Gentlemanly Capitalism and British Expansion Overseas I: The Old Colonial System, 1688–1850," *Economic History Review* 2d ser., 39 (November 1986), 501–25.

Rita Katherine Carey, "Samuel Jarvis Peters," *Louisiana Historical Quarterly* 30 (April 1947), 439–80.

David L. Carlton and Peter A. Coclanis, "Capital Mobilization and Southern Industry, 1880–1905: The Case of the Carolina Piedmont," *Journal of Economic History* 49 (March 1989), 73–94.

"The Uninventive South? A Quantitative Look at Region and American Inventiveness," *Technology and Culture* 36 (April 1995), 302–26.

William W. Chenault and Robert C. Reinders, "The Northern-born Community of New Orleans in the 1850s," *Journal of American History* 51 (September 1964), 232–47.

John G. Clark, "New Orleans and the River: A Study in Attitudes and Responses," *Louisiana History* 8 (Winter 1967), 117–35.

James C. Cobb, "Beyond Planters and Industrialists: A New Perspective on the New South," *Journal of Southern History* 54 (February 1988), 45–68.

Peter A. Coclanis, "In Retrospect: Ransom and Sutch's *One Kind of Freedom*," *Reviews in American History* 28 (September 2000), 478–89.

Michael P. Conzen, "The Maturing Urban System of the United States, 1840–1910," *Annals of the Association of American Geographers* 67 (March 1977), 88–108.

E. Merton Coulter, "The Effects of Secession upon the Commerce of the Mississippi Valley," *Mississippi Valley Historical Review* 3 (December 1916), 275–300.

"Commercial Intercourse with the Confederacy in the Mississippi Valley, 1861–1865," *Mississippi Valley Historical Review* 5 (March 1919), 377–95.

Leonard P. Curry, "Urbanization and Urbanism in the Old South: A Comparative View," *Journal of Southern History* 40 (February 1974), 43–60.

Thomas Ewing Dabney, "The Butler Regime in Louisiana," *Louisiana Historical Quarterly* 27 (April 1944), 487–526.

Douglas F. Dowd, "A Comparative Analysis of Economic Development in the American West and South," *Journal of Economic History* 16 (December 1956), 558–74.

Tom Downey, "Riparian Rights and Manufacturing in Antebellum South Carolina: William Gregg and the Origins of the 'Industrial Mind,'" *Journal of Southern History* 65 (February 1999), 77–108.

Elisabeth Joan Doyle, "Greenbacks, Car Tickets, and the Pot of Gold: The Effects of Wartime Occupation on the Business Life of New Orleans, 1861–1865," *Civil War History* 5 (December 1959), 347–62.

L. Tuffly Ellis, "The New Orleans Cotton Exchange: The Formative Years, 1871–1880," *Journal of Southern History* 39 (November 1973), 545–64.

Harry Howard Evans, "James Robb, Banker and Pioneer Railroad Builder of Antebellum Louisiana," *Louisiana Historical Quarterly* 23 (January 1940), 170–258.

Robert Evans Jr., "Some Economic Aspects of the Domestic Slave Trade, 1830–1860," *Southern Economic Journal* 27 (April 1961), 329–37.

Explorations in Economic History 38 (January 2001) [Special issue devoted to Ransom and Sutch's *One Kind of Freedom*, 2d edition].

Susan Feiner, "Factors, Bankers, and Masters: Class Relations in the Antebellum South," *Journal of Economic History* 42 (March 1982), 61–7.

Louis Ferleger, "Farm Mechanization in the Louisiana Sugar Sector after the Civil War," *Louisiana History* 23 (Winter 1982), 21–34.

"Capital Goods and Southern Economic Development," *Journal of Economic History* 45 (June 1985), 411–17.

"Sharecropping Contracts in the Late-Nineteenth-Century South," *Agricultural History* 67 (Summer 1993), 31–46.

"The Problem of 'Labor' in the Post-Reconstruction Louisiana Sugar Industry," *Agricultural History* 72 (Spring 1998), 140–58.

Barbara J. Fields, "The Nineteenth-Century South: History and Theory," *Plantation Society in the Americas* 2 (April 1983), 7–27.

Julie Flaherty, "A Good Credit History, Indeed: Opening the Books on American Business, 1841–1891," New York *Times*, August 21, 1999.

Richard Follett, "'Give to the Labor of America, the Market of America': Marketing the Old South's Sugar Crop, 1800–1860," *Revista de Indias* 65 No. 233 (2005), 117–46.

Lacy K. Ford, "Rednecks and Merchants: Economic Development and Social Tensions in the South Carolina Upcountry, 1865–1900," *Journal of American History* 71 (September 1984), 294–318.

Herman Freudenberger and Jonathan Pritchett, "The Domestic United States Slave Trade: New Evidence," *Journal of Interdisciplinary History* 21 (Winter 1991), 447–77.

Donna Gabaccia, "A Long Atlantic in a Wider World," *Atlantic Studies* 1 No.1 (2004), 1–27.

Robert E. Gallman, "Self-Sufficiency in the Cotton Economy of the Antebellum South," *Agricultural History* 44 (January 1970), 5–23.

Alison Games, "Atlantic History: Definitions, Challenges, and Opportunities," *American Historical Review* 111 (June 2006), 741–57.

Pierre Gervais, "Neither Imperial, Nor Atlantic: A Merchant Perspective on International Trade in the Eighteenth Century," *History of European Ideas* 34 (December 2008), 465–73.

William E. Highsmith, "Louisiana Landholding during War and Reconstruction," *Louisiana Historical Quarterly* 38 (January 1955), 39–54.

D. Clayton James, "The Tribulations of a Bayou Boeuf Store Owner, 1836–1857," *Louisiana History* 4 (Summer 1963), 243–68.

John A. James, "Financial Underdevelopment in the Postbellum South," *Journal of Interdisciplinary History* 11 (Winter 1981), 443–54.

Howard Palmer Johnson, "New Orleans under General Butler," *Louisiana Historical Quarterly* 24 (April 1941), 434–536.

Ludwell H. Johnson, "Northern Profits and Profiteers: The Cotton Rings of 1864–1865," *Civil War History* 12.2 (1966), 101–15.

Walter Johnson, "The Pedestal and the Veil: Rethinking the Capitalism/Slavery Question," *Journal of the Early Republic* 24 (Summer 2004), 299–308.

Lu Ann Jones, "Gender, Race, and Itinerant Commerce in the Rural New South," *Journal of Southern History* 66 (May 2000), 297–320.

Lane C. Kendall, "The Interregnum in Louisiana in 1861, Part I," *Louisiana Historical Quarterly* 16 (April 1933), 175–208.

"The Interregnum in Louisiana in 1861, Part II," *Louisiana Historical Quarterly* 16 (July 1933), 374–408.

"The Interregnum in Louisiana in 1861, Part III," *Louisiana Historical Quarterly* 16 (October 1933), 639–69.

Louis M. Kyriakoudes, "Lower-Order Urbanization and Territorial Monopoly in the Southern Furnishing Trade: Alabama, 1871–1890," *Social Science History* 26 (Spring 2002), 179–98.

Lawrence H. Larsen, "New Orleans and the River Trade: Reinterpreting the Role of the Business Community," *Wisconsin Magazine of History* 61 (Winter 1977–78), 112–24.

Stanley Lebergott, "Through the Blockade: The Profitability and Extent of Cotton Smuggling, 1861–1865," *Journal of Economic History* 41 (December 1981), 867–88.

"Why the South Lost: Commercial Purpose in the Confederacy, 1861–1865," *Journal of American History* 70 (June 1983), 58–74.

Alex Lichtenstein, "Right Church, Wrong Pew: Eugene Genovese's Defense of Southern Conservatism," *New Politics*, n.s. 6 (Summer 1997), 59–68.

"Proletarians or Peasants?: Sharecroppers and the Politics of Protest in the Rural South, 1880–1940," *Plantation Society in the Americas* 5 (Fall 1998), 297–331.

Nelson Lichtenstein, "The Return of Merchant Capitalism," *International Labor and Working-Class History* 81 (March 2012), 8–27.

E. E. Liebhafsky, "The Influence of Charles Sanders Peirce on Institutional Economics," *Journal of Economic Issues* 27 (September 1993), 741–54.

Diane Lindstrom, "Southern Dependence upon Interregional Grain Supplies: A Review of the Trade Flows, 1840–1860," *Agricultural History* 44 (January 1970), 101–13.

James H. Madison, "The Evolution of Commercial Credit Reporting Agencies in Nineteenth-Century America," *Business History Review* 48 (Summer 1974), 167–76.

"The Credit Reports of R. G. Dun & Co. as Historical Sources," *Historical Methods Newsletter* (September 1975), 128–31.

Scott P. Marler, "Merchants in the Transition to a New South: Central Louisiana, 1840–1880," *Louisiana History* 42 (Spring 2001), 165–92.

"Fables of the Reconstruction: Reconstruction of the Fables," *Journal of the Historical Society* 4 (Winter 2004), 113–37.

"Après Le Déluge: New Orleans and the New Environmental History," *Journal of Urban History* 32 (March 2006), 477–90.

"Stuck in the Middle (Class) with You," *Historical Methods* 39 (Fall 2006), 154–58.

"Two Kinds of Freedom: Mercantile Development and Labor Systems in Louisiana Cotton and Sugar Parishes during Reconstruction," *Agricultural History* 85 (Spring 2011), 225–51.

Lawrence T. McDonnell, "The Janus Face of *Fruits of Merchant Capital*," *Labour/Le Travail* 15 (Spring 1985), 185–90.

George L. Mehren, "Market Organization and Economic Development," *Journal of Farm Economics* 41 (1959), 1307–15.

James M. Merrill, "Confederate Shipbuilding in New Orleans," *Journal of Southern History* 28 (February 1962), 87–93.

David R. Meyer, "The Industrial Retardation of Southern Cities, 1860–1880," *Explorations in Economic History* 25 (1988), 366–86.

Philip Mirowski, "The Philosophical Bases of Institutional Economics," *Journal of Economic Issues* 21 (September 1987), 1001–38.

Harry A. Mitchell, "The Development of New Orleans as a Wholesale Trading Center," *Louisiana Historical Quarterly* 27 (October 1944), 933–63.

J. Preston Moore, "Pierre Soulé: Southern Expansionist and Promoter," *Journal of Southern History* 21 (May 1955), 203–23.

Irene D. Neu, "J. B. Moussier and the Property Banks of Louisiana," *Business History Review* 35 (Winter 1961), 550–7.

"Edmond Jean Forstall and Louisiana Banking," *Explorations in Economic History* 7 (Summer 1970), 383–98.

Arthur G. Nuhrah, "John McDonogh: Man of Many Facets," *Louisiana Historical Quarterly* 33 (January 1950), 5–144.

Thomas H. O'Connor, "Lincoln and the Cotton Trade," *Civil War History* 7 (March 1961), 20–35.

Rowena Olegario, "'That Mysterious People': Jewish Merchants, Transparency, and Community in Mid-Nineteenth-Century America," *Business History Review* 73 (Summer 1999), 161–89.

George S. Pabis, "Delaying the Deluge: The Engineering Debate over Flood Control on the Lower Mississippi River, 1846–1861," *Journal of Southern History* 64 (August 1998), 421–54.

Jane H. Pease, "A Note on Patterns of Conspicuous Consumption among Seaboard Planters, 1820–1860," *Journal of Southern History* 35 (August 1969), 381–93.

Lawrence N. Powell, "Reinventing Tradition: Liberty Place, Historical Memory, and Silk-Stocking Vigilantism in New Orleans Politics," *Slavery & Abolition* 20 (April 1999), 127–49.

Merl E. Reed, "Footnote to the Coastwise Trade: Some Teche Planters and Their Atlantic Factors," *Louisiana History* 8 (Spring 1967), 191–7.

Joseph D. Reid, "Sharecropping as an Understandable Market Response: The Post-Bellum South," *Journal of Economic History* 33 (March 1973), 106–30.

William L. Richter, "James Longstreet: From Rebel to Scalawag," *Louisiana History* 11 (Spring 1970), 215–30.

John C. Rodrigue, "More Souths?" *Reviews in American History* 30 (March 2002), 66–71.

Charles P. Roland, "Difficulties of Civil War Sugar Planting in Louisiana," *Louisiana Historical Quarterly* 38 (October 1955).

Michael A. Ross, "Resisting the New South: Commercial Crisis and Decline in New Orleans, 1865–85," *American Nineteenth-Century History* 4 (Spring 2003), 59–76.

Morton J. Rothstein, "Antebellum Wheat and Cotton Exports: A Contrast in Marketing Organization and Development," *Agricultural History* 40 (April 1966), 91–100.

"The New South and the International Economy," *Agricultural History* 57 (Fall 1983), 385–402.

Jerry Purvis Sanson, "White Man's Failure: The Rapides Parish 1874 Election," *Louisiana History* 31 (Winter 1990), 39–58.

Judith Kelleher Schafer, "New Orleans Slavery in 1850 as Seen in Advertisements," *Journal of Southern History* 47 (February 1981), 33–56.

Louis B. Schmidt, "The Influence of Wheat and Cotton on Anglo-American Relations during the Civil War," *Iowa Journal of History and Politics* 16 (July 1918), 400–39.

"Internal Commerce and the Development of [a] National Economy Before 1860," *Journal of Political Economy* 47 (December 1939), 798–822.

Larry Schweikart, "Secession and Southern Banks," *Civil War History* 31 (June 1985), 111–25.

Manisha Sinha, "Eugene D. Genovese: The Mind of a Marxist Conservative," *Radical History Review*, No. 88 (Winter 2004), 4–29.

Leon C. Soulé, "The Creole-American Struggle in New Orleans Politics, 1850–1862," *Louisiana Historical Quarterly* 40 (January 1957), 54–83.

Raleigh A. Suarez, "Bargains, Bills, and Bankruptcies: Business Activity in Rural Antebellum Louisiana," *Louisiana History* 7 (Summer 1966), 189–206.

Richard Tansey, "Southern Expansionism: Urban Interests in the Cuban Filibusters," *Plantation Society in the Americas* I (June 1979), 227–51.

"Bernard Kendig and the New Orleans Slave Trade," *Louisiana History* 23 (Spring 1982), 159–78.

E. P. Thompson, "Time, Work-Discipline, and Industrial Capitalism," *Past and Present* 38 (December 1967), 56–97.

Bennett H. Wall, "Leon Godchaux and the Godchaux Business Enterprises," *American Jewish Historical Quarterly* 66 (September 1976), 50–66.

Warren Whatley, "Southern Agrarian Labor Contracts as Impediments to Cotton Mechanization," *Journal of Economic History* 47 (March 1987), 45–70.

Kenneth Weiher, "The Cotton Industry and Southern Urbanization, 1880–1930," *Explorations in Economic History* 14 (1977), 120–40.

"West Feliciana [Railroad]: A Century Old," *Illinois Central Magazine* (March/April 1931), 3–5.

Jonathan M. Wiener, "Class Structure and Economic Development in the American South, 1865–1955," *American Historical Review* 84 (October 1979), 970–1006.

T. Harry Williams, "The Louisiana Unification Movement of 1873," *Journal of Southern History* 11 (August 1945), 349–69.

James Winston, "Notes on the Economic History of New Orleans," *Mississippi Valley Historical Review* 11 (September 1924), 200–26.

Harold D. Woodman, "Sequel to Slavery: The New History Views the Postbellum South," *Journal of Southern History* 43 (November 1977), 523–54.

"Post-Civil War Southern Agriculture and the Law," *Agricultural History* 53 (January 1979), 319–37.

"Postbellum Social Change and Its Effects on Marketing the South's Cotton Crop," *Agricultural History* 56 (January 1982), 215–30.

"The Political Economy of the New South: Retrospects and Prospects," *Journal of Southern History* 67 (November 2001), 789–810.

Gavin Wright, "New and Old Views on the Economics of Slavery," *Journal of Economic History* 33 (June 1973), 452–66.

Michael Zakim, "The Dialectics of Merchant Capital: New York City Businessmen and the Secession Crisis of 1860–61," *New York History* 87 (Winter 2006), 67–87.

Jan Luiten van Zanden, "Do We Need a Theory of Merchant Capitalism?" *Review* 20 (Spring 1997), 255–67.

VII. Unpublished Dissertations and Theses

Floyd M. Clay, "Economic Survival of the Plantation System within the Feliciana Parishes, 1865–1880" (M.A. thesis, Louisiana State University, 1962).

Elizabeth Joan Doyle, "Civilian Life in Occupied New Orleans, 1862–65" (Ph.D. diss., Louisiana State University, 1955).

Peter W. FitzRandolph, "The Rural Furnishing Merchant in the Postbellum United States: A Study in Spatial Economics" (Ph.D. diss., Tufts University, 1979).

Leslie A. Lovett, "From Merchant to Sugar Planter: The Rise and Success of Jacob Lemann and Son" (unpubd. honors thesis, Tulane University, 1990).

Linda Kay Murphy, "The Shifting Economic Relationships of the Cotton South: A Study of the Financial Relationships of the South During Its Industrial Development, 1864–1913" (Ph.D. diss., Texas A&M University, 1999).

Robert Earl Roeder, "New Orleans Merchants, 1800–1837" (Ph.D. diss., Harvard University, 1959).

Joel M. Sipress, "The Triumph of Reaction: Political Change in a New South Community [Grant Parish, La.], 1865–1898" (Ph.D. diss., University of North Carolina at Chapel Hill, 1993).

Van Mitchel Smith, "British Business Relations with the Confederacy, 1861–1865" (Ph.D. diss., University of Texas, 1949).

Index

African Americans. *See* free blacks; race; slaves and slavery
agriculture, 16, 39–40, 93–4, 229; cotton and sugar parishes compared, 236–55; crop liens, 232; mixed-farming parishes, 114–5. *See also* grain trade; merchants, rural; names of particular crops; *One Kind of Freedom* (1977); sharecropping; slaves and slavery
Alabama, 224, 227, 235
Alexandria, La., 90, 96, 100, 108, 133
Andrews, Israel D., 16, 23–4, 38, 46
Ascension Parish, La., 94, 97, 102, 103, 107, 274; demography of, 236–7, 242–3; geography of, 236; postbellum stores in, 236–55. *See also* merchants, rural
Ashe, Thomas, 21
Assumption Parish, La., 243
Atchafalaya Bay, 212
Atherton, Lewis, 92, 98, 103
Atkinson, Edward, 195
Atlantic world, 21–2, 26, 36, 110; decline of, 279–81; diplomacy and, 163–4; King Cotton ideology and, 134–5; merchant capital and, 260, 264–5, 279–80; New Orleans in, 280–1
Avoyelles Parish, La., 97–8, 105, 107, 114–15

Bach, L., & Co., 110
Ball, Douglas B., 153
Bankers' Magazine, 153

banks and banking, 30–5, 46, 49–51; Confederacy and, 128, 130–2; criticisms of, 31–2; Gen. Butler and, 152–6; New Orleans specie reserves, 34–5, 128–30, 153; postbellum, 187–8, 209–10, 221–2, 227–9, 276; rural, 104. *See also* names of particular banks
Banks, Nathaniel P., 7, 167, 172–3; background of, 175; banking policies of, 176, 193–4; critical of Gen. Butler, 165; priorities as commander of New Orleans, 175–6; Red River campaign of, 180
Baring Brothers, 20, 32–3, 49, 51, 124, 141, 164
Barker, Jacob M., 51, 158n.14; background of, 156; emancipation fears of, 160; in postbellum New Orleans, 192, 194, 196–7; relations with Gen. Butler, 156–8
Baton Rouge, La., 177, 236; postbellum stores in, 244
Bayou Sara, La.. *See* St. Francisville, La.; West Feliciana Parish, La.
Beard, Charles, 257
Beauregard, P. G. T., 199, 212, 215
Beckert, Sven, 181
Behan, William J., 204
Bell, John, 122
Bell, William A., 200, 203–4
Bellocq, Nobblom & Co., 238–9
Belmont, August, 124

CPSIA information can be obtained
at www.ICGtesting.com
Printed in the USA
LVOW03s2014270617

539561LV00001B/132/P